AF324691

STEPHEN HANNOCK

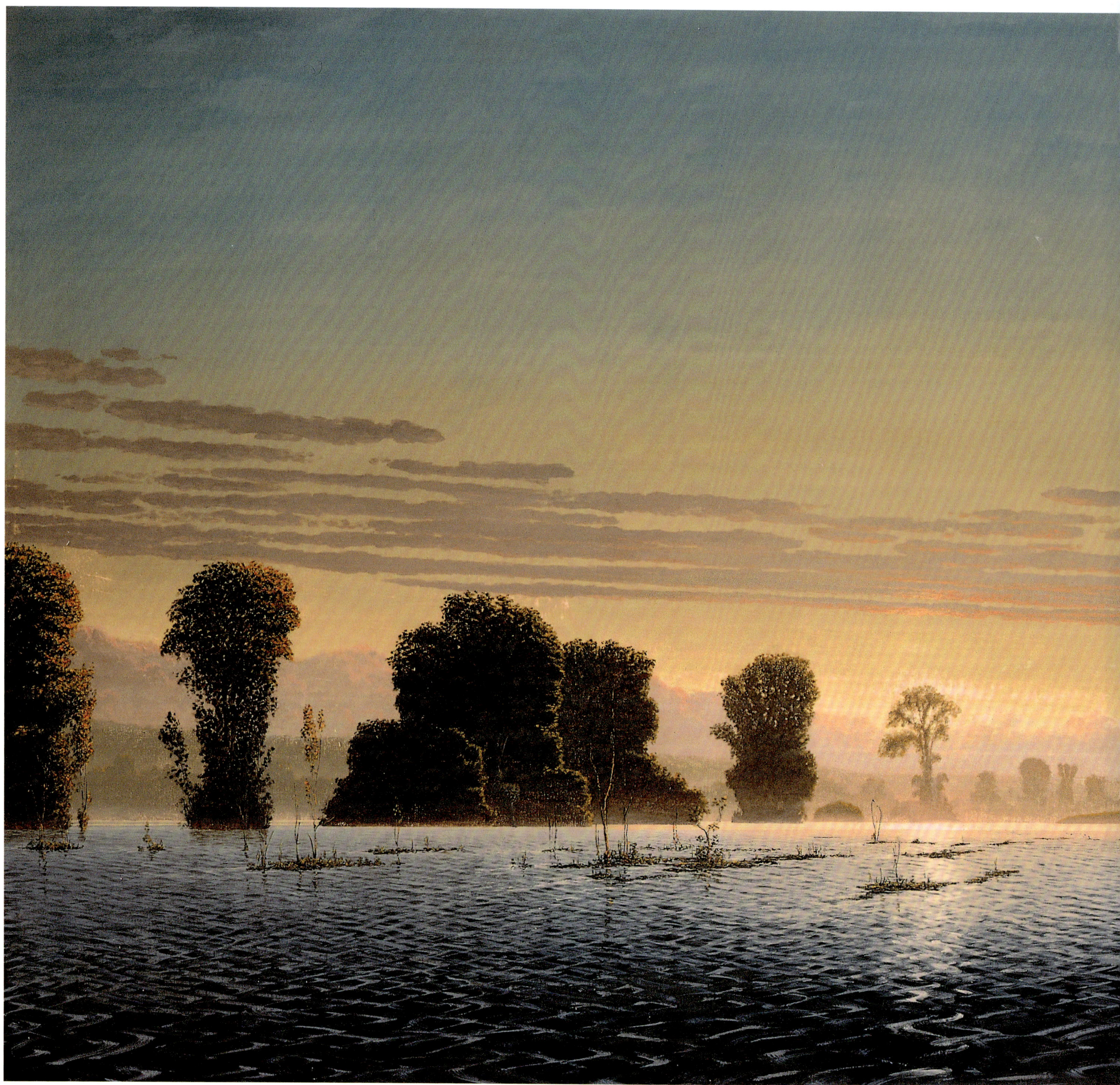

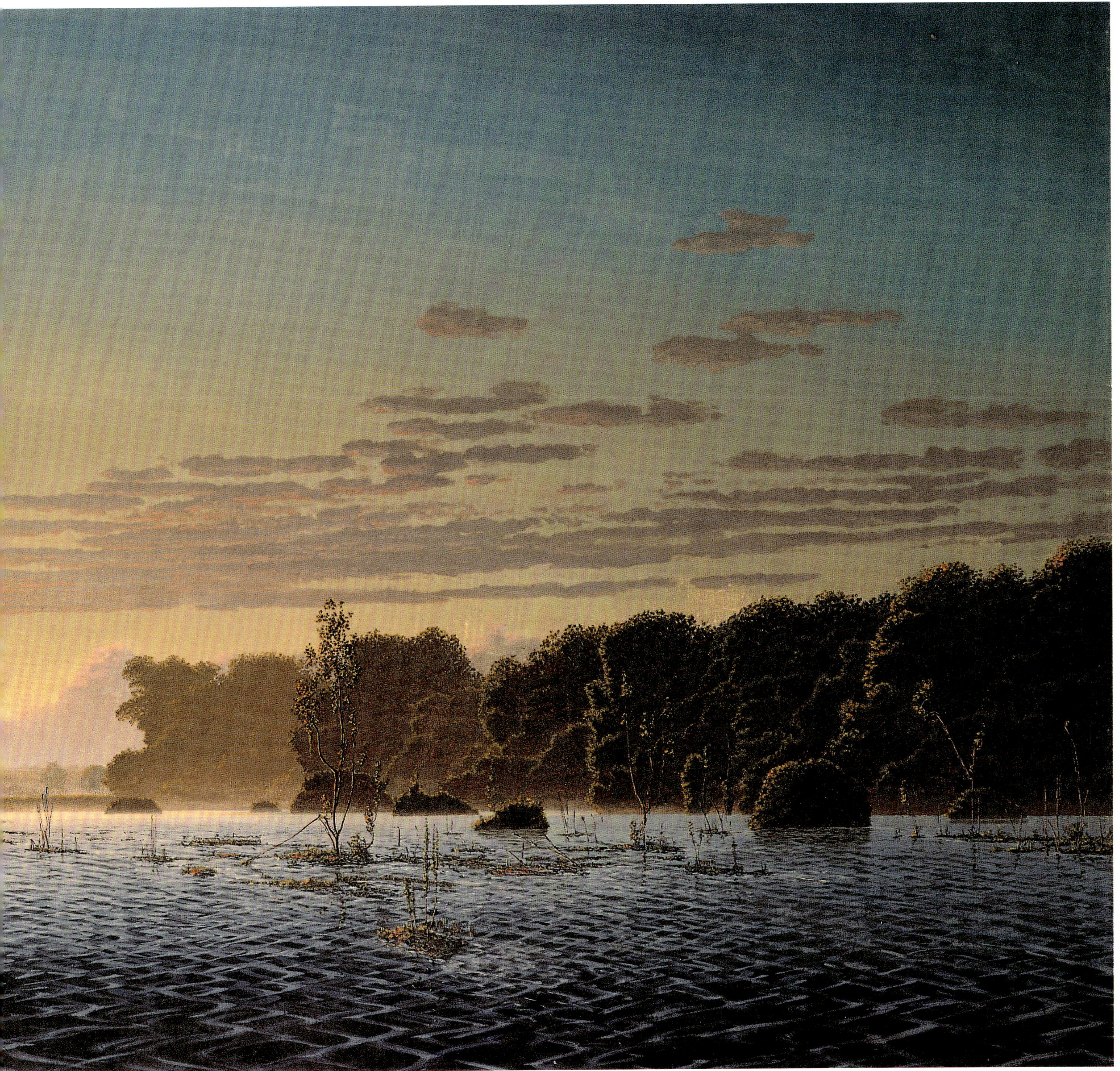

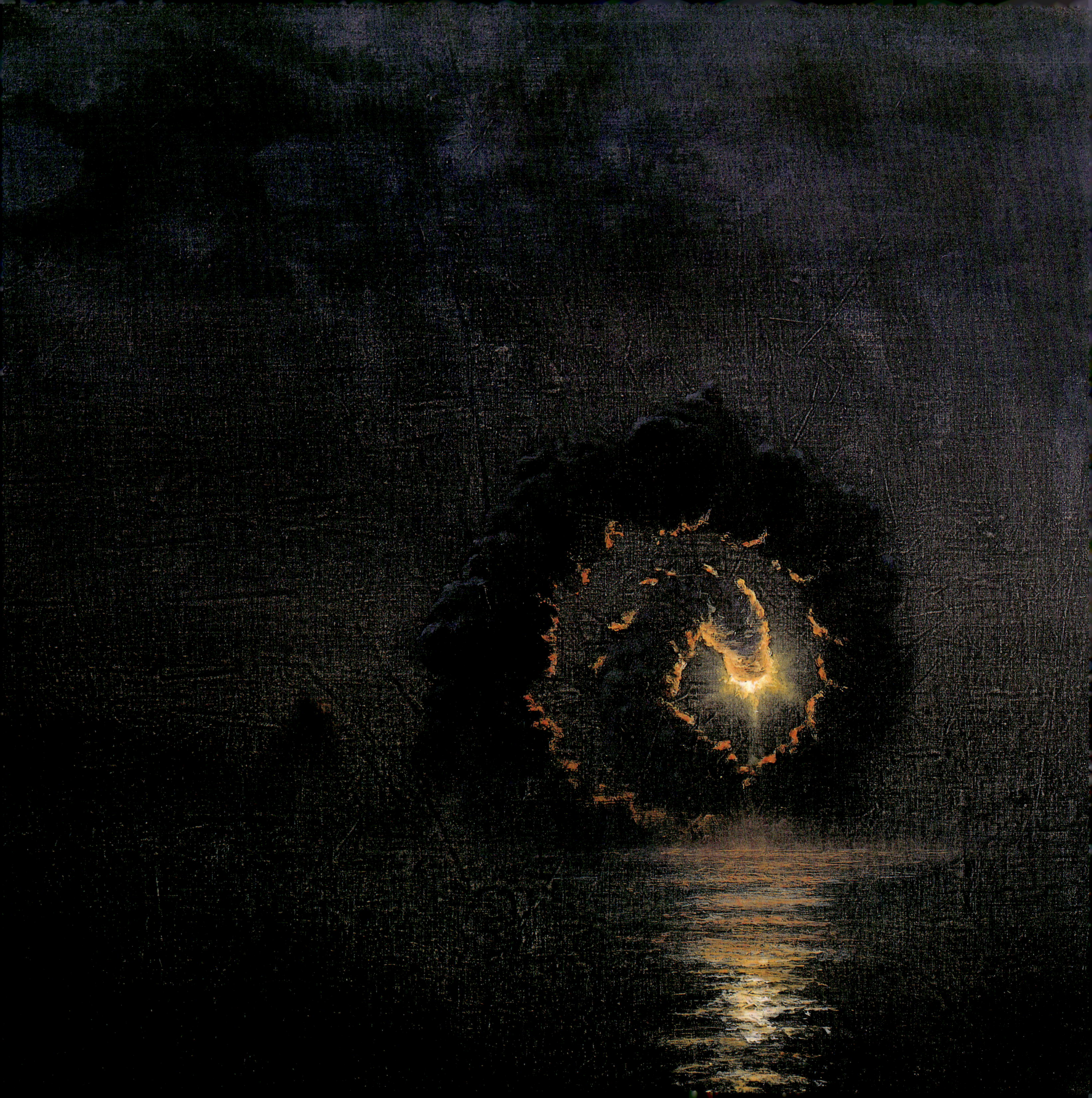

STEPHEN HANNOCK

Jason Rosenfeld   Martha Hoppin   Garrett White

Foreword by *Mark C. Taylor*

HUDSON HILLS PRESS

NEW YORK AND MANCHESTER

First Edition

Copyright © 2009 by Stephen Hannock

Published in the United States by Hudson Hills Press, LLC
P.O. Box 205, 3556 Main Street, Manchester, Vermont 05254

Distributed in the United States, its territories and possessions, and Canada by
National Book Network, Inc.
Distributed outside of North America by Antique Collectors' Club, Ltd.

Publisher and Executive Director: Leslie Pell van Breen
Production Manager: David Skolkin
Design: Arnold Skolnick
Editor: Martha Hoppin
Proofreader: Amanda Sparrow
Production Editor: Marisa Crumb
Production Assistance: David Lachman
Printed and bound by Mondadori, Verona, Italy
Founding Publisher: Paul Anbinder

Manufactured in Italy.

Library of Congress Cataloging-in-Publication Data

Hoppin, Martha J.
  Stephen Hannock / by Martha Hoppin, Jason Rosenfeld, Garrett White ; foreword by
Mark C. Taylor.
      p. cm.
  Includes bibliographical references and index.
  1. Hannock, Stephen, 1951—Criticism and interpretation. I. Hannock, Stephen,
1951—II. Rosenfeld, Jason. III. White, Garrett, 1960— IV. Title.
ND237.H293H67 2008
759.13--dc22
2008048305

ISBN: 13: 978-155595-291-4

(PAGES 2–3) FLOODED RIVER ABOVE THE OXBOW, 1990
POLISHED OIL ON CANVAS, 44 X 96 INCHES (112 X 244 CM). PRIVATE COLLECTION

(FRONTISPIECE) VORTEX AT DAWN, 1996
POLISHED OIL ON CANVAS, 31 X 38 INCHES (79 X 97 CM). PRIVATE COLLECTION

Contents

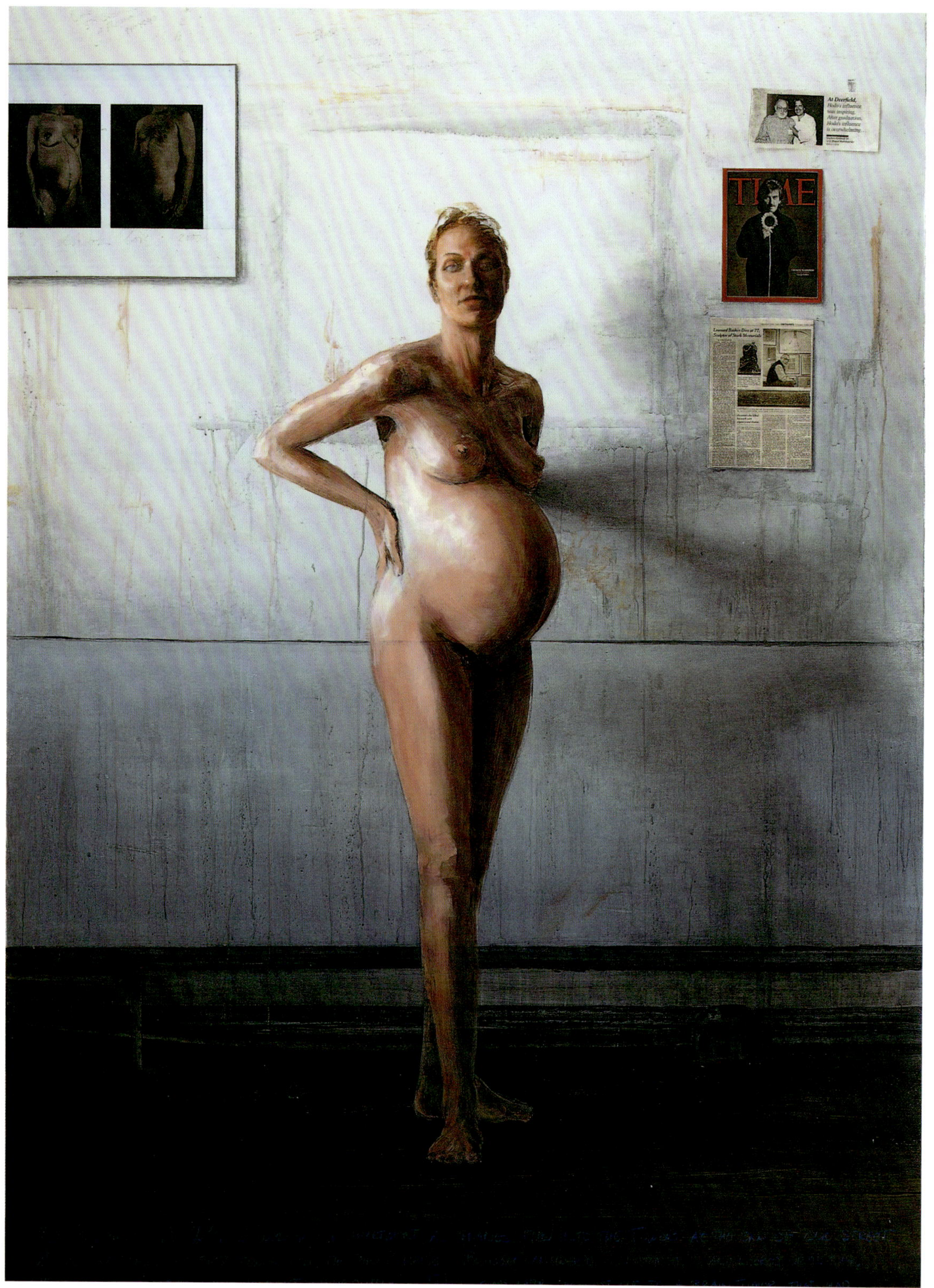

HEROIC WOMAN, 2002

Mixed media on canvas, 84 x 60 inches (213 x 152 cm). Deerfield Academy, Deerfield, Massachusetts

Landscape of Self-Portraiture

Mark C. Taylor

On the morning of September 11, 2001, Stephen Hannock was in his Manhattan apartment watching plumes of smoke rising from the towers of the World Trade Center when his wife, Bridget, received a call from her doctor informing her that she had an inoperable brain tumor. Hanging up the phone, she turned to Stephen and said simply, "Honey, we have to get to a neurologist immediately."[1] Bridget had been noticing some changes in her body but did not think they were unusual; however, when she developed double vision, she knew something serious was wrong. The problem with her vision seemed uncanny—only a few months earlier, Stephen had begun to have trouble seeing out of both eyes. His condition, which would be not properly diagnosed for five years, continues to affect his vision and poses the possibility that he may become blind. In the three years after that fateful morning, Bridget's condition steadily worsened until August 2004, when the malignancy raged out of control. By October, she was dead, and Stephen was left to ponder the baffling intersection of personal and global catastrophe.

In the months prior to the diagnosis of Bridget's tumor, Stephen had started a painting that is unlike the so-called moody landscapes for which he is well known. Late in her pregnancy, Bridget, eight-and-a-half months pregnant, stands in a shadowy room completely naked and staring directly at the viewer. Over the course of the next several years, the painting evolved with her illness and was not completed until the day of her memorial service. The final version, entitled *Heroic Woman*, is haunted by death—Bridget's figure is framed on the left by a picture of matching portraits of her and Stephen, a Chuck Close daguerreotype, and on the right by reproductions of the obituaries of Dan Hodermarsky, Stephen's Deerfield teacher who first encouraged him to pursue art, and Leonard Baskin, the sculptor and printmaker with whom Stephen studied at Smith College. Between these two notices is a picture of George Harrison on the cover of *Time* on the occasion of his death, which had occurred less than two months after 9/11. Across the bottom of the painting, five lines matter-of-factly recounting the story of Bridget's illness and death conclude: "Three years later she lost out to a brain tumor that had shifted gears during her third trimester with Georgia while work on this piece was underway. The life she lived during those three years as a mother, wife and professional, as well as daughter, sister and friend was truly heroic. 10-10-2004." As Stephen reworked this remarkable painting, his understanding of it and the rest of his work began to change. Though ostensibly a portrait of Bridget, *Heroic Woman* is, in fact, Stephen's self-portrait. Looking back from the perspective of this painting, it becomes clear that his entire oeuvre is an extended exercise in self-portraiture.

Stephen Hannock's art has been consistently misunderstood. Critics, eager to forge continuities where there are disruptions and even subversions, are quick to categorize him as a landscape artist whose work derives from nineteenth-century Luminism, Tonalism, and, above all, the Hudson River School. There are, of course, superficial similarities between Hannock's paintings and the work of these precursors. When pressed about his artistic preoccupations, he explains, "Art is an adventure in seeing short-lived light that creates an incomparable mood." Acutely aware of the transience of light and the fragility of vision, Hannock is preoccupied with what Wallace Stevens aptly describes as "evanescent symmetries" that reveal "a permanence composed of impermanence." With humor and courage as admirable as they are rare, Hannock finds insight even in his impending blindness: what he calls his "funky eye," he explains, enables him to "see the fluid nature of light, which sometimes creates a flare like one of Turner's explosions or a rocket stopped in mid-launch." Rendering the fleeting instant when light appears by disappearing is the aim of all his work. This task is, of course, impossible and, thus, the work of art is endless.

Hannock's comment on the importance of mood in art is reminiscent of an observation by George Inness, an artist to whom he is often compared. "The arrangement of colors," Inness insisted, "must be kept in harmony because it must reproduce not merely the facts of the landscape, either separately or in mass, but, rather, the effect of the scene upon the painter's feelings, the emotion it evokes. Not alone the grass and trees, with whatever delicate recog nition of gradation of color, but the mood, of which they are the embodiment and cause, it is to be transferred to the canvas."[2] In the work of Luminists like Frederic Edwin Church, John F. Kensett, and Fitz Henry Lane as well as Tonalists like Albert Pinkham Ryder and James Abbott McNeill Whistler, the interplay of sky, water, and landscape creates a misty atmosphere designed to evoke a sense of timelessness or even transcendence. By contrast, for Hannock the challenge is not to lift viewers out of the paradoxes and contradictions of time but to create the conditions for thoughts about everyday life that immerse viewers ever more deeply in the tensions of temporality.

The persistent misinterpretation of Hannock as a landscape artist and association of him with the Hudson River School is in some ways understandable. In 1994, he completed what remains his best-known painting, *The Oxbow, after Church, after Cole,*

Flooded, 1979–1994 (Flooded River for the Matriarches: E. and A. Mongan) (p. 14). As the title suggests, this work is a response to Thomas Cole and his student Frederic Edwin Church. In 1836, Cole painted a view of Mount Holyoke in Northampton, Massachusetts, often called simply *The Oxbow*, which quickly became one of the most influential landscapes of the nineteenth century. Cole's panoramic canvas depicts a magnificent vista of the Connecticut River Valley during a midday thunderstorm. Infatuated by Romanticism, Cole juxtaposes the beautiful and the sublime by dividing the canvas in half. On the left side of the river, a violent storm rages over a dark wilderness, and on the right side carefully cultivated and ordered fields bathe in golden sunlight. Cole leaves no doubt that civilization is progressively taming the dangerous forces of nature. Two nearly inconspicuous details are especially important. First, Cole paints his own figure, with back turned toward the viewer, at the approximate point where he had sketched the scene three years earlier. Jason Rosenfeld suggests that Cole's self-portraiture "represents an intimate dialogue in *The Oxbow* that implies far more than a casual integration with the motif but, rather, a vivid and personal association of place, time, and experience, as well as a formative suggestion of his future tangent in art—one that produced his greatest works, the grand historical landscapes of the mid-1830s." Second, Cole interrupts the painting's naturalistic representation by etching the Hebrew word *Shaddai* (the Almighty) on the distant mountain. The letters are inverted as if to suggest that they are only legible from the heavens.[3]

Over the years, Cole's work has become something of an obsession for Hannock. He has repeatedly returned to this painting and now has completed twenty-one versions of *The Oxbow*. This ongoing dialogue and the series of works it has produced offer ample evidence of the subtle ways in which Hannock's thinking is developing and art is evolving. His first encounter with Cole was at least in part accidental. Having lived and studied in the Connecticut River Valley for seventeen years, it was impossible to avoid Cole's famous painting. But Hannock took offense with Cole's attempt to claim territory the artist had only visited briefly. By painting and repainting the Oxbow, Hannock is, of course, staking a claim that is more about art than geography. His work differs from Cole's in both obvious and not-so-obvious ways. Hannock does not sharply divide his canvas between nature (the sublime) and culture (the beautiful); rather, cultivated fields extend on both sides of the river and are joined by four bridges. Instead of a midday storm, the painting depicts the glow of the sky at twilight, reflected in the tranquil water of the river. The name of the Almighty has been erased and, most important, there is no human figure in the painting. Hannock consistently elides images of people and distinct objects in order to expand the range of vision and, as he explains, to make it possible for the viewer "to blow through the surface of the painting." When the mood of the work transports viewers into a different space, they can think new thoughts. The absence of human figures does not, however, mean that there is no self-representation in these paintings; on the contrary, Hannock is present everywhere in his works. Indeed, all of his apparent landscapes are variations of an extended self-portrait.

As one examines Hannock's Oxbow painting more closely, it quickly becomes clear that the landscape is riddled with script bordering on calligraphy. What first seem to be furrows in newly plowed fields and leafy mountain ridges are actually lines of text, which, if carefully examined, are legible. Hannock creates this evocative "landscape" by weaving together brief descriptions of people and things as well as seemingly inconsequential events in his everyday life. His prose is as plain and direct as what he describes; the account is, in effect, a diary or series of snapshots of what was going on in his life at a particular time. Some notes are serious; others are lighthearted. Some events are consequential; others, inconsequential.

Came down from Bowdoin and hockey to study art at
Smith College…and got my eyes fucked out, while being totally
humbled by the fairer sex
a speed trap on Interstate 91
Gordo the Wacko almost blew Jimmy's head off with an M-80
Barry Moser's house

As things and events accumulate, it is impossible to know what matters and what does not. Hannock makes no effort to find a thread that unifies or integrates what takes place; the narrative is episodic—a recording of fragments in search of a whole that never comes together. The coincidence of events and juxtaposition of people as well as things continue to grow until the substance of life itself appears to be a series of inexplicable accidents. "The text tells stories," Hannock explains, "which are euphoric but not always in a good sense." After all, how can you ever grasp the meaning of a phone call informing you that the person you love most dearly has a fatal brain tumor that arrives while you are watching a deadly disaster whose global consequences we may never fully comprehend?

While resisting self-representation through painted figures, Hannock fashions complex patterns from simple events to create an open-ended self-portrait. Having developed this strategy in the first Oxbow painting, he continually refines it in later works. In many cases, words seem to flow freely in a stream of consciousness that recalls the Surrealists' automatic writing; in other cases, the text is more deliberately crafted. In *American City with Restored Park* (2004–2006, p. 126), for example, the underlying text recounts twenty years of Hannock's life in New York both before and after he knew Bridget. Though the large canvas depicts a familiar cityscape on an early spring day with the slightest hint of buds on the trees, the muted tones create a November mood. The text traces every building and lines every street, creating a melancholy if not foreboding mood. Embedded in the painting between the words and images are two concrete fragments related to Bridget's life and death. The first is a torn paper towel on which she had recorded the doctor's description of how the tumor's growth was shutting the capacity of fluid to circulate through her brain, and the second is the actual letter Stephen wrote to their daughter, Georgia, when Bridget slipped into a coma after suffering a stroke while recovering from brain surgery. Words and image combine to form figures more haunting than either could convey alone.

Accident, chance, serendipity, paradox, coincidence, fragments, connections, disconnections—such is the stuff of life. Not content to make this the substance of his art, Hannock has developed a distinctive technique that enacts the chance of life in the process of painting. While the canvasses seem fixed, Hannock's paintings are, in important ways, traces of a performance no one ever observes. He combines machine and hand to create what he describes, in a remarkably evocative phrase, as "accidents that happen within the cataclysm of paint." The work of art is not merely an object or finished product but an endless process in which creativity can be neither planned nor programmed but is spontaneous and, thus, occurs by chance. Among the many lessons that Hannock's art teaches us is that the unexpected not only harbors the specter of death but also expresses the pulse of life. Far from deterministic, chance and accident are the condition of the only freedom we can ever know. This is not to imply that artistic creation involves no deliberation or discipline; to the contrary, discipline and freedom are mutually implicated in such a way that neither is possible apart from the other. Discipline provides the parameters within which to exercise the freedom without which creativity is impossible.

Over the years, the technique Hannock has developed has become something like a ritual process that sets the stage for the creative emergence of his art. He begins by stretching canvas over a panel and then applying layers of modeling paste until the teeth of the canvas are wiped away. He then covers the canvas

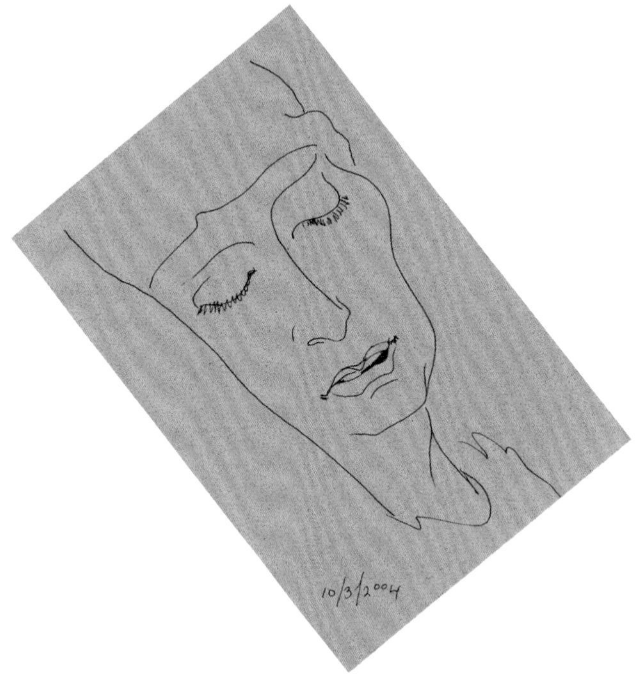

with water and works it smooth with industrial-strength power sanders. When the canvas has dried, he starts applying multiple layers of acrylic paint, each of which forms something like a wave of paint, which Hannock shapes and reshapes in a manner as sculptural as it is painterly. Recalling Pollock, the canvas is always placed horizontally on the floor or on sawhorses. Hannock's relation to the canvas, however, is closer to Serra's industrial activity than Pollock's ritualistic dance. Machine intervenes between hand and surface to mechanically produce the glow of paintings that seem auratic. What makes this process even more intriguing is that Hannock is ambidextrous and always works with both hands at the same time. As the layers build up or, in Hannock's terms, the waves overlap, an environment emerges in which accidents happen. In the moment of creativity, the artist lets go and allows the work to form by itself. One of the many reasons Hannock resists association with the artists of the Hudson River School is that he is convinced they know nothing of the freedom involved in this creative moment. Their aim was total control of the work of art—each element is carefully calculated to express the feeling of the artist or to trigger an emption in the viewer. For a child of the sixties, devoted friend and fan of Sting, and erstwhile hockey and Ultimate Frisbee player, stuff happens only when you let go.

A finished painting comprises between eight and twelve layers, each of which is worked over with an orbital sander. When three layers have accumulated, Hannock applies a resin consisting of a clear acrylic gel, which he first builds up and, after it sets, polishes. The result is surfaces that are profound at the points where figures emerge from the interplay of waves that run deep. This complex production process lends his paintings a realism that is quite different from that characterizing the work of painters with whom he is usually compared. Hannock does not represent life in readily discernible images; he reenacts it on a stage carefully crafted to allow the unexpected to occur.

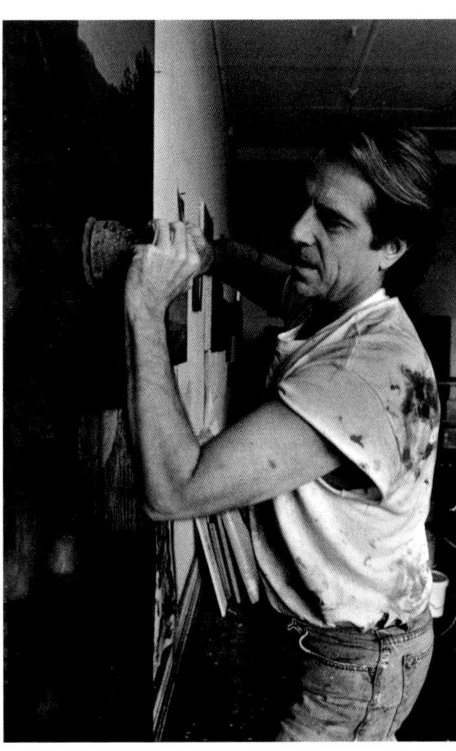

What lends Hannock's work its depth is the friction between and among the layers of his work. His paintings heighten, rather than relax, tensions. In some, figures harbor penumbral traces that leave everything obscure; in other paintings, figures are clear and crisp but when studied closely appear to be composed of braided threads of texts whose fragments simultaneously create and resist the whole they form. As noted earlier, these textual shards record events in Hannock's life in a way that transforms his landscapes into self-portraits. But these works are not merely self-referential, for in presenting himself, he enacts the life we all share. When we "blow through the surface" of Hannock's paintings, art does not lift us out of the complexities and contradictions of life, but rather opens us to the unexpected—in all its glory and terror—in ways that leave the future open and renders the work of art forever incomplete. The timeless is a lunar landscape that is deadly; the temporal is an earthy landscape that is vital.

> *It is fatal in the moon and empty there.*
> *But, here, allons. The enigmatical*
> *Beauty of each beautiful enigma*
> *Becomes amassed in a total double-thing.*
> *We do not know what is real and what is not.*[4]

In the beautiful enigma of life, everything is a double-thing, and we can never be sure what is real and what is not. By painting this cloud of unknowing, Hannock shows us who we are by endlessly probing who he is.

Notes

1. All quotations from Stephen Hannock are from a conversation that took place in his studio in North Adams, Massachusetts, on June 25, 2007.

2. Harvey Jones, *Twilight and Reverie: California Tonalist Painting 1890–1930* (Oakland: Oakland Museum of California, 1995).

3. Jason Rosenfeld, "Imaginary Realism, Meaningful Contradictions," in *Stephen Hannock* (New York: McKenzie Fine Arts, Inc., 2002), p. 8.

4. Wallace Stevens, "An Ordinary Evening in New Haven," in *The Collected Poems* (Originally published: New York: Knopf, 1954), p. 465.

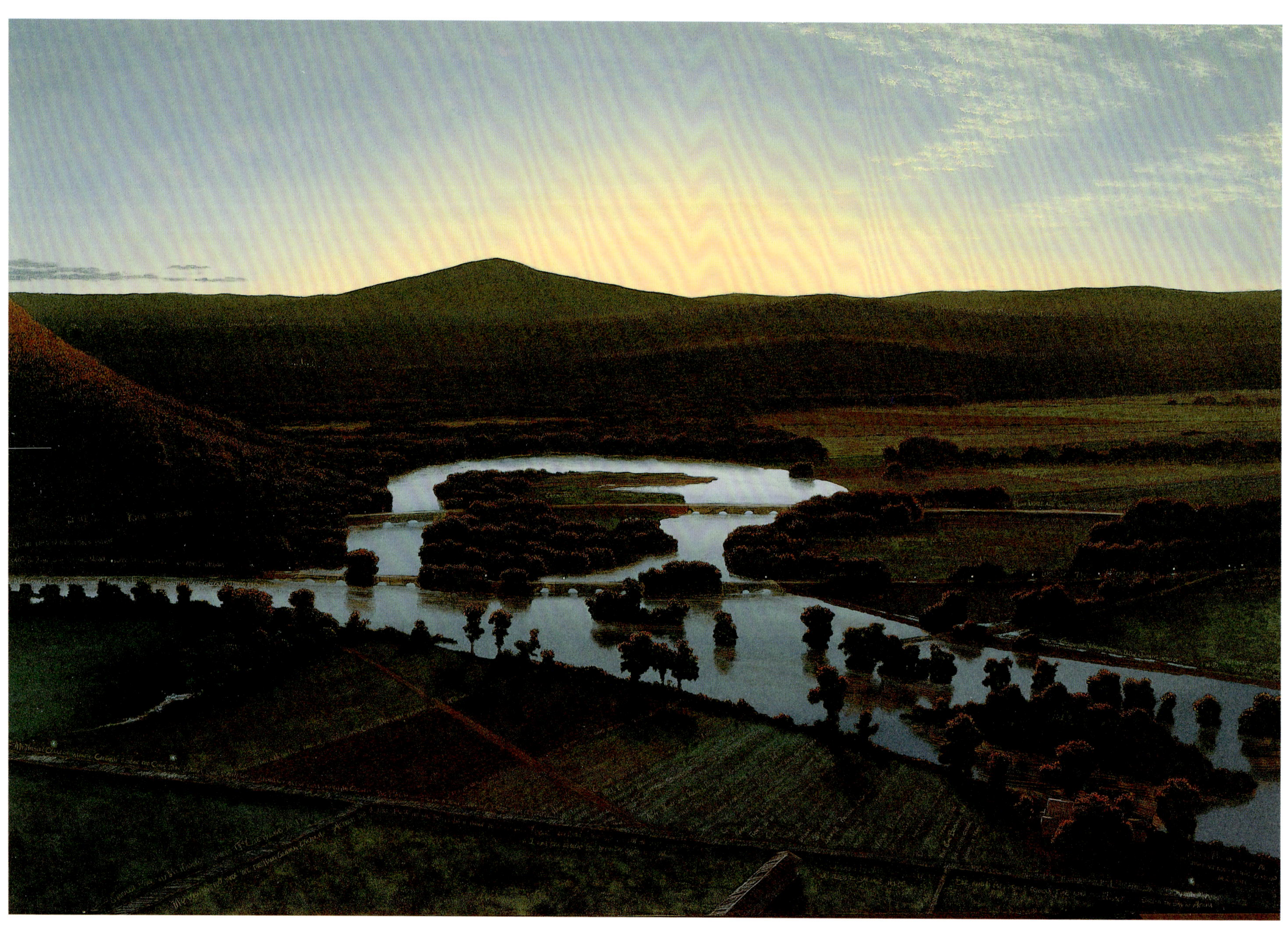

The Oxbow, after Church, after Cole, Flooded, 1979–1994 (Flooded River for the Matriarchs, E. and A. Mongan), 1994
Polished oil on canvas, 54 x 81 inches (137 x 206 cm). Smith College Museum of Art, Northampton, Massachusetts, Gift of Irene Mennen Hunter (Class of 1939), 1995

Variations on a Theme: The Oxbow

Martha Hoppin

A climb up Mount Holyoke affords a spectacular view of the Oxbow, the distinctive loop in the Connecticut River near Northampton, Massachusetts. As a formation the Oxbow is not unique—meandering rivers produce them—but this particular oxbow has attracted tourists for more than 175 years. Set amid fields and farmland, it forms the centerpiece of a pastoral landscape compared by nineteenth-century writers to a garden and still celebrated by artists today. By the 1870s, visitors could reach Mount Holyoke's summit through a combination of train, steamship, carriage, and cog railway, and they could stay at a comfortable hotel. While the mountain is now a state park, the hotel a museum, and the region more developed, the vista remains one of exceptional beauty.

Stephen Hannock has made the Oxbow, as seen from Mount Holyoke, the defining motif of his art. Even though he paints other landscapes, he is most identified with his Oxbow views.[1]

In a series of works—twenty-one canvases over thirteen years—he has explored different light and color effects as they ring changes in mood across the framework of the Oxbow. He uses these paintings to link his art to the past, to develop new techniques, and to explore his personal associations with nature.

His first Oxbow piece, now in the Smith College Museum of Art, evolved over a number of years, as its title reflects: *The Oxbow, after Church, after Cole, Flooded, 1979–1994 (Flooded River for the Matriarchs, E. and A. Mongan)* (p. 14). Although Hannock had lived in Northampton since 1971 and climbed Mount Holyoke often, the idea of painting the view came to him only after he stayed one day to watch the sunset, when fading light illuminated the river and land forms grew dark against the sky. Similarly, he had long been aware of the most famous depiction of the site, Thomas Cole's *View from Mount Holyoke, Northampton, Massachusetts, after a Thunderstorm—The Oxbow*, dating from 1836 (p. 15),

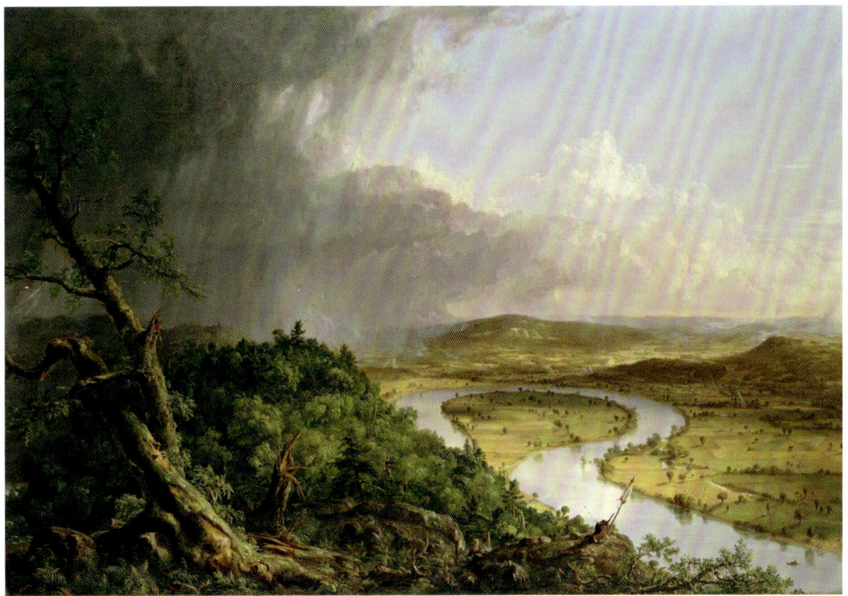

Thomas Cole, View from Mount Holyoke, Northampton, Massachusetts, after a Thunderstorm—The Oxbow, 1836
Oil on canvas, 51½ x 76 inches (131 x 193 cm). The Metropolitan Museum of Art, Gift of Mrs. Russell Sage, 1908 (08.228) Image ©The Metropolitan Museum of Art

but he did not decide to reinterpret Cole's work until 1992, six years after moving to New York. Hannock composed from memory, guided by rough, on-the-spot drawings he had executed in the early 1980s. In a series of drawings and small paintings, he distilled the Oxbow loop to what he felt was its essence—a U-shape that resembles an omega (pp. 16, 17). Next he made small and medium-size oil studies of the whole composition. Then, in 1994, he painted the final version belonging to Smith College.

In his lengthy title Hannock acknowledged his twin inspirations: the art historians Elizabeth and Agnes Mongan and the painter Thomas Cole. The Mongan sisters, prominent print and drawing curators at the Smith College Museum of Art and the Fogg Art Museum, became his mentors. They advised him to leave Northampton for New York. In addition to the Cole painting, Hannock referred to another then thought to be by Frederic Edwin Church after Cole's example. By including both names Hannock aligned himself with the Hudson River School, a group of nineteenth-century artists known for panoramic views of pastoral or wilderness expanses. Cole and his pupil Church were its leading practitioners. Hannock's realistic description of the landscape follows in Hudson River School tradition, though he did not adopt their nationalist or religious overtones.

Hannock may have taken Cole's painting as his starting point, but his end result is quite different. While both artists idealized the landscape, Cole sought drama where Hannock sought preternatural serenity. In place of Cole's swirling clouds, thunderstorms, and sun, Hannock pictured glowing skies, peaceful fields, and soft light. Cole had manipulated perspective and topography to abruptly juxtapose river and mountain and create a perfect oxbow shape. Hannock eliminated Cole's foreground stage, instead suspending the viewer over the scene below. He also raised Cole's horizon line and showed the river as it flows between Mount Holyoke and Mount Tom. These new features place more emphasis on the Oxbow's surroundings. Like Cole, however, Hannock tipped up the Oxbow to make its far edge visible. He turned Cole's paddle form into an irregular arc with an irregular interior island. Hannock may have wanted to avoid pure geometric shapes, but his view also reflects changes in the topography

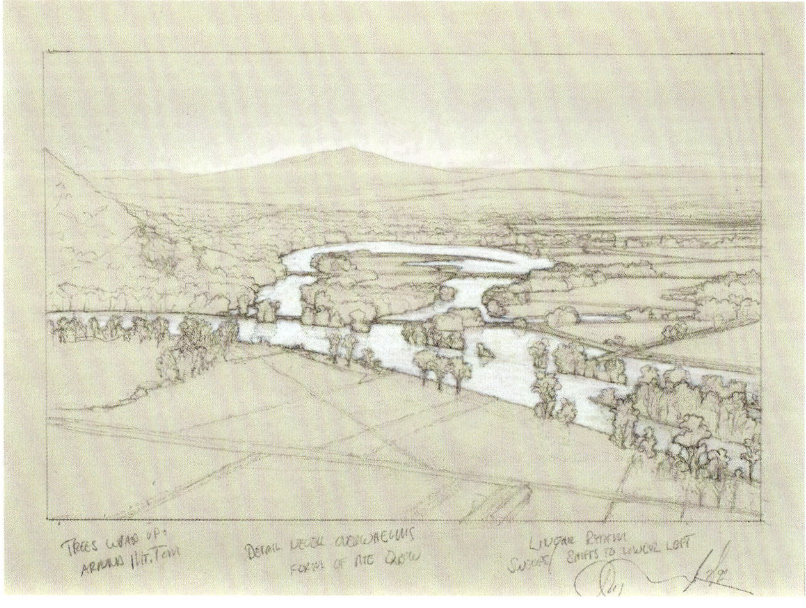

Study for The Oxbow, 1992

Pencil and gouche on paper, 12 x 18 inches (31 x 46 cm). Smith College Museum of Art, Northampton, Massachusetts, Gift of Stephen Hannock in Memory of Jodie Faison, Class of 1934

since Cole's day. Some changes occurred naturally, as oxbows form and reform over long periods of time. Four years after Cole painted his view, the Connecticut River cut through the narrow neck of land that had created the Oxbow configuration. As a result, the center turned into an island and the river shortened its course (and the whole became what is more properly called an oxbow lake). Soil deposits soon filled in the entrance to the Oxbow's north arm, and in the 1850s, a rail line was built across the Oxbow's opening.

The mid-twentieth century brought additional man-made alterations. A road was laid parallel to the railroad, a four-lane interstate highway was cut across the middle of the Oxbow, and a large chunk of the island was removed for a marina. Hannock's composition incorporates the new features, but in keeping with his elegaic mood, he made the highways things of beauty, transforming them into arched aqueducts that hint of ancient civilizations. Small streetlights provide the only signs of habitation, other than half-hidden structures in the lower right, and of modern life. Where Cole included boats and people in his painting as evidence of bounty and industry, Hannock presented a silent, mysterious world, its lights resembling fireflies at dusk, more poetic than real.

Hannock added one more key element: he depicted the river at flood stage. Flooding allowed him to restore the Oxbow's island, but his true motive was to introduce as much reflective surface as possible, for Hannock's overriding subject is light— a luminous glow that radiates to all corners of the picture and animates selected parts. The Connecticut River's annual flooding occurs in spring, not fall. Hannock prefers the fall color palette, which accords with his favorite time of day: sunset. In his Oxbow painting, he picked out backlit trees with pink and red touches and suffused the scene with reddish-gold evening light. Like Cole, he manipulated the landscape in other ways. He placed a mountain at the horizon, on axis with the Oxbow, to bring the viewer's eye back to the central focus of the composition (he was pleased to discover that Cole, too, had added a mountain where none exists). Hannock also removed the many trees that now obscure the Oxbow's form and placed them where he wanted them, in the river and along its banks.

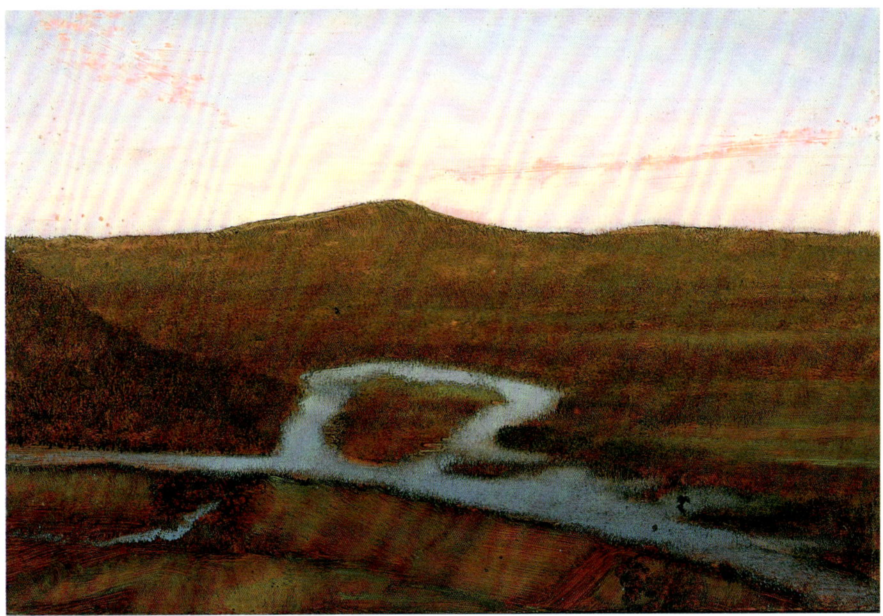

Study #2 the Oxbow, 1992

Polished oil on panel, 4 x 6 inches (10 x 15 cm). Collection of the Artist

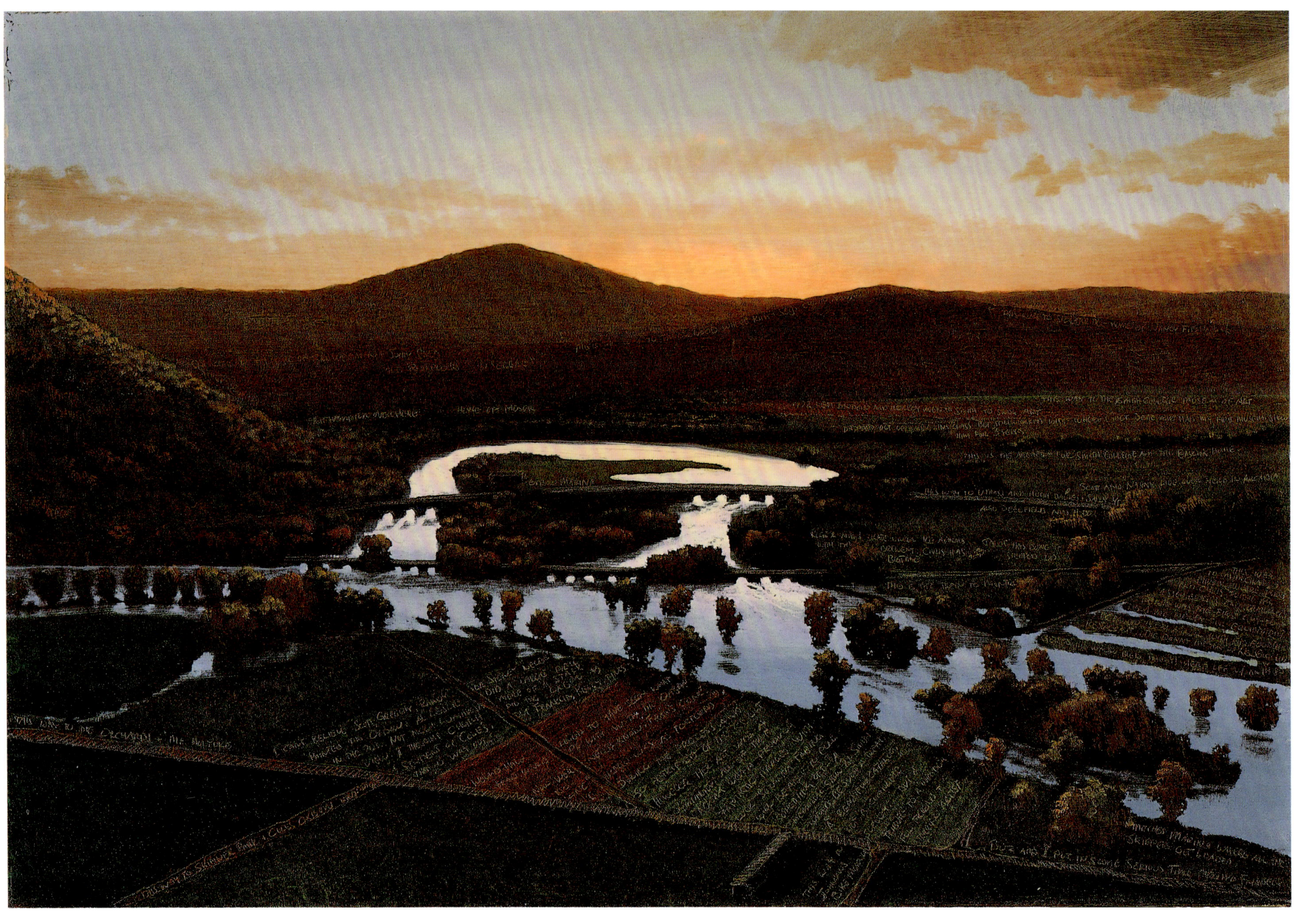

The Oxbow: After Church, After Cole, Flooded (Flooded River for Fran), 1998
Polished oil on canvas, 24 x 36 inches (61 x 91 cm). Museum of Fine Arts, Boston, Gift in Memory of Francis Cohen Gillespie, 1999 (1999.681)

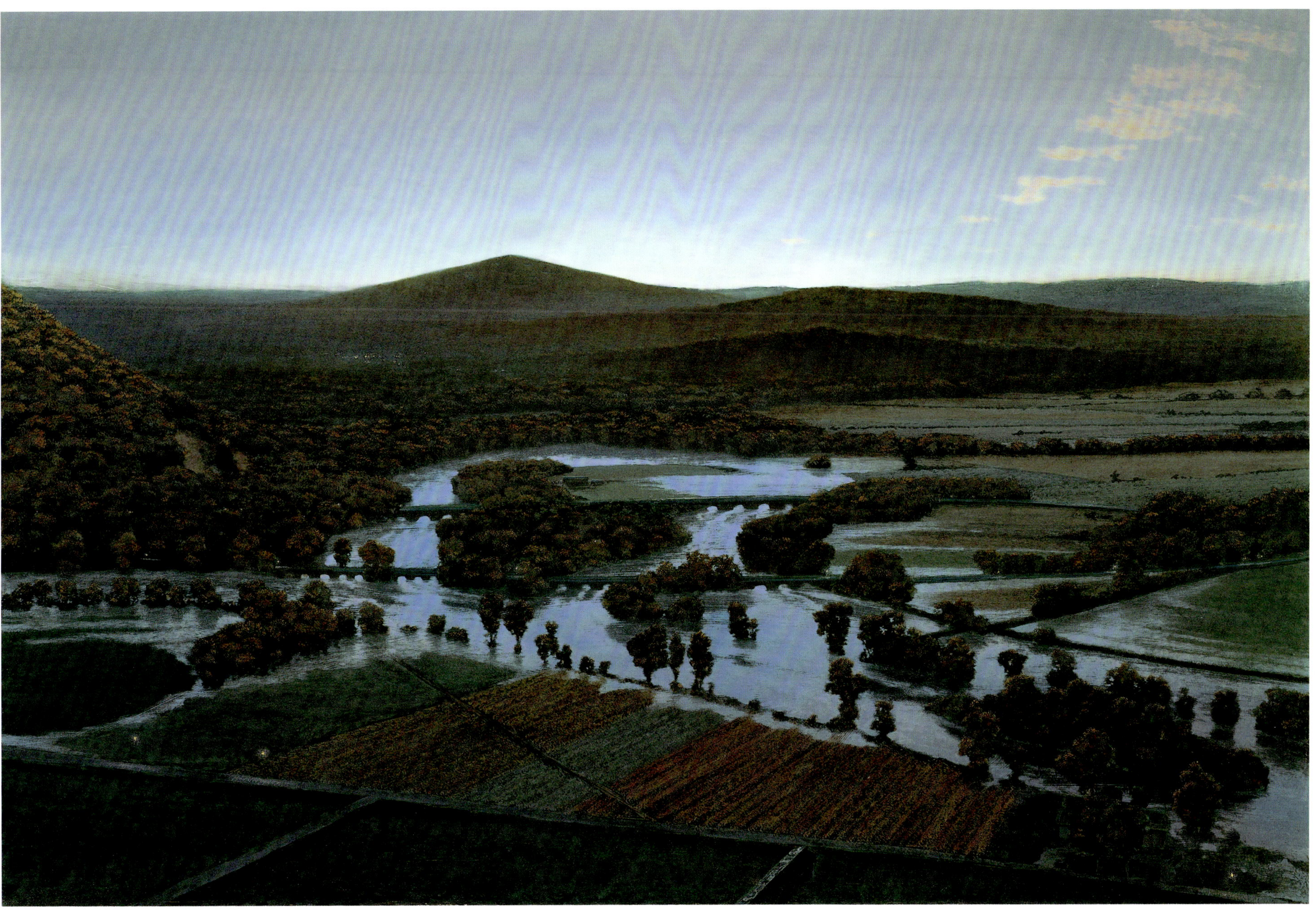

Evening Oxbow: Flooded (for Rockwell Kent at the Smith College Museum), 1996
Polished oil on canvas, 40 x 60 inches (102 x 152 cm). Private Collection

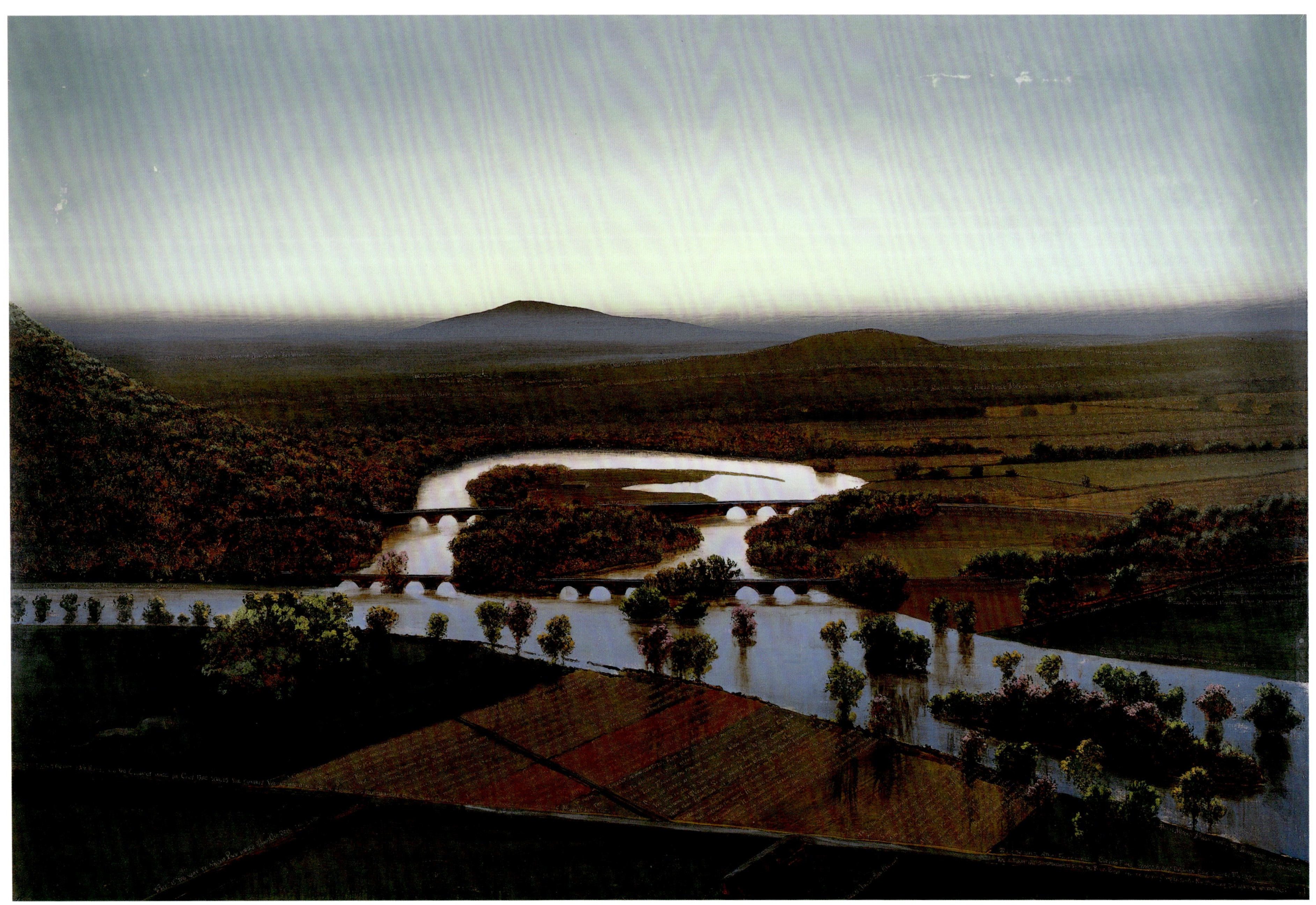

The Oxbow: After Church, after Cole, Flooded (Flooded River for the Matriarchs E. & A. Mongan), Green Light, 2000
Acrylic with oil glazes on canvas, 96 x 144 inches (244 x 366 cm). The Metropolitan Museum of Art. Purchase, Moore Capital Management Inc. Gift, 2001 (2001.153)

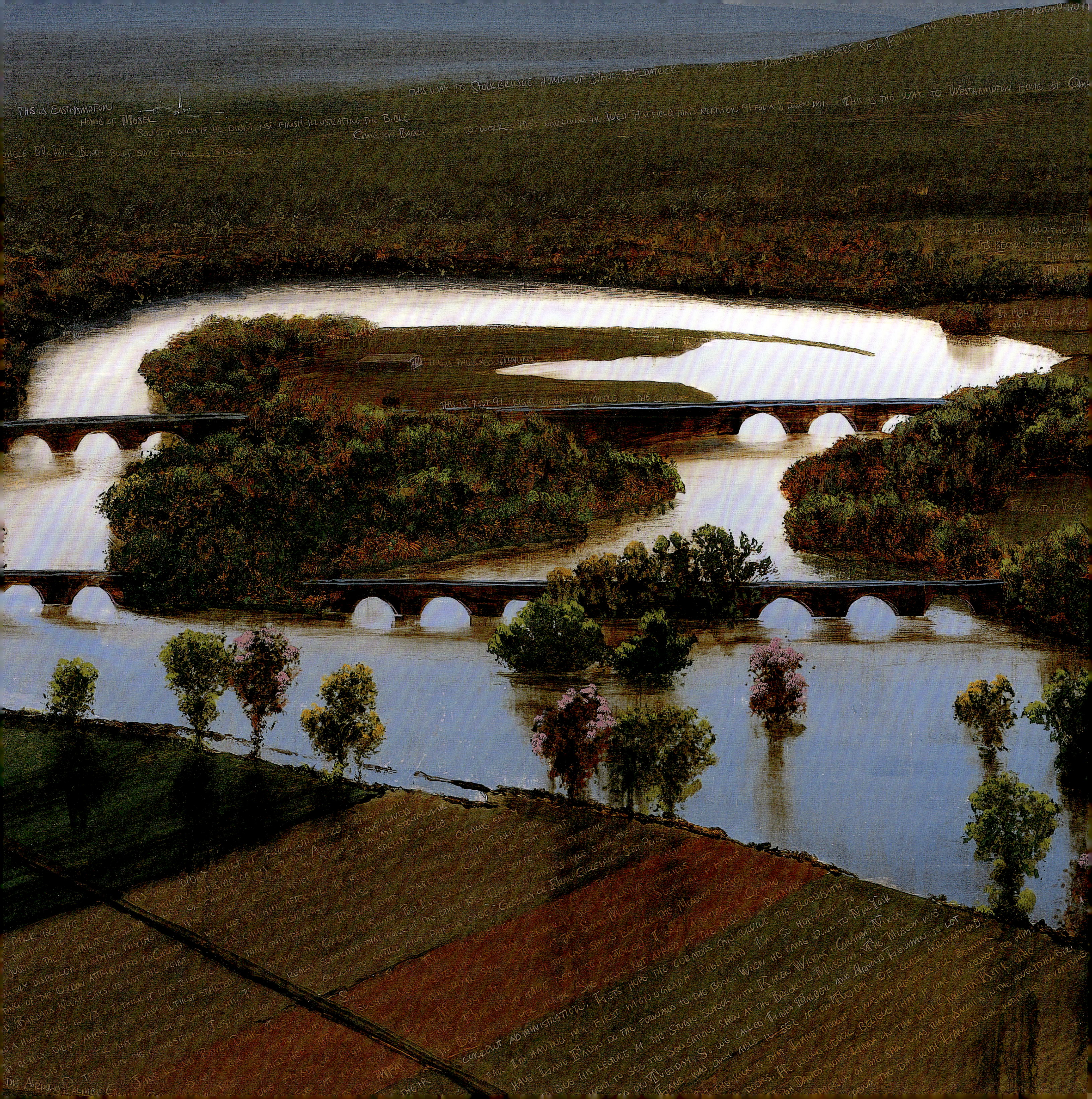

THIS IS EASTHAMPTON
HOME OF MOSER
SON OF A BITCH IF HE DIDN'T JUST FINISH ILLUSTRATING THE BIBLE
COME ON BARRY
...BLE MC WILL BUNEY BUILT SOME FABULOUS STUDIOS
THIS WAY TO STOCKBRIDGE HOME OF NANCY FITZPATRICK ... ALSO TO TANGLEWOOD WHERE SEIJI ...
THIS IS THE WAY TO WESTHAMPTON HOME OF OM...
BIBLE ... GET TO WORK.. WE'RE NOW LIVING IN WEST HATFIELD, THEN NORTH ON 91 FOR A ½ DOZEN MI...

Two aspects of Hannock's Oxbow painting profoundly distance him from the nineteenth century—his paint application and his inclusion of his handwritten commentary on the canvas. By 1994, he had developed a highly personal technique that combined brushwork and industrial tools. Using a power sander, Hannock polished successive layers of paint and gel medium, aiming to create a translucent surface that would trap light but not produce a distracting glare. As part of his process, he incorporated erasures or unconventional textures along the way. Broad, rough strokes of paint are clearly visible. Under and over the layers he wrote his thoughts. Cole had pictured himself as an artist sketching in the foreground. Hannock inserted himself more insistently, turning the canvas into a diary. His sentences follow the composition's main lines, appearing diagonally in foreground fields and along the horizontals of roads or tree groupings. The words are readable from up close, but they are not noticeable from a distance. The viewer discovers the text almost by chance. Hannock identified his location: "My view is 100 yards off the hang- gliding launch" (on the ridge south of the Summit House). He indicated directions, as in "this way to the Berkshires." He recounted events that happened there, such as "Gordo the wacko almost blew Jimmy's head off with an M-80." He expressed his feelings about his contemporaries, noting that, also in response to Cole's work, Alfred Leslie had painted a large view of the Oxbow from Mount Holyoke; he called Leslie's work a "nice piece" that "didn't do it for me."

All Hannock's later paintings of the Oxbow build on his first one. Until 2002, he usually titled them in the same manner, honoring Cole and the Mongans. He continues to write on his canvases. He always uses the same configuration of the Oxbow, which he projects onto the canvas from a template he created based on his first drawings of the site. Thus certain constants remain—the course of the river, the alignment of the fields, the position of Mount Tom at the left, and the mountain in the distance—while light, color, time of day, amount of flooding,

placement and number of trees, and cloud formations change. He essentially invents these features, keying the whole to how he envisions the sky.

At the time he was painting *The Oxbow: After Church, After Cole, Flooded (Flooded River for Fran)* (p. 18), late in 1998, he was experimenting with how much of the setting sun he would leave visible. When artist Frances Cohen Gillespie, a friend and former Northampton colleague, died of cancer at the age of 59, he was moved to dedicate the work to her memory. He focused on her in the handwritten commentary that now spreads to the far banks of the river and the hills beyond. "I would love to have seen what Fran would do with the Oxbow. Now we'll never know. Fran's gone," he inscribed, and added, "No one I know was as tortured during the process and so petrified of the result." The painting is chiefly distinguished by the many orange clouds lit by a sun that has just disappeared behind the horizon. Water spills further into the nearby fields, and the Oxbow's surface shines particularly brightly against the dark hills. These elements—flood, sunset, glowing river—serve as metaphors for death and renewal.

Oxbow subjects painted between 1994 and 2000 show Hannock's preoccupation with color and light variations. *The Oxbow Flooded at the End of the Day* (1996; 40 x 60 inches, Museum of Fine Arts, Houston) represents the setting sun visible over the horizon. *Evening Oxbow: Flooded (for Rockwell Kent at the Smith College Museum),* 1996 (p. 19), was inspired by the green cast of light in Kent's *Dublin Pond,* a 1903 painting (owned by the Smith College Museum of Art) that features a dark mountain against a lighted sky. Two others, both bearing titles identical to the Smith College painting but measuring 48 x 72 inches, express contrasting moods. One, painted in 1998 (private collection), features a dramatic sunset with darkened clouds and a path of reflected light in the Oxbow channel. In the other, painted in 1999 (private collection), a tonality of greens and a cloudless sky heighten the starkness of land forms.

The Oxbow: After Church, after Cole, Flooded (Flooded River for the

Matriarchs E. & A. Mongan), Green Light, of 2000 (p. 20), is his largest Oxbow painting at 96 x 144 inches. The viewer is catapulted into space and confronted directly by the river. As before, the time of day is twilight and the season autumn, but now a striking blue haze envelops the horizon, partly obscuring the mountain there. The words "green light" in the title refer to the same painting by Rockwell Kent that had interested him before. He felt the need to elaborate further on the feeling of Kent's painting, to make the sky a stronger green. The fields display a range of green tones accented by peach and coral. Other, more nuanced adjustments include the spit of land at the far side of the island that now extends in an elegant, fingerlike curve.

Stillness permeates Hannock's Oxbow paintings. The foreground road, the river, the two highways, and the fields beyond provide horizontal axes, although these are not rigid and are further softened by diagonal lines of fields. The horizontal bands, sense of quietude, and emphasis on light link Hannock to other nineteenth-century landscape painters known as Luminists. He is also well aware of their work—of Martin Johnson Heade and Sanford Gifford, for instance, who were contemporaries of his Hudson River School favorites. Hannock openly admires past art, reveling in both the associations that accrue to his work and the challenge of recasting tradition.

In successive paintings of the Oxbow, Hannock enlarged the role of his diaristic observations, covering more passages with words. He repeated many of the identifying labels ("this way to Easthampton") and stories ("Gordon the wacko") and references to artists, but added new information. On the Metropolitan picture he wondered again why his former Northampton colleagues had not painted the Oxbow: "I'm really surprised that none of the other New England painters have sunk their teeth into the composition. Just the light is enough to rattle any painter's cage. Gregory, or Fran Gillespie, Scott Prior, Jane Lund, Randy Deihl, Greg Stone." By this time he had changed his mind about Alfred

Leslie's painting *View of the Connecticut River as Seen from Mount Holyoke*, of 1972 (in the Museum Moderner Kunst, Vienna). "It really didn't appeal to me when I first started studying the Oxbow at Smith. But I've grown to appreciate it for its total disregard for any sense of Romanticism." He referred to Cole's painting, pointing out that "Cole may have drawn the Oxbow from Skinner Park but he sure as hell didn't paint it from up there." (As he knows, Cole painted the view in his studio three years after having drawn it on site.) He also went further in correcting the record about his reference to Frederic Edwin Church, having learned from Franklin Kelly that the painting was now attributed to an anonymous copyist after a print by William Bartlett. "It really does suck," Hannock wrote. He had continued to include Church in his titles to symbolize the Hudson River School tradition.

Two years later, Hannock painted another Oxbow piece for another mentor, S. Lane Faison Jr., a revered art scholar and professor at Williams College (p. 24). Although Hannock taught at Williams as a visiting artist in 1982, he did not meet Faison until the late 1980s, when his parents began summering in Williamstown. In 2002, Hannock bought his own place there and left New York for Williamstown the next year. *The Oxbow, After Church, After Cole, Flooded (Flooded River for S. Lane Faison Jr.)* pictures the river so flooded that it has doubled in width. Luminous surfaces dominate the composition. Mini-islands and peninsulas, as well as stranded trees, stand out against the golden river. In a curving band of orange sky, a brighter orange disk hovers at the horizon. Hannock's writing is largely confined to foreground and distant fields, where entries at first glance resemble rows of corn. Many of the artist's observations center on associations with Faison and Williams College. He recalled, for instance, going with Faison to see the controversial *Sensations* exhibition at the Brooklyn Museum. "We had a great time but came away with the overwhelming impression that Charles Saatchi is in the advertising business." He delights in discovering connections among the people in his life,

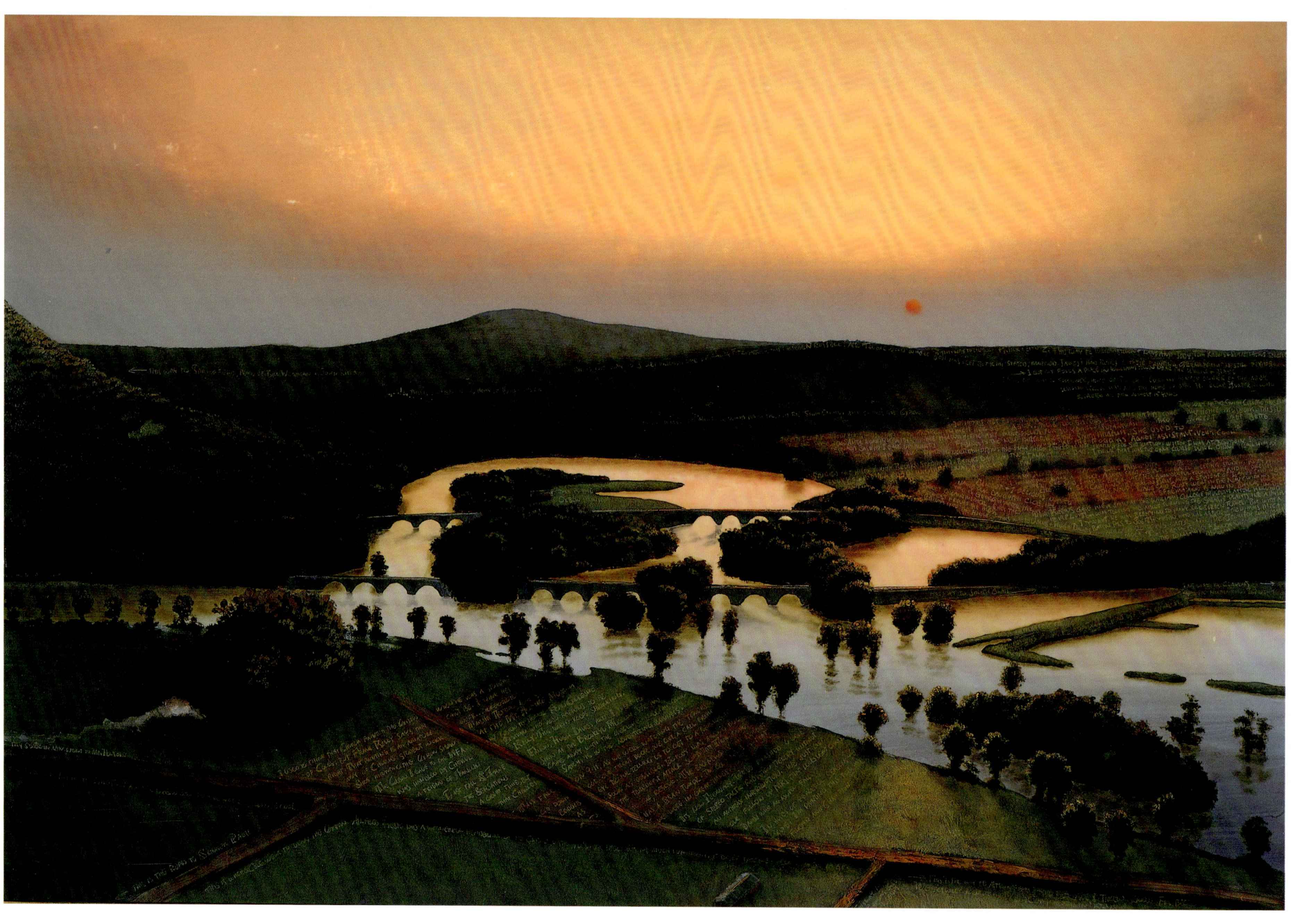

The Oxbow, After Church, After Cole, Flooded (Flooded River for S. Lane Faison Jr.), 2002

Polished oil on canvas, 40 x 60 inches (102 x 152 cm). Williams College Museum of Art, Williamstown, Massachusetts, Gift of the Artist in Honor of S. Lane Faison Jr. (M. 2002.5)

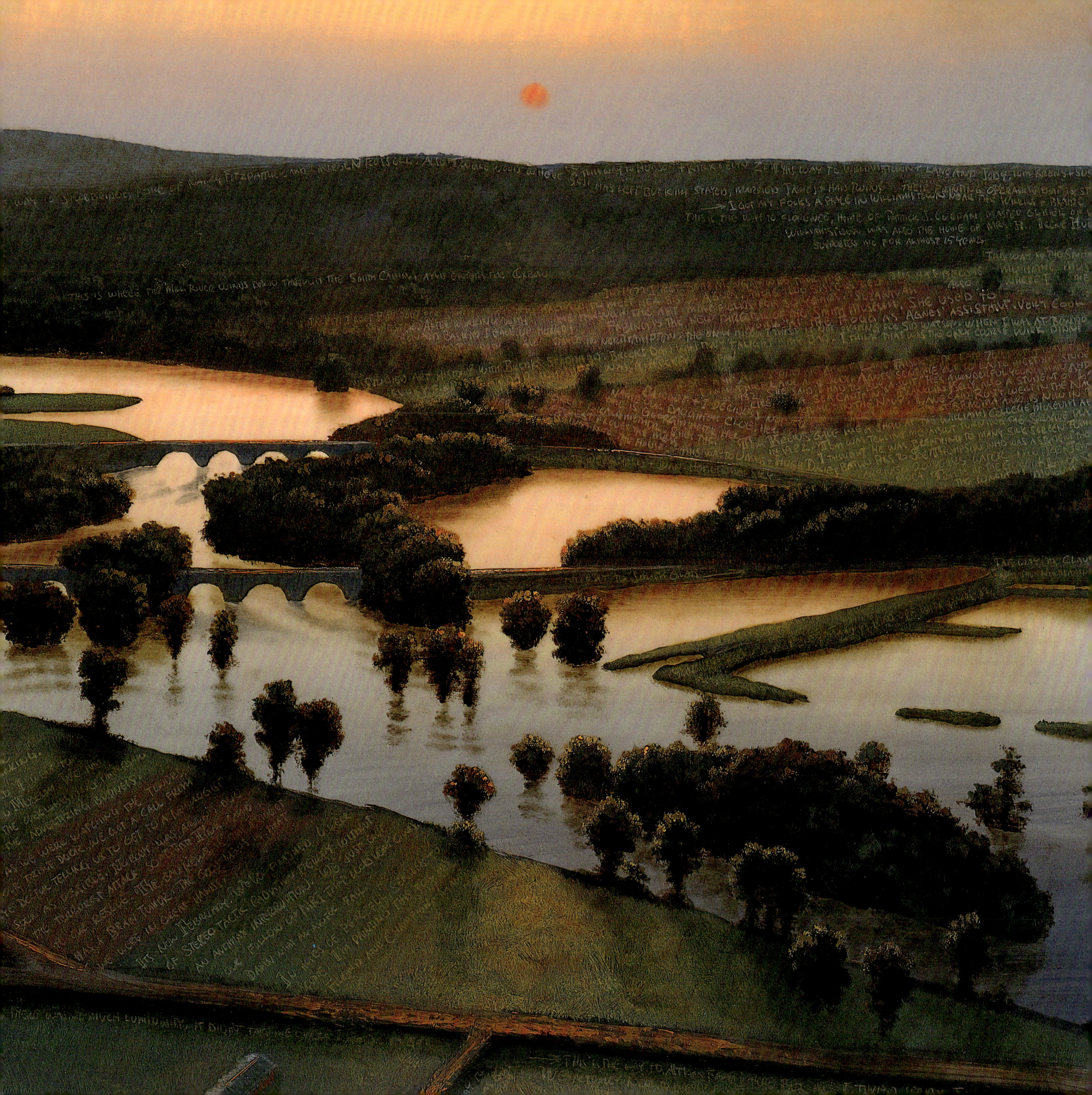

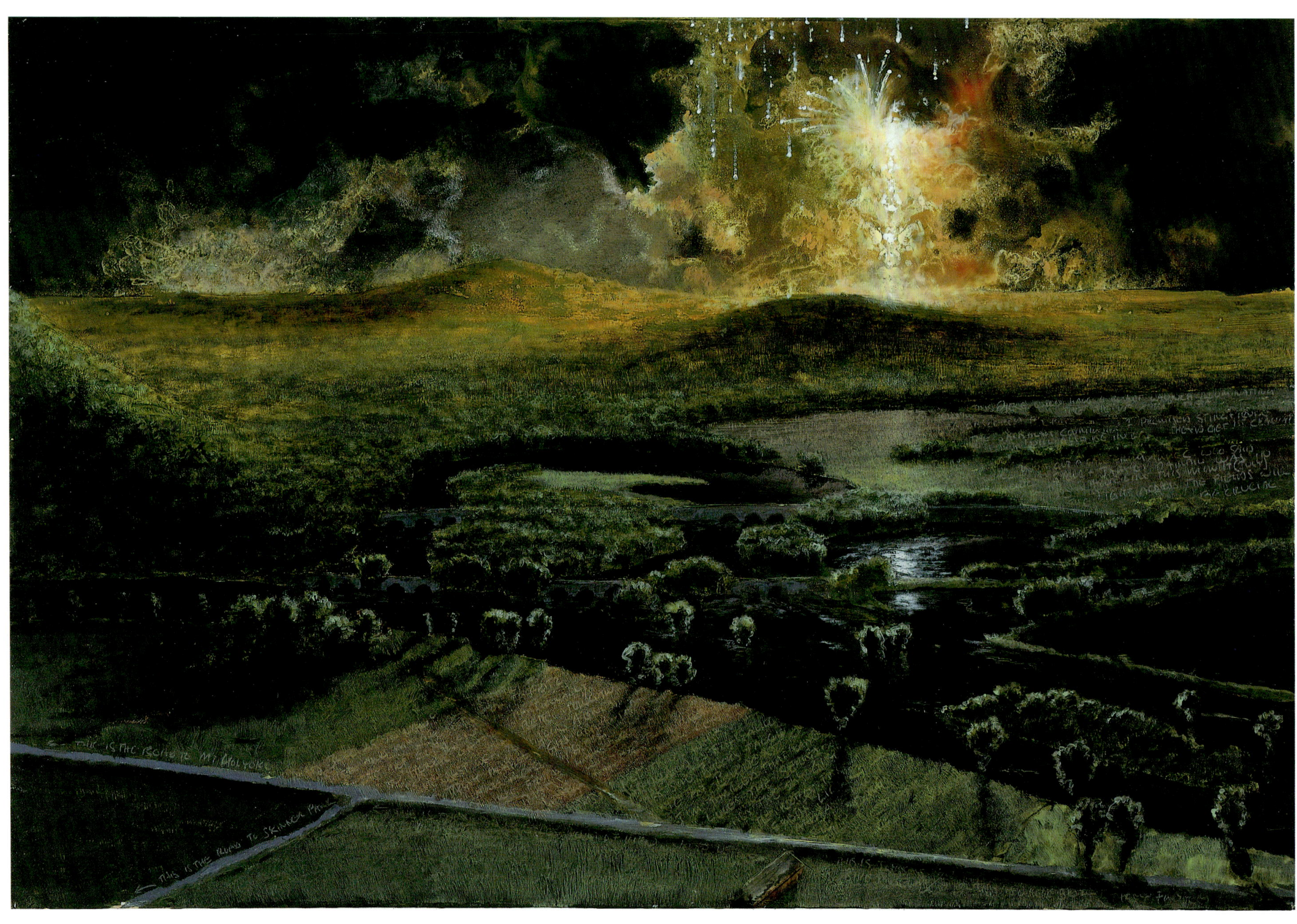

Study for Evening Launch over the Oxbow (Flooded River for Agnes & Bette Mongan), 2002
Polished oil on canvas, 12 x 22 inches (31 x 56 cm). Private Collection

26

pointing out on the canvas that before meeting Faison, "Agnes sent me out to L.A. to meet his student Rusty Powell in 1982. She said I had to buy a suit because he dresses like a sea captain." On the background hills he included the names of other successful Faison students with whom he had an association. Running alongside these lighthearted memories was a darker note. In his direct manner he referred to the stereotactic radiation treatments his wife, Bridget Watkins Hannock, was receiving for a brain tumor diagnosed the previous year.

In 2002, Hannock was also pursuing a radically different vision of the Oxbow: a night scene lit by rockets. Intrigued by J. M. W. Turner's painting of fiery night skies, *The Battle of Waterloo* in the Tate Gallery, London, he tried out the idea in *Study for Evening Rockets near Salisbury* (1999–2002; 14 x 21 inches; private collection) using oil and acrylic on a digital print of another of his paintings. Here the rolling English countryside, seen from a promontory, resembles the Oxbow terrain. For *Study for Evening Launch over the Oxbow (Flooded River for Agnes & Bette Mongan)*, Hannock introduced cataclysmic skies, showers of tiny lights, and deep green fields lit by light green streaks (p. 26). In a reversal of his usual color scheme, the river runs black. By the time he painted the larger (64 x 96 inches) version, *Evening Launch over the Oxbow* (2002; private collection), he toned down the pyrotechnics and made the darkened meadowlands a rich medley of greens. Although he continued to paint rocket-lit landscapes, Hannock did not feature rockets in any of the seven Oxbow views he produced after 2002. These works, all in private collections, represent a range of sizes, color harmonies, and personalized inscriptions (pp. 28, 29). His ongoing concentration on nuances of light is obvious from some of their titles: *Oxbow with Blue Bridge* (2005; 32 x 48 inches), *Oxbow with Peach Dusk* (2006; 24 x 36 inches), and *Oxbow with Peach Afternoon* (2006; 48 x 72 inches).

Hannock conceived his most recent Oxbow subject, *The Oxbow for Bowdoin College; Flooded River for Leonard Baskin and David P. Becker (Mass MoCA # 84)* (p. 30), to inaugurate the reopening of the Bowdoin College Art Museum in October 2007. For the Bowdoin canvas he returned to his by-now classic formulation, but pushed his diaristic dimension to a new level. Not only did he devote more of the topography to handwritten commentary, but he also embedded photographs and other scraps of paper into the painting's surface. The additions are more or less visible, some faint, some overrun with text. He had introduced collage items in previous paintings, but never in an Oxbow scene.

Collage pieces and text center on Hannock's connections to Bowdoin College, which he attended before transferring to Smith in 1971, and on the two men honored in the work's title. Art curator and print specialist David Becker was a Bowdoin College friend. As Hannock wrote on the canvas, "In 2005 DPB curated a show of old master drawings from Bowdoin at the Timken Museum in San Diego." Becker appears in photographs as well; one toward the lower edge of the canvas shows him with some prints. Both text and photographs also document Hannock's connections to his former teacher Leonard Baskin, well-known printmaker and member of the art faculty at Smith College. Hannock noted that Bowdoin "gave Baskin his first museum show in 1962." A picture of a Baskin self-portrait in woodcut also appears in the canvas. Other embedded photographs show his favorite Rockwell Kent painting, which he partially hid by blending it into a curving hillside, and Hannock himself, seated on the railing of the Summit House atop Mount Holyoke. Faison appears standing before his Oxbow painting. Commentary there reads: "Williams Museum has an Oxbow in honor of Lane. I really miss him." Faison died in 2006.

More personal still is the section of the painting Hannock devoted to his wife, who died in 2004. "This Oxbow was completed three years after the day we lost Bridget." He included a photograph of his painting of Bridget when pregnant, and he noted that his daughter Georgia had been born ten days after

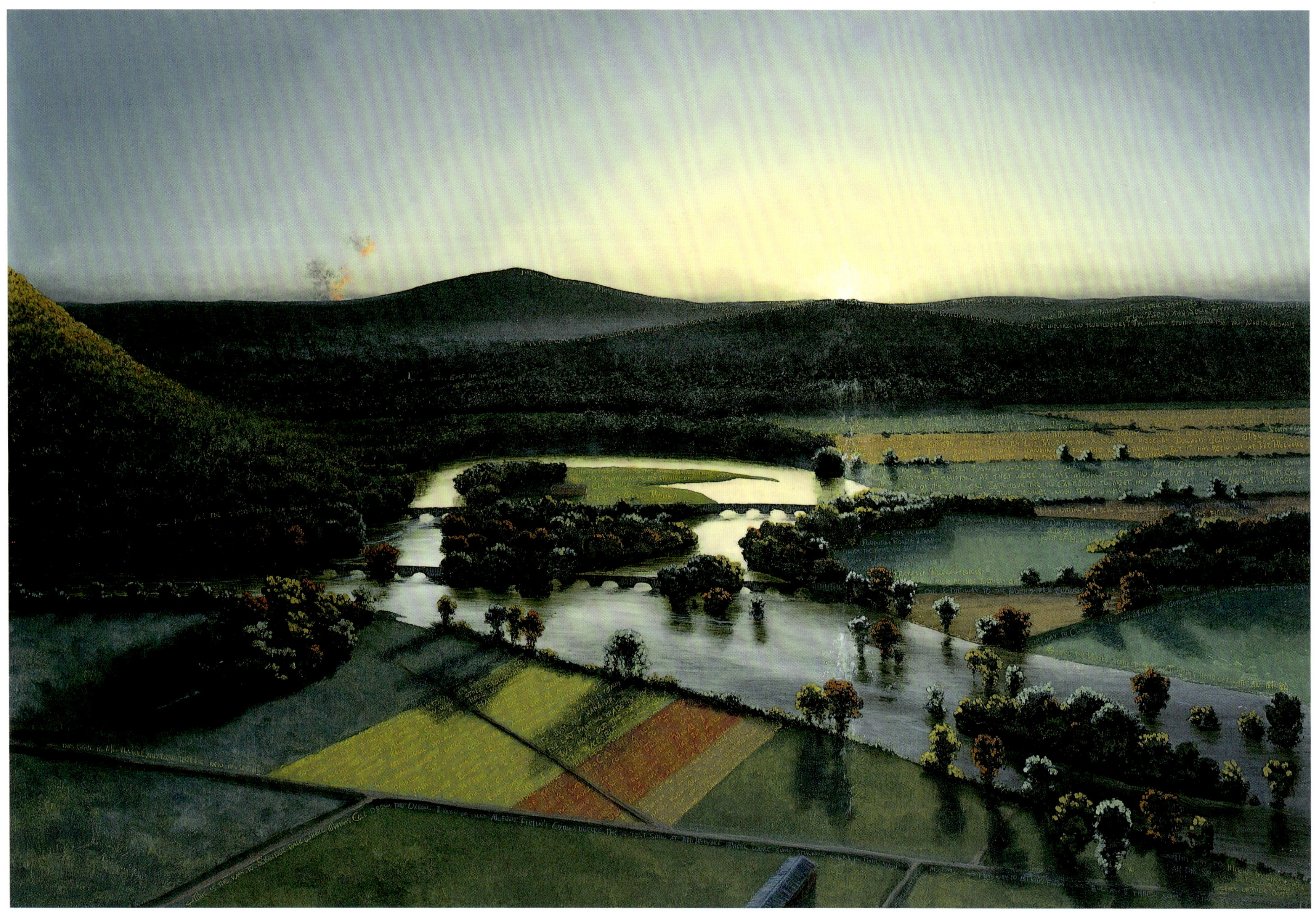

The Oxbow with Solo Cloud, 2003
Polished oil on canvas, 48 x 72 inches (122 x 183 cm). Private Collection

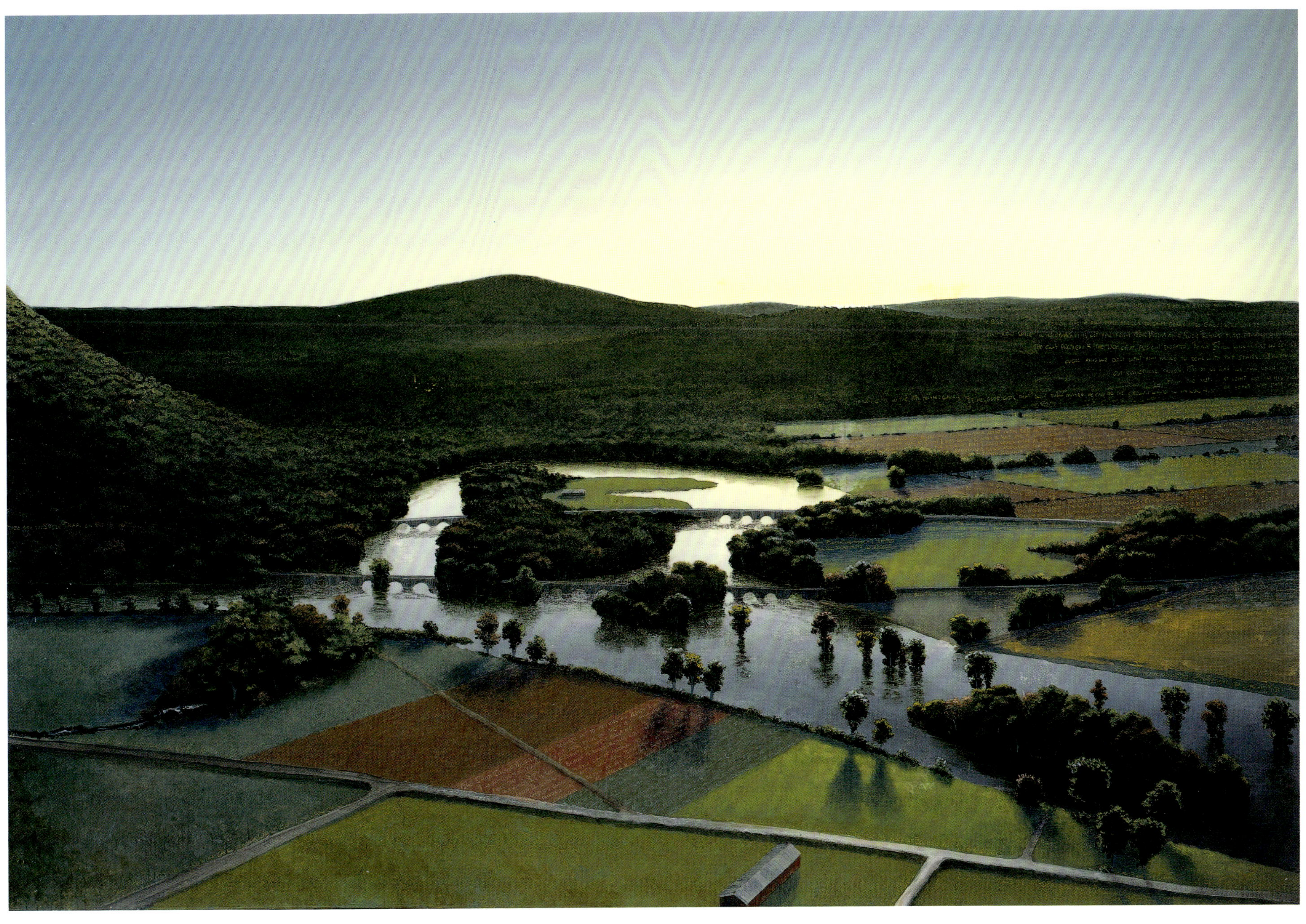

Twilight Oxbow, Before the Move, 2003
Polished oil on canvas, 64 x 96 inches (163 x 244 cm). Private Collection

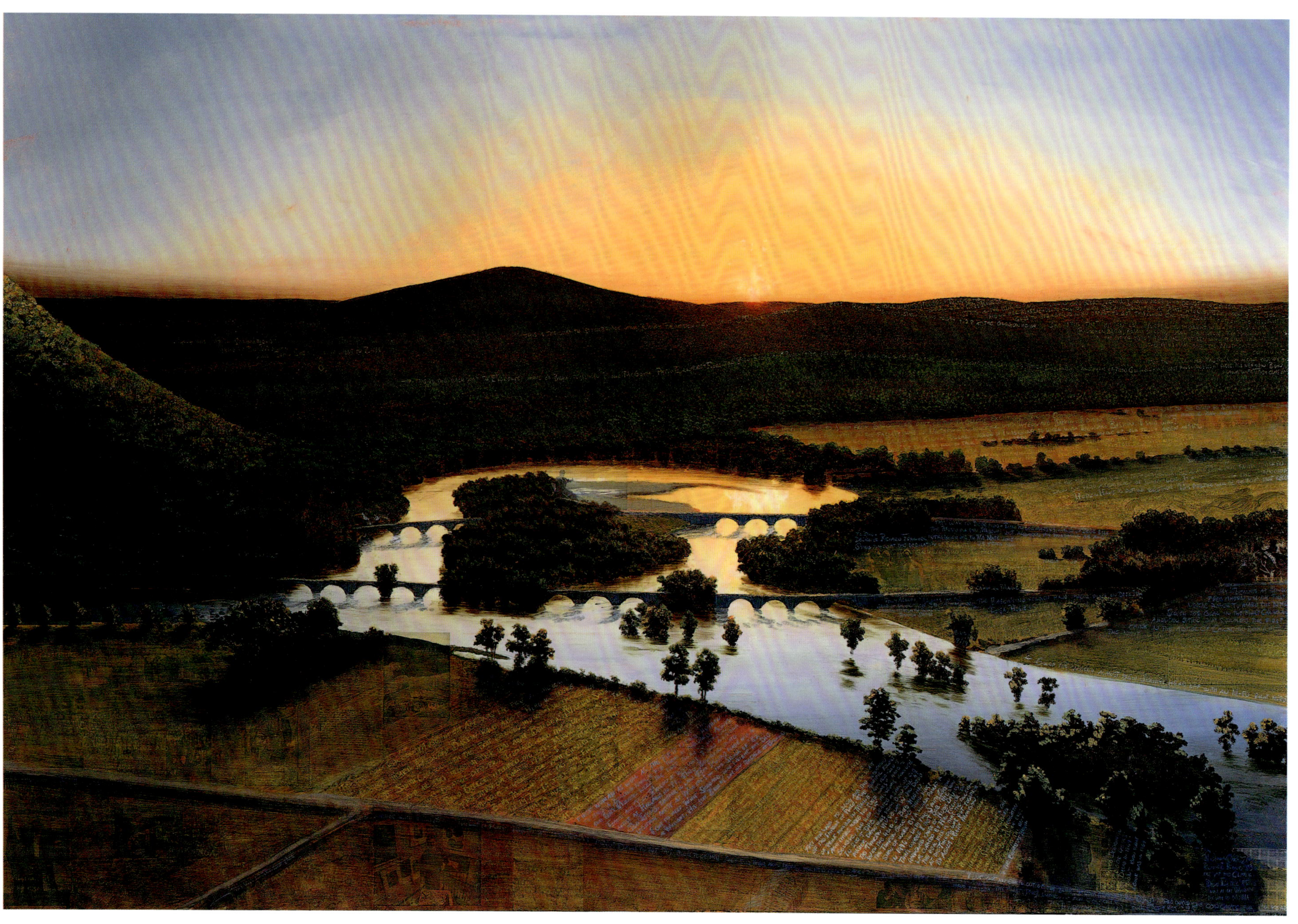

The Oxbow for Bowdoin College; Flooded River for Leonard Baskin and David P. Becker (Mass MoCA # 84), 2007
Polished mixed media on canvas, 64⁹/₁₆ x 96⁷/₁₆ inches (164 x 245 cm). Bowdoin College Museum of Art, Brunswick, Maine. Gift of the Artist (2007.18)

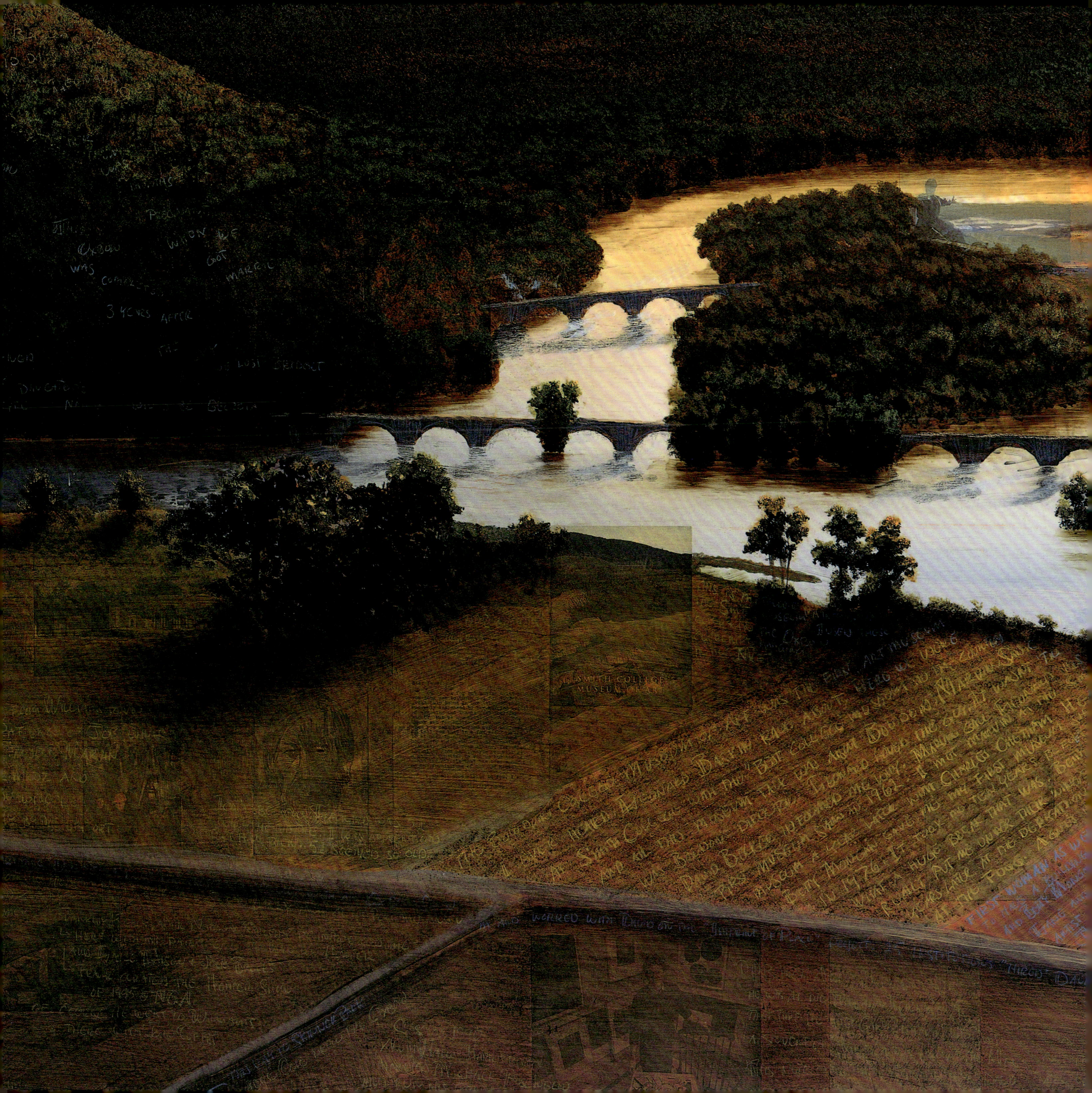
SMITH COLLEGE
MUSEUM OF ART

Baskin died. Georgia wrote her own name on the canvas. Of a photograph that disappeared during the painting process, he commented: "You can't see it now but this is our last picture as a family." In a previous painting dedicated to his wife, *The Oxbow: Warm Light, Flooded Fields (for Bridget)* (2004; 48 x 72 inches; private collection), he described getting the phone call that announced her illness minutes after watching the second airplane hit the World Trade Center on September 11, 2001. By now, Hannock has established his own iconographical tradition—the use of the Oxbow as memorial tribute.

While the Oxbow paintings form a series with its own evolution, they also relate directly to the rest of Hannock's work.[2] The subject grew out of his early focus on the Connecticut River, on the close-up views of it he began producing in 1989. In his early Northampton days, he would go out in a small boat and submerge himself literally up to his eyeballs to capture the sensation of water merging with sky. This experience led him to depict flooded rivers, either the Connecticut or another real or imagined place, as the purest means of capturing light. His compositions feature water as the immediate foreground, sharply receding banks, and ethereal trees floating across a tonal expanse. Like his views of the Oxbow, these works have no foreground stage. He has painted flooded river imagery steadily since 1989, moving back and forth between two poles: amorphous, atmospheric, tonal rivers and their counterpoint, the firm structure and predictability of the Oxbow. On a technical level, Hannock's Oxbow paintings also influence, and are influenced by, his work as a whole. He has lately applied techniques developed in the Oxbow subjects to other landscape paintings, most notably the use of writing on the canvas. In 2005, he incorporated words in *A Recent History of Art in Western Massachusetts; Flooded River for Lane Faison (Mass MoCA #12)* (p. 83) and now extends the practice to large paintings that he calls "vistas with text." In turn, he used collage elements in his latest Oxbow scene.

Hannock is not alone in painting the Oxbow today. In the last thirty years, the view from Mount Holyoke has become a popular subject. Almost all artists, like Hannock, remove the obvious traces of encroachment—traffic, roads, telephone wires, distant towns— inevitably associating their works with the modern environmental movement. Whether intentional or not, Hannock's paintings promote preservation or at least controlled development of the land. At the same time, he incorporates elements repeatedly depicted by nineteenth-century landscape artists: sunset, autumn, river, and radiant light, all signifying natural cycles of birth and death. Flooding and the Oxbow's formation itself symbolize destruction and rebirth. In suggesting the possibility of loss while expressing the sublime loveliness of nature, Hannock's views of the Oxbow are unabashedly romantic.

Notes

1. This essay is based on the author's conversations with Stephen Hannock in January 2002, September 2007, and December 2007. Hannock's Oxbow paintings are discussed in Duncan Christy, *Luminosity* (San Francisco: Chronicle Books, 2000) and the following exhibition catalogues: Robert Atkins, *After Church, After Cole, Stephen Hannock's Oxbow* (San Diego: Timken Museum of Art, 1995); Robert Atkins, *Stephen Hannock* (New York: James Graham & Sons, 1996); Hal Fischer, *Stephen Hannock, Space & Time* (Dayton, Ohio: Dayton Art Institute, 1998); Marianne Doezema, ed., *Changing Prospects, The View from Mount Holyoke* (Ithaca, NY: Cornell University Press, 2002); Jason Rosenfeld, *Stephen Hannock* (New York: MacKenzie Fine Art, 2002); and *The Harrison Gallery* (Williamstown, MA: Harrison Gallery, 2005).

2. Of the twenty-one Oxbow paintings measuring 24 x 36 inches and larger, those not mentioned in the text are: *The Oxbow, After Church, After Cole, Flooded, 1979–1994 (Flooded River for the Matriarchs, E. and A. Mongan)*, 1994, 24 x 36 inches, collection of the artist; *The Oxbow, After Church, After Cole, Flooded, 1979–1994 (Flooded River for the Matriarchs, E. and A. Mongan)*, 1998, 24 x 36 inches, private collection; *The Oxbow, After Church, After Cole, Flooded, 1979–1994 (Flooded River for the Matriarchs, E. and A. Mongan)*, 2000, 48 x 72 inches, private collection; *The Oxbow, Flooded: Red Flare, Green Light, 2003–04*, 64 x 96 inches, private collection; *The Oxbow for Bowdoin College; Flooded River for Leonard Baskin and David P. Becker (Mass MoCA #78)*, 2007, 32 x 48 inches, private collection.

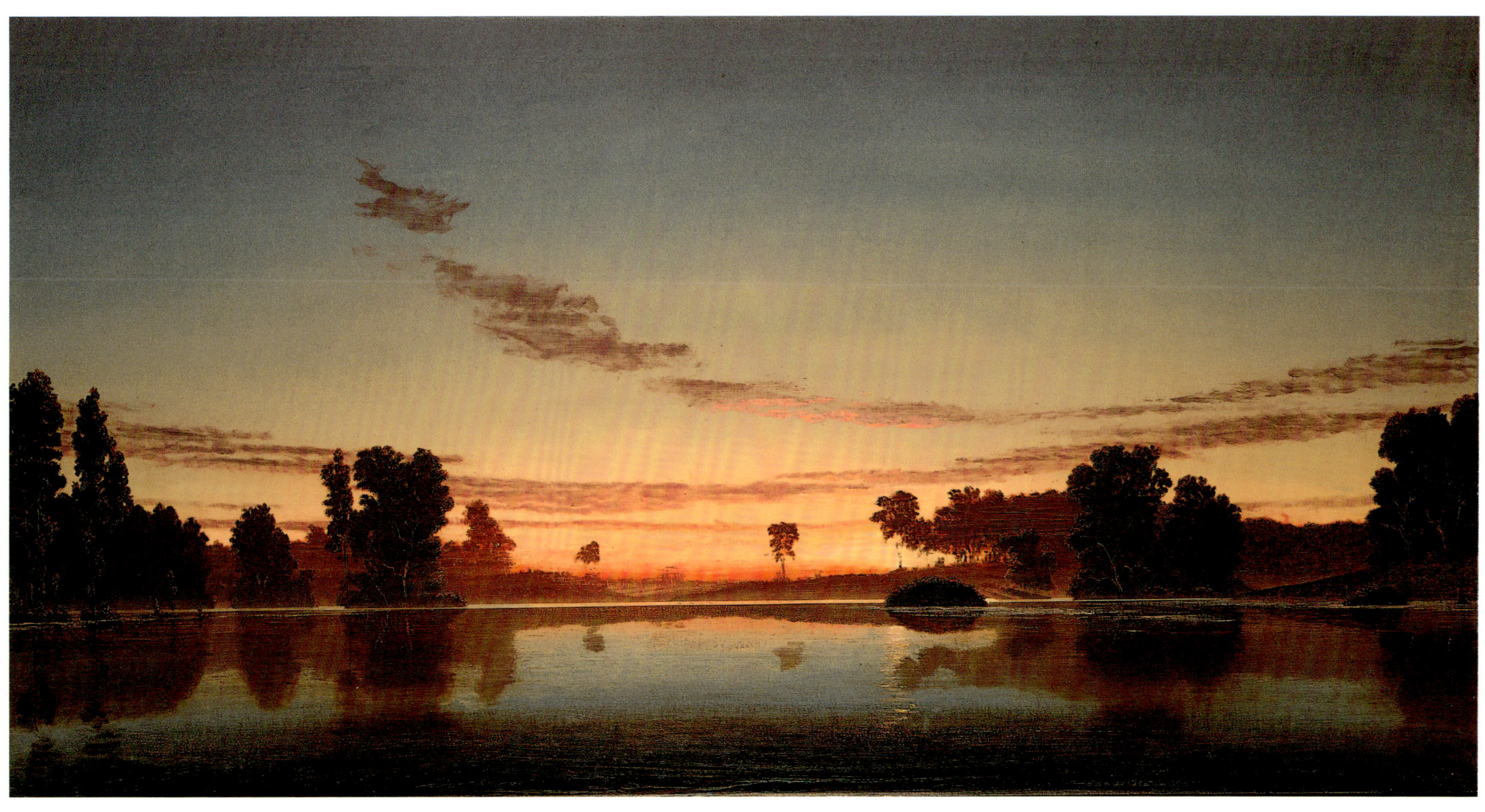

Flooded River: Entering the Oxbow (Rose Horizon at Dawn), 1990

Polished oil on canvas, 36 x 70 inches (61 x 178 cm). Private Collection

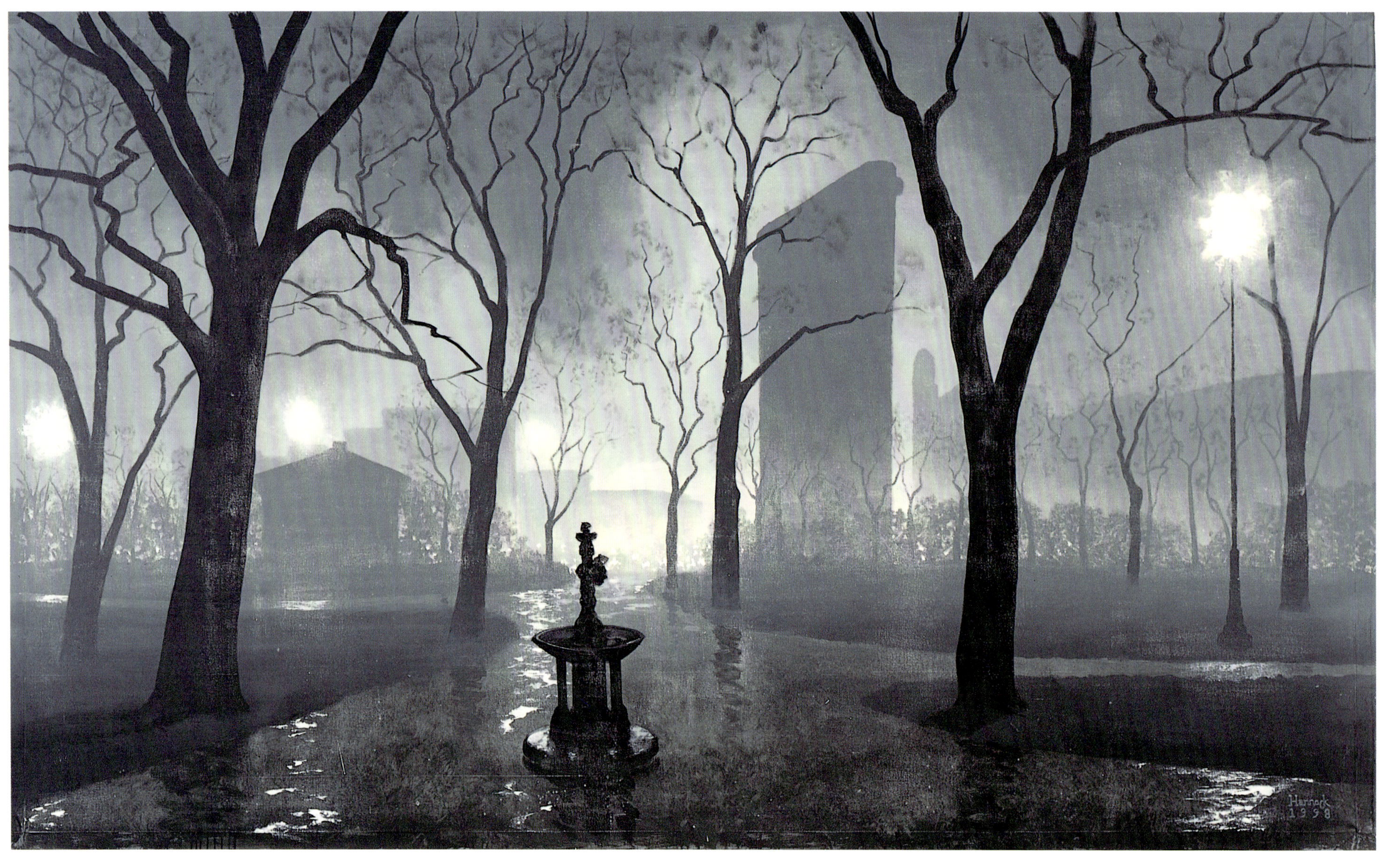

Madison Square Park at the Turn of the Century (View South), 1997
Acrylic on canvas, 84 x 144 inches (213 x 366 cm). Private Collection

Stephen Hannock: New England/New York

Jason Rosenfeld

*I*N 1766, THE EMINENT ENGLISH PAINTER JOSHUA REYNOLDS, soon-to-be first president of London's Royal Academy of Arts, recognized the young Boston painter John Singleton Copley's artistic promise and advised him that if he availed himself of the…

> …advantages of the Example and Instruction which you could have in Europe, You would be a valuable Acquisition to the Art, and one of the first Painters in the World, provided you could receive these Aids before it was too late in Life, and before your Manner and Taste were corrupted or fixed by working in your little way at Boston.[1]

Thus did an established authority in the world's then most important city goad a developing artist from provincial Massachusetts. Eight years later, Copley would sail to London for good and, confirming Reynolds's prescience, prove to be one of North America's most gifted exports.

In the fall of 1981, the Mongan sisters, prominent curators and art historians Elizabeth and Agnes, took aside the budding Northampton, Massachusetts, painter Stephen Hannock, who had just concluded a successful show at Harvard University, and told him to go south to New York City.[2] His manner and taste were not in danger of being corrupted, his training was already well advanced, but his promise demanded a fuller challenge. Hannock did not need more encouragement, nor near a decade to deliberate. He moved to Manhattan and lived there full time until 2002, when he moved back to Massachusetts. This much is known. But less recognized is the degree to which form and idea in Hannock's mature art were decisively inflected by advanced art in New York in the 1980s and 1990s. His subject may at times be Massachusetts, or that state's representation in art over the centuries, but so much of what he has made over the past twenty years has been a sharp, and novel, response to the New York scene. Hannock's style and preferences were not corrupted by western Massachusetts, nor New York, but the blend of the two has resulted in something original and complex in technique and subject, an intricate art of mood, reflection, and considerable power.

Hannock's present, mature technique is very different from the strategies of his earlier art from before his Harvard show. In the 1970s, he developed a radical mode of using highly unstable phosphorescent acrylic paints for pictures that bore extravagant light effects when seen under black light. These were painted in the dark (p. 36)[3], a tradition in art stretching back to Johannes Vermeer in his camera obscura or Georges Seurat, who sought the perception of increased luminosity in his paintings by working at night. Often on a mural scale, Hannock's early works are difficult to photograph, and their subjects are bizarre landscapes with superficial affinities to rock 'n' roll album covers, Symbolism, Surrealism, science fiction illustration, experimental film, and the visual impact of how film in general illuminates a screen. It was not until the early 1980s that Hannock began experimenting with polishing his surfaces, at first to remove mistakes and then as a formal technique to break down any calculated quality in his brushwork while simultaneously increasing their radiance. The challenge was to match the range of tones of the phosphorescent pictures in a more conventional medium, one that through this innovative method overcame the tendency of oils to reflect light.

Hannock's paintings of the first decade of the twenty-first century are, in most cases, made of acrylic or oil used alone or together, alternately built up and sanded down in many levels of glazes. They bear inscribed text in the artist's distinctive, blocky,

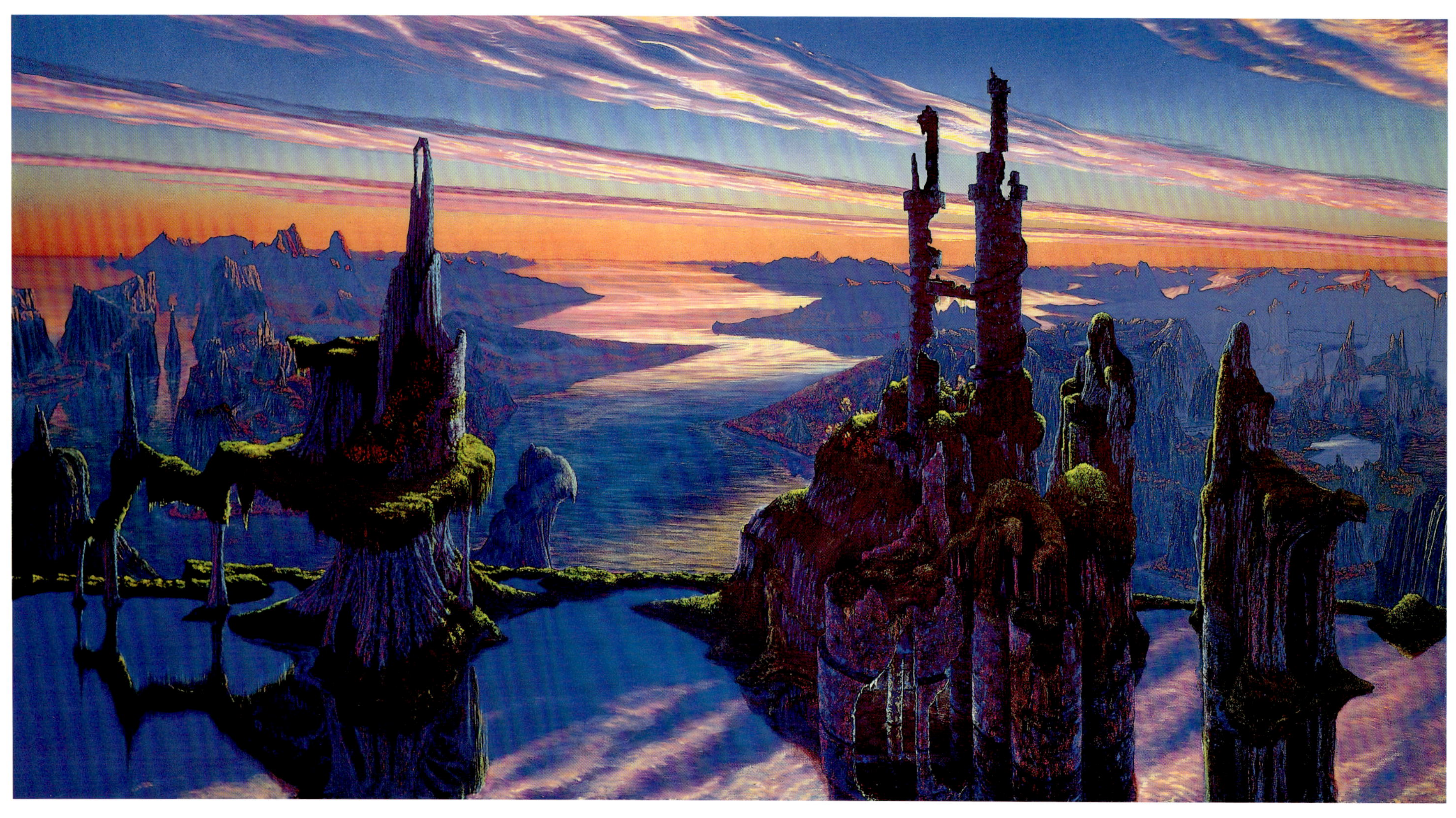

Mural III, 1974

Phosphorescent acrylic on canvas, 91 x 144 inches (231 x 366 cm). Private Collection

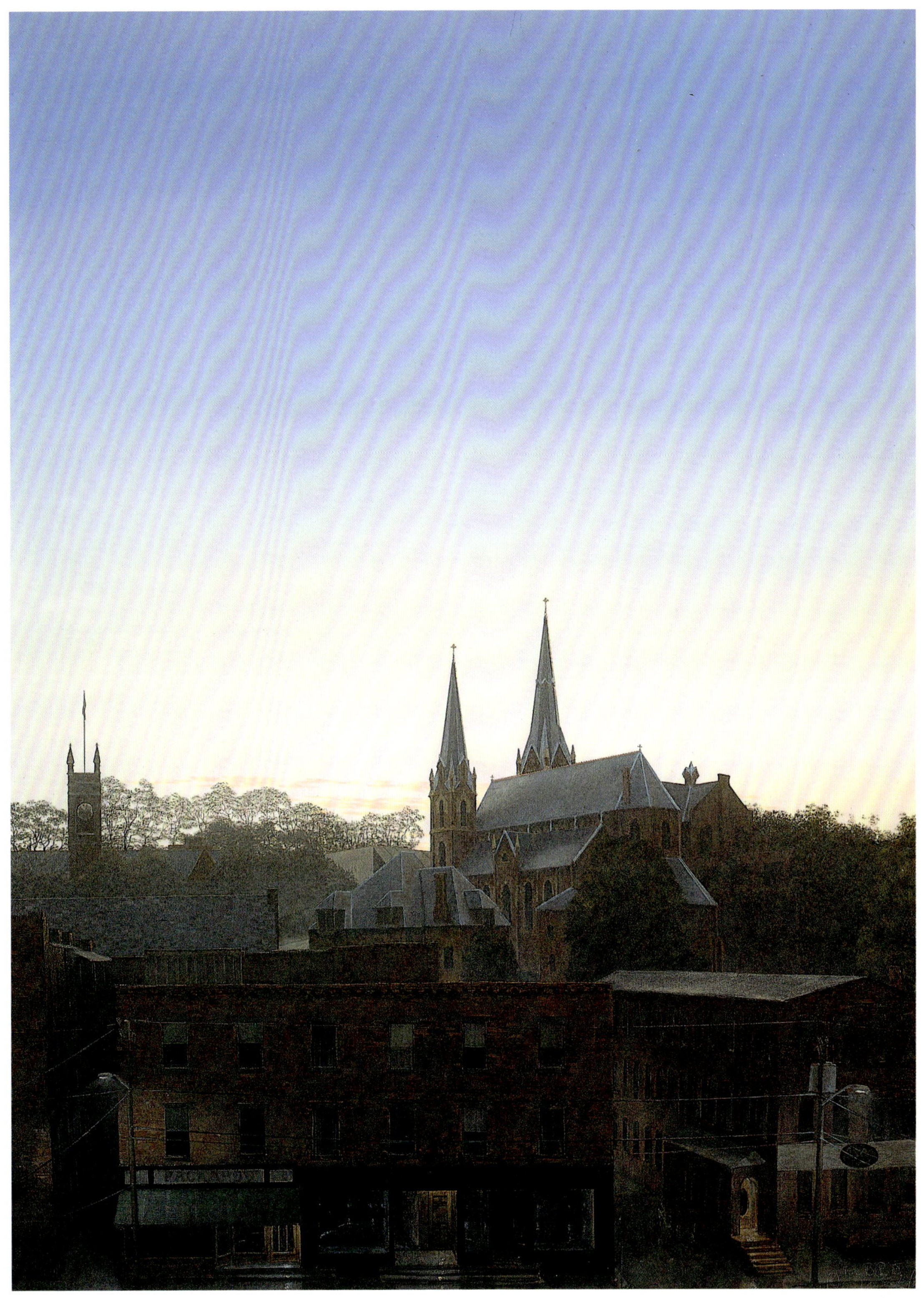

New England City (Northampton, Massachusetts), 1983

Polished oil on canvas, 72 x 54 inches (183 x 137 cm). Private Collection

37

all-caps script written across and flowing in harmony with descriptive passages. The pictures usually include pasted materials—photographs, magazine articles, letters, envelopes—that are submerged with varying levels of legibility between the painted layers. The most recognizable motif is some kind of landscape, and the overarching effect sought is a quality of light that bursts out from the support in a luminous and emanative glow. The specific landscapes set the stage for stories that emerge through the texts and collaged materials. The pictures become narrational. The repeated building up and grinding down of the surface tamps down the reflectivity of traditional painting as well as glare. It is commensurate to the difference between marble and bronze sculpture. Marble can absorb light up to one-and-a-half inches in depth and then return it to the eye transformed into a crystalline gleam. Conversely, light does not penetrate bronze but instead glints off its surface. The concentration on dark areas of Hannock's compositions allows the highlights to emit even more fully. For Hannock, this effect establishes mood. There is a continuity with his earlier work, but also a disjuncture: his subjects are at once recognizable—the Oxbow, Kaaterskill Falls, Sundance Canyon in Utah—but they are treated so as not to become singular in meaning. They are instead open-ended settings. Such theoretical aspects of Hannock's mature work owe much to his experience of art in New York City.

When Hannock arrived in New York in 1981, initially sharing a loft and then moving for good to his own place in 1983, he did what most artists without an agent did—he made the rounds, bearing his portfolio, trying to get a gallery interested in his art. It took him a few years. I imagine his hands glowing with phosphorescence, hair shaggy, a post-hippie entering ever-changing hipsterdom, and he perhaps did not seem out of place in a city with a burgeoning, if difficult to define, arts scene. Like many new arrivals to New York, he keyed into the aspects that seemed so alien to his own rural experience: subways, vertiginous scale,

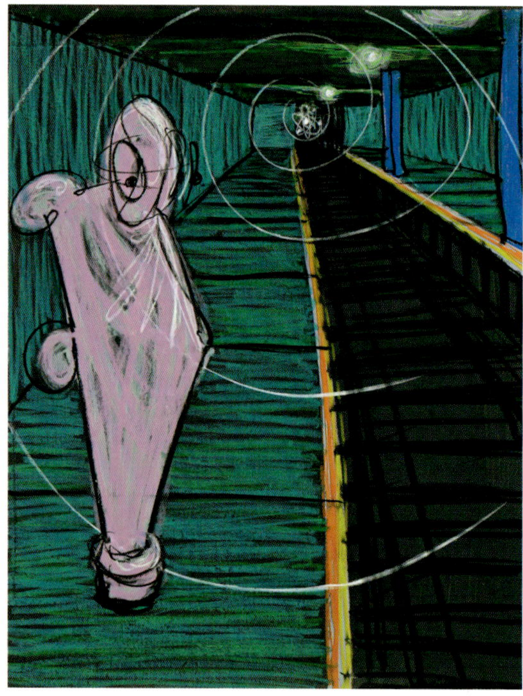

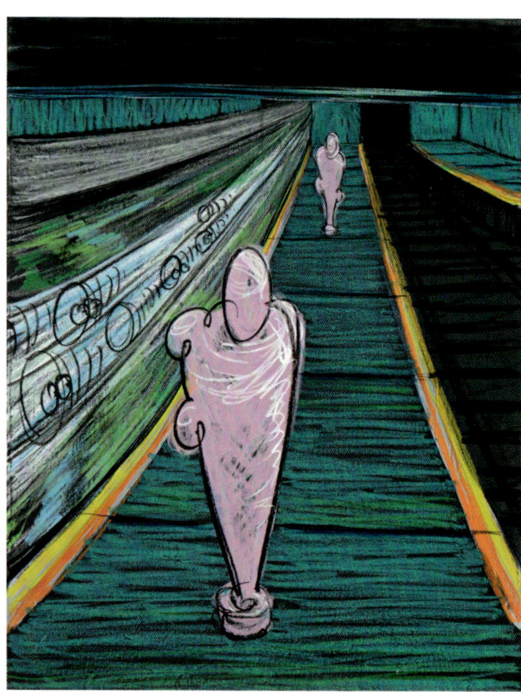

(TOP) WAITING IN THE NUCLEAR AGE, 1985

PASTEL AND OIL STICK ON PAPER, 45 X 35 INCHES (114 X 89 CM). COLLECTION OF THE ARTIST

(BOTTOM) TWO MEN WAITING, 1985

PASTEL AND OIL STICK ON PAPER, 45 X 35 INCHES (114 X 89 CM). COLLECTION OF THE ARTIST

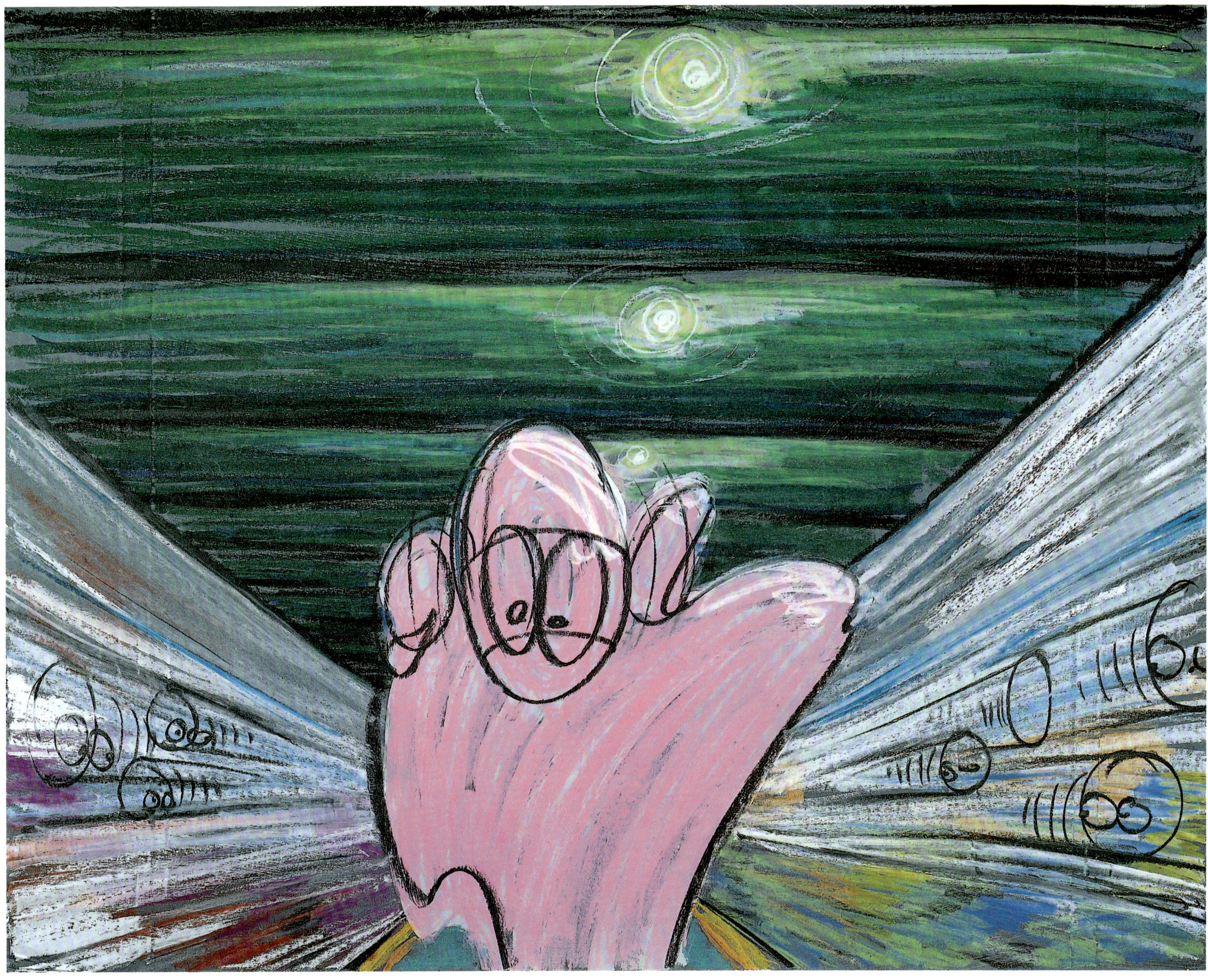

The Scream (Welcome to New York), 1985
Pastel and oil stick on paper, 35 x 45 inches (89 x 114 cm). Collection of the Artist

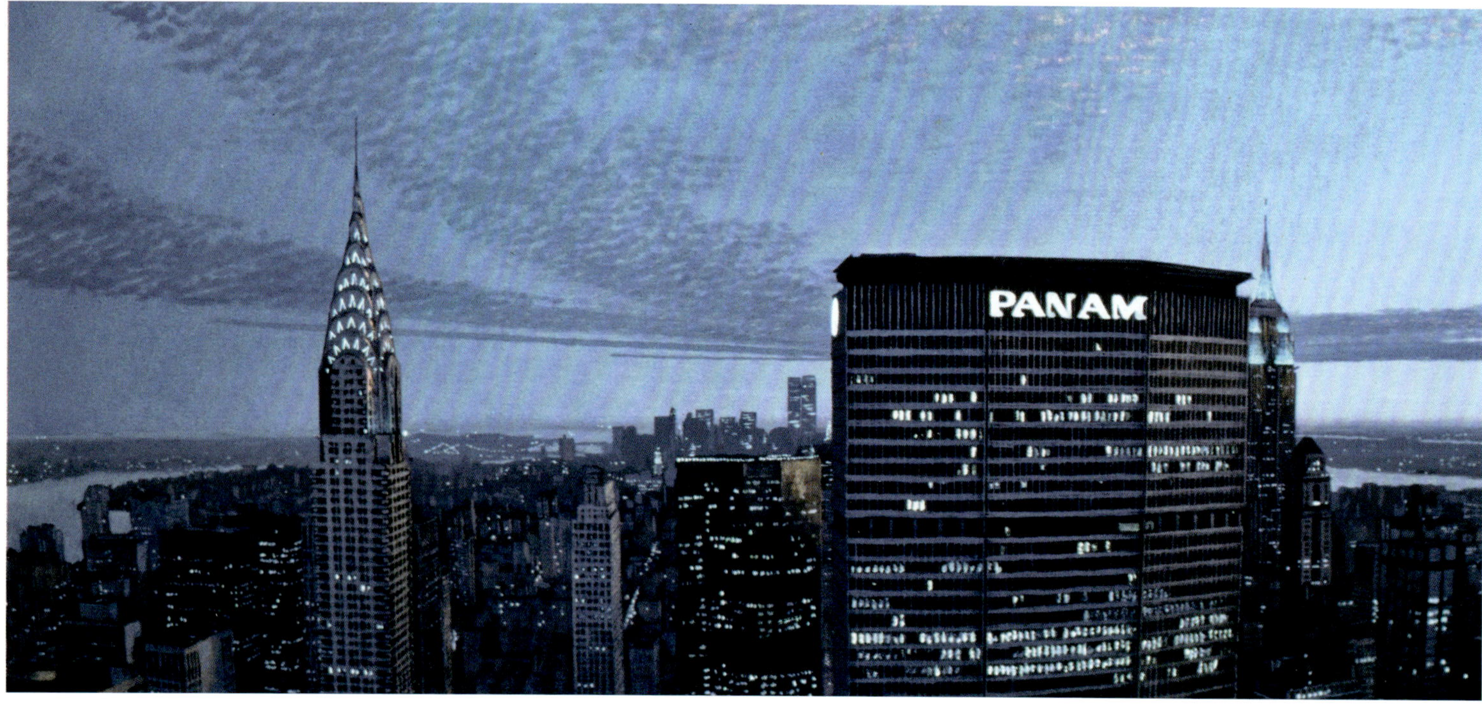

AMERICAN CITY, 1986
PHOSPHORESCENT ACRYLIC ON CANVAS, 48 X 96 INCHES (122 X 244 CM). PRIVATE COLLECTION

noise, bombast, and contemporary art in a range of different media on all kinds of surfaces. For a time he seesawed, residentially and thematically, painting northern landscapes such as the early, polished *New England City (Northampton, Massachusetts)* of 1985 (p. 37) while up in those environs and beginning the subway series with works such as *The Scream* two years later (p. 39). This was a period of indeterminacy—one not simply inflected by the underground world of mass transit, but also by the Soho world of what we now think of as postmodern art—marked by "neoexpressionist" proclivities. Hannock's immediate experience of careening around the city shopping art to galleries is treated metaphorically in his subway series, which represent the perfect venue for artistic intervention, as Keith Haring was revealing in that more illicit medium of the subway walls themselves. The stations were

also ideal settings in which to record an itinerant existence. Thus, as with so much of Hannock's work, the pictures bear elements of self-portraiture—not literally, as the anthropomorphic pink blobs do not resemble reality any more than the platforms themselves do actual MTA stations.[4] The only parameter Hannock set for the series was that the hand could never rest for a second; the pastels and oil sticks needed to be in constant motion over the gray gesso ground, thus blending the spontaneity of action painting with the caricatural facility of Haring's hieroglyphic chalk lines.[5] The resultant pictures are a cross between Gerald Scarfe's animations for Pink Floyd's film *The Wall* (1982, dir. Alan Parker), Edvard Munch's hourglass-headed, adrift figures and feverishly rendered landscapes, and mid-twentieth-century subway scenes by George Tooker and Mark Rothko that traded in human alienation. But the latter lack

Hannock's delirium in the speed of the trains as well as residual Day-Glo aesthetics from his phosphorescent art (which jived nicely with the graffiti-laden subway cars that snaked as splays of color through the system). The subway pictures represent sublime bewilderment in the "fundamental landscape" of New York City, in Hannock's term—its ruling orthogonality.[6] They layer chaos on a backdrop of order, a consistent theme in the artist's subsequent work.

The subway pictures do not resemble the simultaneously painted New England landscapes that would within a decade win out as Hannock's presiding motif. Yet they represent a tangent in his art that parallels his larger theme. They are transitional. A related example is *American City* (1986, private collection, p. 40), whose generalized title, like the supposed anonymity of Batman's Gotham, can hardly cloak the truth of its locale due to the cadence of the Chrysler, Pan Am, and Empire State Buildings flowing across this view from Park Avenue's Chemical Bank Building.[7] At eight feet wide, such works recall the panoramas of the late

eighteenth and early nineteenth centuries, and on a scale of Hannock's imagined landscapes of the 1970s. But they also have moved from the subterranean anonymity and prosaism of the subways to a winged view of the most celebrated monuments of the metropolis. This is also evident in the Robert Longo–influenced *Take Me to the River* of 1987 (p. 41)—a picture both phosphorescent and of New York. Invited to contribute to a celebration of the centenary of the Statue of Liberty, Hannock juxtaposed an image from the New Wave band Talking Heads' mainstream crossover hit film *Stop Making Sense* (1984, dir. Jonathan Demme) with a neon translation of Frédéric Bartholdi's colossal allegorical figure, made with phosphorescent paint and an airbrush. Meant to be viewed by black light, the diptych appeared to signal new concerns.

As a subject, however, New York may ultimately have been too obvious, too lacking in depth, and in the last two decades it has occupied the artist infrequently: spectral works from 1997 based on

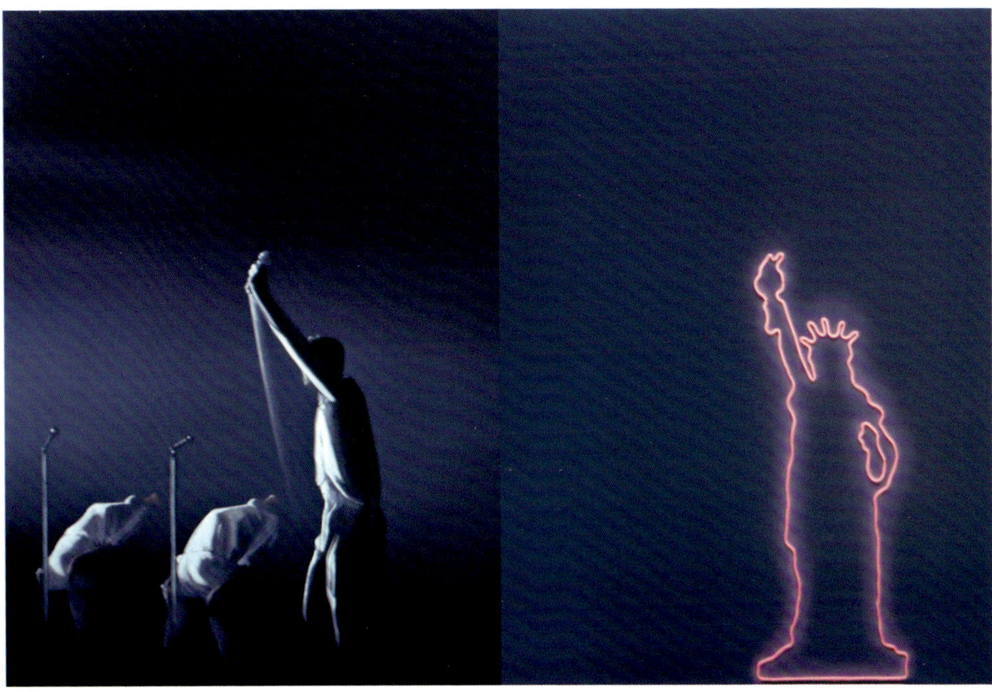

TAKE ME TO THE RIVER, 1987

(FILM STILL [LEFT] TAKEN FROM *Stop Making Sense*, JONATHAN DEMME, 1984)

PHOSPHORESCENT ACRYLIC ON CANVAS, 48 x 72 INCHES (122 x 183 CM). PRIVATE COLLECTION

41

Jessie Tarbox Beals's early twentieth-century photographs at Danny Meyer's Eleven Madison Park; a massive and soaring 2006 vision of the in-progress High Line park at Tom Colicchio's Craftsteak; five fantastical imagined landscapes, completed in 1993, of old and current New York at the Knickerbocker Club. Or the city appears in a single instance of deeply personal and specific meaning such as *American City with Restored Park* of 2005 (p. 126), a shimmering view of Madison Square painted as a cathartic memorial to his wife.[8]

Nevertheless, for Hannock New York is central to the Connecticut River Valley, and to recognize that is to explore more fully meaning in his art. The New York art scene of the 1980s coupled with his earlier decade in Massachusetts, as an apprentice to Leonard Baskin, resulted in works that intersect with trends in art and represent the essential gambit in Hannock's oeuvre. The decision to embrace realism was not a scheme or strategy. In fact, one would have expected that the experience of art in New York in the 1980s would have resulted in something opposed to realism, a denial of fidelity, a shift further toward irresolution.[9] But Hannock's work since 1990 has been both about modes of legibility and a fixation on abstract moods. The painted landscapes with layered text and media are palimpsests that are never easily decoded. And it took him until 1994 to settle on the defining subject of his art. Since then, for example, in producing twenty-one paintings of the Oxbow, Hannock has not particularly helped viewers better understand the course of the Connecticut River, but he has used the waterway as a stage for his stories.[10] The history is there. The traditions of art are there. The luminosity is there. But the pictures are not literally about the earth any more than Paul Cézanne's numerous Mont Sainte-Victoires are about geological time or historical and artistic human endeavor in Provence. Instead, the art operates within a number of strategies consistent with aspects of postmodernism in the 1980s as well as recent art—appropriation, figurative repetition, identity, and narrative disjuncture evident

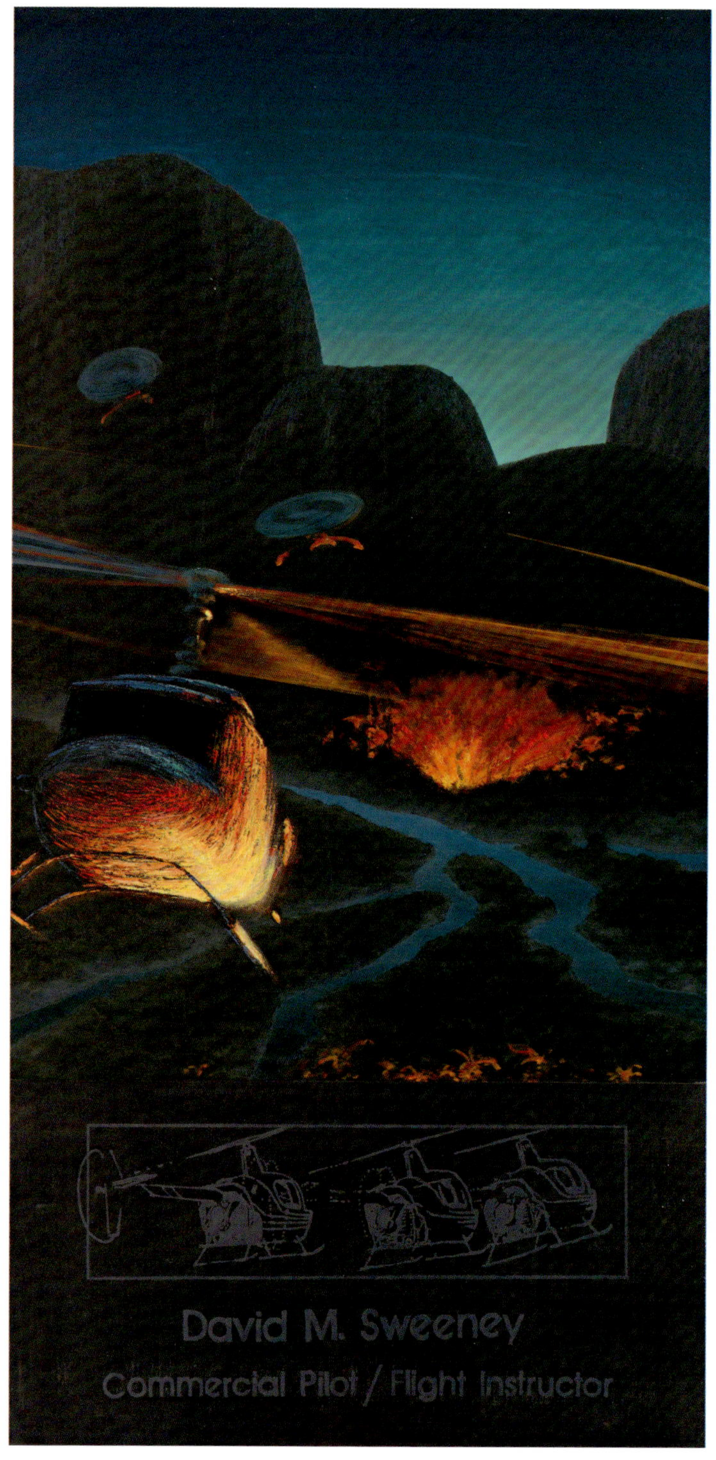

in artists as disparate as David Salle, Julian Schnabel, Eric Fischl, and Richard Prince.

The Oxbow pictures are appropriation of a kind. The frequently used phrase in titles—*The Oxbow, After Church, After Cole*—presents that plainly. But here "after" is not equivalent to "as." Not to acknowledge the lineage would be omissive. Yet Hannock's Oxbow does not resemble Cole's, nor Church's (who Hannock later discovered, somewhat appropriately, had not painted the site)—it is a conceptual recycling. If appropriation is seen as the artist looking "to ready-made images or ideas as the data of personal experience as well as the raw material of one's own expressive work,"[11] then there is a disconnect in Hannock's imaging of the natural formations. They are not direct liftings from earlier pictures. But the transformation of canonical landscape subjects and use of original materials pasted under the surface moves closer to a technically innovative act of appropriation. It is a return to nature as the primary, backgrounding reference via a picturesque accessing of landscapes of American art history—a reference, it must be noted, that would have been perceived as deeply uncool in the New York art world of the time.[12] But it is the Oxbow used as a sign. It is an adoption of the package in order to explore the personal. The landscape backdrops function as springboards for stories, vignettes, references that ultimately can be far removed from the specific sites Hannock depicts.[13] But unlike the layered imagery in Salle's work, for example, Hannock's paintings do not deny the source of the images. It is in the multiplicity of reference that the pictures operate. The reference, identified, is simply part of the meaning. And like Salle or Prince or Vernon Fisher, the use of text over the images is a displacement strategy, a kind of pictorial equivalent to the prismatic workings of the mind.

Hannock's work employs repetition and is also figuration without once-radical and now-traditional gesture, far different in its aims than the active surfaces of the preceding American generation of Alex Katz, Grace Hartigan, Fairfield Porter, and Larry Rivers. However, it is the apparent stability that is, paradoxically, upset by Hannock's building up and piling on of stories until fixity is dispersed. The tension lies in the confluence of text, collaged images, and canonical natural monuments, whether the Oxbow or Kaaterskill Falls (p. 91).[14] This is what gives Hannock's art its complexity. Hannock takes something seemingly universal, like the view from Mount Holyoke of the Oxbow based on a sketch from 1993,[15] and renders its form inert and devoid of resonance through coming back over and over to the motif. He has chosen not to fragment the presiding image, so that it becomes through repetition a tabula rasa for the artist's experience. He does not uncomplicatedly adapt the images of earlier painters. Instead, the imagistic setting becomes a kind of film set for his recorded experiences, tweaked, through luminosity, for mood. This serial use of the Oxbow has precedents in modernism's preference for newly constructed universal truths—those of Claude Monet's grain stacks and Cézanne's Mont Sainte-Victoires, of Andy Warhol's soup cans and Jasper Johns's flags.[16] But outside those ideas of absolute realities based on observation, technics, standardization, or languages of representation, Hannock's visual language bears a core Romanticism, the idea of art as the emanation of the personal. This is where he is most traditional, not in the appearance of expressive gesture on his surfaces.

Hannock counts as influences Chuck Close, Wayne Thiebaud, Gregory Gillespie; Haring, Schnabel, Don van Vliet (better known as Captain Beefheart); Eric Fischl, Mark Tansey, and David Hockney—the first generation of painters in New York freed of New York School influence. Closer perhaps is the work of Robert Longo and then Duncan Hannah, who showed at the Semaphore Gallery, under Barry Blinderman's direction, on West Broadway and Houston, a kind of haven for artists not interested in expressionist trends in painting. Yet Hannock's art has more frequently been linked to long-dead painters Cole, Church, George Inness, Sanford Robinson Gifford, James McNeill Whistler, and the like, with closer connections manifesting themselves in the work of contemporaries April Gornik and Mark Innerst, as recognized in an article in *Newsweek* in 1988.[17] Hannock's work—whose apparent verisimilitude is belied by an artificiality that comes to the forefront with patient looking—bears different, more chaotic aims and embraces slippages. And it fulfils conditions of postmodernism in its lack of autonomy and denial of subject of modernism. His is an art of rehabilitation and relevance. It does not shy from the past.

Hannock's novel technique has been discussed elsewhere.[18] His adoption of the power sander is commensurate with Chuck Close and Audrey Flack beginning to use airbrushes in the late 1960s and early 1970s as a way of moving beyond the finicky concision and polish of photorealism. But there are affinities with the premise of work like that of Schnabel, whose large, crockery-laden, gestural paintings of the late 1970s and 1980s fulfilled that artist's stated goal: "I want my life to be embedded in my work… crushed into my painting, like a pressed car."[19] Schnabel, however, was left ultimately with a "diffuse sense of identity" as Jonathan Fineberg has written, a byproduct of the confusion of the period.[20] For Schnabel—whose paintings now seem particularly to stand for a strand of uncontrolled grandiosity in the art of early-1980s New York—this meant bombast and facture and a continuation of the modernist collage tradition.[21] For Hannock, embedding and crushing meant subtlety and submersion and *fini* and, in his most recent work, a continuation of

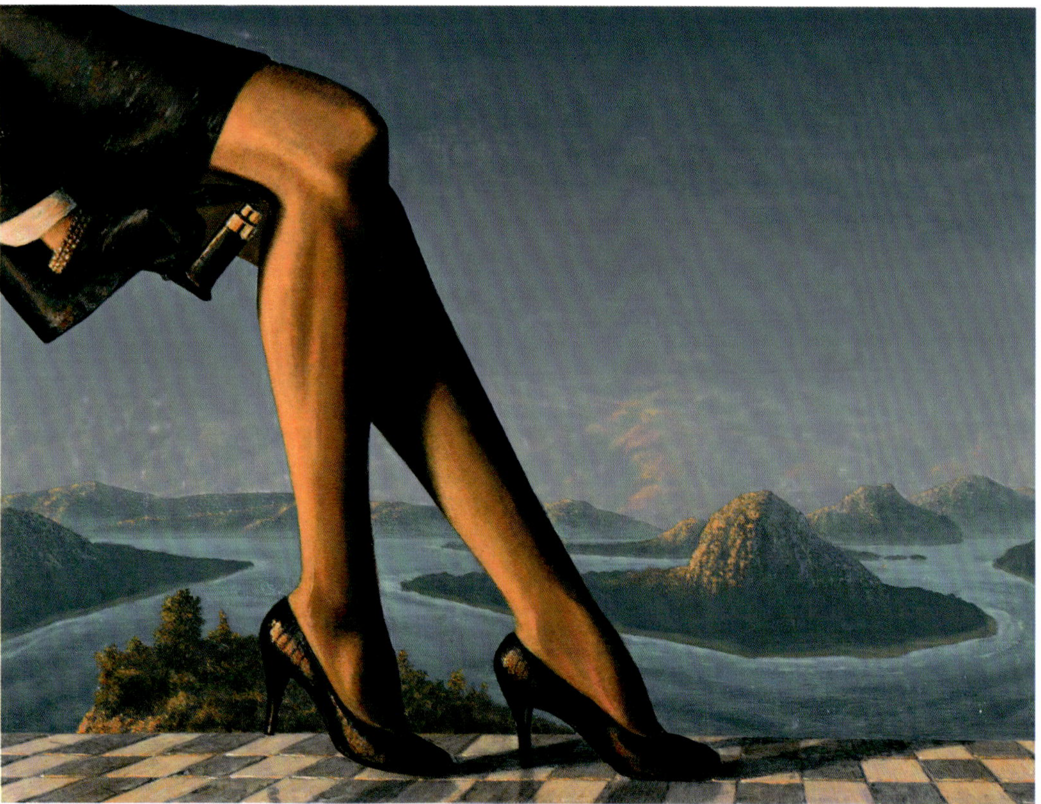

Polished oil on canvas, 15 x 20 inches (38 x 51 cm). Collection of the Artist

the modernist papier collé tradition.[22] Schnabel's pictures reside in the world of abstract figuration; Hannock's make use of the realm of defined yet symbolic landscape. There is not so very much to separate them. Both spring from the modern, albeit along different visual tangents.

For Hannock, unsurprisingly, the easel painter who most impacted him in the early 1980s was Fischl, whose disjunctive narratives as in *Bad Boy* of 1981 (private collection, p. 45) showed both resurgent energy and the relevance of realism. Fischl's elliptical and unresolved stories, a perverse reprise of the famously popular and open-ended "problem picture" tradition in late-Victorian and Edwardian English art, realigned aesthetic forces in the 1980s, making the actual permissible. And Fischl's generalized suburbia is commensurate with Hannock's imagined Connecticut River Valley—both function as artificial and somewhat banal templates for narrative exploration and self-revelation.

Hannock's art is part of this generation of New York artists. The reason why it has eluded such interpretation before remains the issue of the status of landscape painting as a genre. This is the story of a long-running battle. For seventeenth-century artists such as Nicholas Poussin and Claude Lorrain, landscape was the fit setting for history, the evolving category of *paysage historique* in the French Academy. It was not a venue for the personal. Not until J.M.W. Turner and John Constable in English Romanticism did pure, depopulated, landscape achieve acceptance into the higher ranks of art as history painting and come to bear the ability to present fundamental states of mind. Since the midnineteenth century, however, the psychological in landscape has been associated with expressionism or abstraction, and in postwar art its greatest practitioners—Robert Smithson, Michael Heizer, Gordon Matta-Clark, Walter de Maria, Richard Long, and Andy Goldsworthy—have not worked in paint. The appearance of

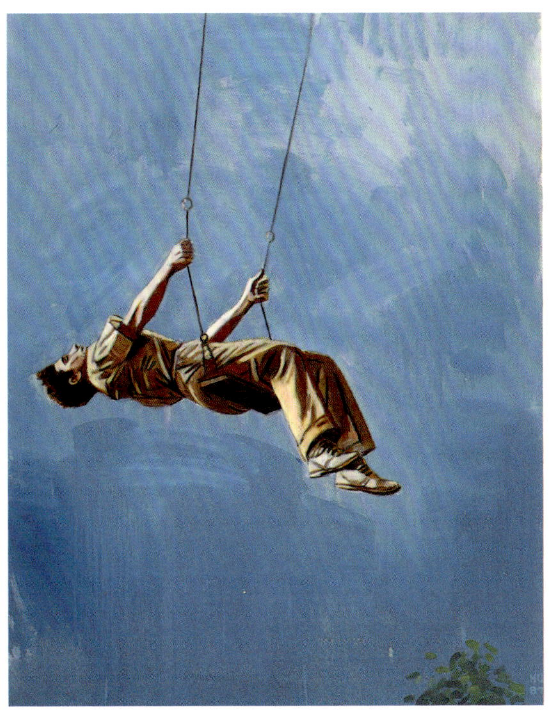

DUNCAN HANNAH, *SWING*, 1988
OIL ON CANVAS, 54 X 40 INCHES (137 X 102 CM). PRIVATE COLLECTION

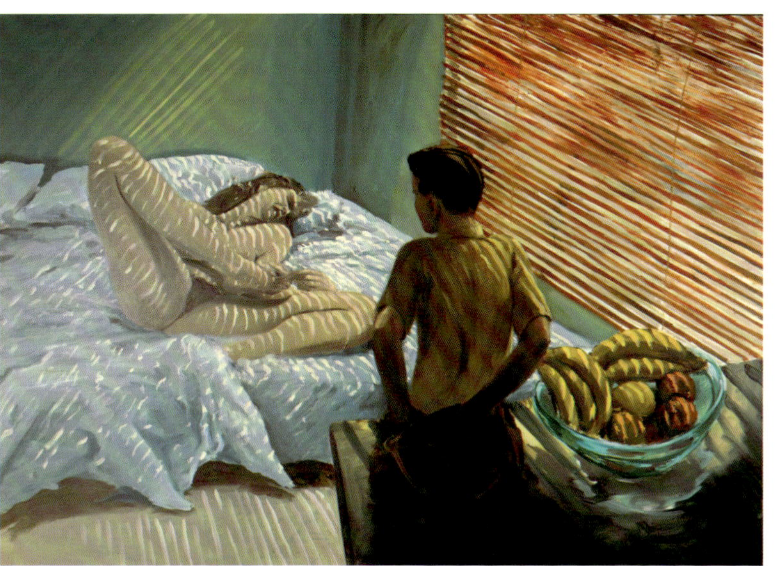

ERIC FISCHL, *BAD BOY*, 1981
OIL ON CANVAS, 66 X 96 INCHES (168 X 244 CM). PRIVATE COLLECTION

fidelity has come to be linked to kitsch, in a perceived motiveless verisimilitude (as in derogatory assessments of Andrew Wyeth), or simply the effects of light and mood. Hannock's work strives to demolish these associations. Its complexity lies in its placidly liquid yet yielding surfaces, its depth of tone, layering of materials, tension between description and inscription, and seriality. In terms of light, the pictures come as close as an artist ever has to painting with light-emitting diodes (LEDs). Their quality of radiance is remarkable, but measured in a manner appropriate to the age of LEDs—unlike the blinding radiance of Turner in *Regulus* (1828, Tate, London, p. 46), or the strobish occlusion of form of Valdemar Schönheyder Møller's (1864–1905), remarkable *Sunset, Fontainebleau* of 1900 (Statens Museum fur Kunst,

Copenhagen, Denmark, a picture that is, like the sun itself, very difficult to look at directly.

John Constable famously remarked that he associated his "careless boyhood" with the valley of the river Stour, that such scenes "made [him] a painter" but his art needed the competitiveness and pressure of London to push him to his greatest advances in landscape.[23] John Singleton Copley's provincial training lent him a sense of clarity and work ethic, but London gave him a range of subject and a creative moxie that shook up the art world of the 1780s. Hannock travels always with New England, but it was New York in the 1980s that gave him the conceptual framework and challenge to elevate his art.

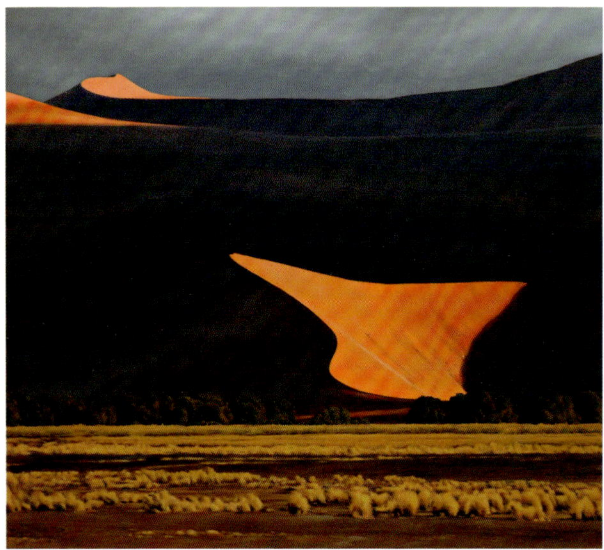

April Gornik, Dune Sky, 2007
Oil on linen, 70 x 81 inches (178 x 206 cm). Collection of April Gornik

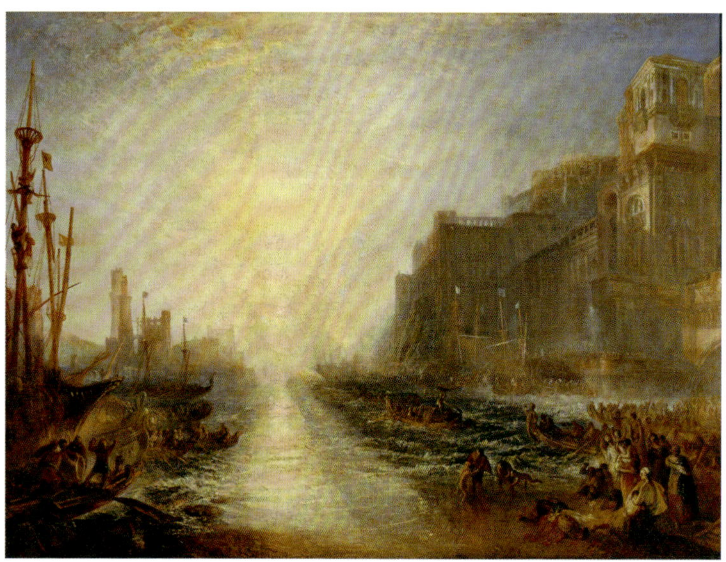

J. M. W. Turner, Regulus, 1828, reworked 1837
Oil on canvas, 35¼ x 48¾ inches (90 x 124 cm). ©Tate, London 2008

Notes

1. *Letters & Papers of John Singleton Copley and Henry Pelham: 1739–1776* (Boston: The Massachusetts Historical Society, 1914), 41–2.

2. At the Carpenter Center for the Visual Arts.

3. *Portrait of the Artist Painting in the Dark* (1988).

4. Hannock calls these "self-portraits comprised of forms that can relate."

5. Haring eventually dabbled in a phosphorescent technique, showing works under black light at Tony Shafrazi Gallery in 1982.

6. There is also a link to the deconstruction of personal identity in Francesco Clemente's macabre self-portraits of the period, such as *Untitled* (1983, Thomas Ammann, Zürich) with its multiple small Clementes peeping out from every orifice in a larger self-portrait.

7. 277 Park Avenue, now a JPMorgan Chase office.

8. It is interesting that, unlike earlier landscapists who often envisioned loss through the potent image of ruins (as in John Constable's *Hadleigh Castle*, 1829 or John Everett Millais's *"The Tower of Strength,"* 1878–79), Hannock in this picture does so through renovation, celebrating the rebirth of Madison Square Park, a project to which his wife contributed much.

9. The period is well summarized in chapters 13 and 14 of Irving Sandler, *Art of the Postmodern Era from the Late 1960s to the Early 1990s* (New York: Icon-Editions/HarperCollins, 1996).

10. The rethinking of the concept of traditional history painting, often involving the personal, has been a persistent trend in postwar art. An early, radical practitioner was Robert Rauschenberg in his combines, where found objects blended with personal elements in sculptural collages that explored the artist's own experience. A good example is *Odalisk* of 1955–58, Museum Ludwig, Cologne. See Thomas Crow's essay on the subject in Paul Schimmel, ed., *Robert Rauschenberg: Combines* (Los Angeles: The Museum of Contemporary Art, 2005).

11. Jonathan Fineberg, *Art Since 1940: Strategies of Being*, 2nd ed. (New York: Harry N. Abrams, Inc., 2000), p. 467.

12. Although, it should be noted, traditional imagery was beginning to creep back into the conversation in the post-Pop scene. Andy Warhol began to introduce an image of Leonardo's *Last Supper* in his paintings in 1984.

13. See "Luminosity: Paintings by Stephen Hannock," *Panorama*, Albany Institute of History & Art (Spring/Summer 2007), p. 7, for a complete transcription of the lengthy text embedded in *Nocturne for the River Keeper, Green Light*, 2001, Albany Institute. The text more than once references the particular Hudson River location, one whose appearance Hannock admits changing, but then moves off onto tangents and snippets of memory dislodged from associations with the landscape imaged.

14. *Kaaterskill Falls for Frank Moore and Dan Hodermarsky* (2005, Metropolitan Museum of Art, New York). This picture is a kind of play on Asher B. Durand's famous *Kindred Spirits* (1849, Walton Family Foundation, Inc.), which imaged the recently deceased Thomas Cole and the poet William Cullen Bryant surveying the landscape with Kaaterskill Falls in the distance. In the right foreground of Hannock's picture are the young Moore and his uncle Hodermarsky, whose painting of a waterfall inspired him to become an artist.

15. This tradition is comprehensively surveyed in an exhibition catalogue from the Mount Holyoke College Art Museum: Marianne Doezema, ed., *Changing Prospects: The View from Mount Holyoke* (Ithaca and London: Cornell University Press, 2002).

16. Hannock's *Flooded River* series is even closer to Monet's permutational *Morning on the Seine* scenes of 1896–97.

17. Cathleen McGuidan, "Transforming the Landscape," *Newsweek*, December 1988, pp. 60–2. In Jason Rosenfeld, *Stephen Hannock*, exhibition catalogue (McKenzie Fine Art Inc., New York; Michael Kohn Gallery, Los Angeles, 2002), p. 5. I have suggested ways to connect Hannock to the modernist tradition and artists such as Barnett Newman and Richard Serra.

18. See Rosenfeld, p. 5, and the essays in this volume.

19. Julian Schnabel, "Writings," from the Madrid notebooks, 1978; in Thomas McEvilley and Lisa Phillips, *Julian Schnabel: Paintings 1975–1987* (London: Whitechapel Art Gallery; New York: Whitney Museum of American Art, 1987), p. 104; quoted in Fineberg, p. 449.

20. *Ibid*.

21. *St. Sebastian – Born in 1951* (1979).

22. Collage refers to materials used expansively in a three-dimensional form on a two-dimensional surface. Papier collé is limited to papers added to a surface. It is generally the difference of materials in synthetic vs. analytic cubism.

23. Quoted in Michael Rosenthal, *Constable: The Painter and his Landscape* (New Haven and London: Yale University Press, 1983), p. 137.

Paintings

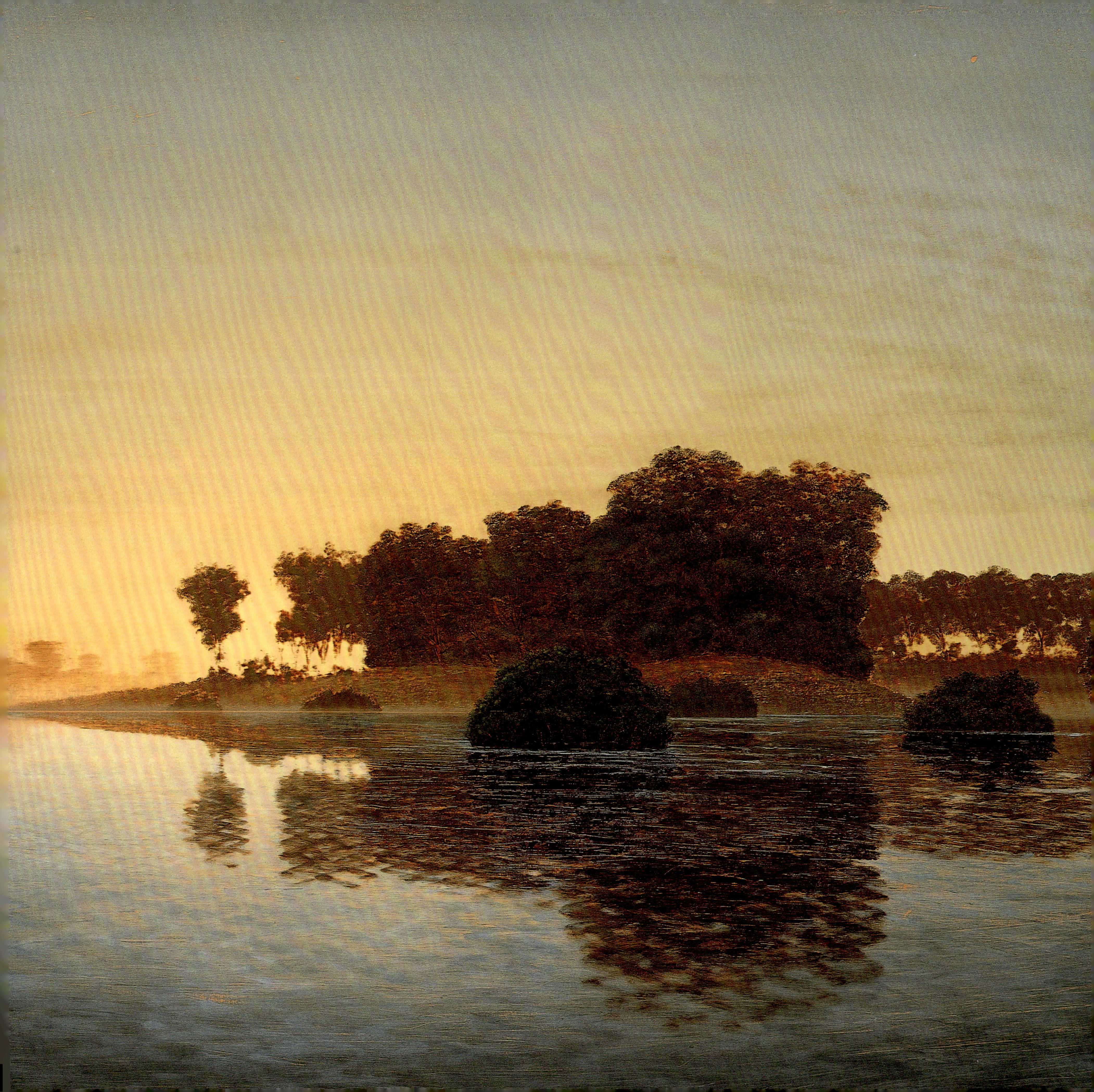

FLOODED RIVERS

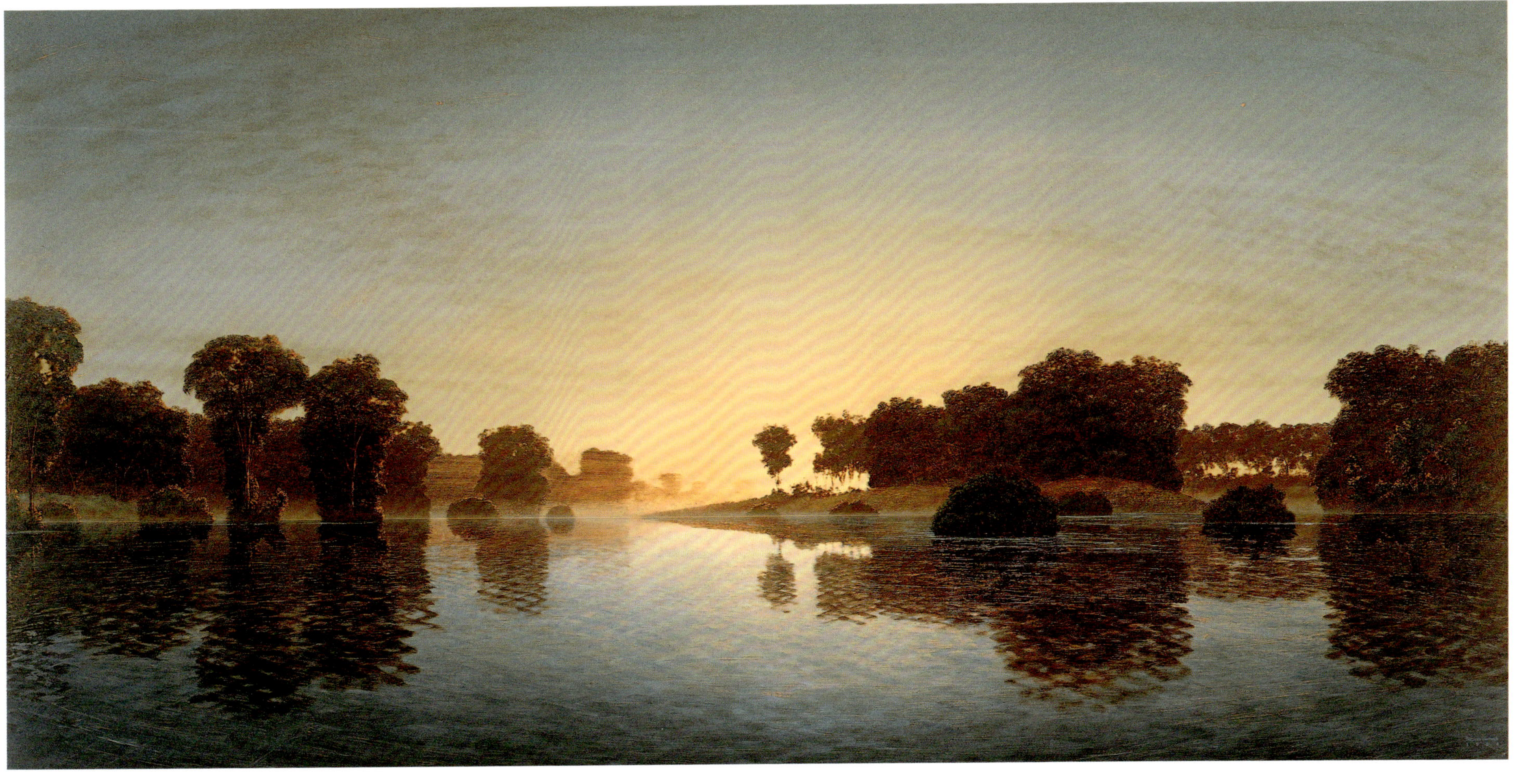

Flooded River with Golden Light, 1994
Polished oil on canvas, 60 x 120 inches (152 x 305 cm). Private Collection

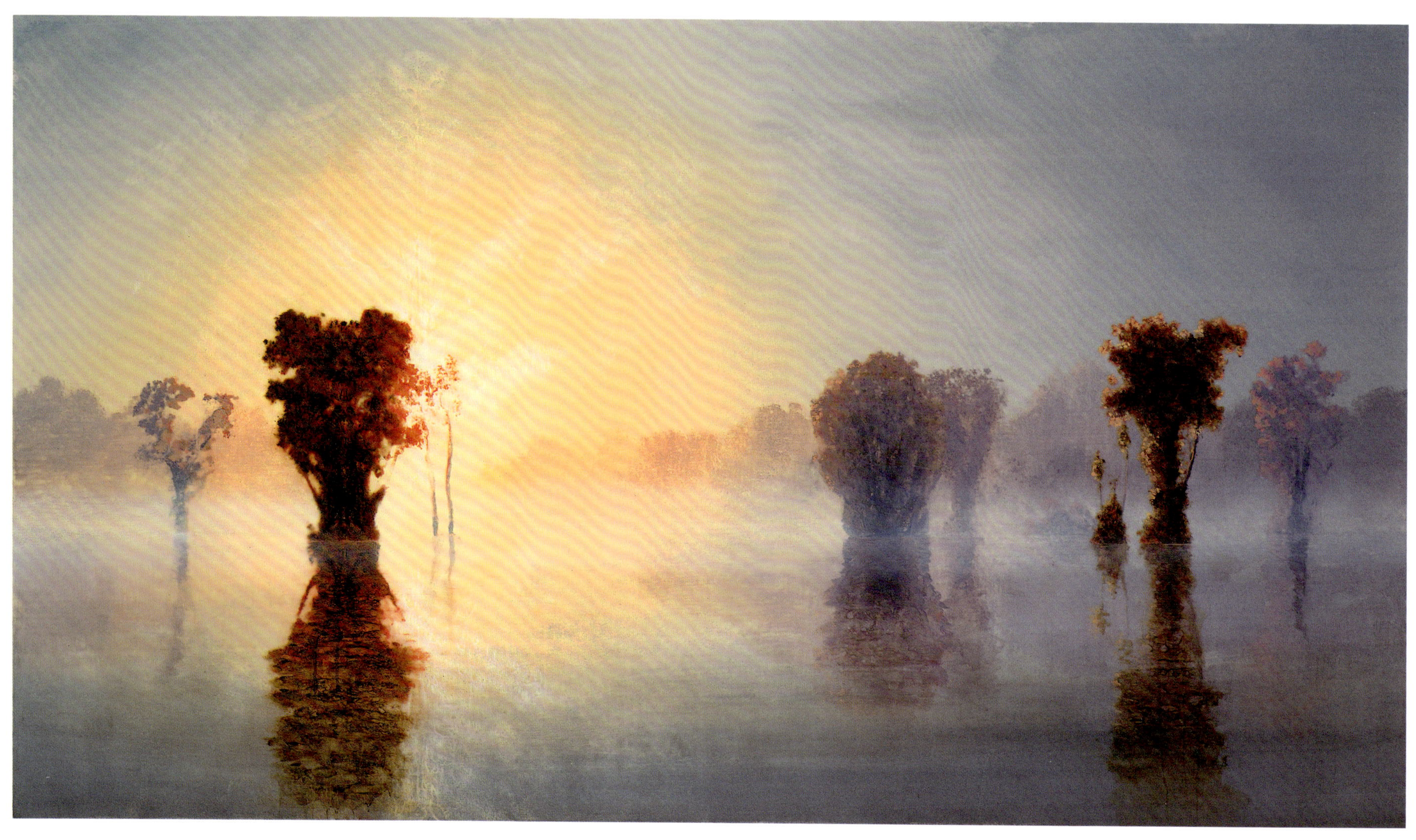

FLOODED FOREST, MORNING LIGHT, 2003

POLISHED OIL ON CANVAS, 40 X 72 INCHES (102 X 183 CM). PRIVATE COLLECTION

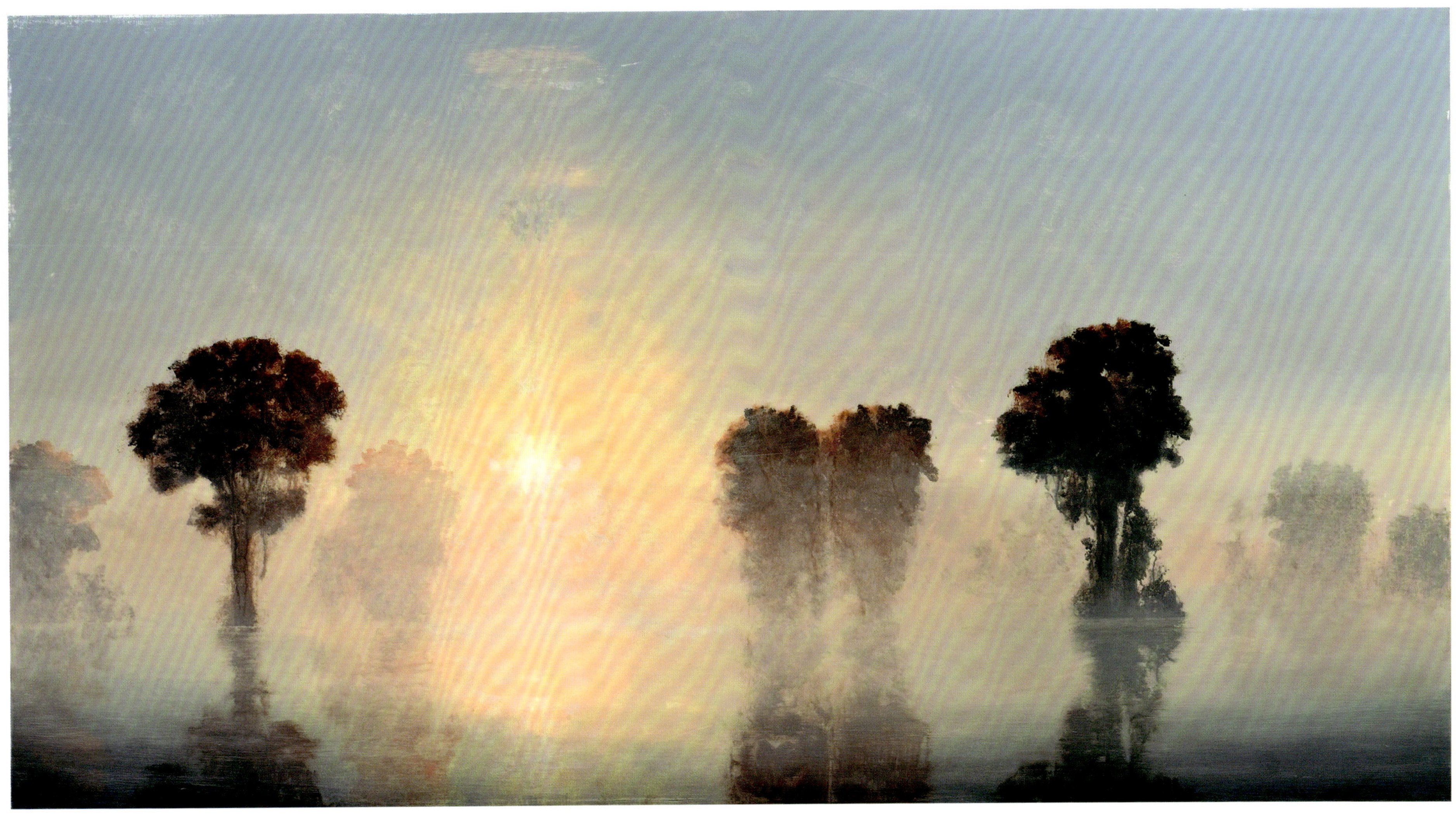

Flooded River, Golden light, 2003

Polished oil on canvas, 36 x 60 inches (102 x 183 cm). Private Collection

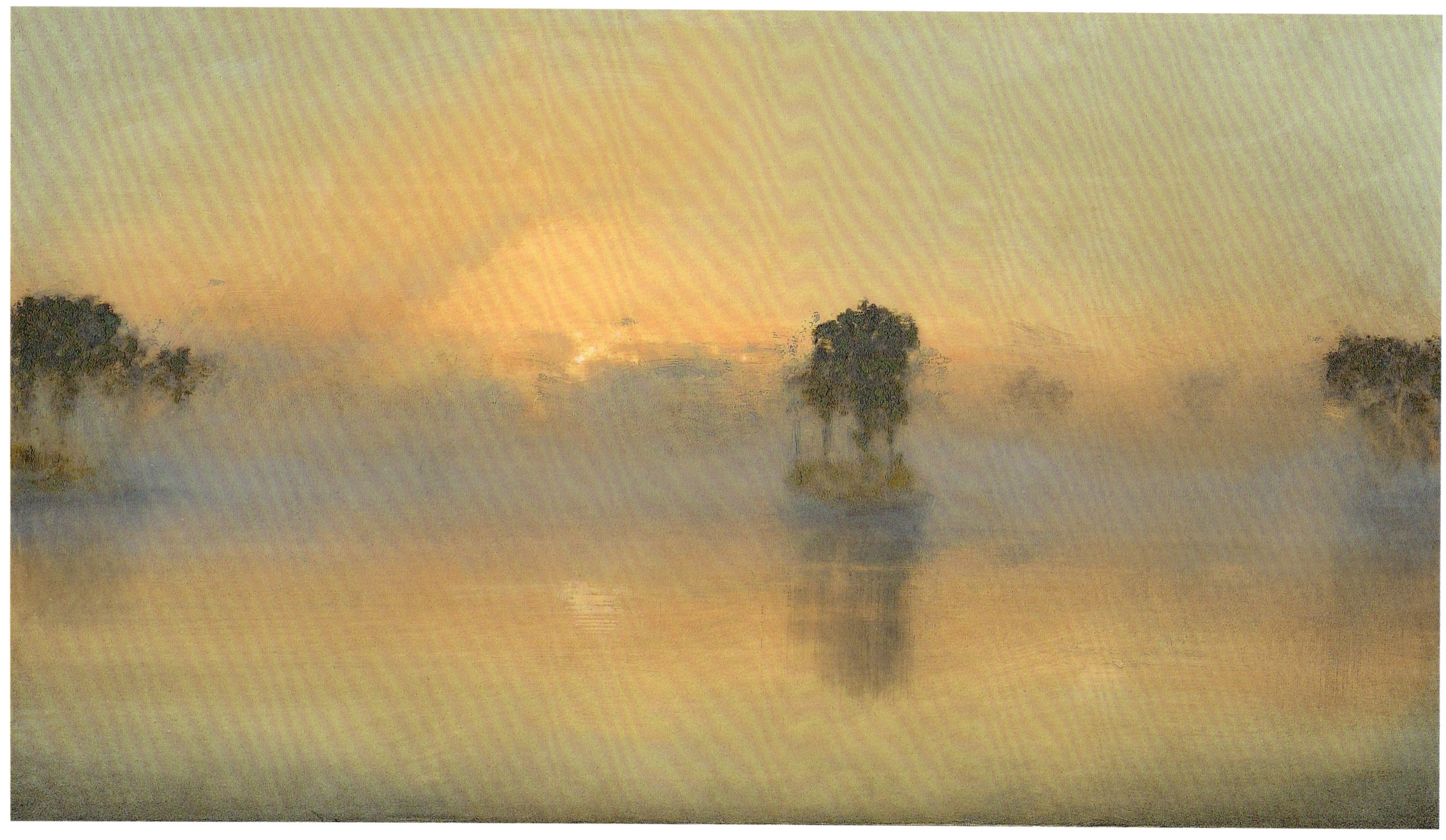

Mauve Morning with Corkscrew Cloud, 2002
Polished oil on canvas, 12 x 22 inches (31 x 56 cm). Private Collection

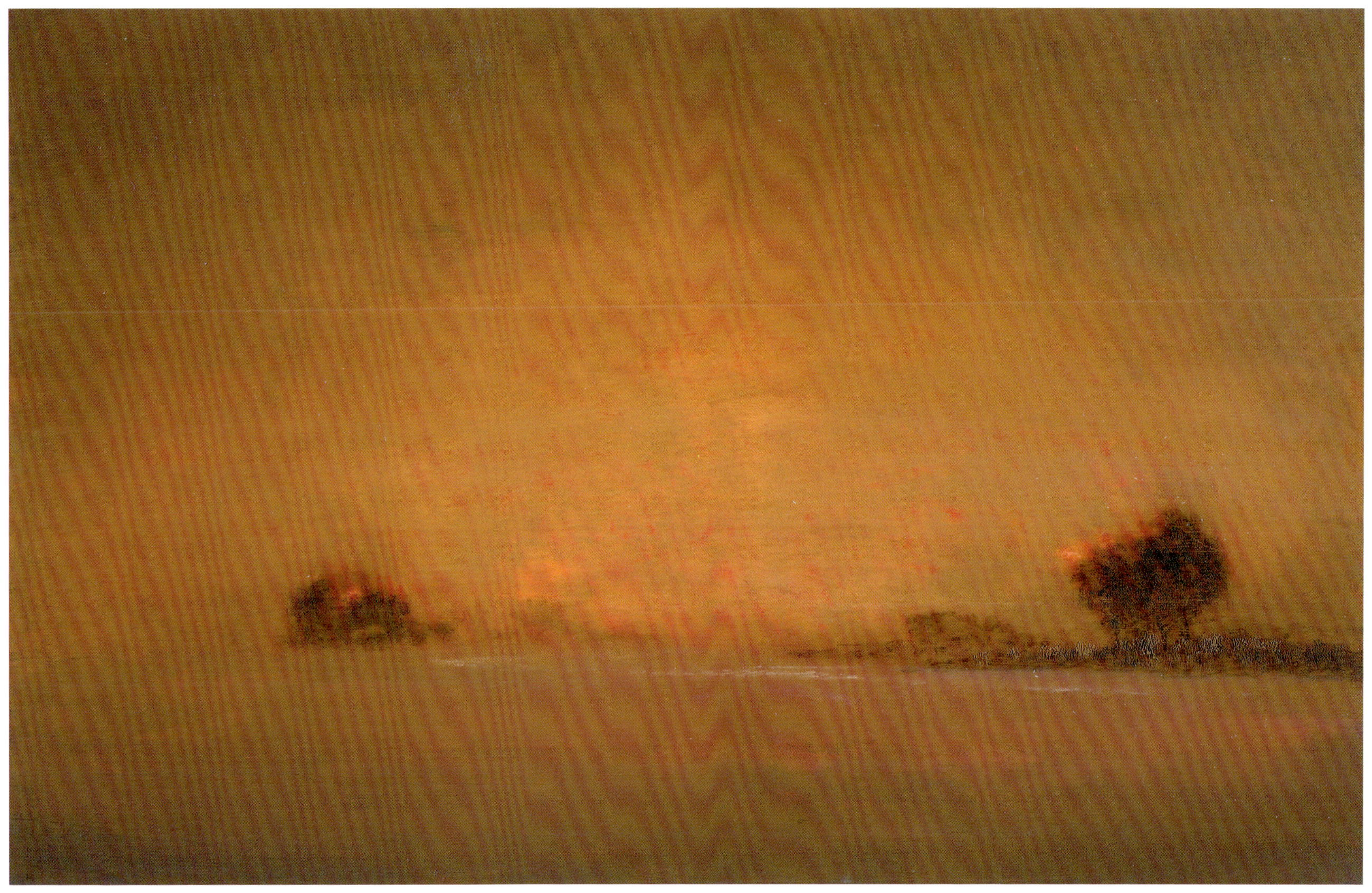

Flooded Marsh: Ginger's Morning, 1996

polished oil on panel, 12 x 22 inches (31 x 56 cm). Worcester Art Museum, Worcester, Massachusetts, Gift of the Artist in Memory of Ginger Cross Shaw

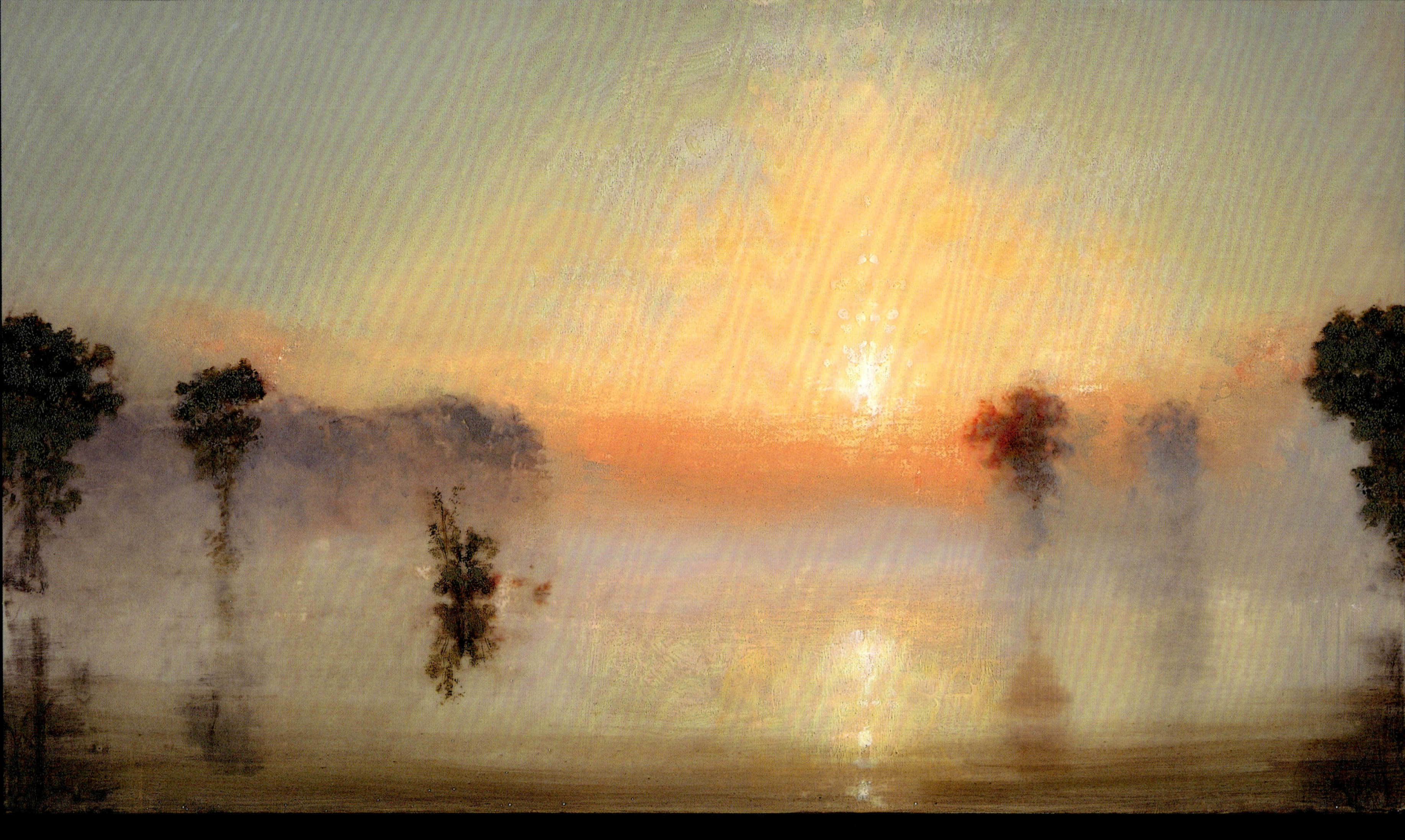

Flooded River at Dawn for Jackson, 2003

Polished oil on canvas, 12 x 22 inches (31 x 56 cm). Private Collection

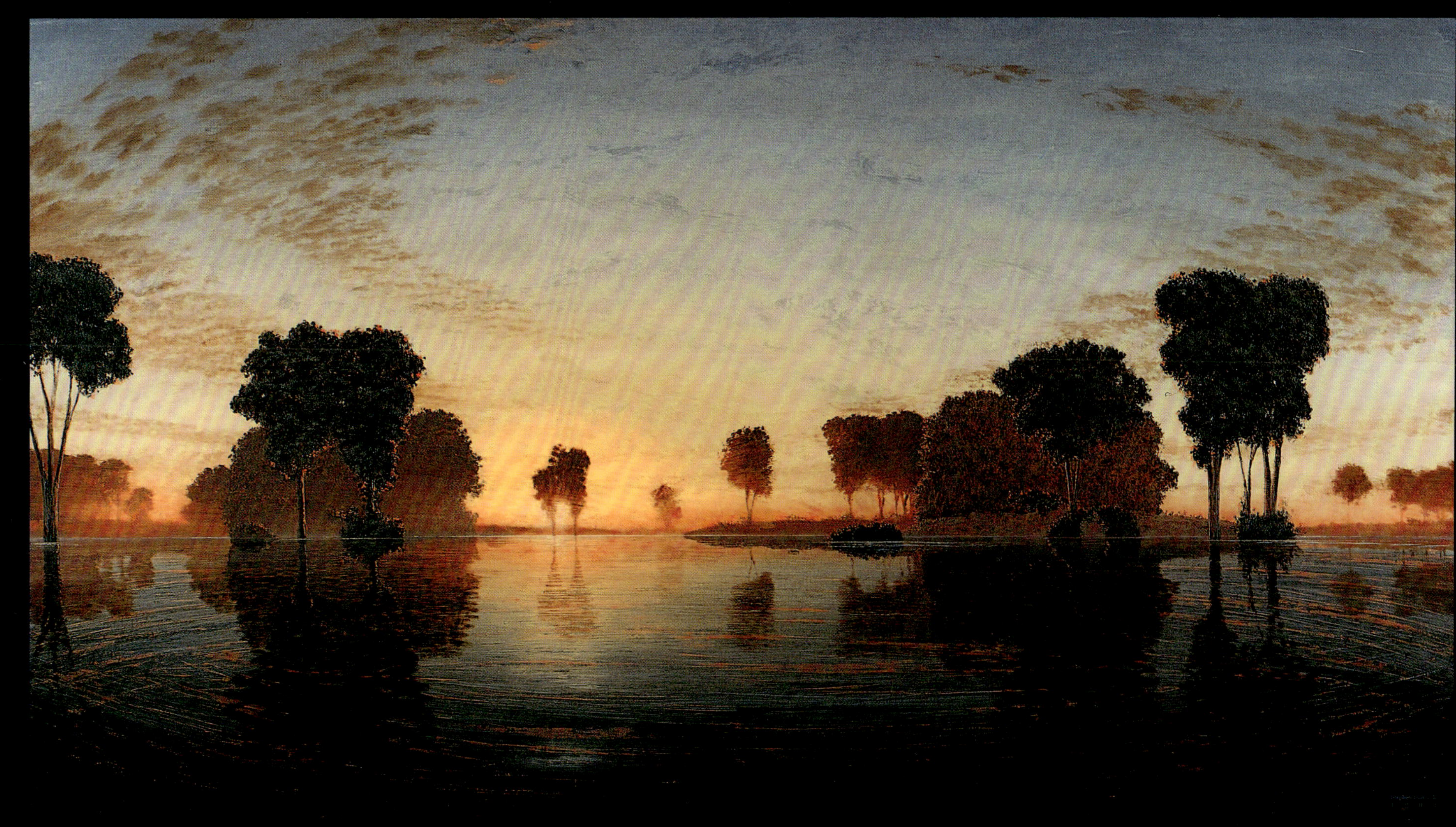

Flooded River for Dante and Hallie, 1994

Polished oil on canvas, 44 x 81 inches (112 x 206 cm), Private Collection

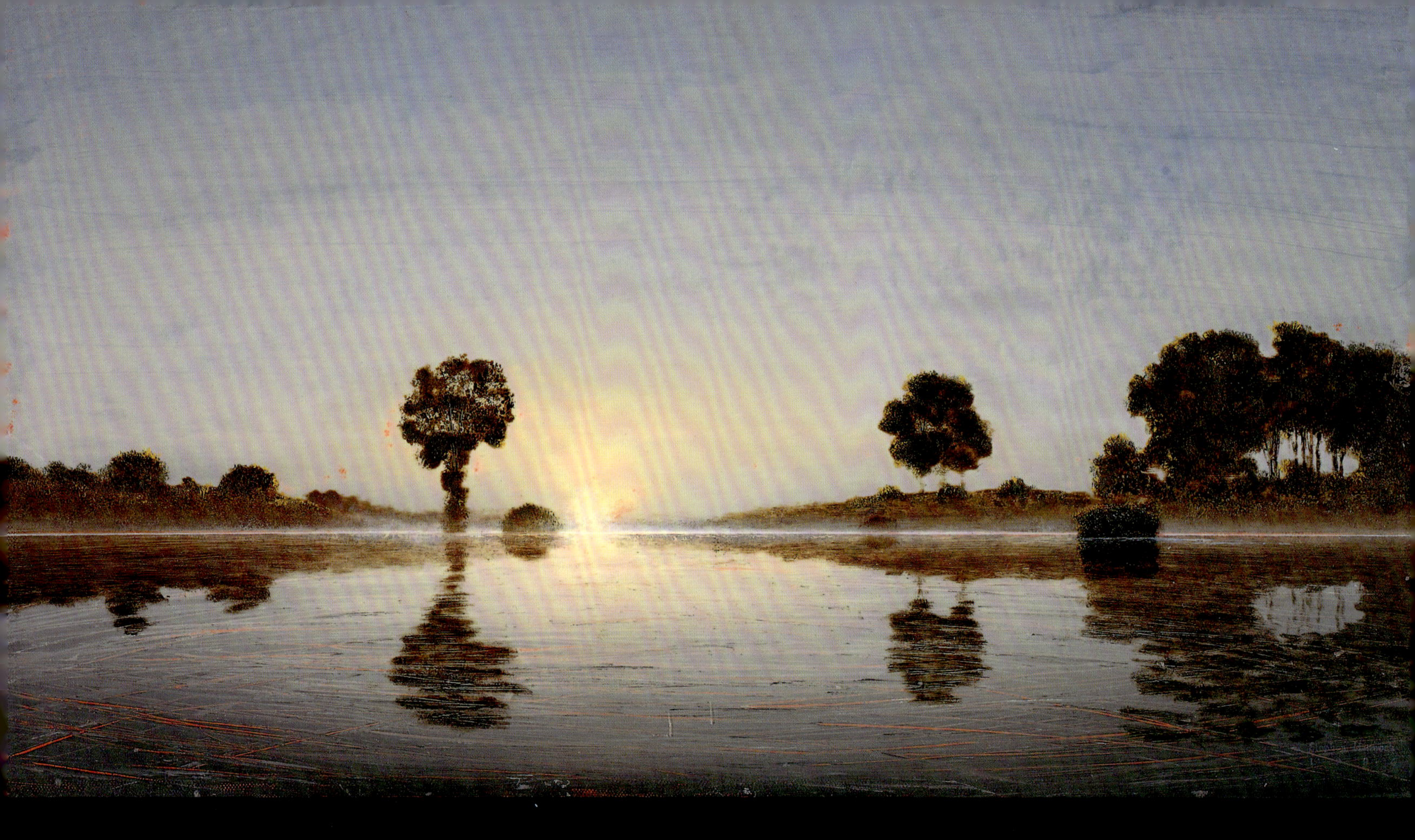

Flooded River Cool Dawn, 1994
Polished oil on canvas, 12 x 22 inches (31 x 56 cm). Collection of the Artist.

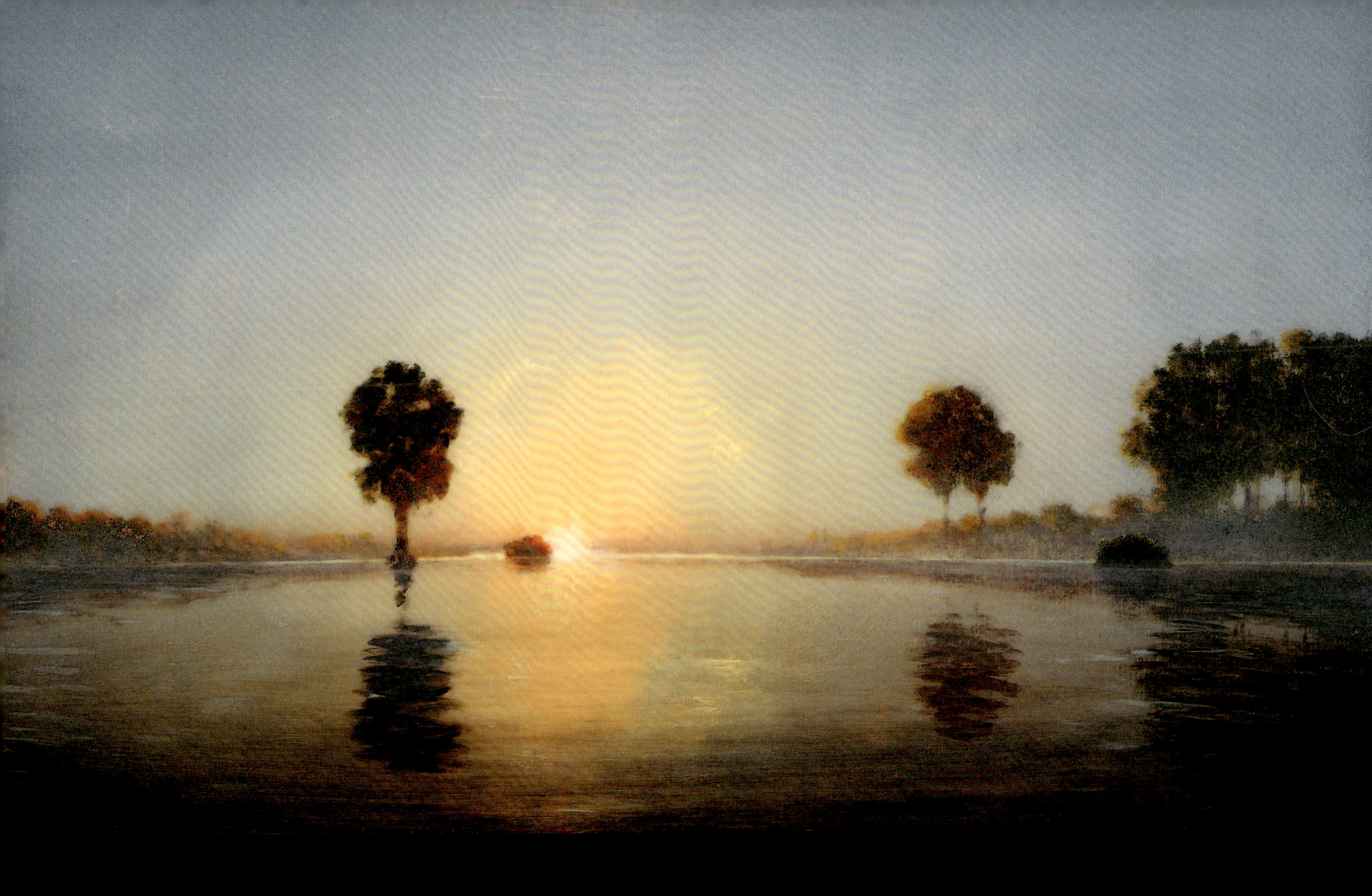

FLOODED RIVER WITH VORTEX AT DAWN, 2002

Polished oil on canvas, 20 x 36 inches (51 x 91 cm). Private Collection

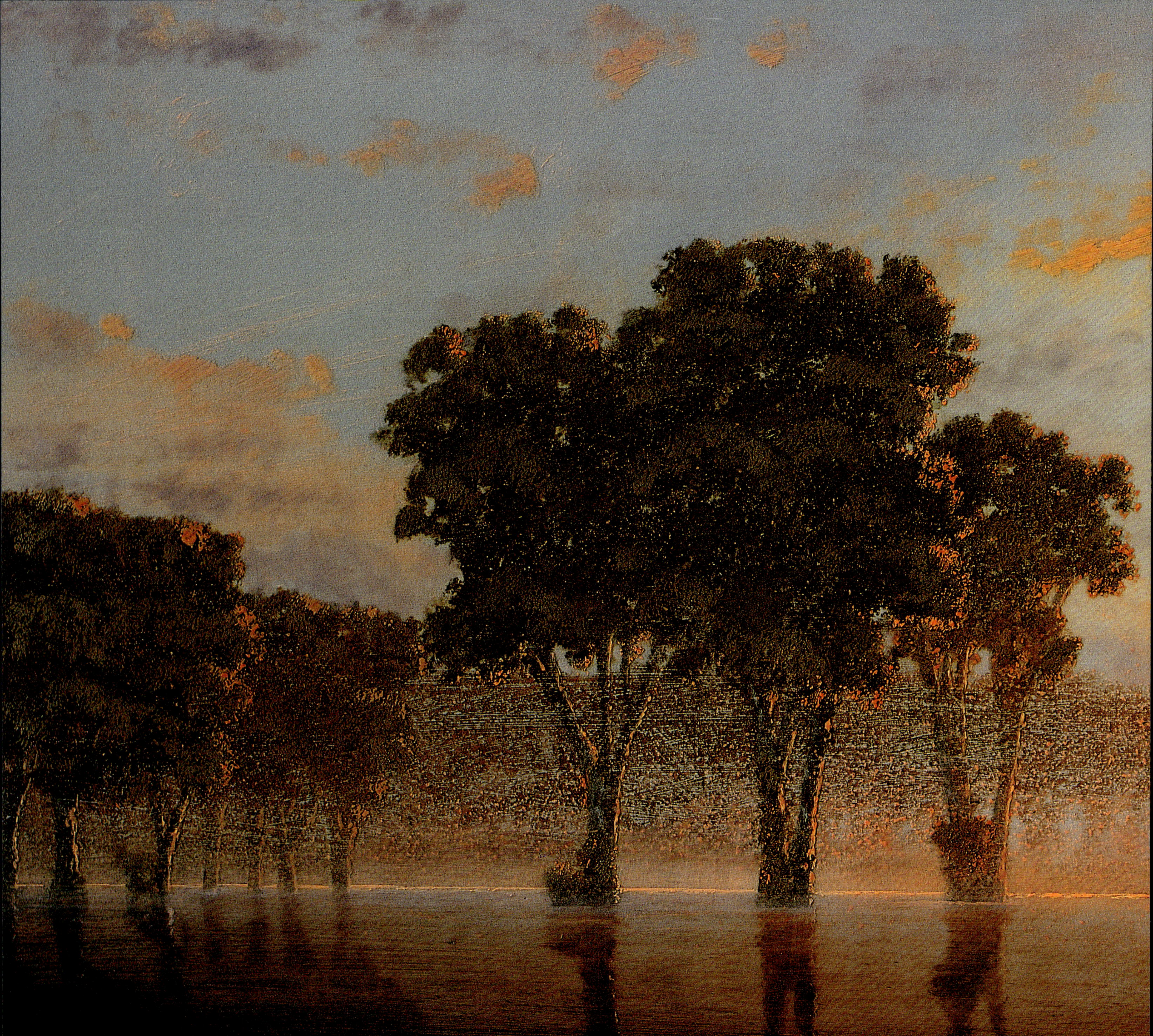

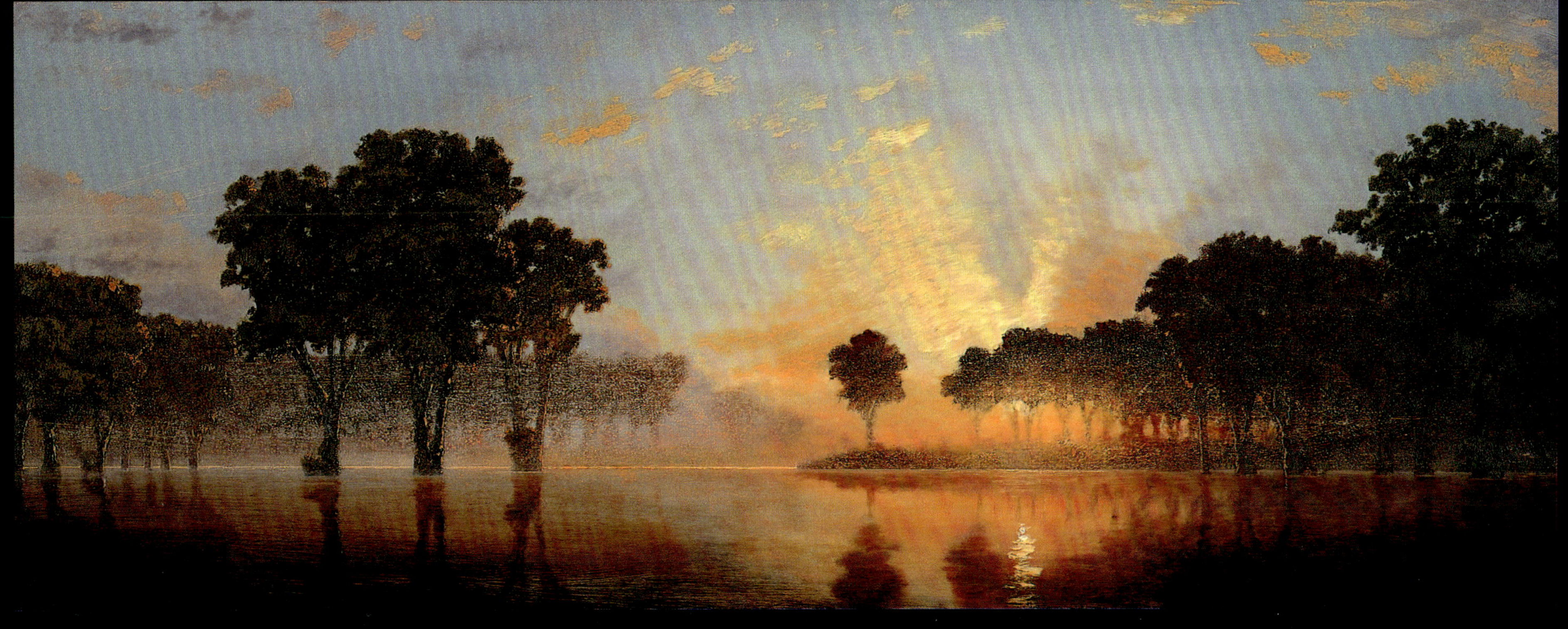

FLOODED RIVER FOR T.M., 1998

Polished oil on canvas, 19½ x 51 inches (50 x 130 cm). Private Collection

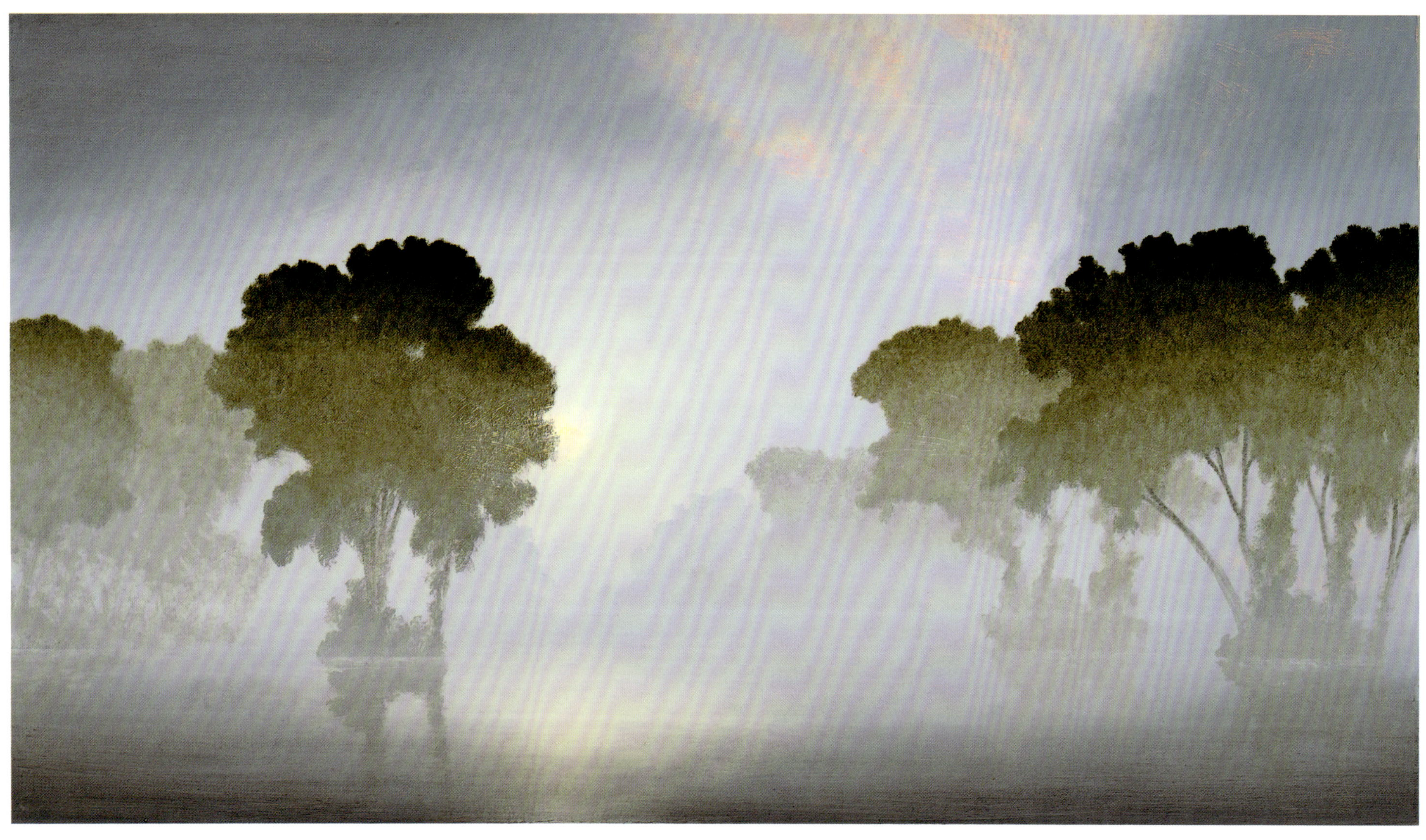

FLOODED RIVER: GOLDEN DAWN, ROSE VEIL, 1997

Polished oil on canvas, 40 x 72 inches (102 x 183 cm). Private Collection

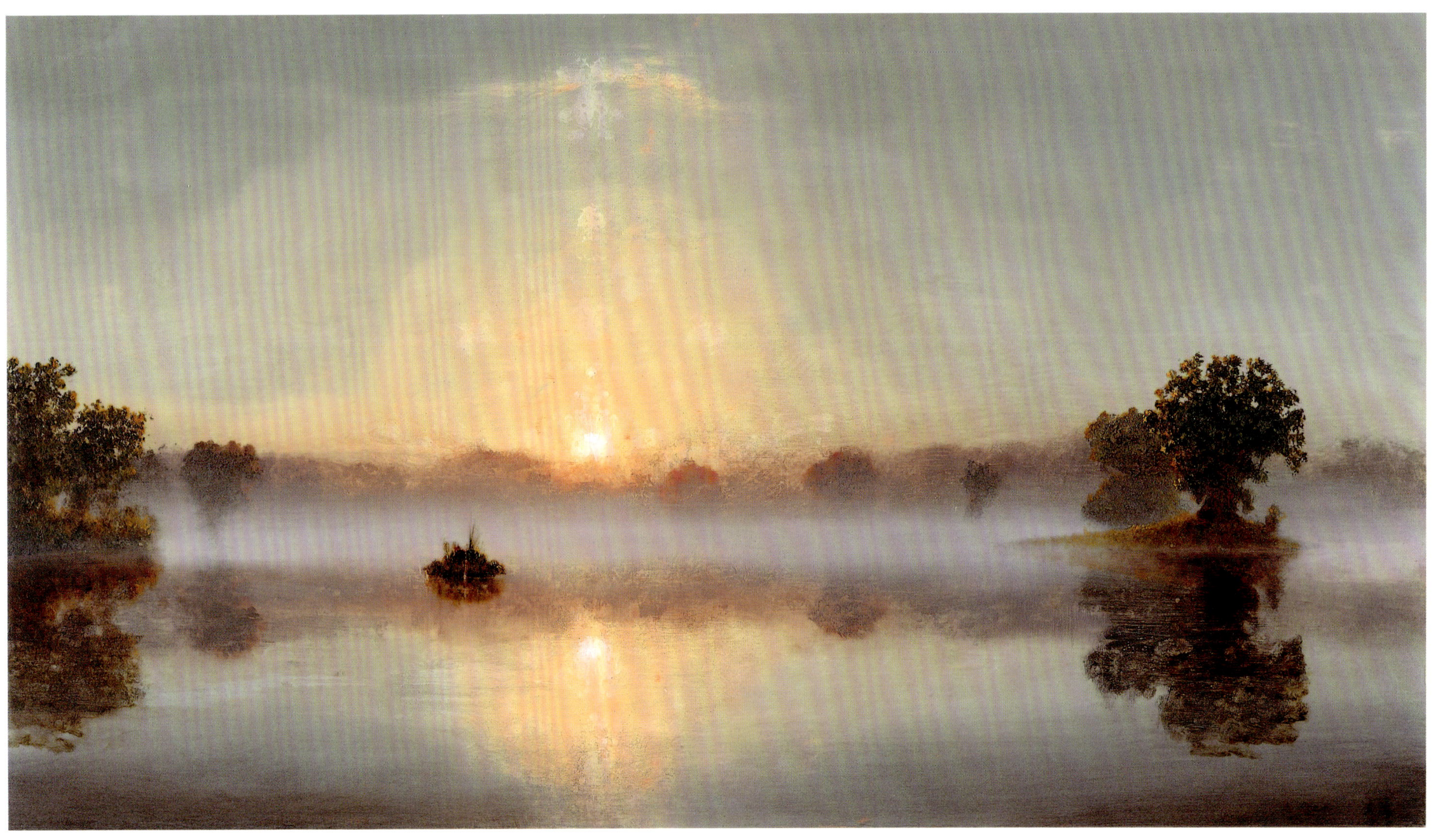

Flooded River at Dawn (Mass MoCA #26), 2005

Polished oil on canvas, 40 x 72 inches (102 x 183 cm). Private Collection

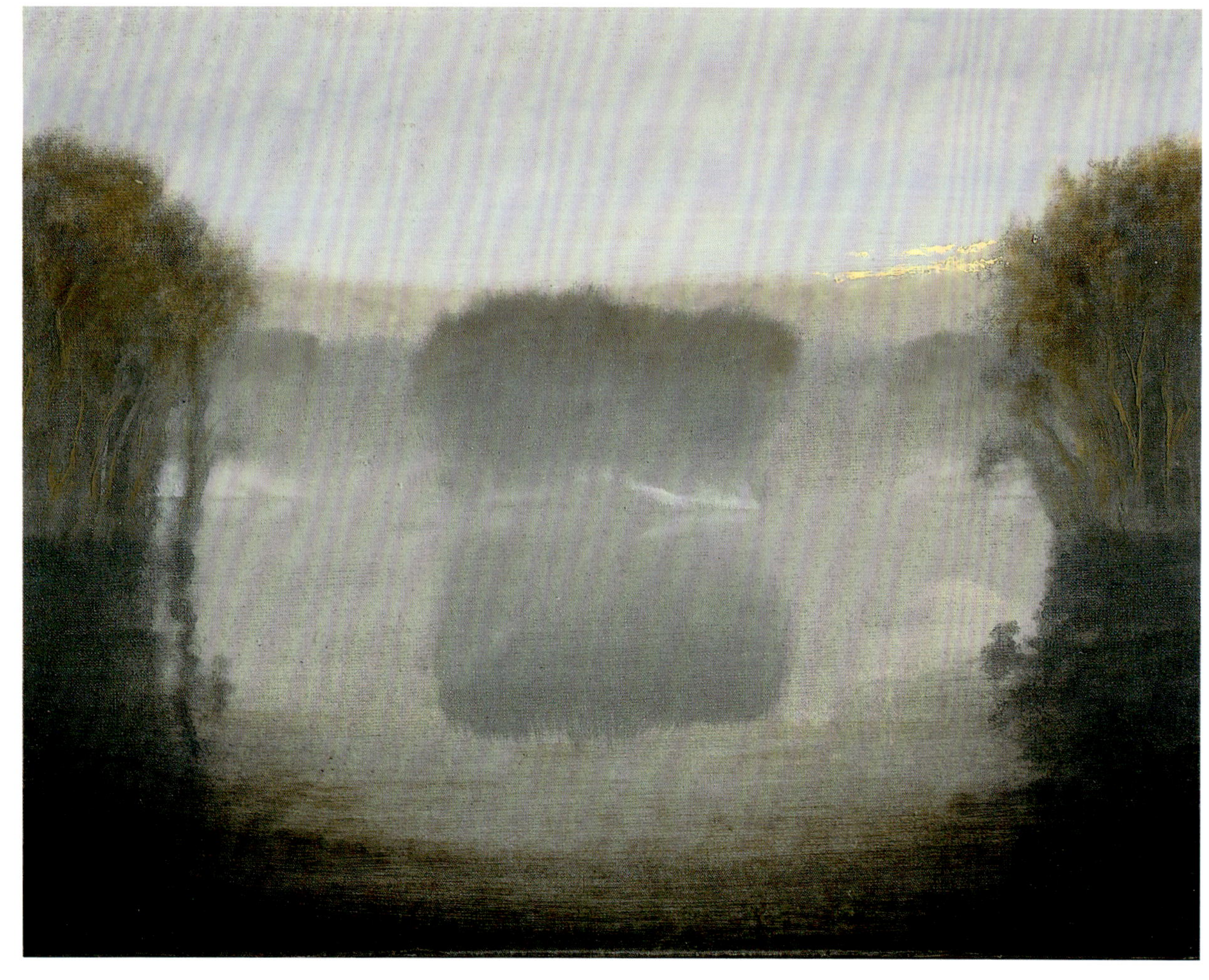

FLOODED RIVER: FEBRUARY THAW, 1997

POLISHED OIL ON CANVAS, 10¼ x 13¼ INCHES (26 x 34 CM). PRIVATE COLLECTION

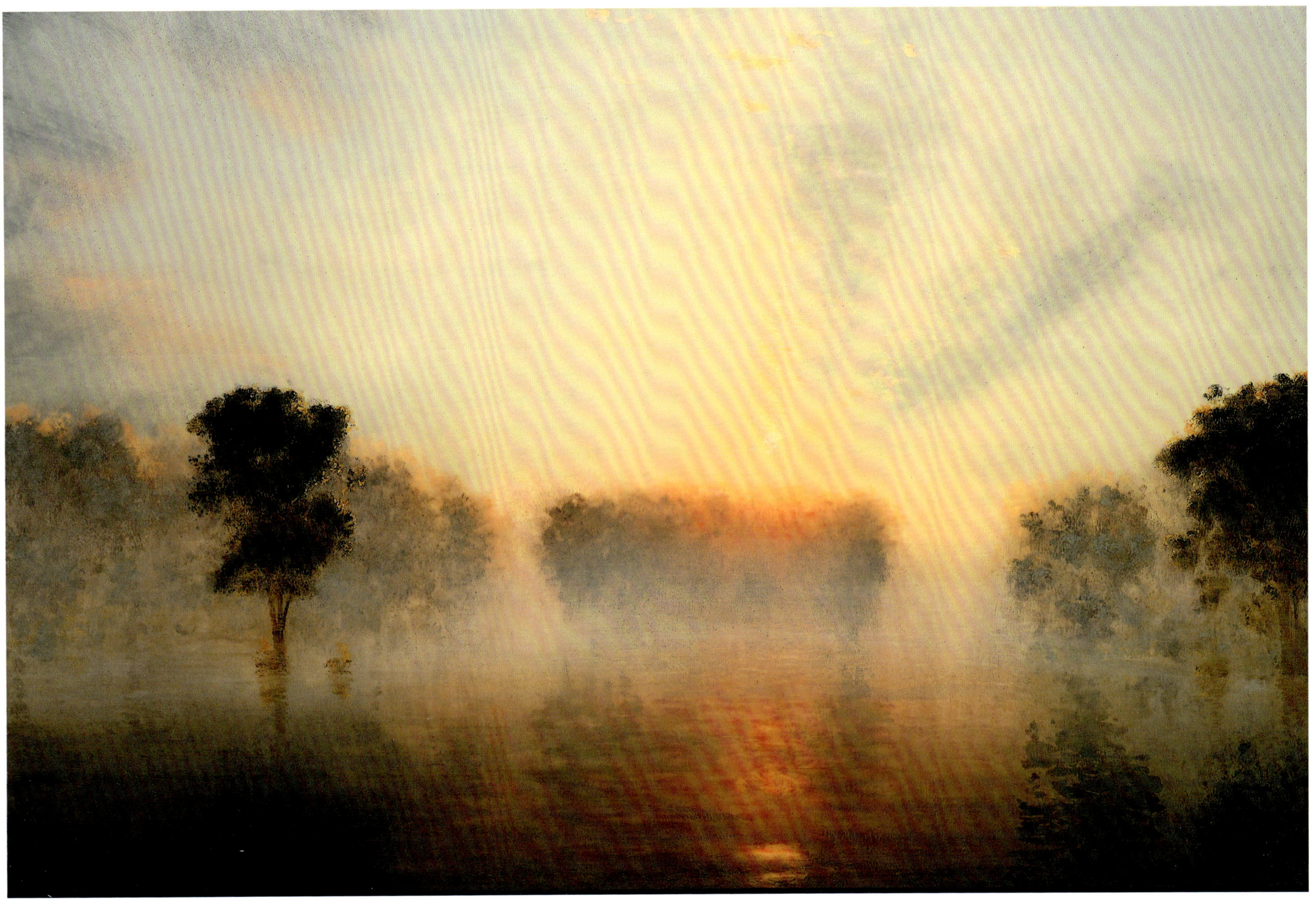

Flooded River: Christmas Morning, 2000

Polished oil on canvas, 23¾ x 35¾ inches (60 x 91 cm). Private Collection

New England City: Flooded River at Dusk, 1999
Polished oil on canvas, 11 ½ x 14 ¾ inches (29 x 38 cm). Private Collection

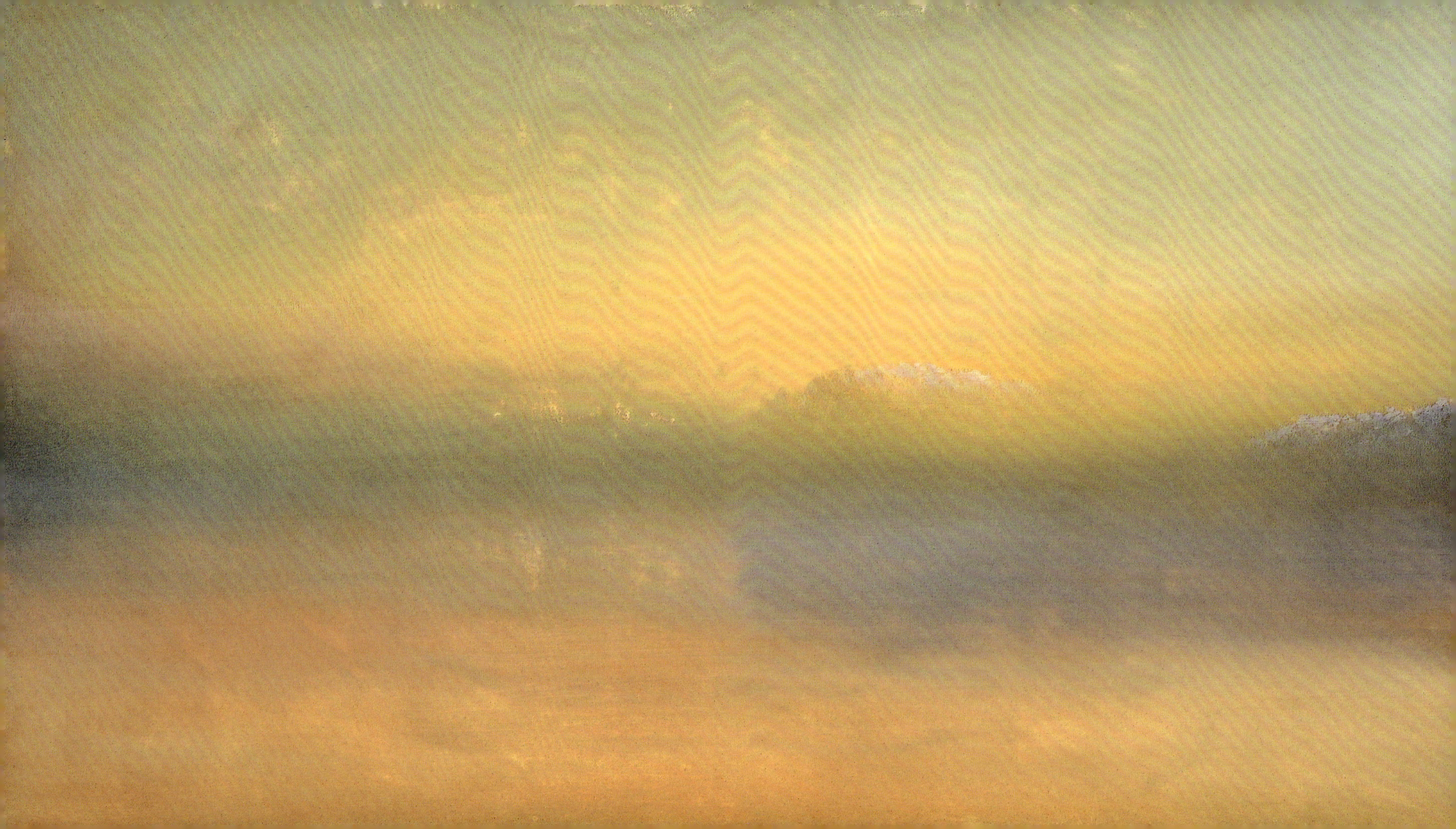

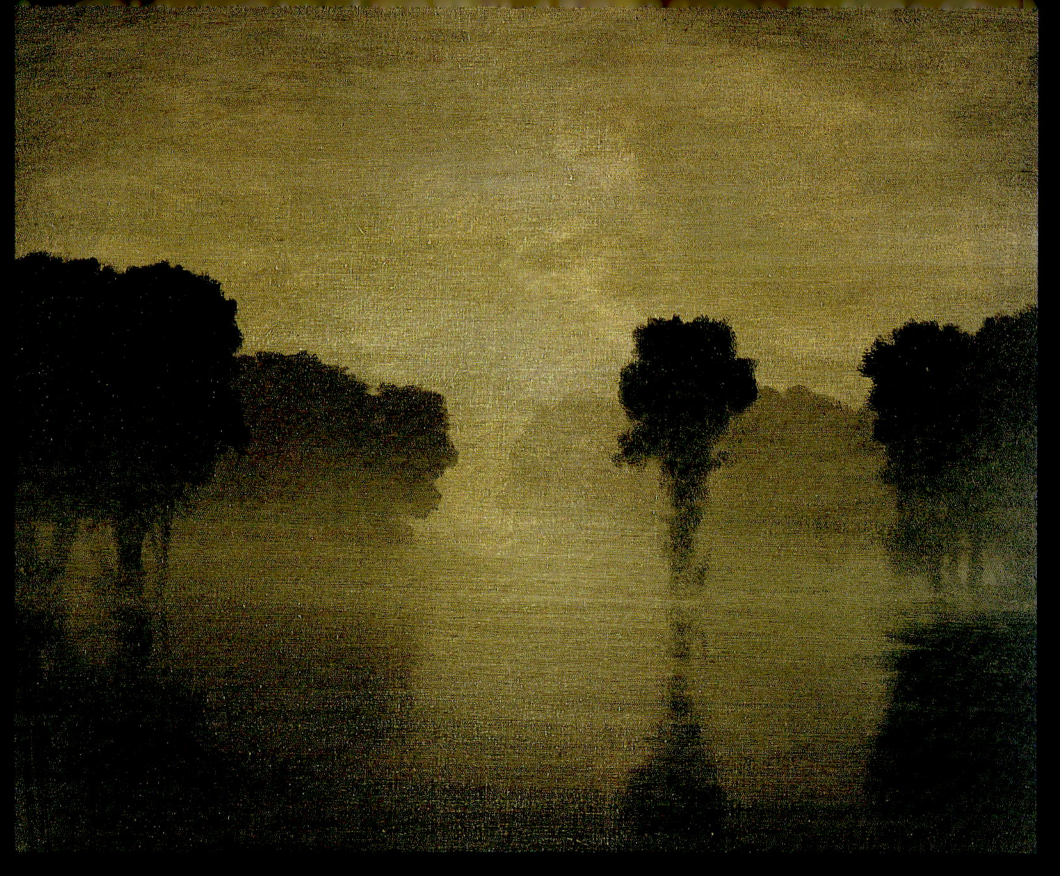

FLOODED RIVER: EVENING RAIN, 1999

Polished oil on canvas, 31 x 37 inches (79 x 94 cm). Private Collection

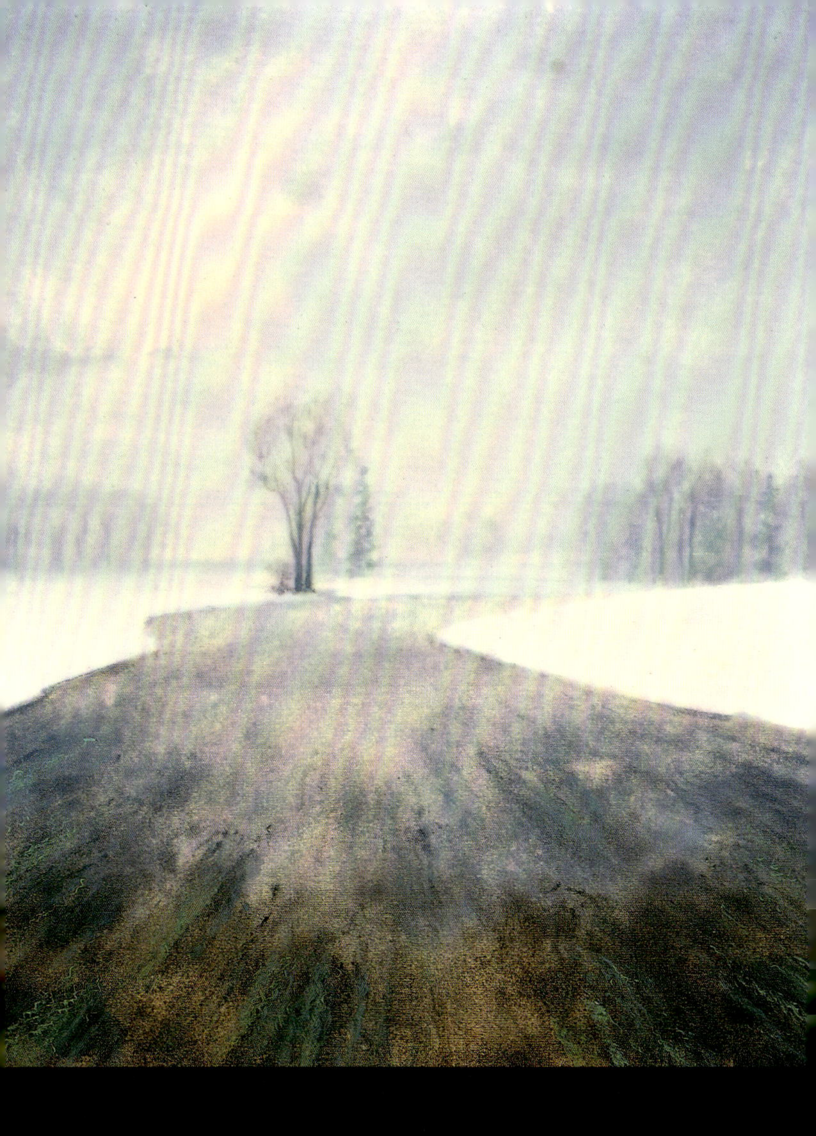

Evening Snow: November, 2001

Polished oil on canvas, 18 x 14 inches (46 x 36 cm). Private Collection

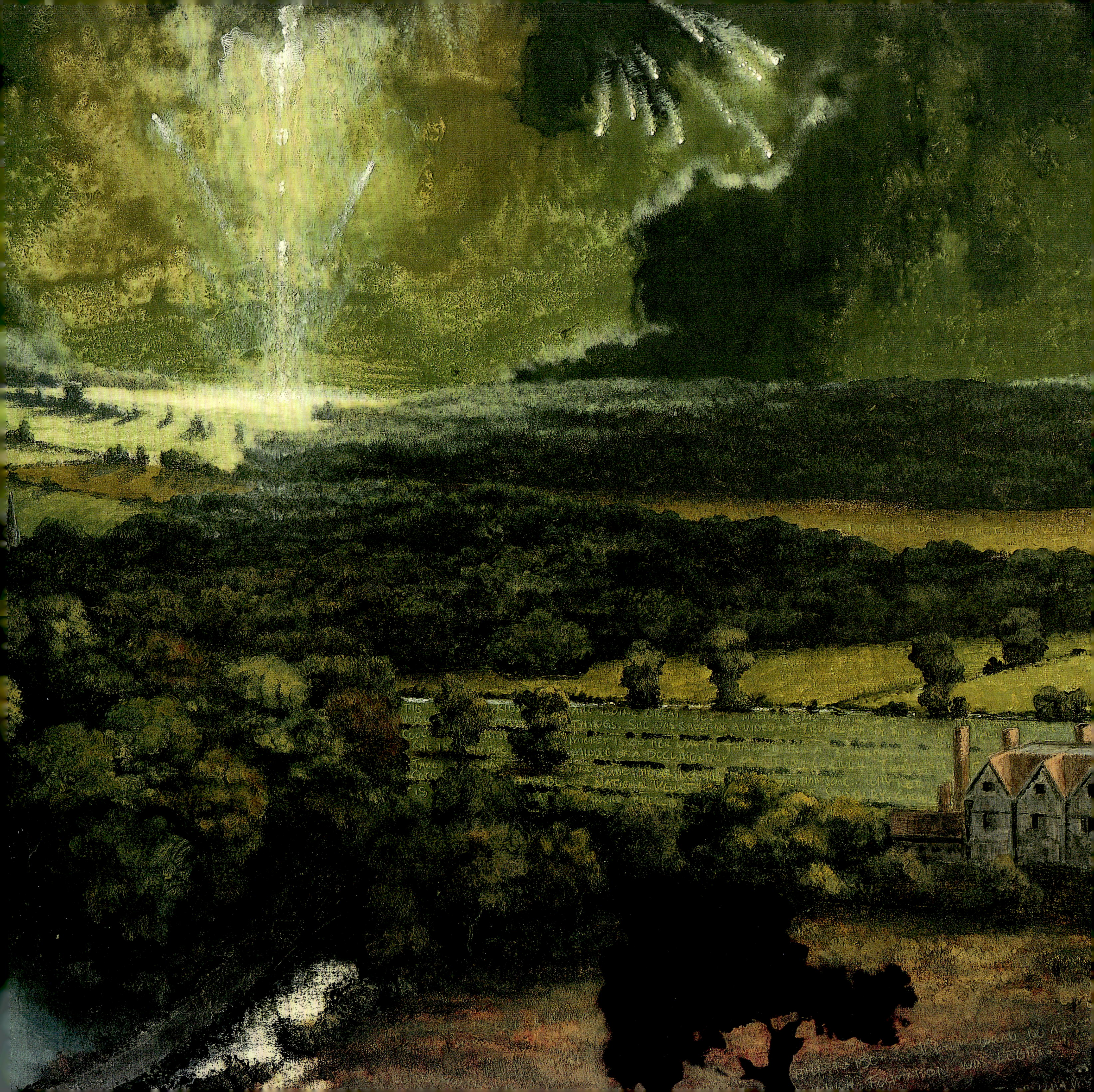

Rockets

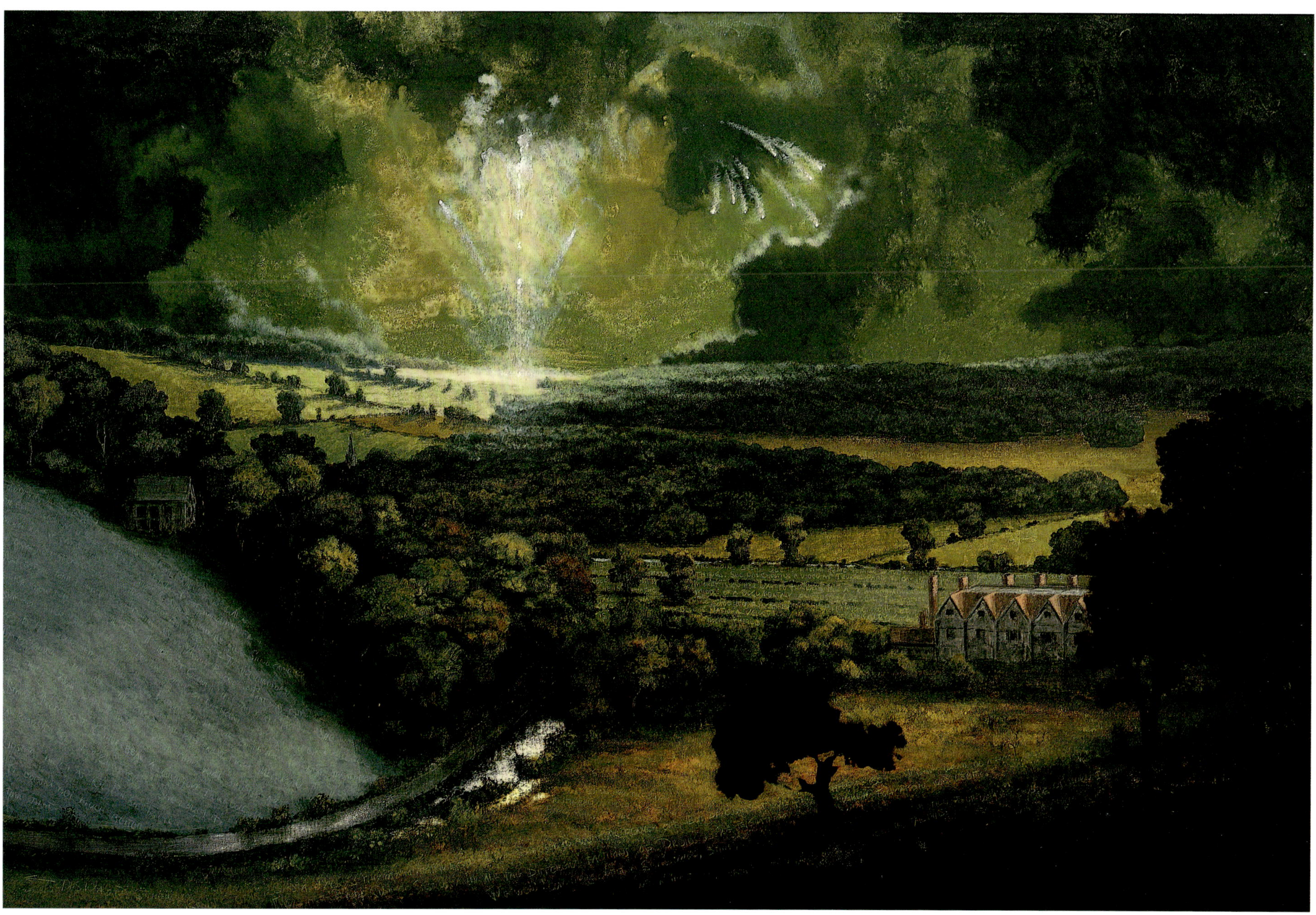

Rockets and Blue Lights, Near Salisbury, 2002
Polished oil on canvas, 48 x 72 inches (122 x 183 cm). Private Collection

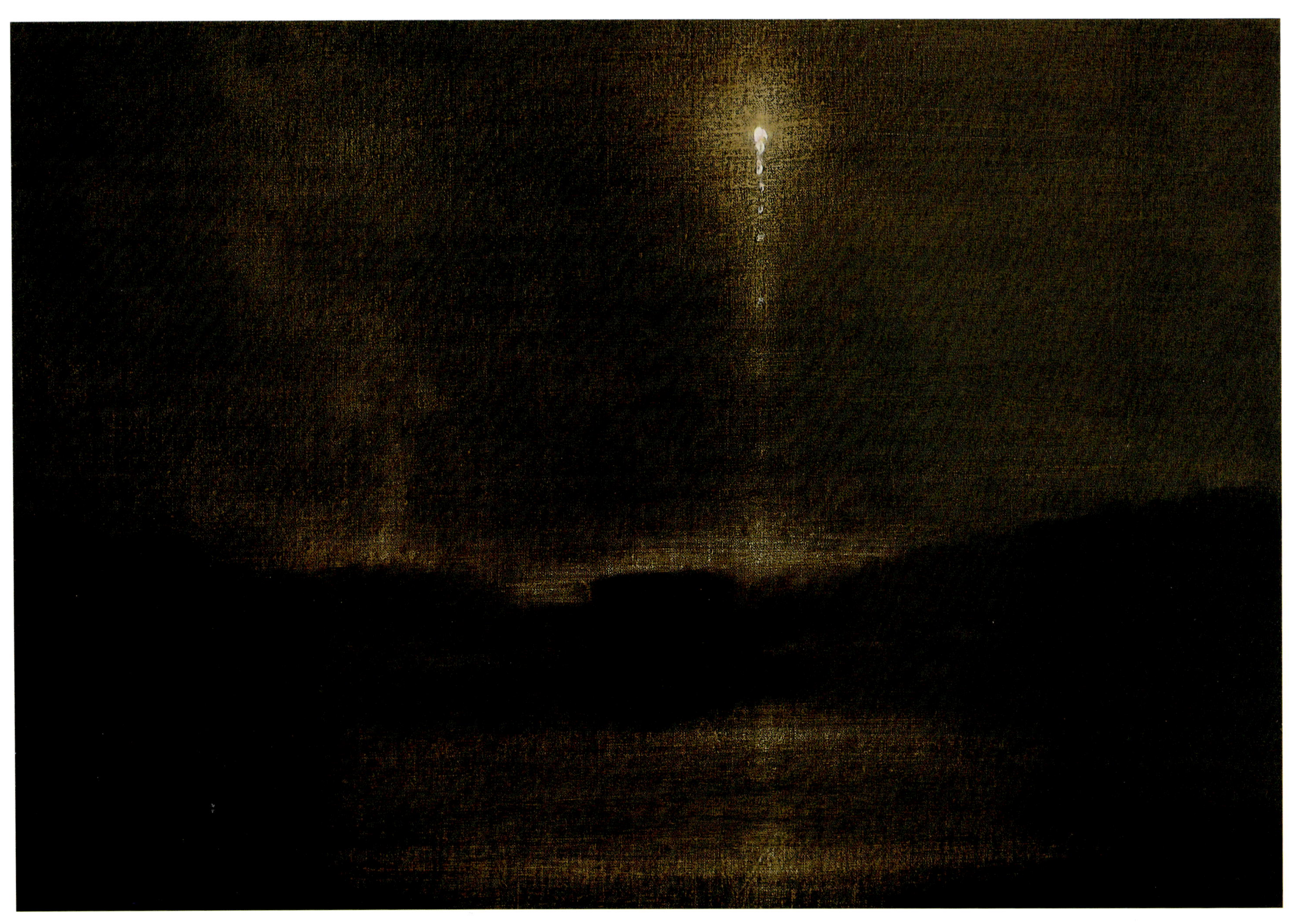

Dual Launch at Dawn, 1995

Polished oil on canvas, 12 x 18 inches (31 x 46 cm). Private Collection

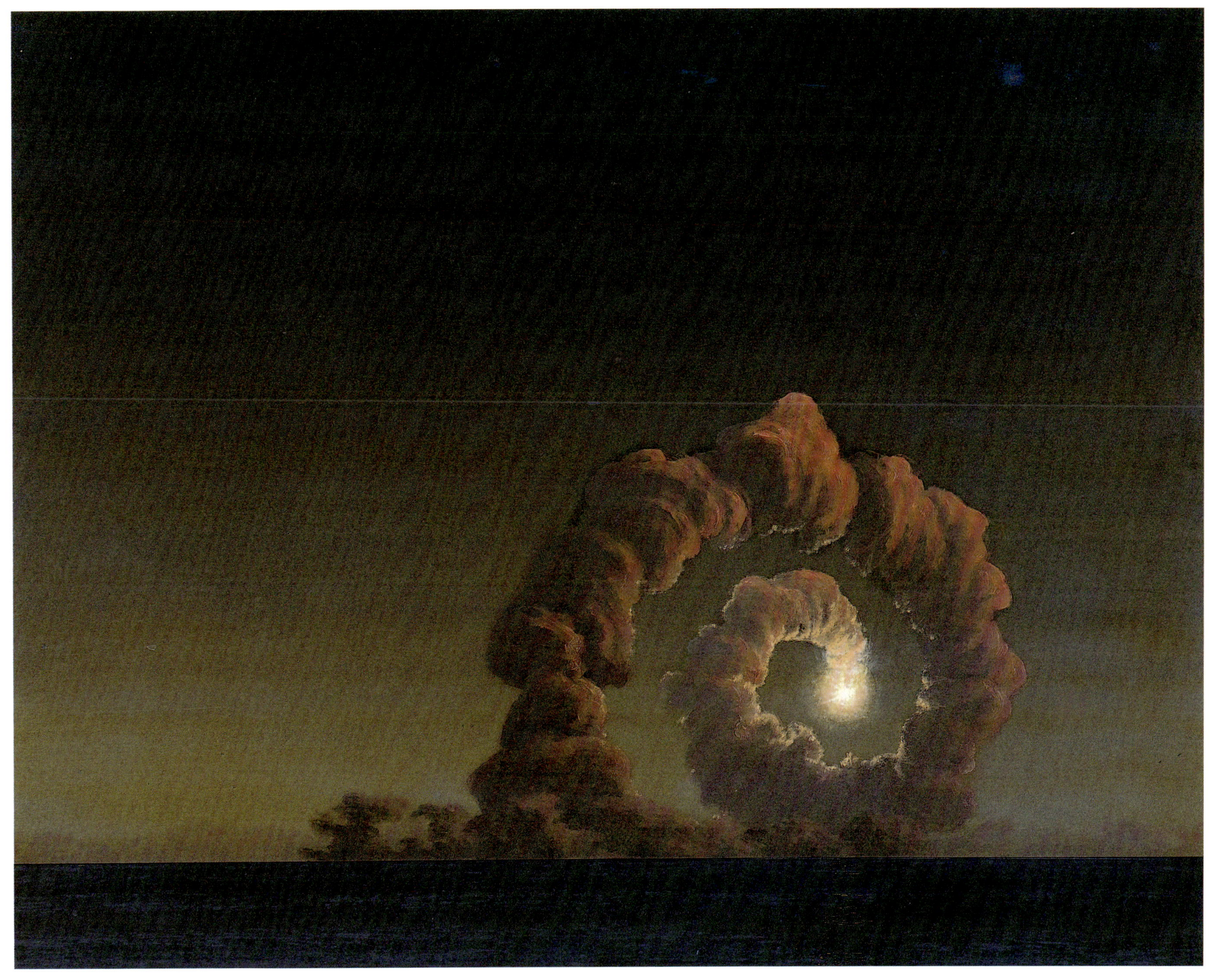

Vortex at Dawn: Green Light, 1993
Polished oil on canvas, 30 x 36 inches (76 x 91 cm). Private Collection

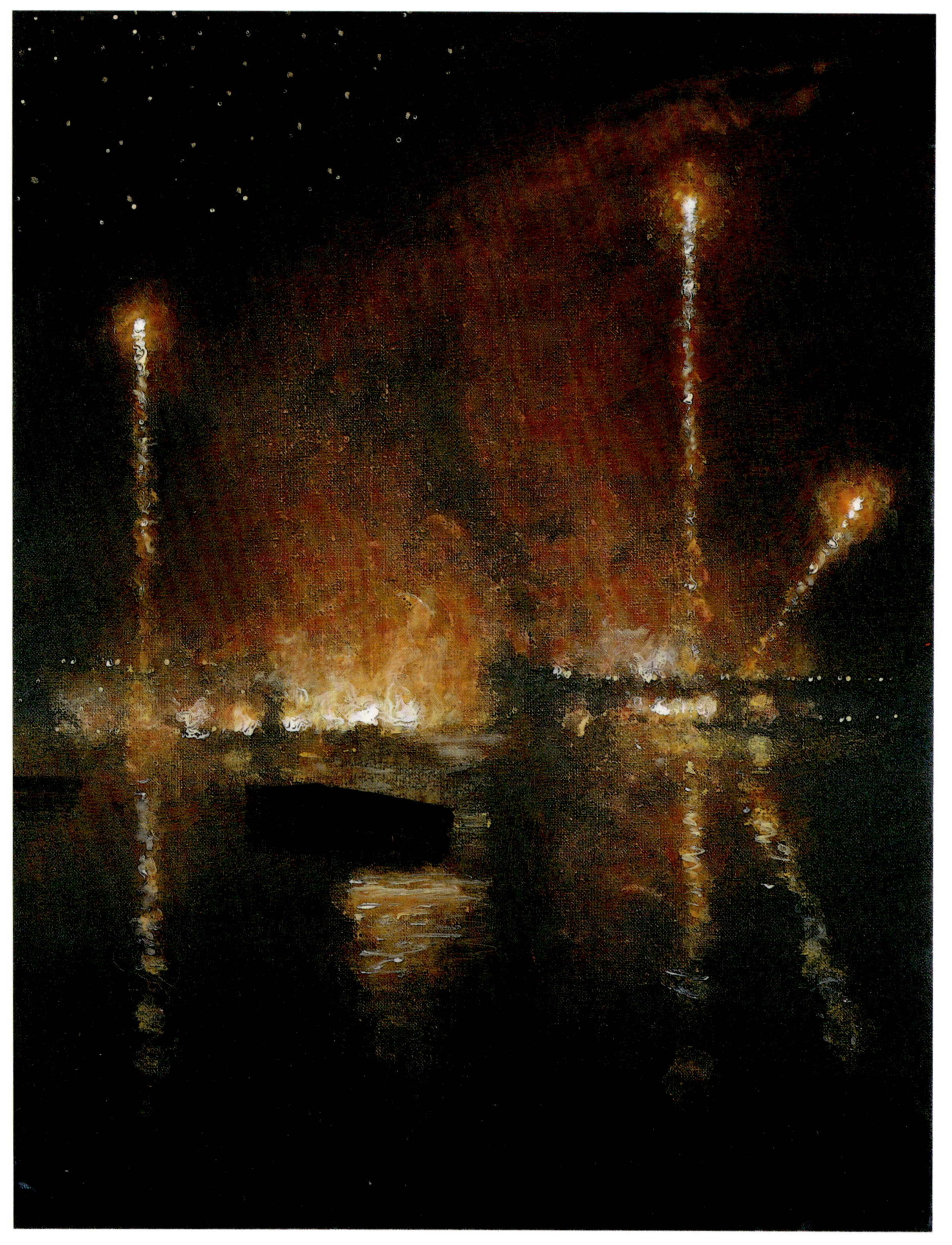

Polished oil on canvas, 12 x 10 inches (31 x 25 cm). Private Collection

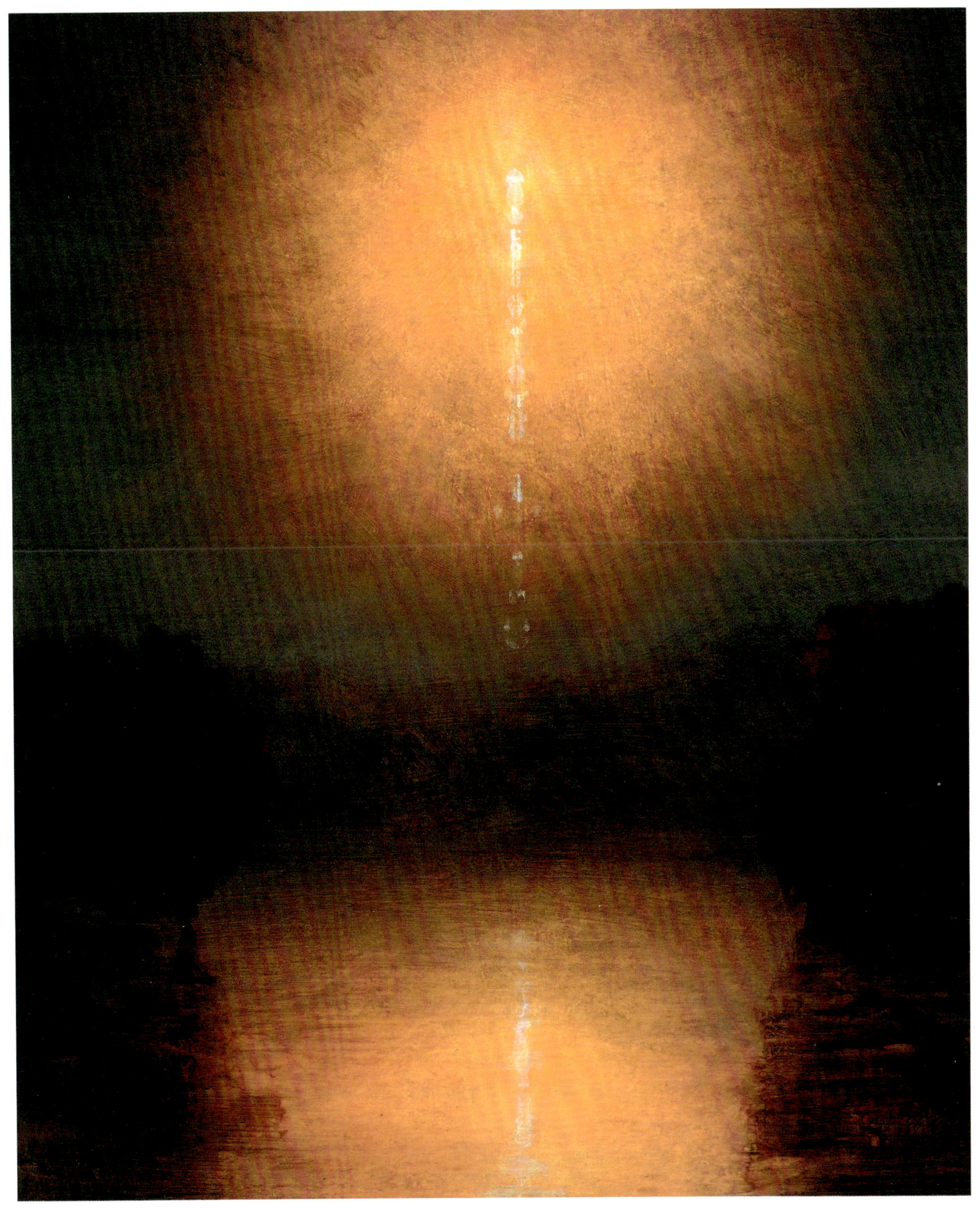

Golden Launch: Green Light (Mass MoCA #74), 2007
Polished acrylic on canvas, 48 x 42 inches (122 x 107 cm). Private Collection

Rockets and Blue Lights, 1989

Polished oil on canvas, 20 x 12 inches (51 x 31 cm). Private Collection

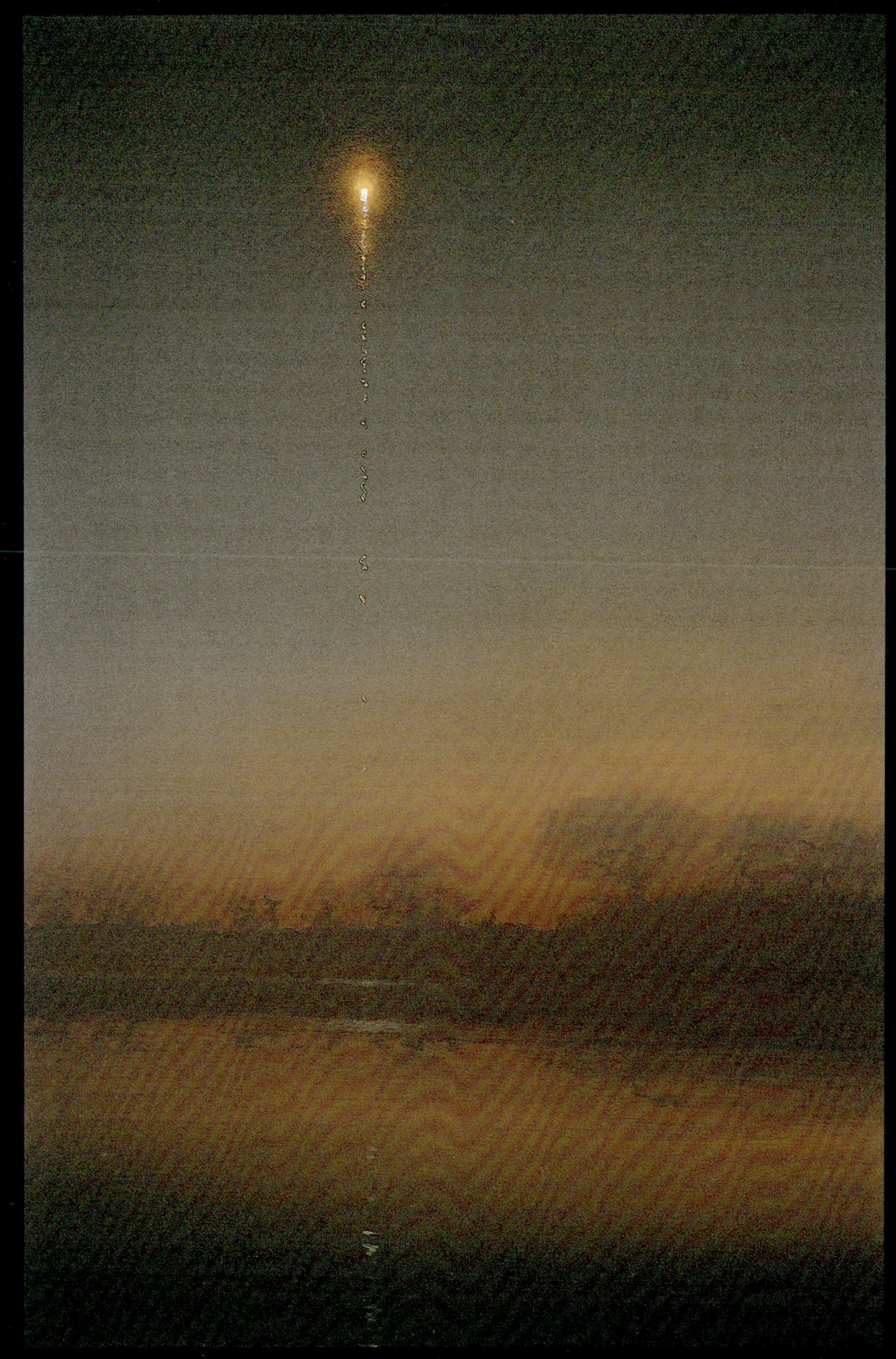

Incendiary Nocturne: Mauve Dusk, 1999
Polished oil on canvas, 54 x 36 inches (137 x 91 cm). Private Collection

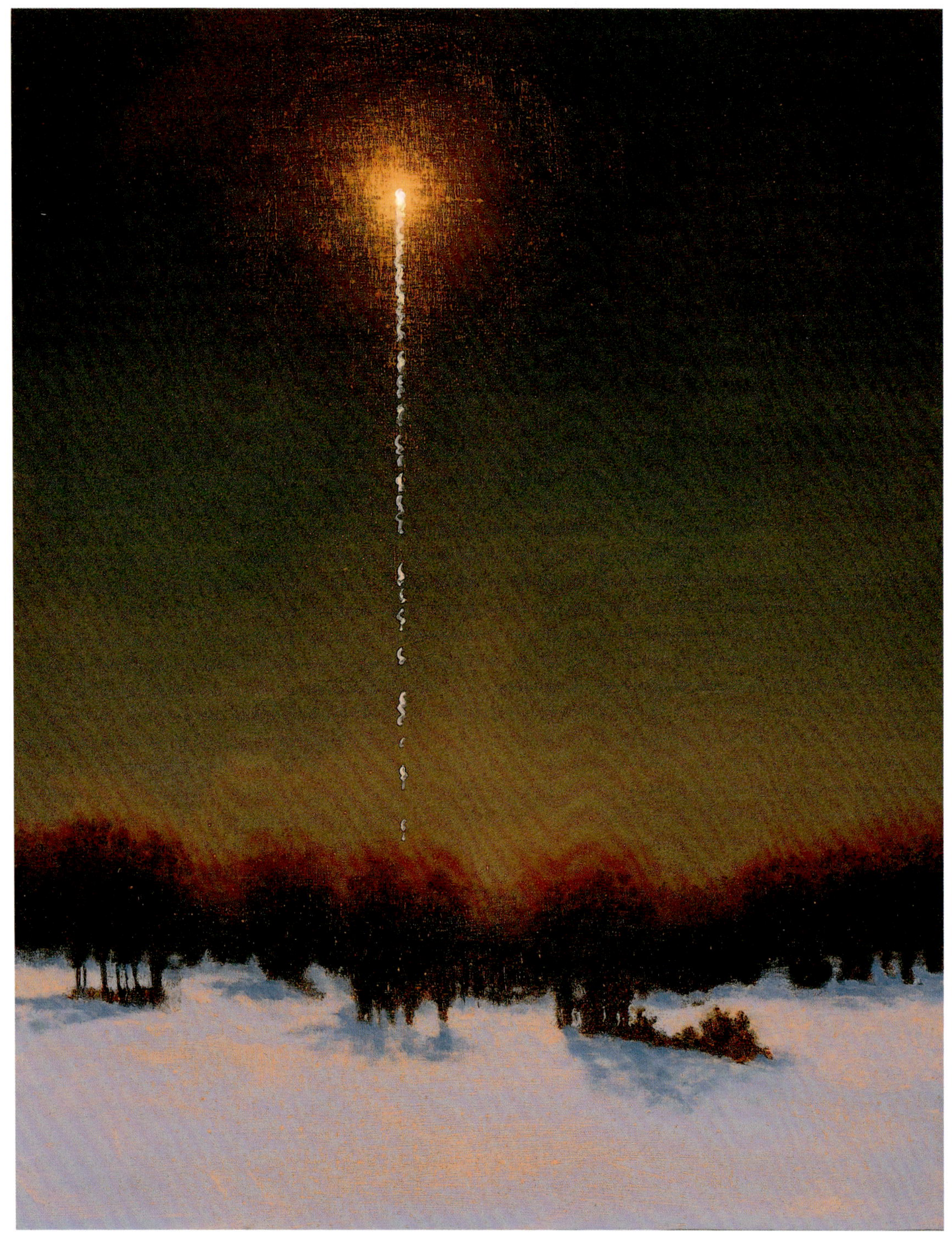

Incendiary Nocturne: Golden Launch at Dawn, 2000
Polished oil on canvas, 40 x 36 inches (102 x 91 cm). Private Collection

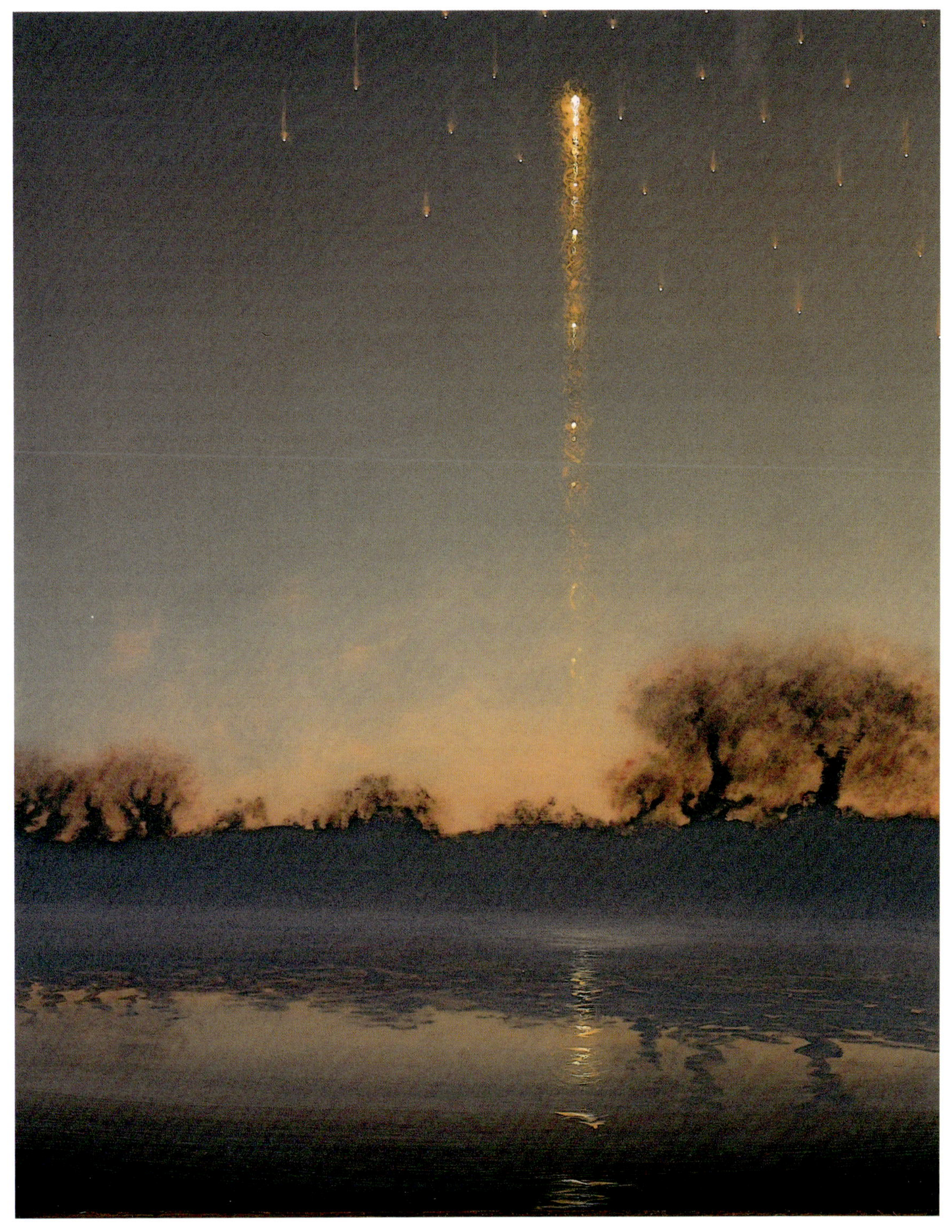

Incendiary Nocturne: Launch at Dawn, 2001
Polished oil on Canvas, 34½ x 26¼ inches (88 x 67 cm). Private Collection

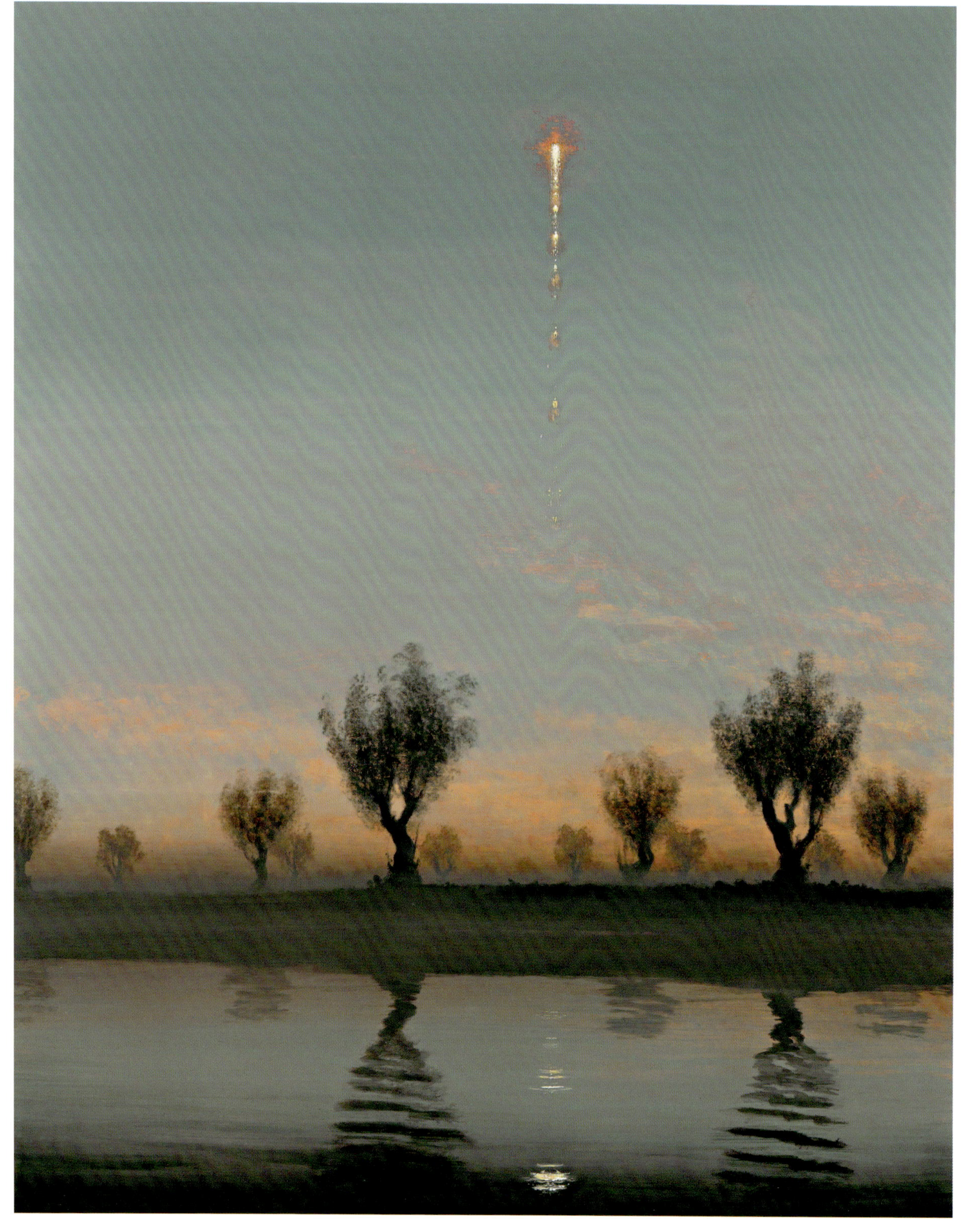

Incendiary Nocturne (Mass MoCA #97), 2008
Polished oil on canvas, 60 x 48 inches (152 x 122 cm). Collection of the Artist

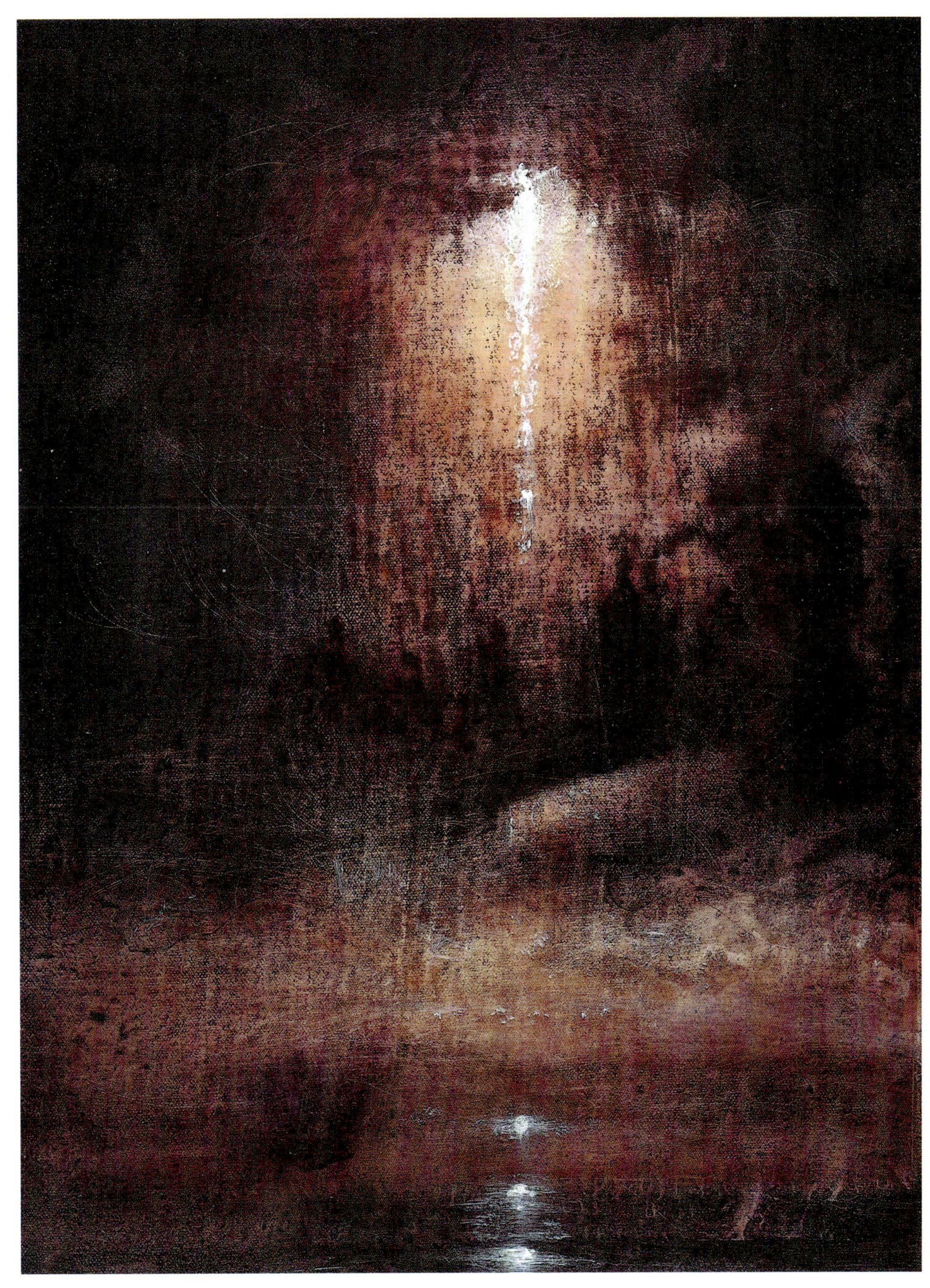

Storm Launch through a Cloud Column (Mass MoCA #90), 2008

Polished acrylic on canvas, 13¾ x 10¼ inches (35 x 26 cm). Collection of the Artist

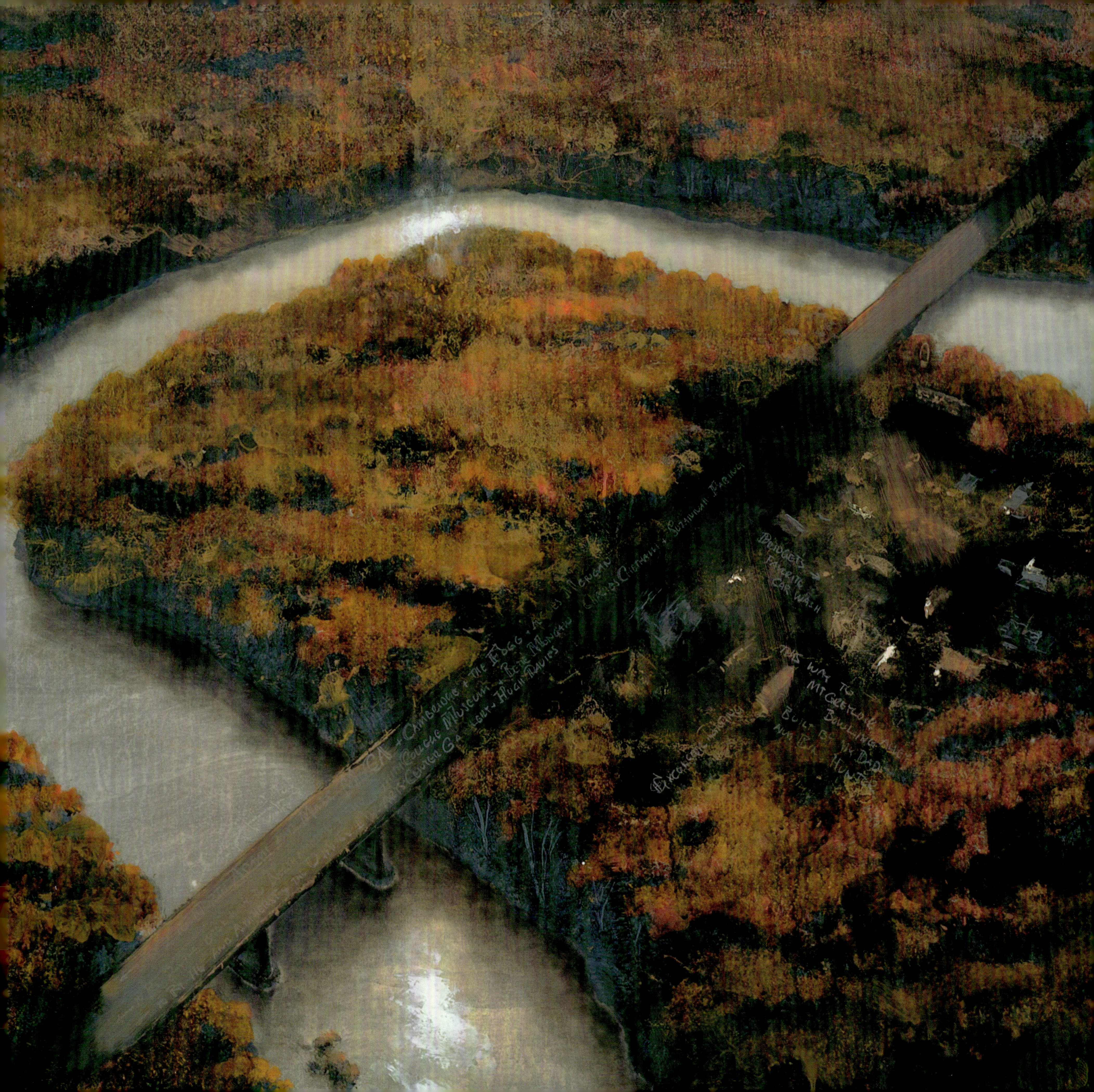
BRIDGETS FAVORITE CAR WASH
THIS WAY TO MT GEELONG BOWLING ALLEY
BUILT BY MY DAD
NUMBER 1 HUNTER
CAMBELONE + THE FOGG + ALLEY MENGAC
KOUCHE MUSEUM + BETE MONDALE
OLOGICAL GALLERY HUGH DAVIES

Vistas and Nocturnes

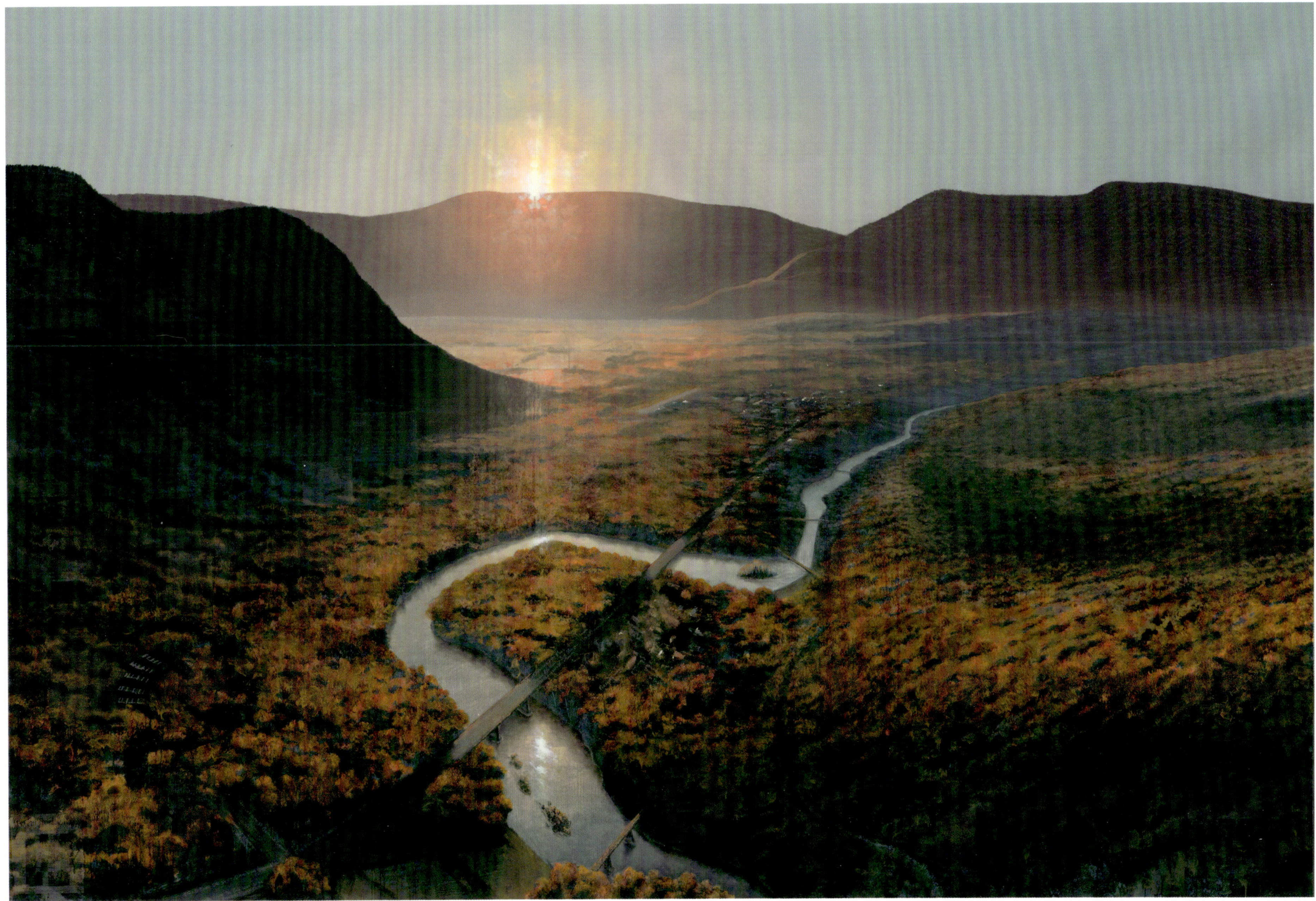

A Recent History of Art in Western Massachusetts; Flooded River for Lane Faison (Mass MoCA #12), 2005
Polished oil over mixed media on canvas stretched over board, 96 x 144 inches (244 x 366 cm). National Gallery of Art, Washington, D.C., Louis M. Bacon Fund (2005.120.1)

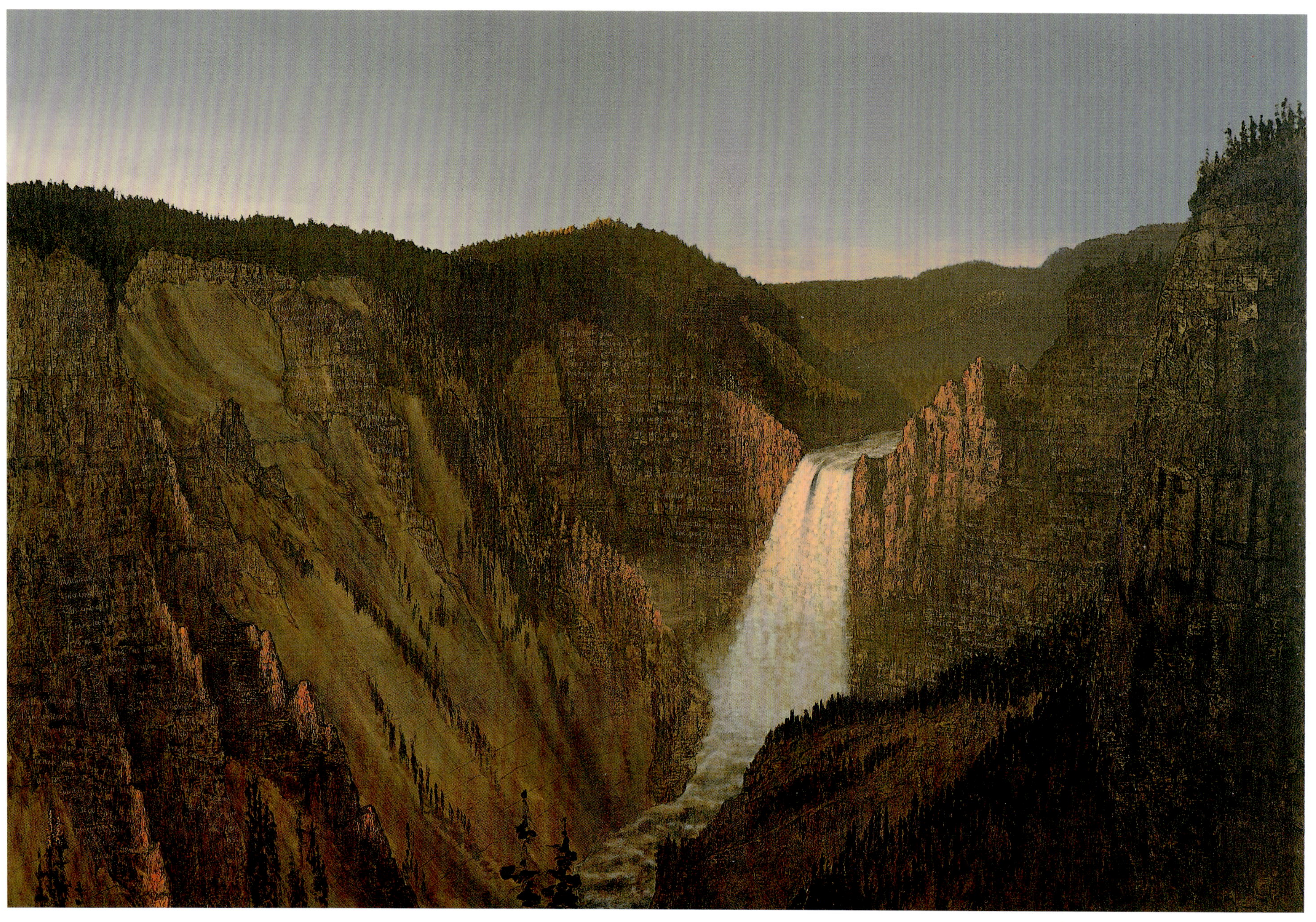

Flooded Canyon: Yellowstone, 1997

Polished oil on canvas, 48 x 72 inches (122 x 183 cm). Smithsonian American Art Museum

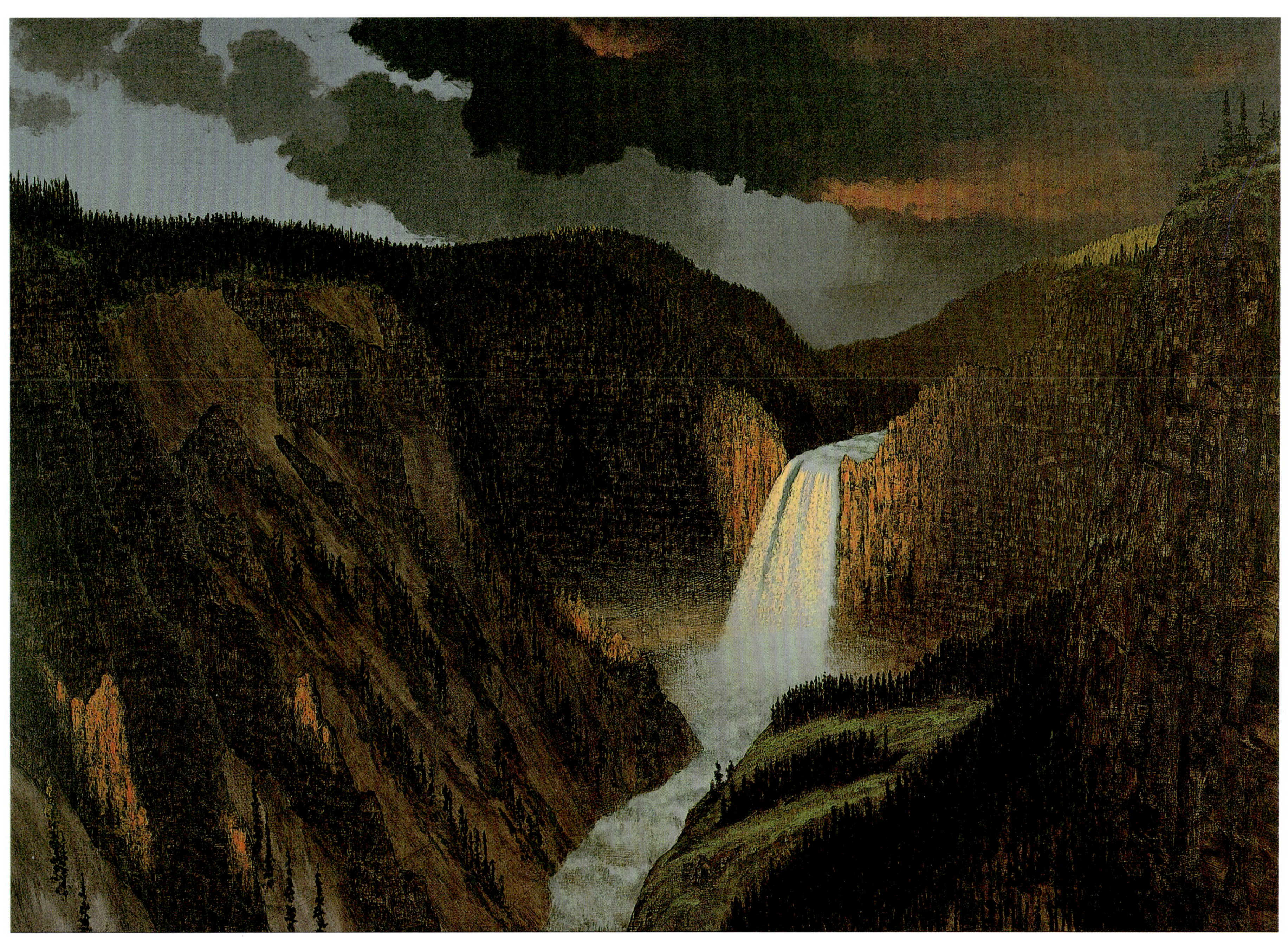

Flooded Canyon: Yellowstone (Storm Approaching), 1998

Polished oil on canvas, 66 x 96 inches (168 x 244 cm). Private Collection

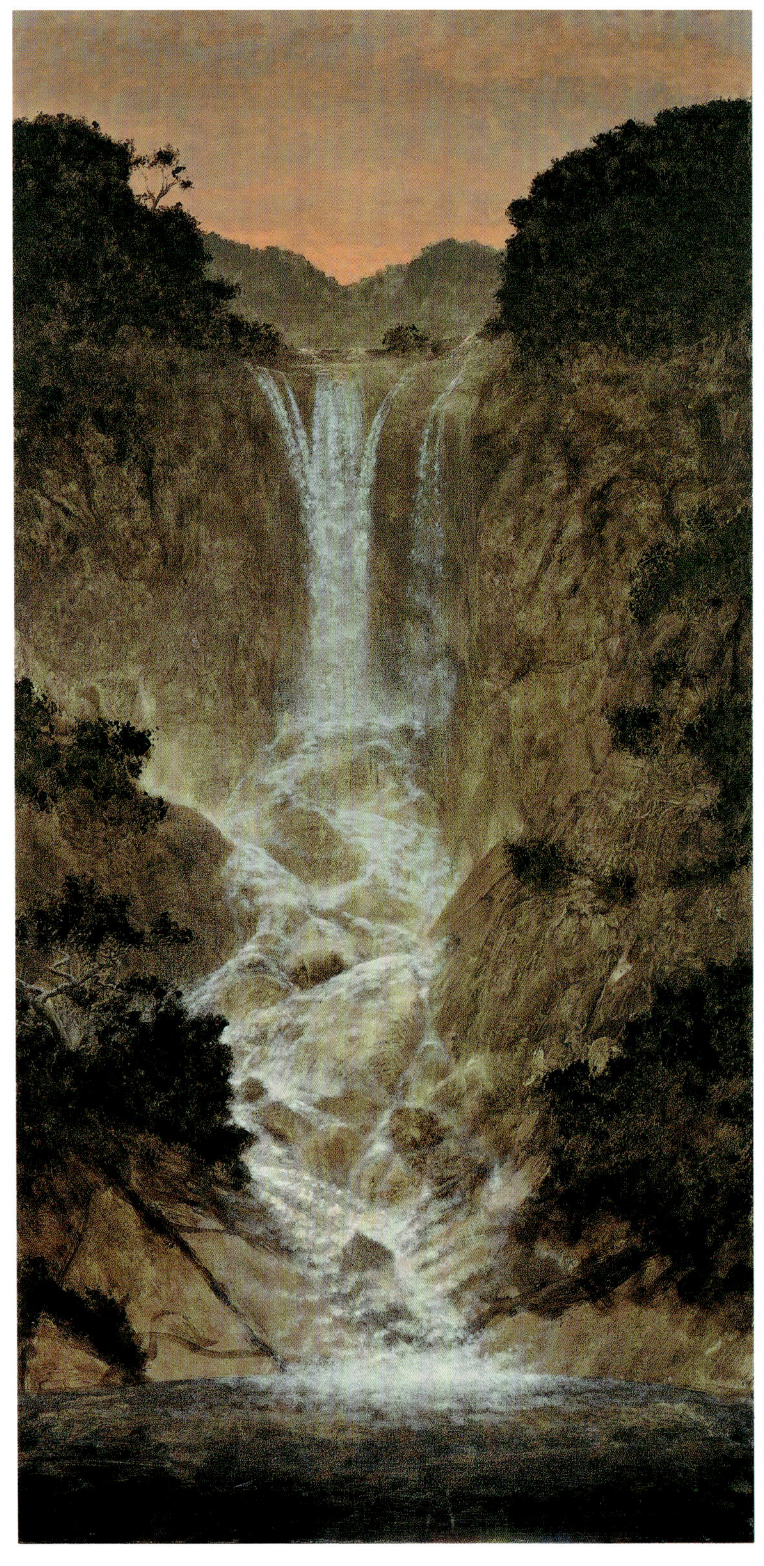

Flooded Cascade on the Way to Robin's House, 1997
Polished oil on canvas, 72 x 36 inches (183 x 91 cm). Private Collection

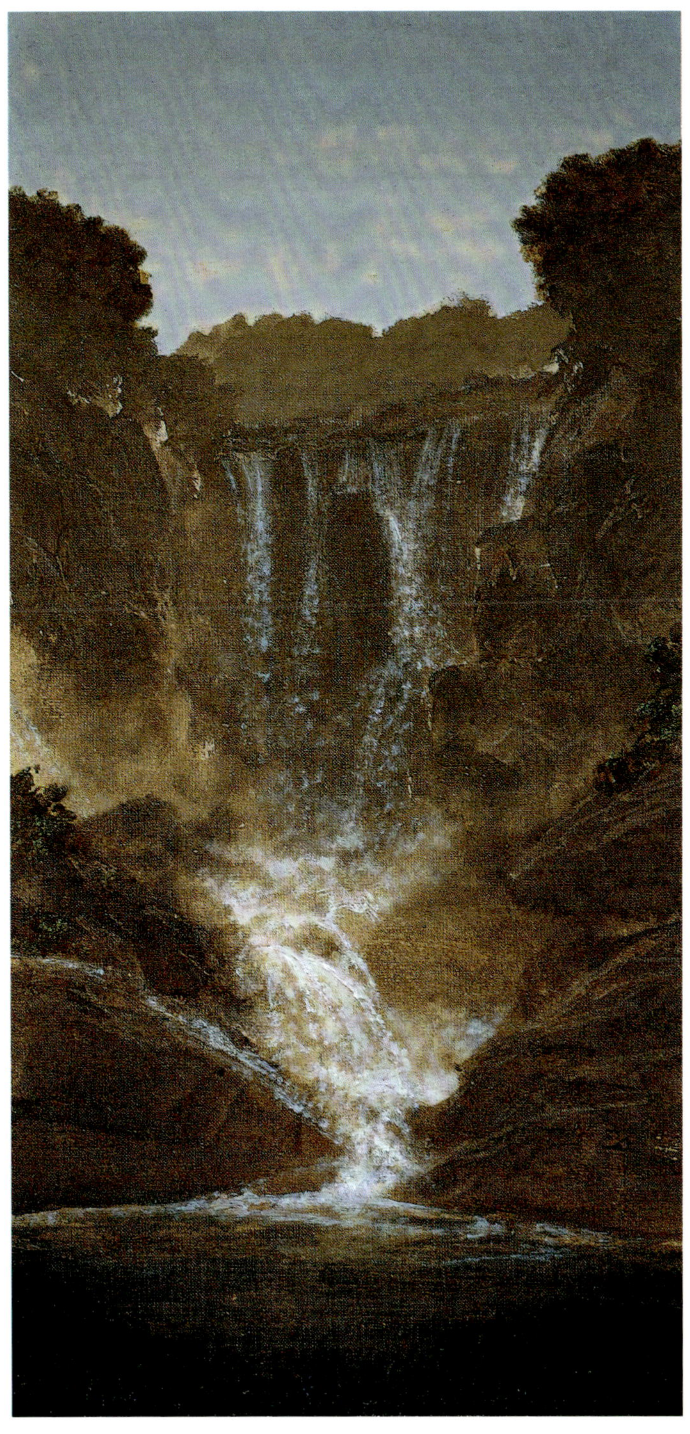

Flooded Cascade: Dawn Light, 1997

Polished oil on canvas, 15¾ x 8 inches (40 x 20 cm). Private Collection

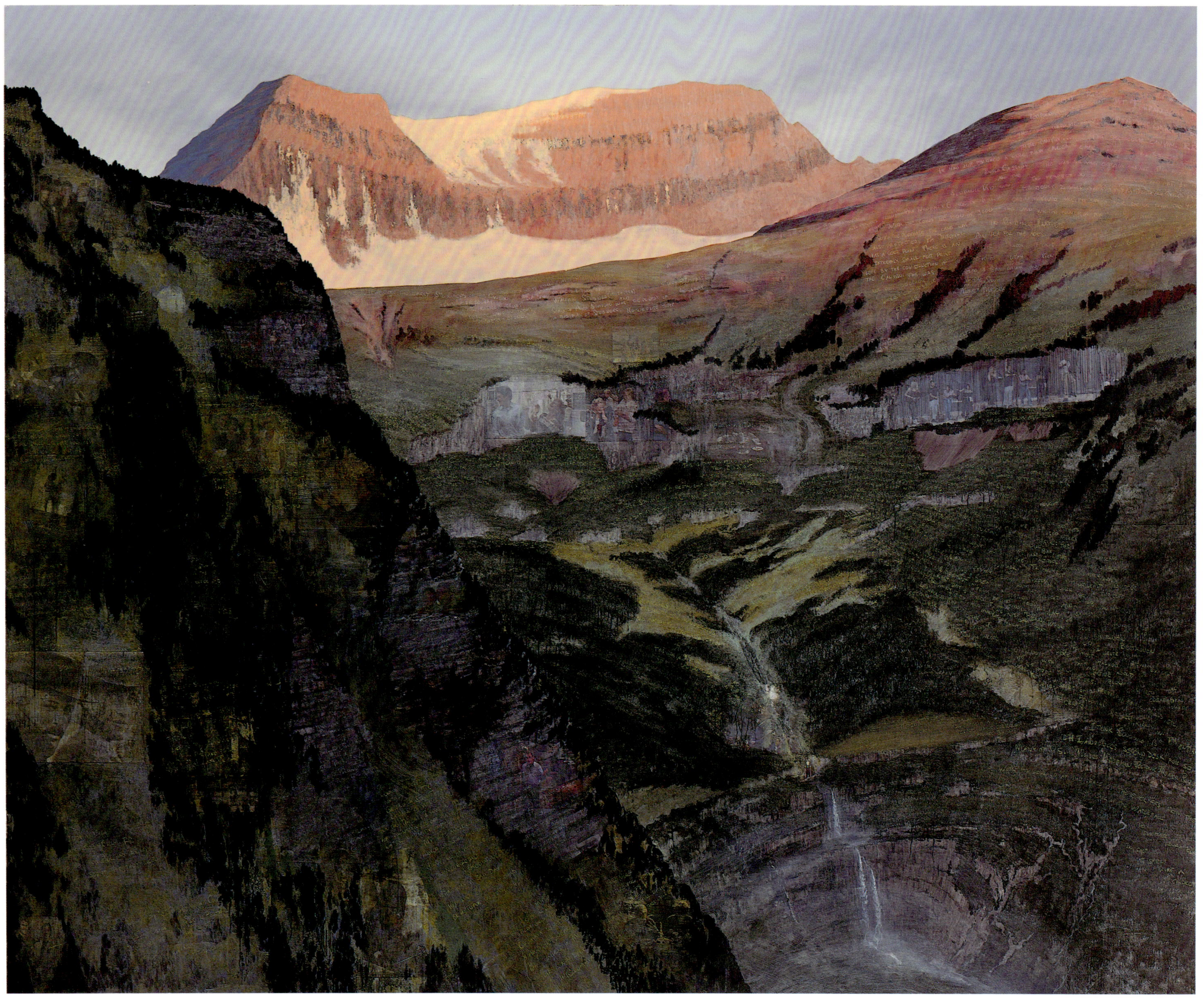

Utah Canyon at Dawn, 2008
Polished mixed media, 96 x 120 inches (244 x 305 cm). Private Collection

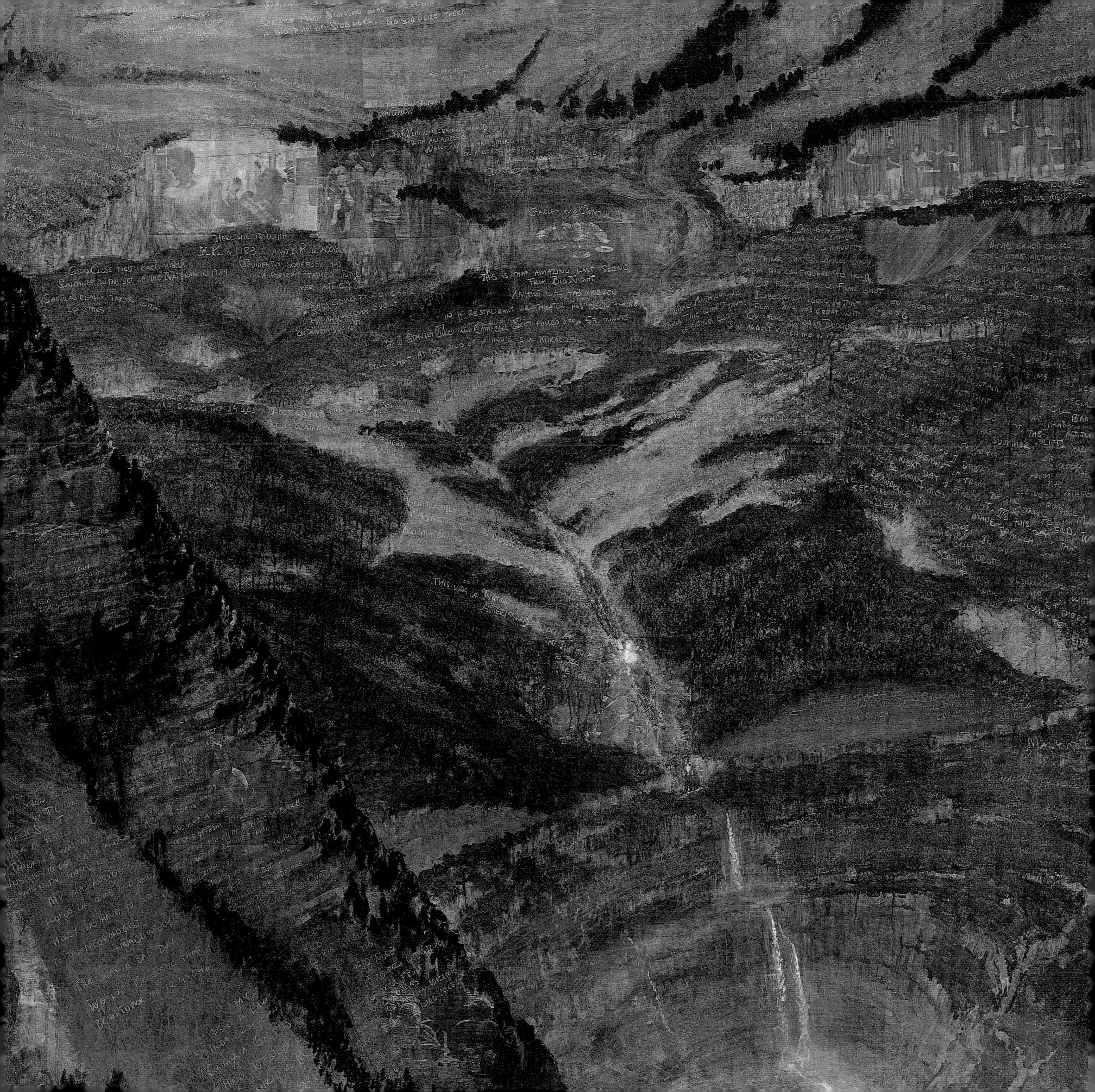

HERE SHE IS WITH
RR IN 1983 AND RR IN 2006
(EVIDENTLY, SOMEBODY HAS
A PORTRAIT STASHED IN
HER ATTIC.)
GLENN CLOSE FIRST HEARD ABOUT
SUNDANCE ON THE SET OF THE NATURAL IN 1984
SHOW WAS REALLY TAKEN
CO-STARS
SHE'S GOING TO CONSIDER THE
25TH ANNIVERSARY EVENT
ON NOVEMBER 6TH.
THIS IS THAT AMAZING LAST SCENE
FROM BIG NIGHT
ANYONE WHO HAS WORKED
IN A RESTAURANT OR THEATER HAS SEEN THIS.
HOW STANLEY TUCCI AND CAMPBELL SCOTT PULLED OFF A 5½ MINUTE
STILL SHOT AT THE END OF A MOVIE IS A MIRACLE.
SENATOR ALAN SIMPSON WAS
A BIG FAN OF SCIENCES. NO SURPRISE THERE.
STANLEY AND TONY
WAS SHOT BY
OF EATING EGGS.
TOUGH TIME WITH 7 TAKES
ISABELLA WAS GOOD IN THAT
FILM AND WAS GREAT WITH
CAMPBELL IN ROGER DODGER.
SHE ALMOST KILLED ME IN 1983.
BEFORE
AND DURING THE 1960s
THIS WAS A NATURAL
AMERICAN
WE LOST BRANDO
BRANDO TURNER ON 10/9/04
MY WIFE ANSWERED
IT WAS A BAD DAY

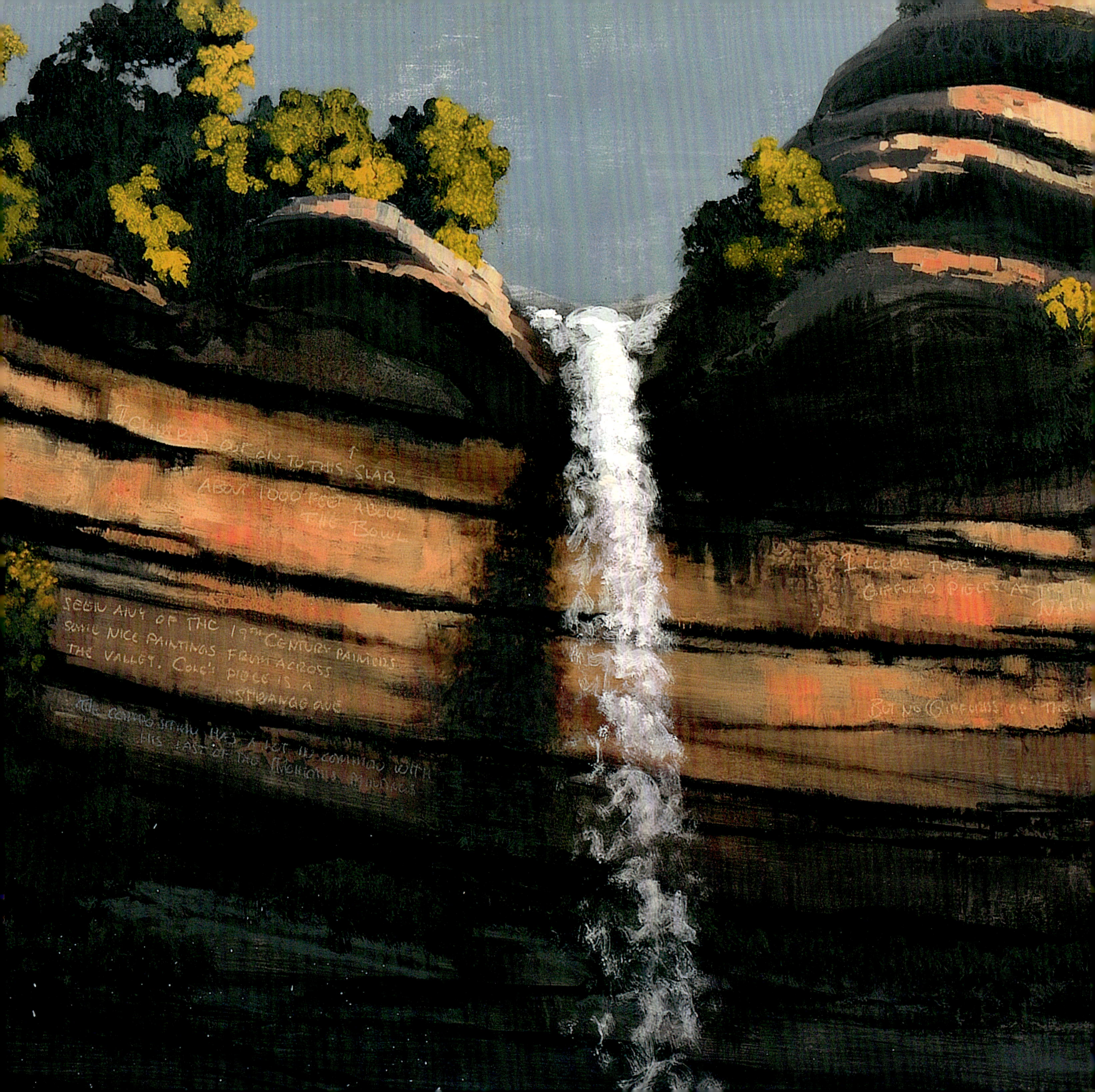

I CLIMBED OUT ON TO THIS SLAB
ABOUT 1000 FEET ABOVE
THE BOWL
SEEN ANY OF THE 19TH CENTURY PAINTERS
SOME NICE PAINTINGS FROM ACROSS
THE VALLEY. COLE'S PIECE IS A
STRANGE ONE
HE CERTAINLY HAS A LOT IN COMMON WITH
HIS LAST OF THE MOHICANS
I LIKED THOSE
GIFFORD PIECES AT
NATL
BUT NO GIFFORDS OF THE

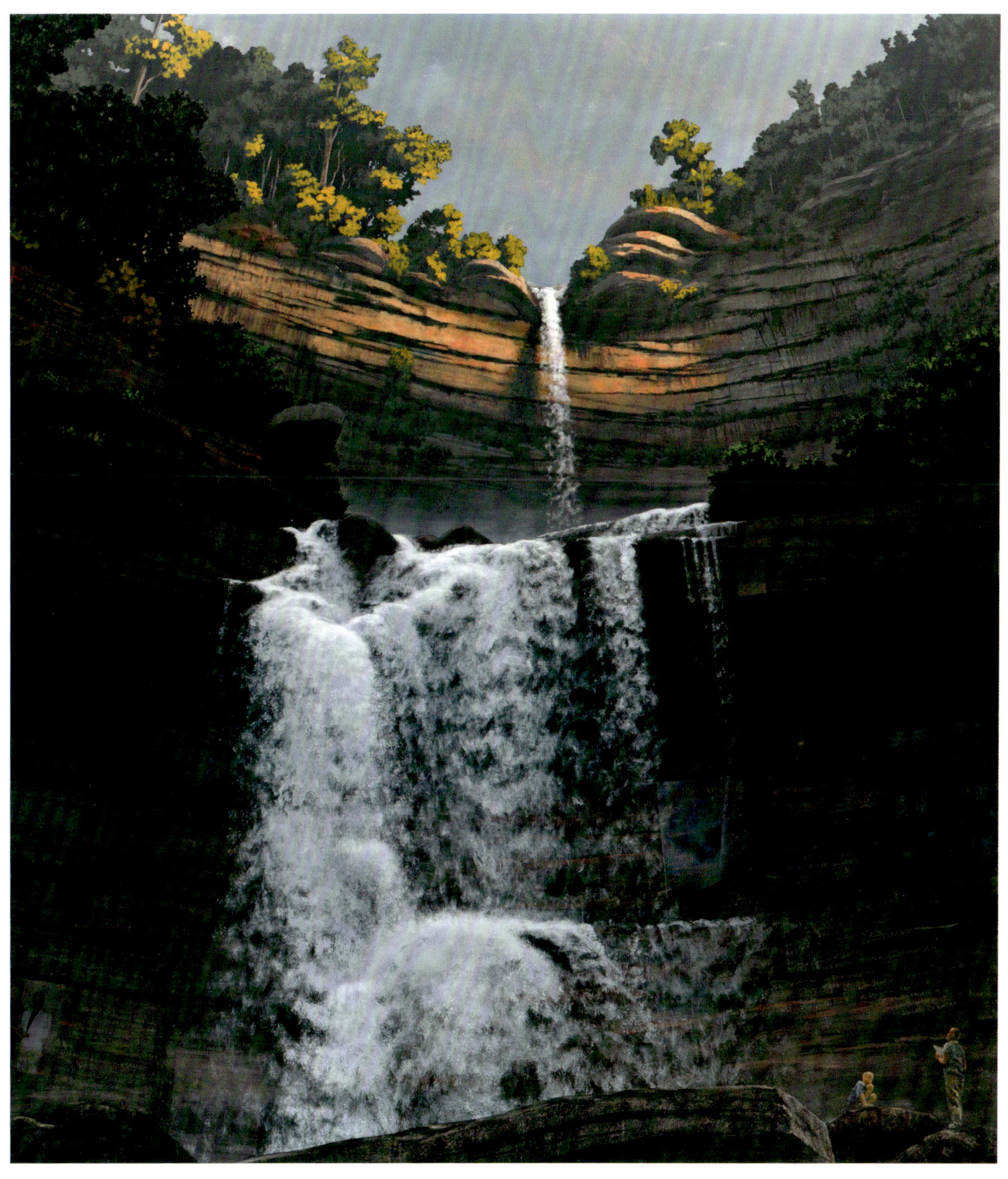

Kaaterskill Falls for Frank Moore and Dan Hodermarsky (Mass MoCA #11), 2005
Acrylic, alkyd, and oil glazes with collage elements on canvas, 108 x 96 inches (274 x 244 cm).
The Metropolitan Museum of Art, New York, Gift of David B. Williams, 2007 (2007.333)

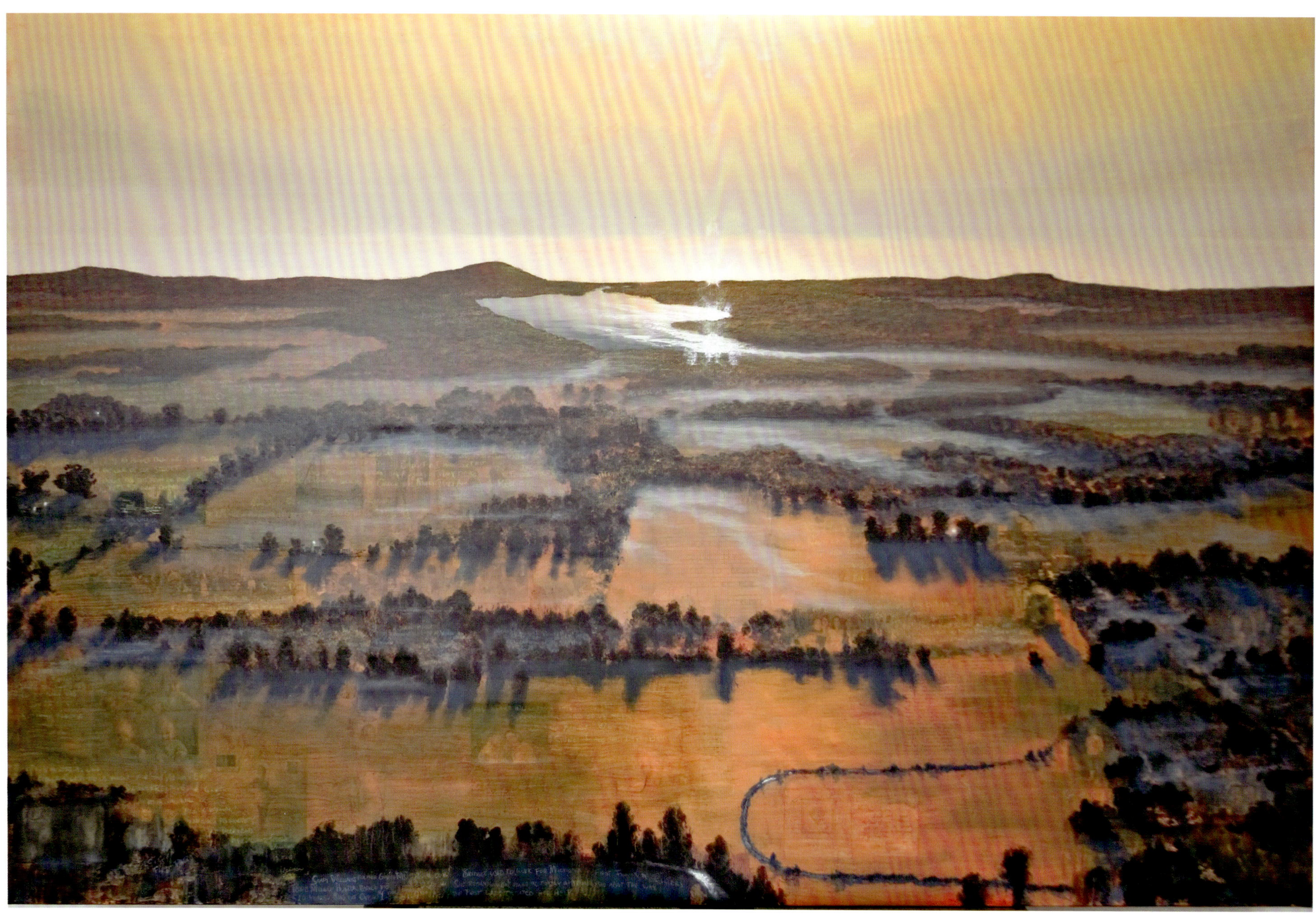

Luminous Afternoon in Western Michigan, for Bridget, 2007

Polished mixed media on canvas, 64 x 96 inches (163 x 244 cm). Grand Rapids Art Museum, Gift of the Artist

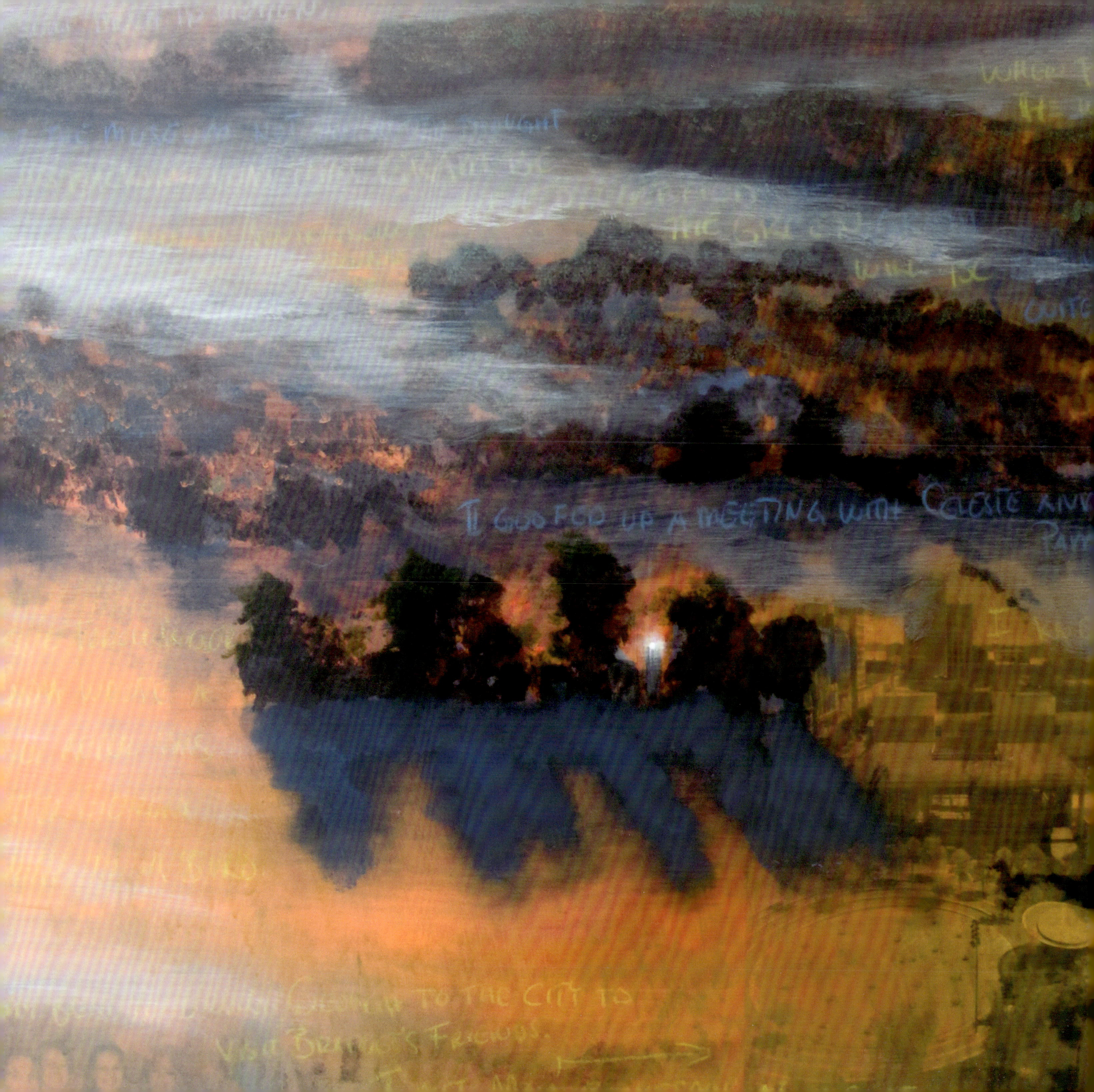
THE MUSEUM WAS THE GREAT
THE GREEN WILL BE
QUITE
I GOOFED UP A MEETING WITH CELESTE AND
GONEW TO THE CITY TO

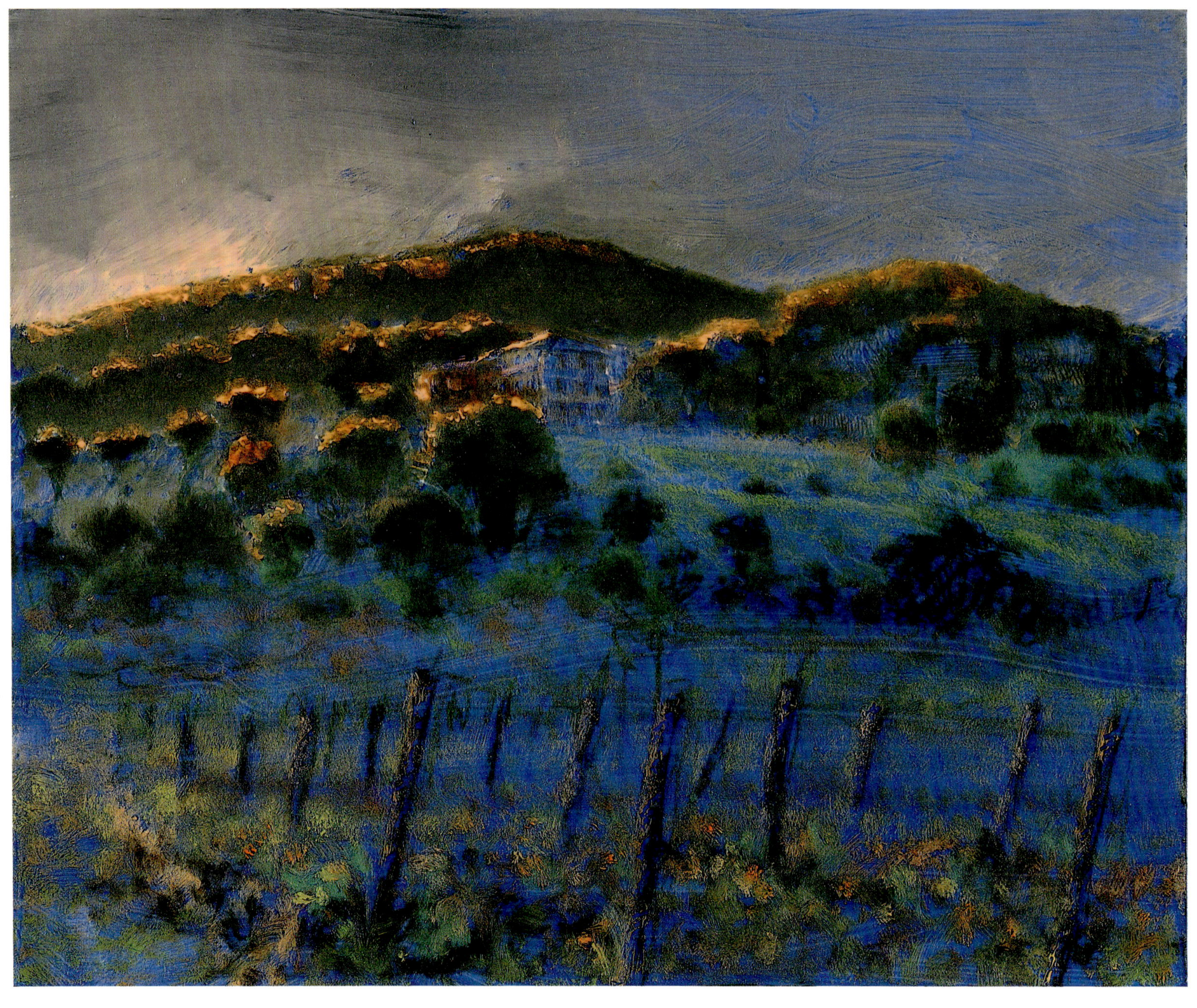

Villa il Palagio: After the Storm, 1999

Polished oil on canvas, 7 x 8½ inches (18 x 22 cm). Private Collection

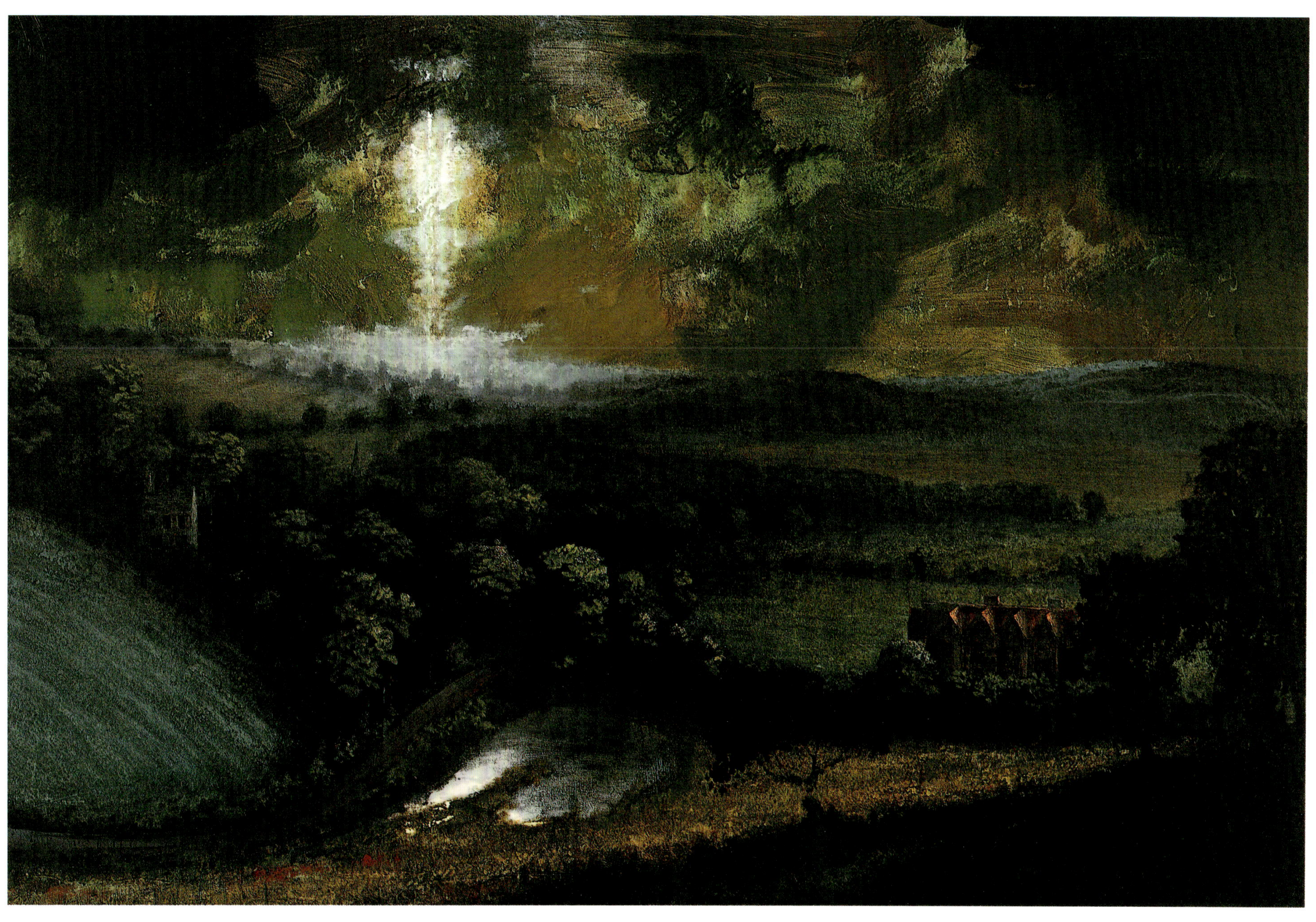

Rockets and Blue Lights over Salisbury, 1999
Polished oil on canvas, 20 x 12 inches (51 x 31 cm). Private Collection

95

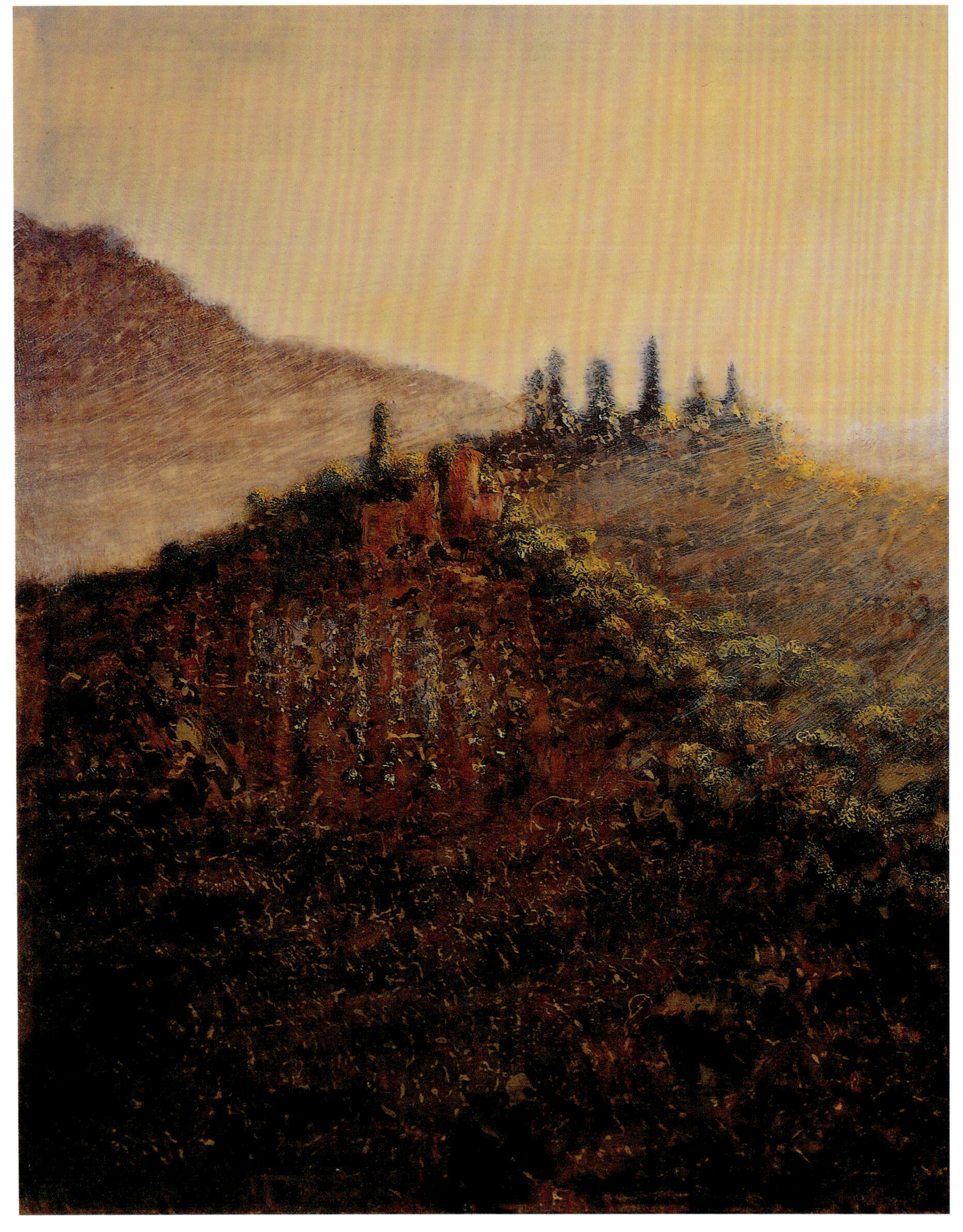

Tuscan Tapestry at Dawn, 1996

Polished oil on canvas, 8 x 7 inches (20 x 18 cm). Private Collection

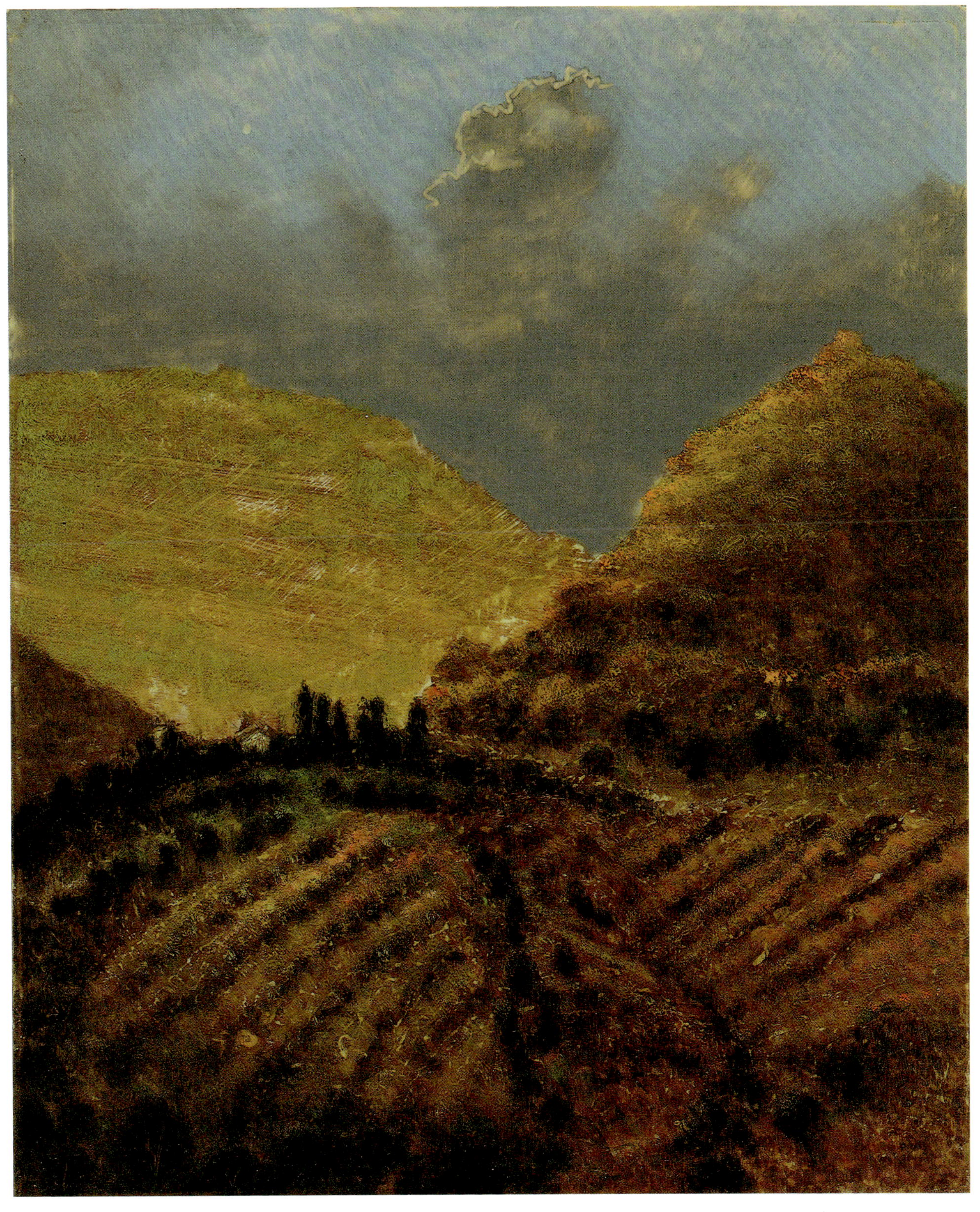

TUSCAN VINEYARD WITH STORM APPROACHING, 1998
POLISHED OIL ON CANVAS, 9¾ X 7¼ INCHES (25 X 18 CM). PRIVATE COLLECTION

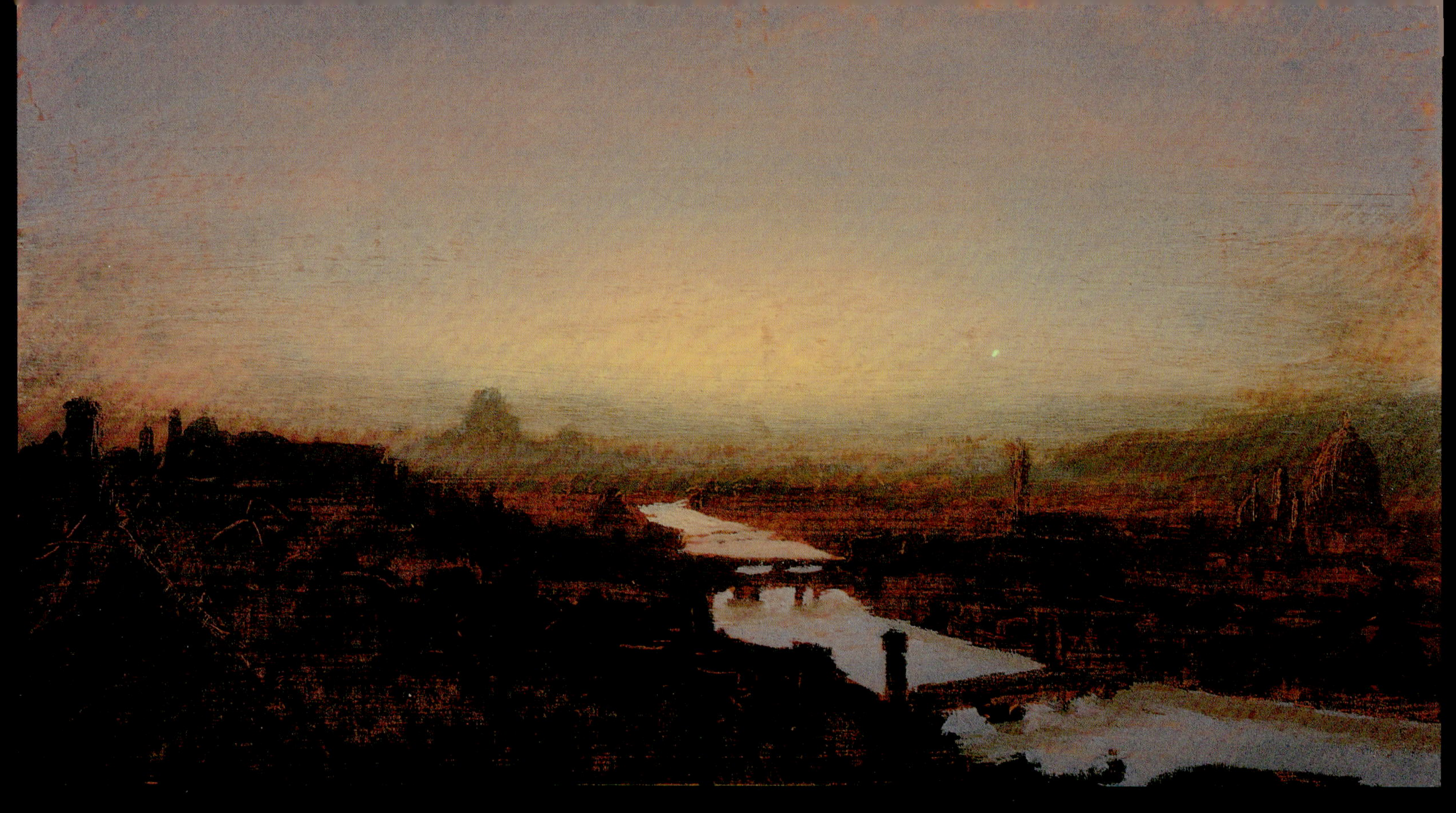

STUDY: FLOODED RIVER, TUSCANY, 1995

Polished oil on canvas, 4¼ x 8 inches (11 x 20 cm). Private Collection

———

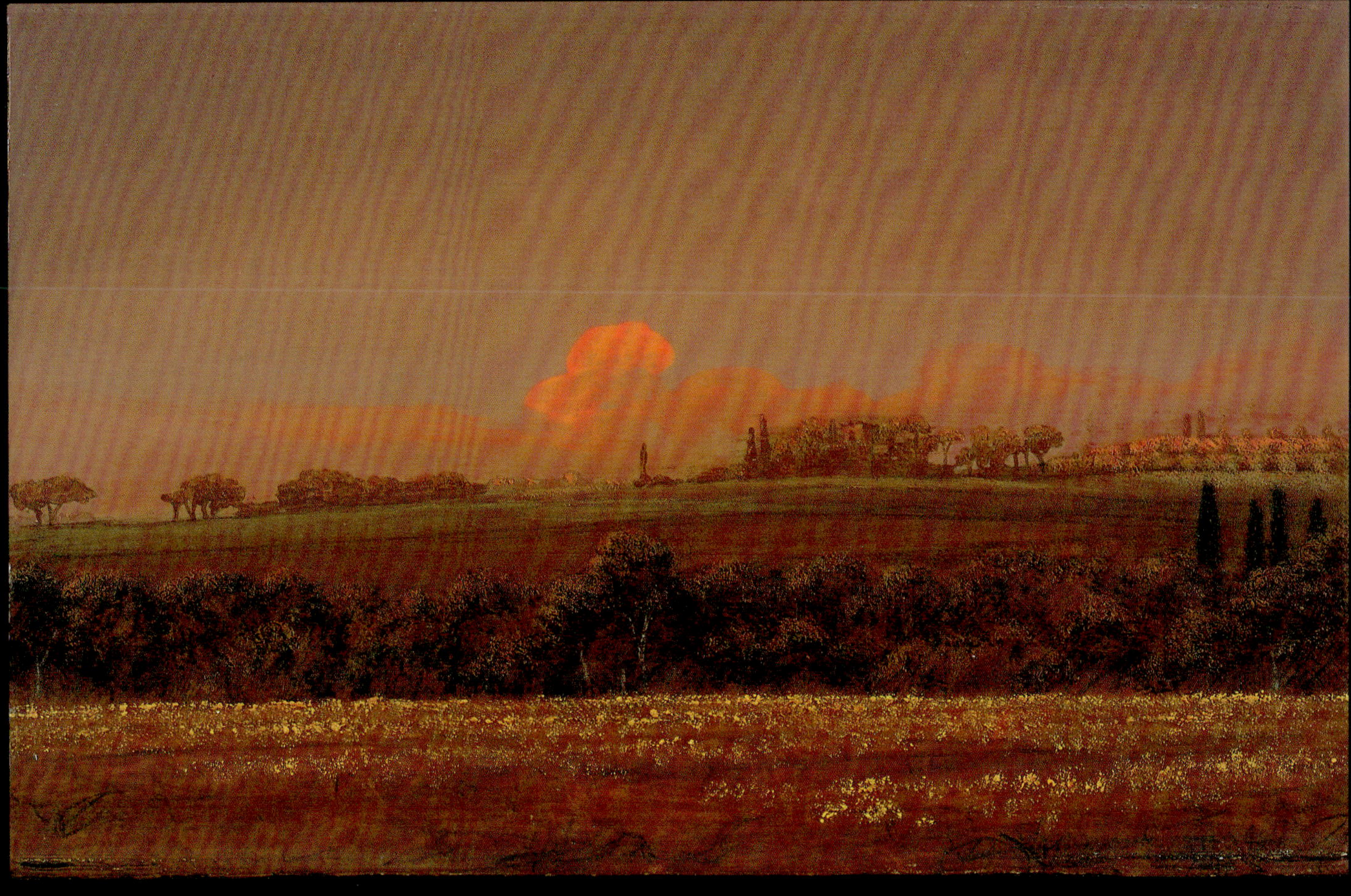

Dusty Dusk in Tuscany, 1996
Polished oil on canvas, 7 x 11 inches (18 x 28 cm). Private Collection

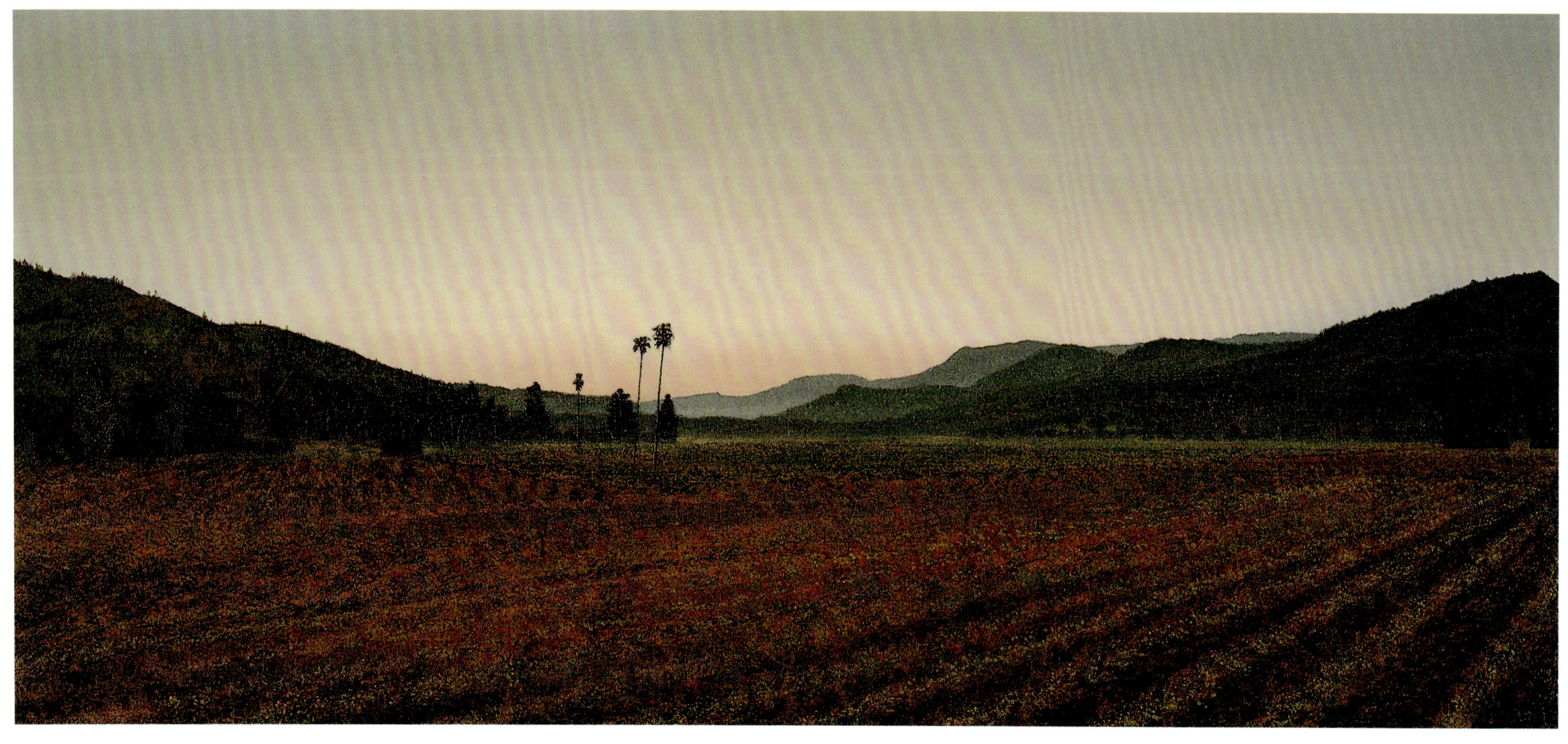

Napa Dawn: Autumn Light, 1997

Polished oil on canvas, 22½ x 50 inches (57 x 127 cm). Private Collection

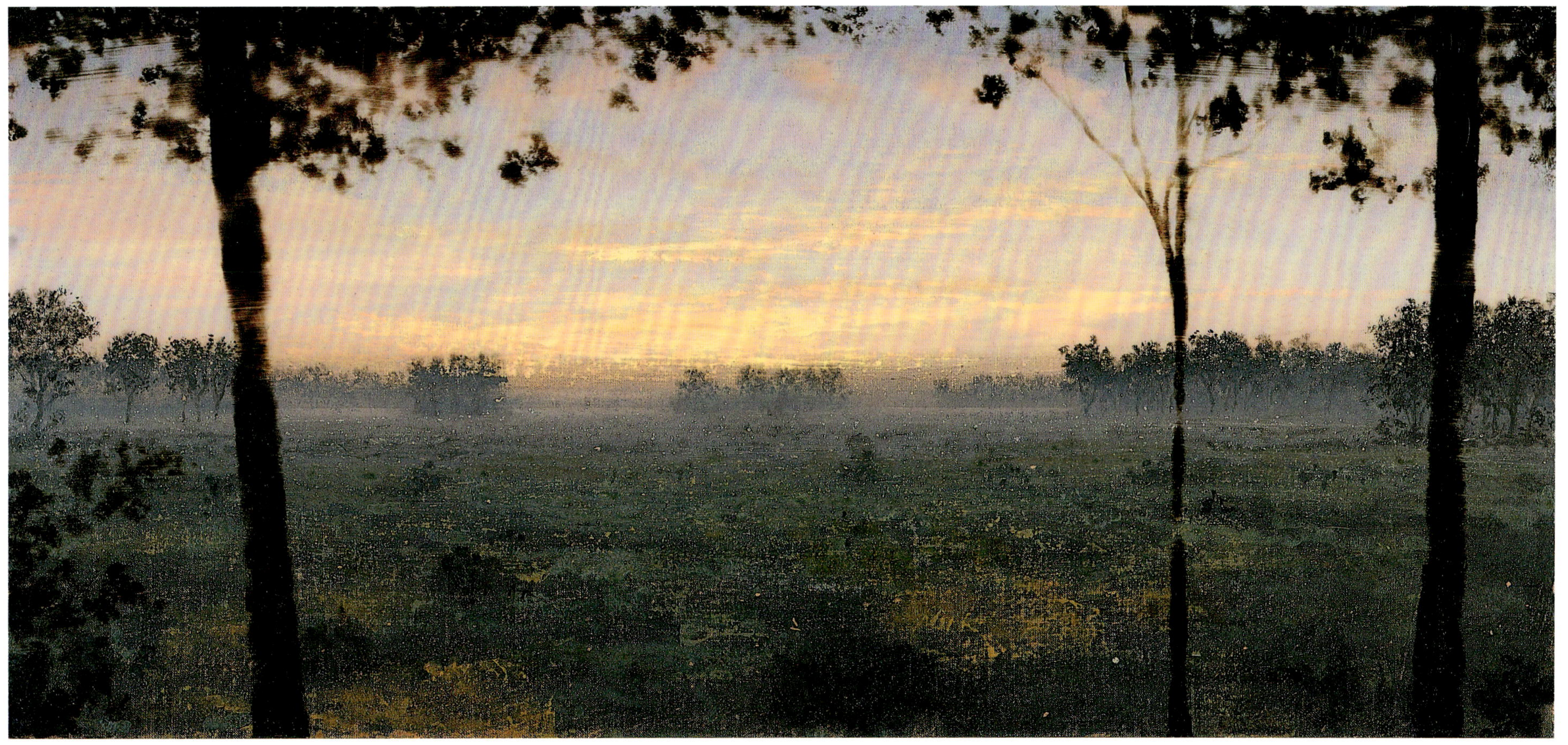

Luminous Field at the End of the Day, 2000

Polished oil on canvas mounted on panel, 11 x 24 inches (28 x 61 cm). Private Collection

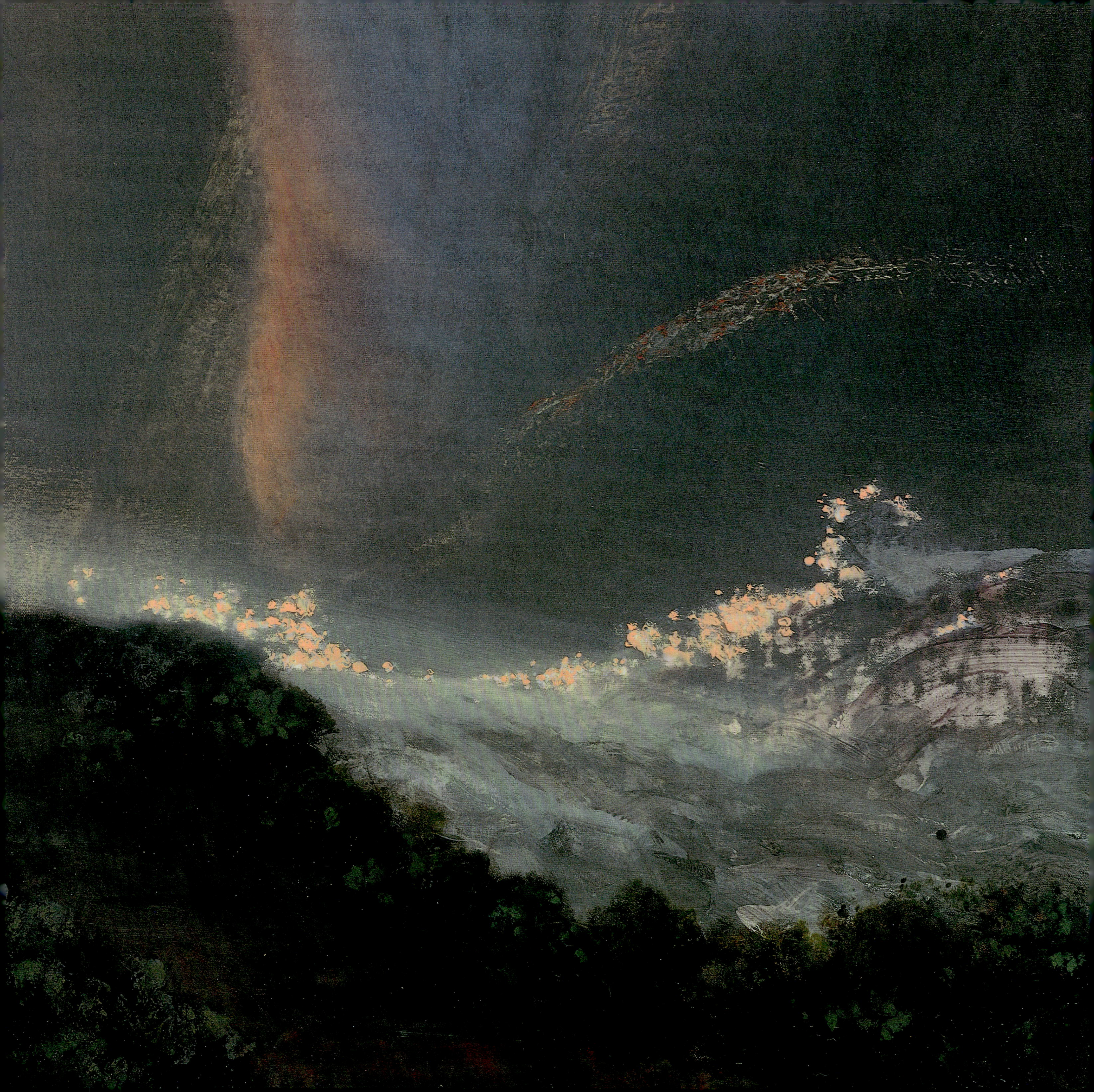

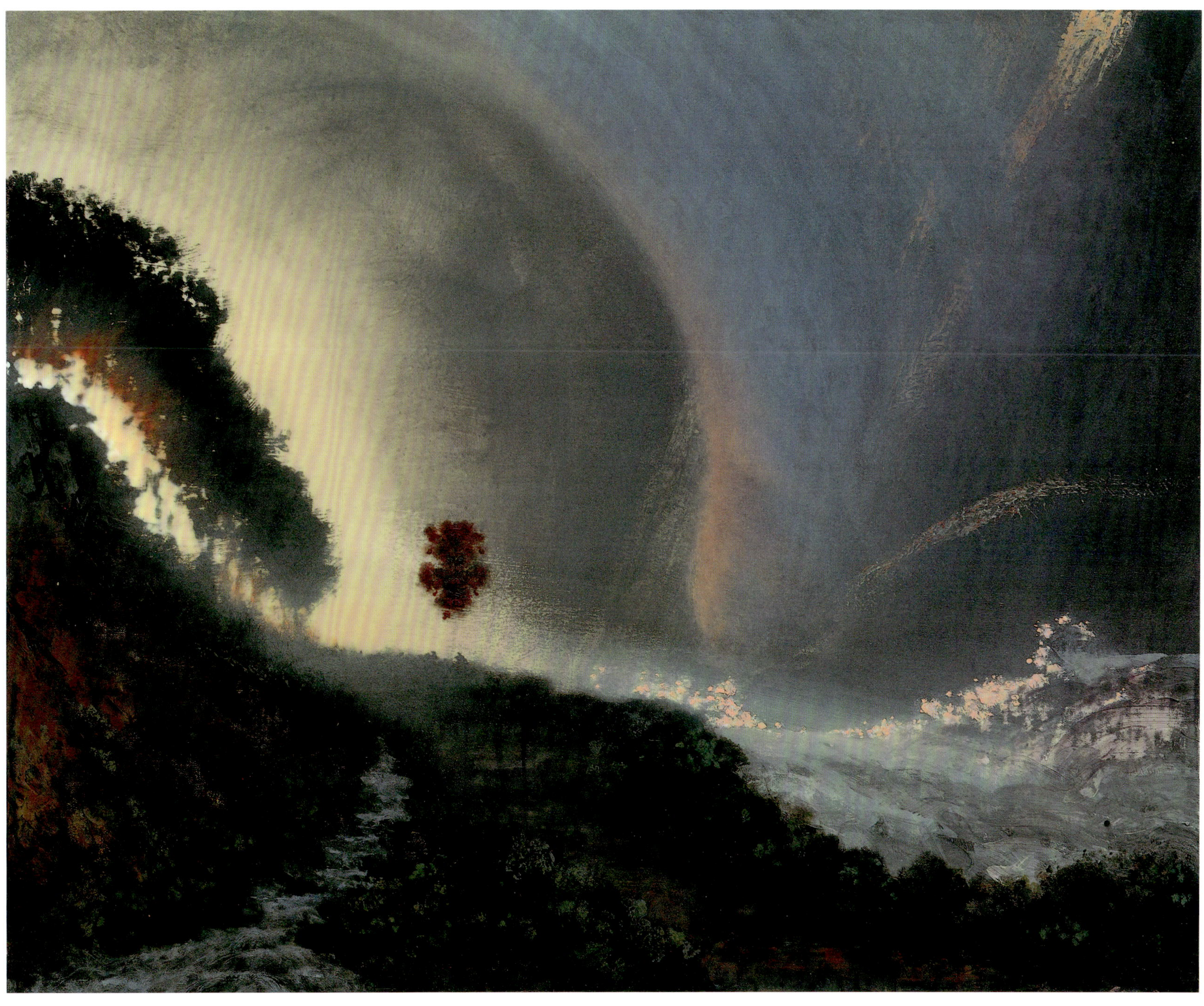

After the Deluge, Red Maple of Peace (For Laurie, Sadly Listening), 2000–2002

Polished oil on canvas, 26 x 32½ inches (66 x 83 cm). Private Collection

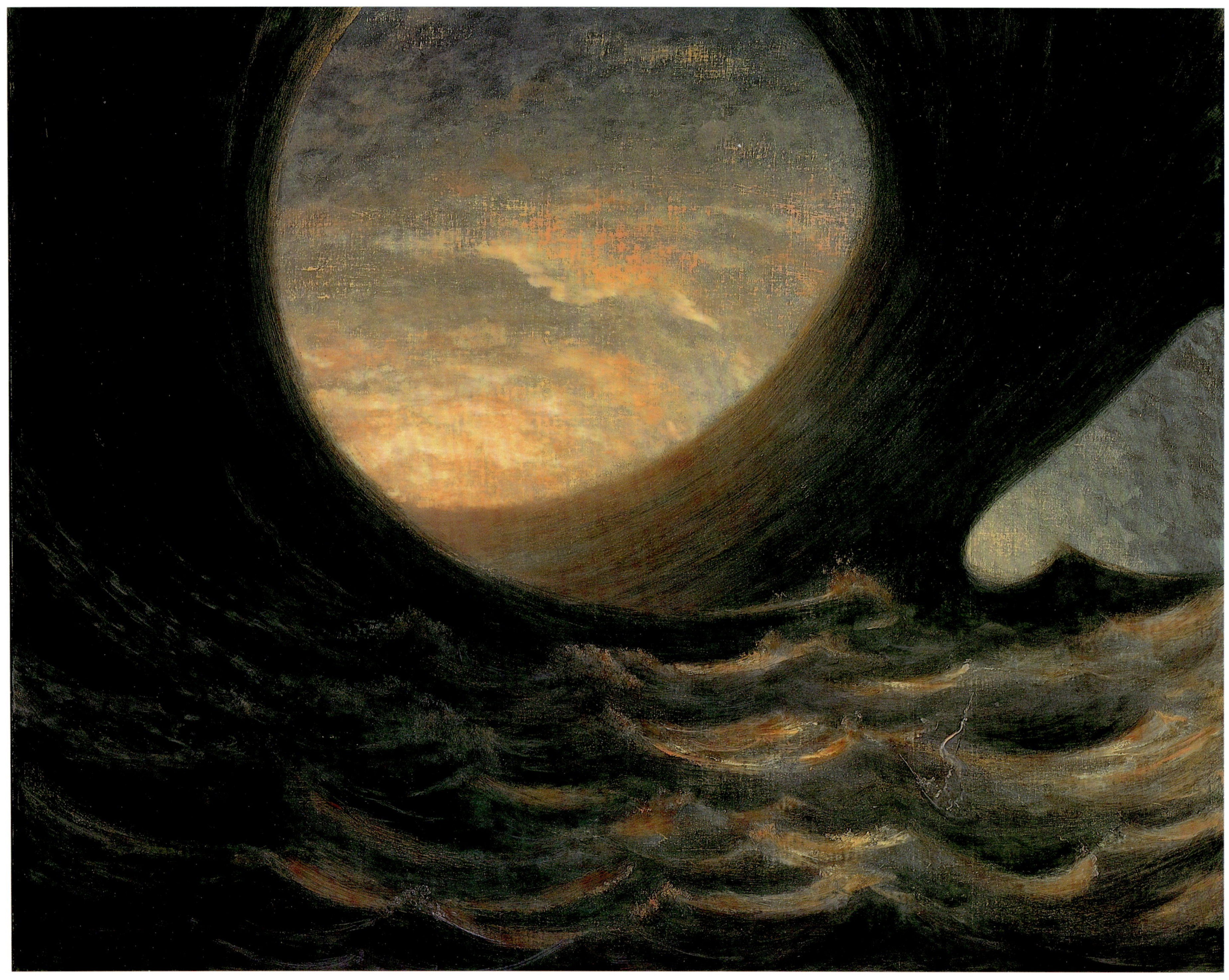

The Raft, 1998
Polished oil on canvas, 45 x 52 inches (114 x 132 cm). Private Collection

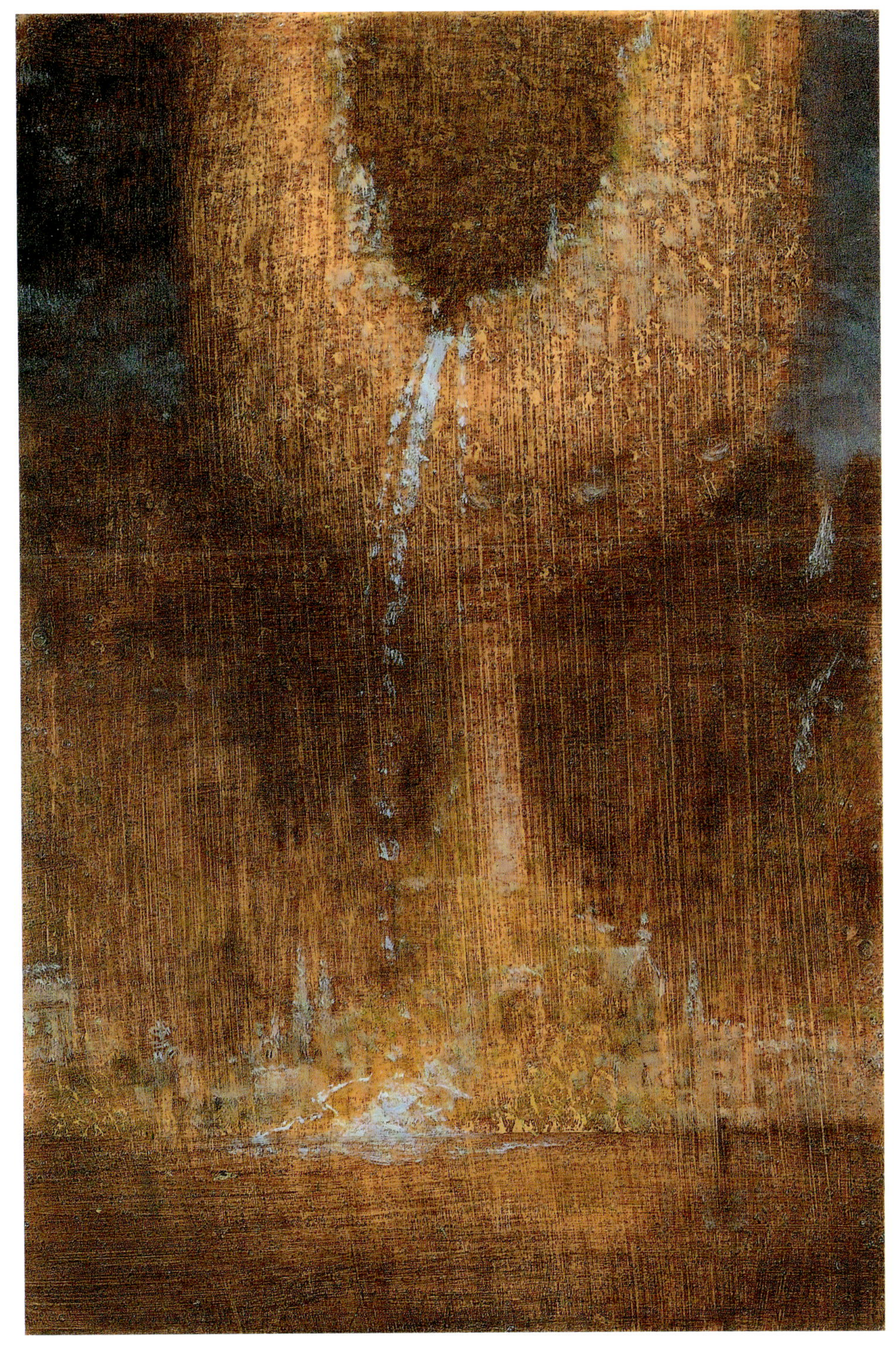

Titan's Goblet at the Approach of the Third Millenium, 1995
Polished oil on panel, 7 x 4¼ inches (18 x 11 cm). Private Collection

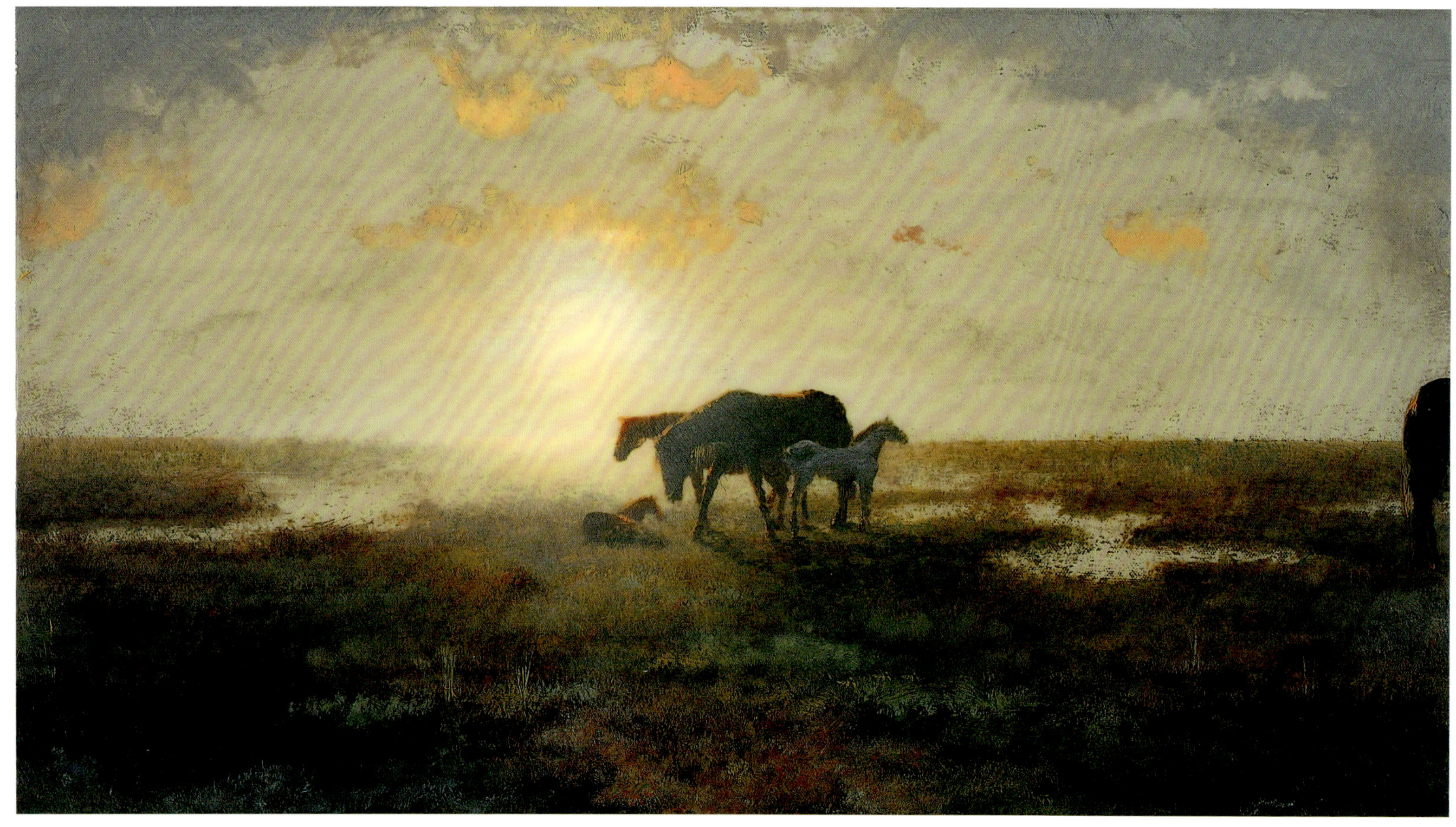

Polished oil on canvas, 12 x 22 inches (31 x 56 cm). Private Collection

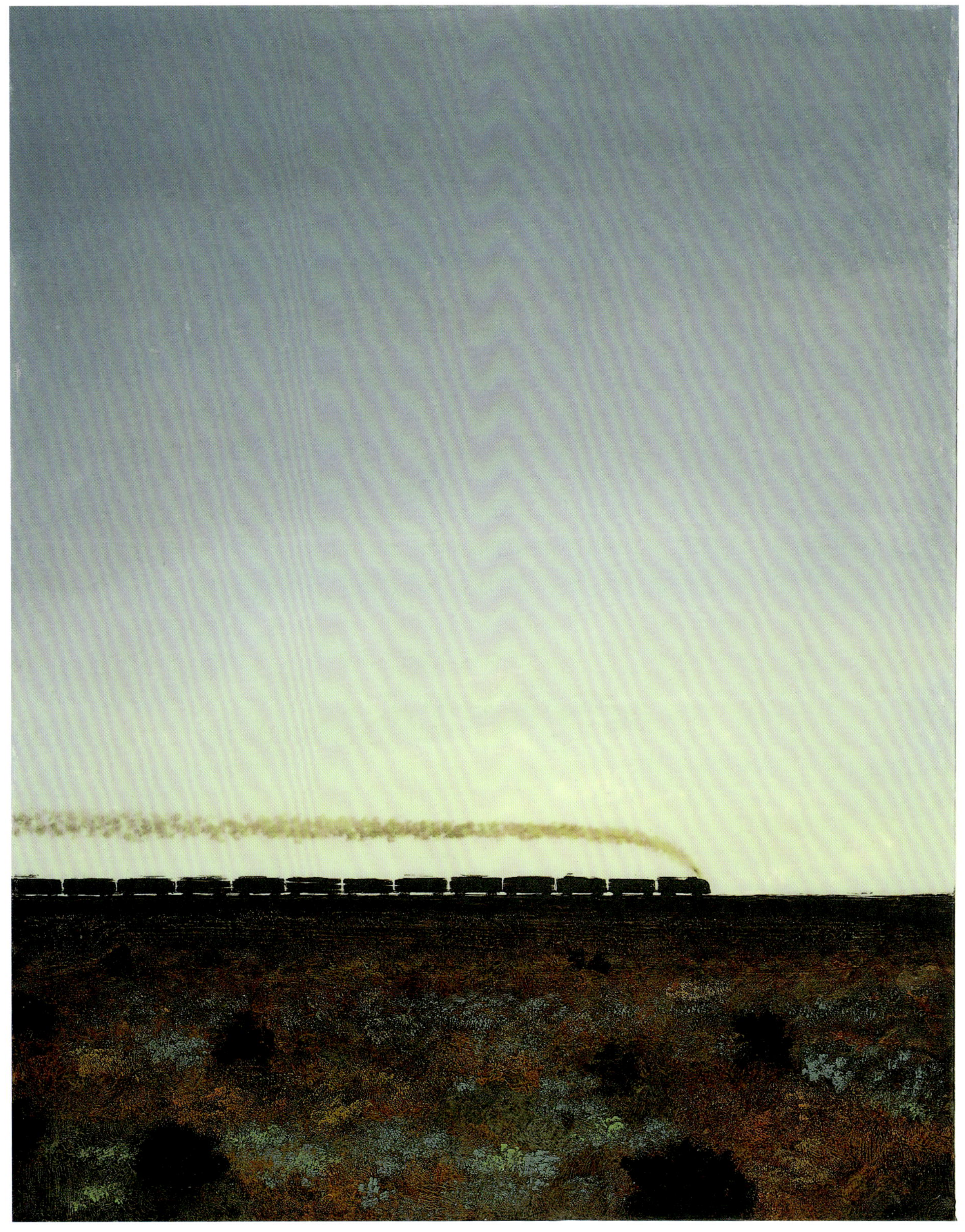

Twilight Train for Barney, 2004

Polished oil on canvas, 56 x 48 inches (142 x 122 cm). Private Collection

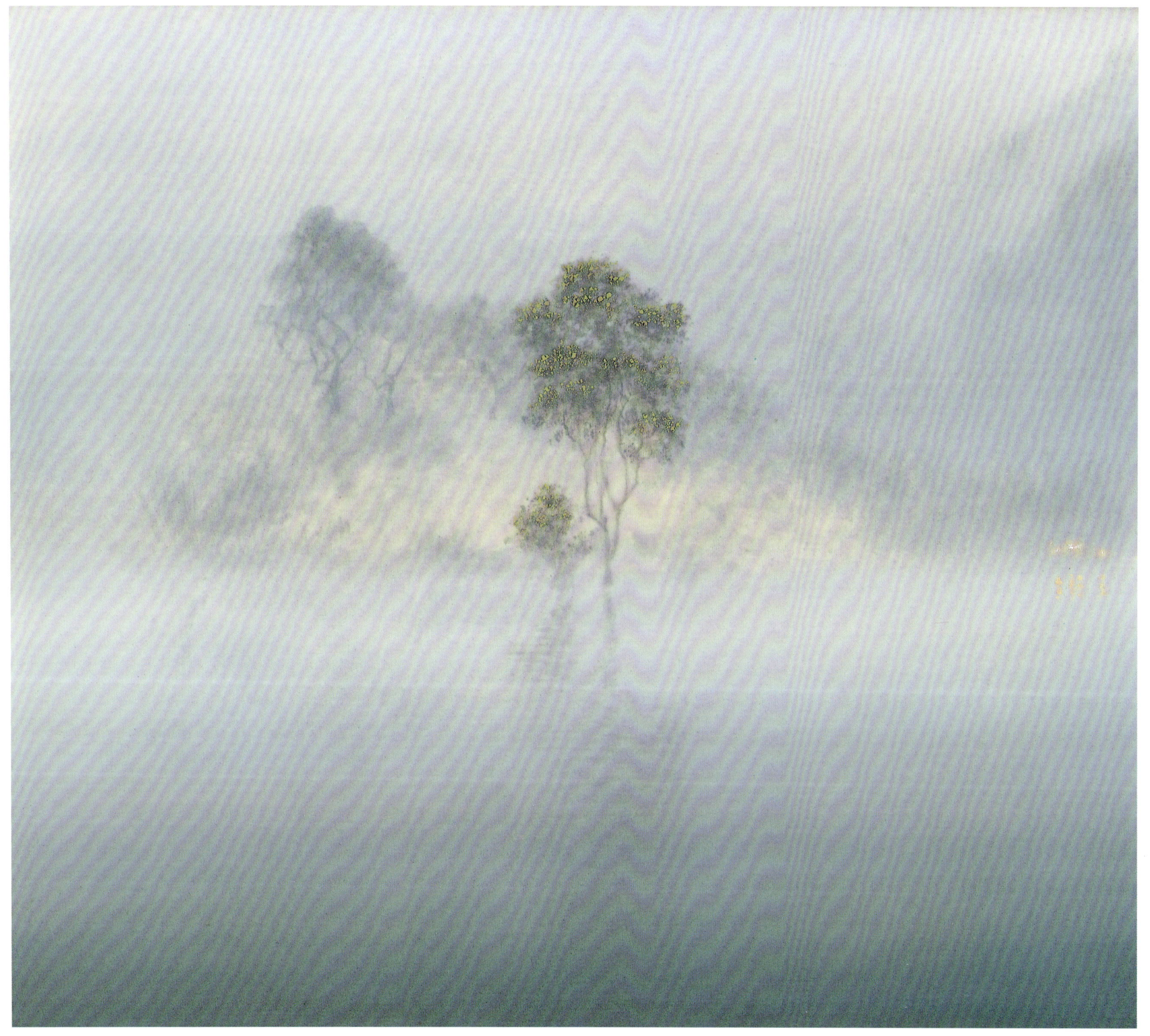

HILLSIDE VINEYARD AT DAWN, 2000
Polished oil on canvas, 23 x 27 inches (58 x 69 cm). Private Collection

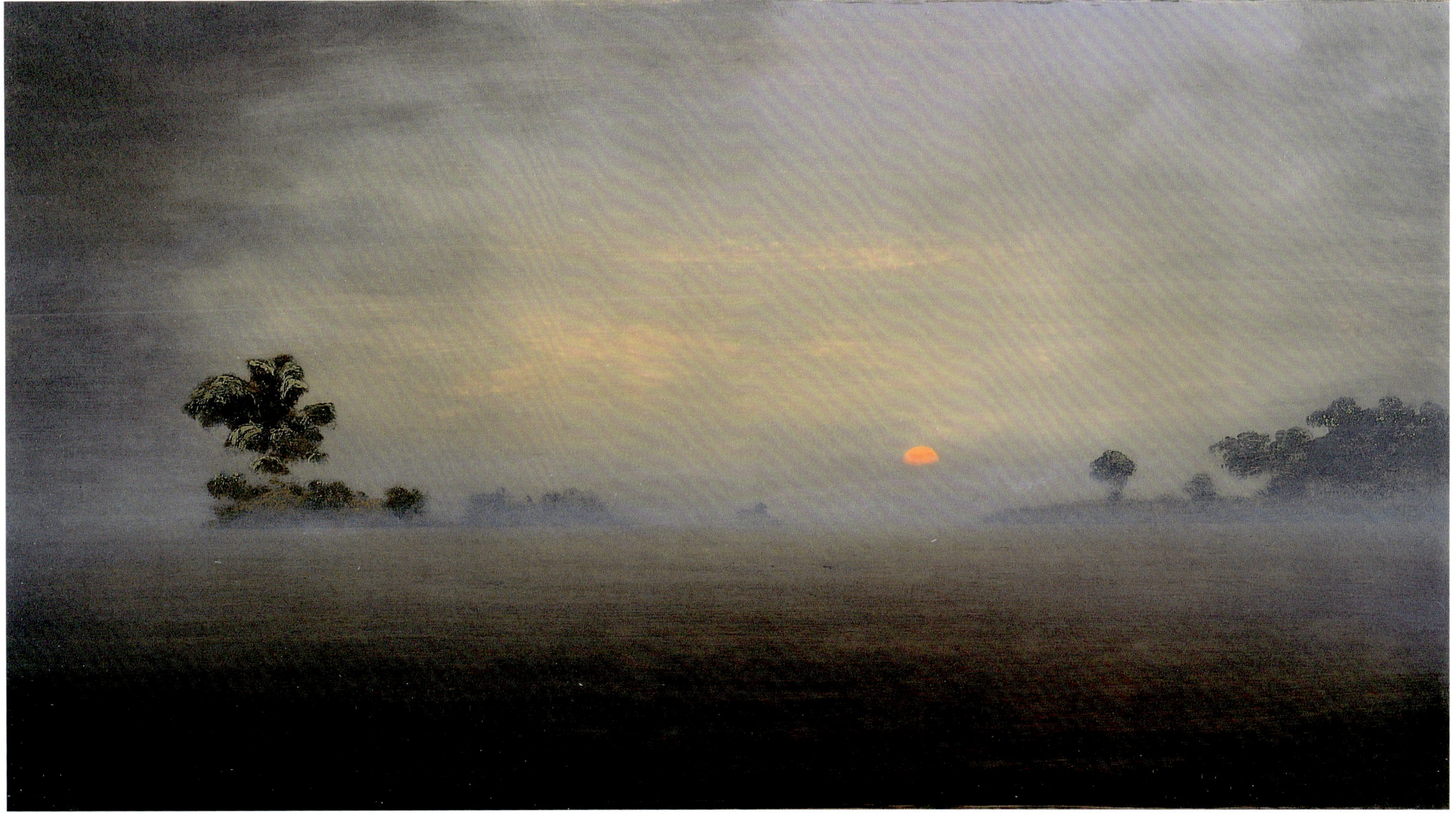

Caribbean Dawn: Storm Clearing, 1995
Polished oil on canvas, 12 x 22 inches (31 x 56 cm). Private Collection

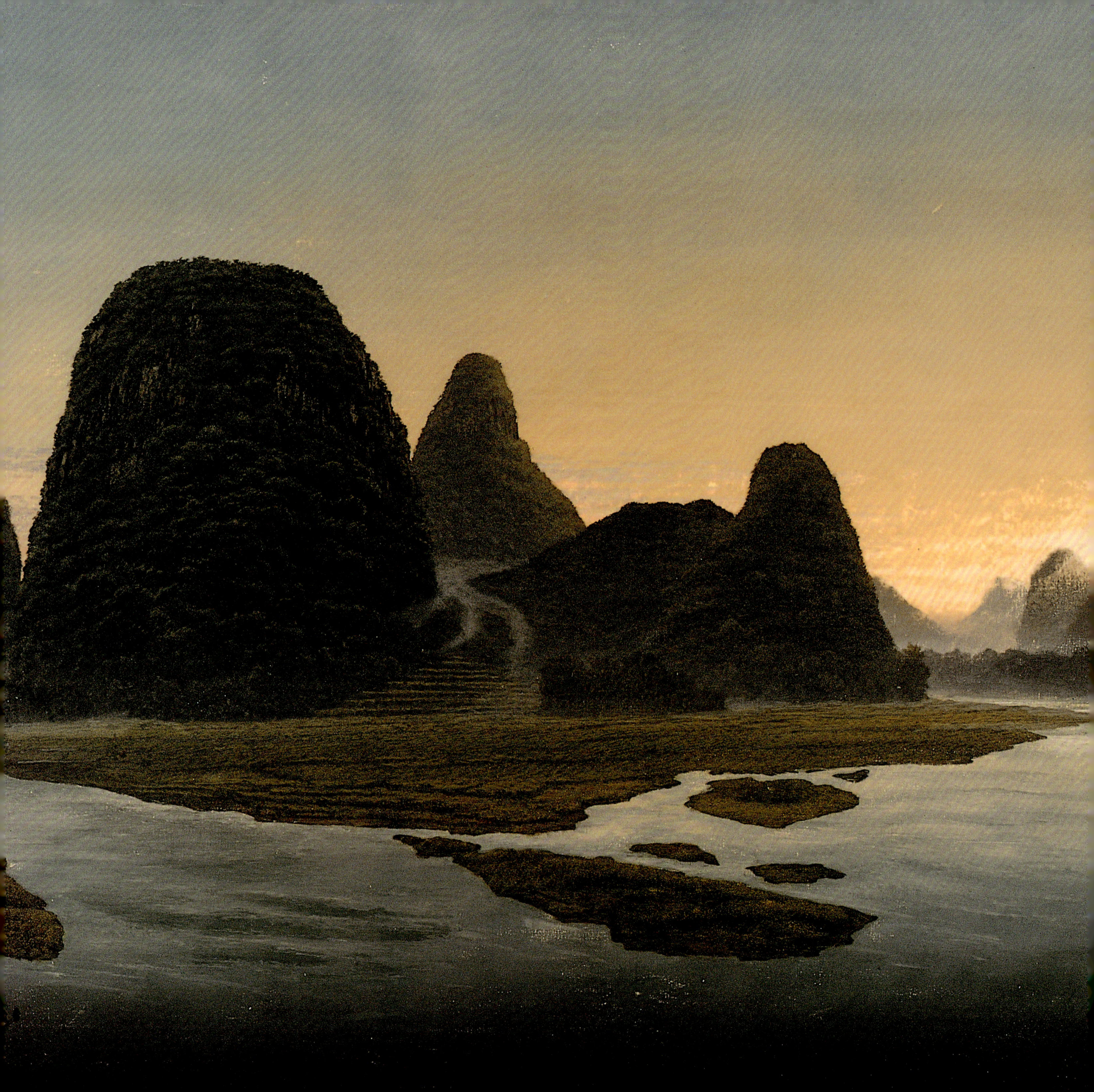

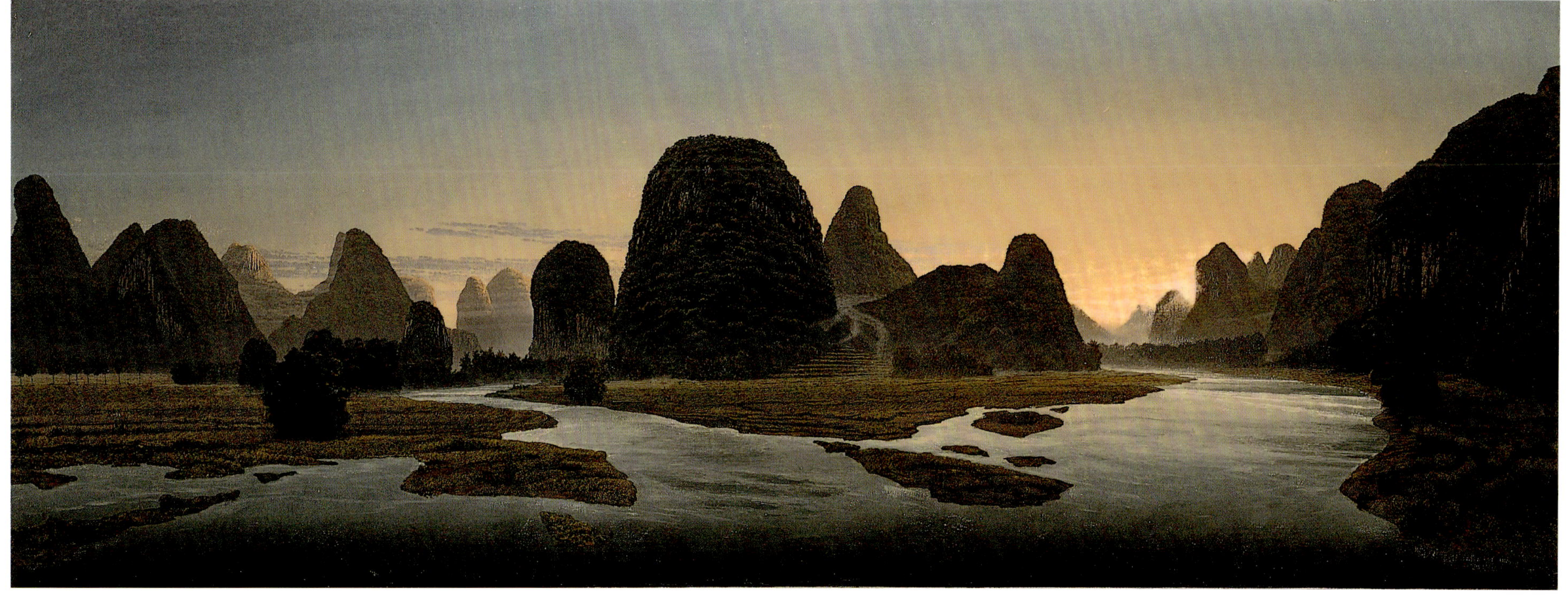

FLOODED RIVER WITH THREE SISTERS, 1990
POLISHED OIL ON CANVAS, 40 X 108 INCHES (102 X 274 CM). COLLECTION OF THE ARTIST

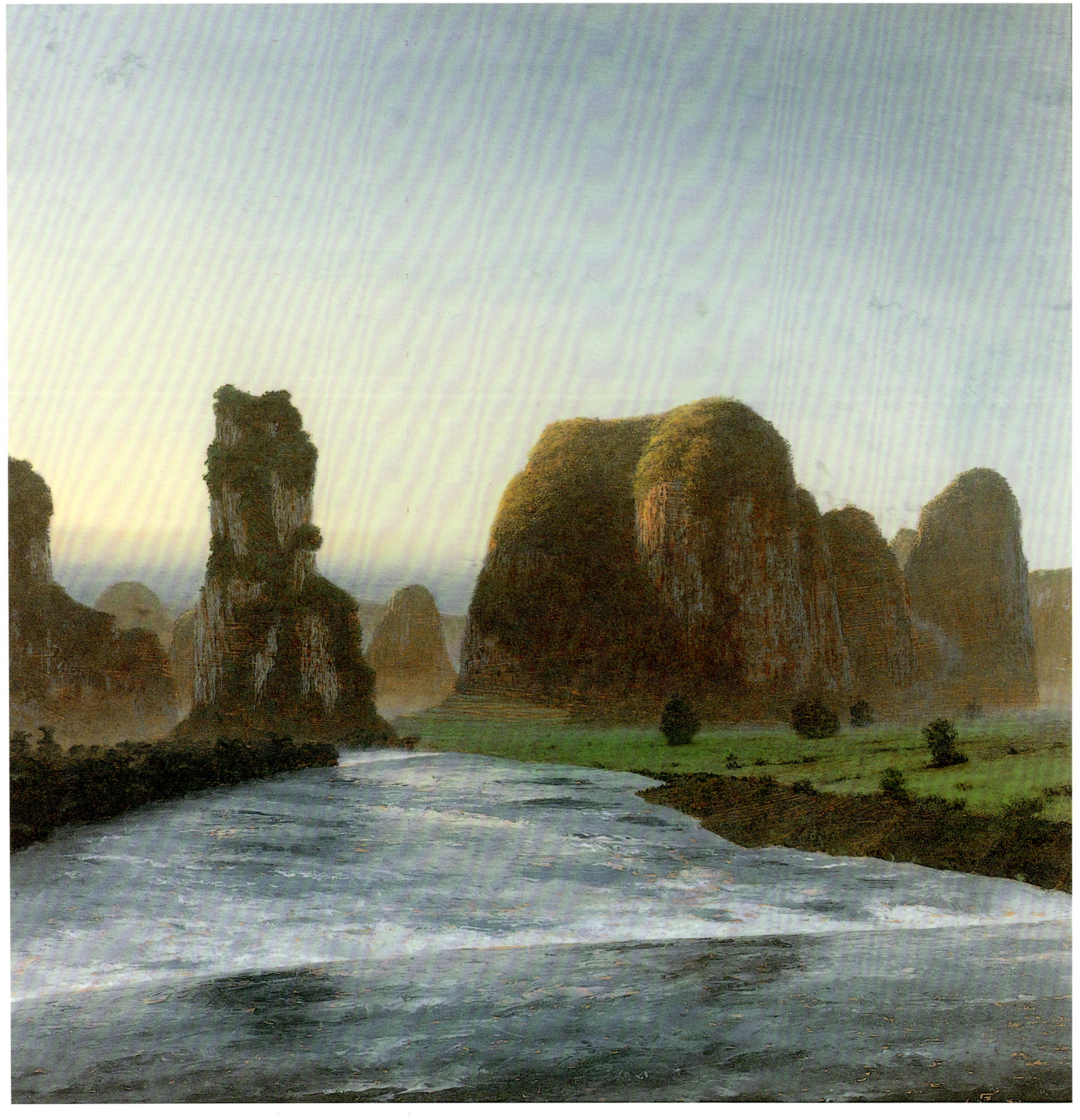

Flooded River, China, 1996
Polished oil on canvas, 40 x 40 inches (102 x 102 cm). Private Collection

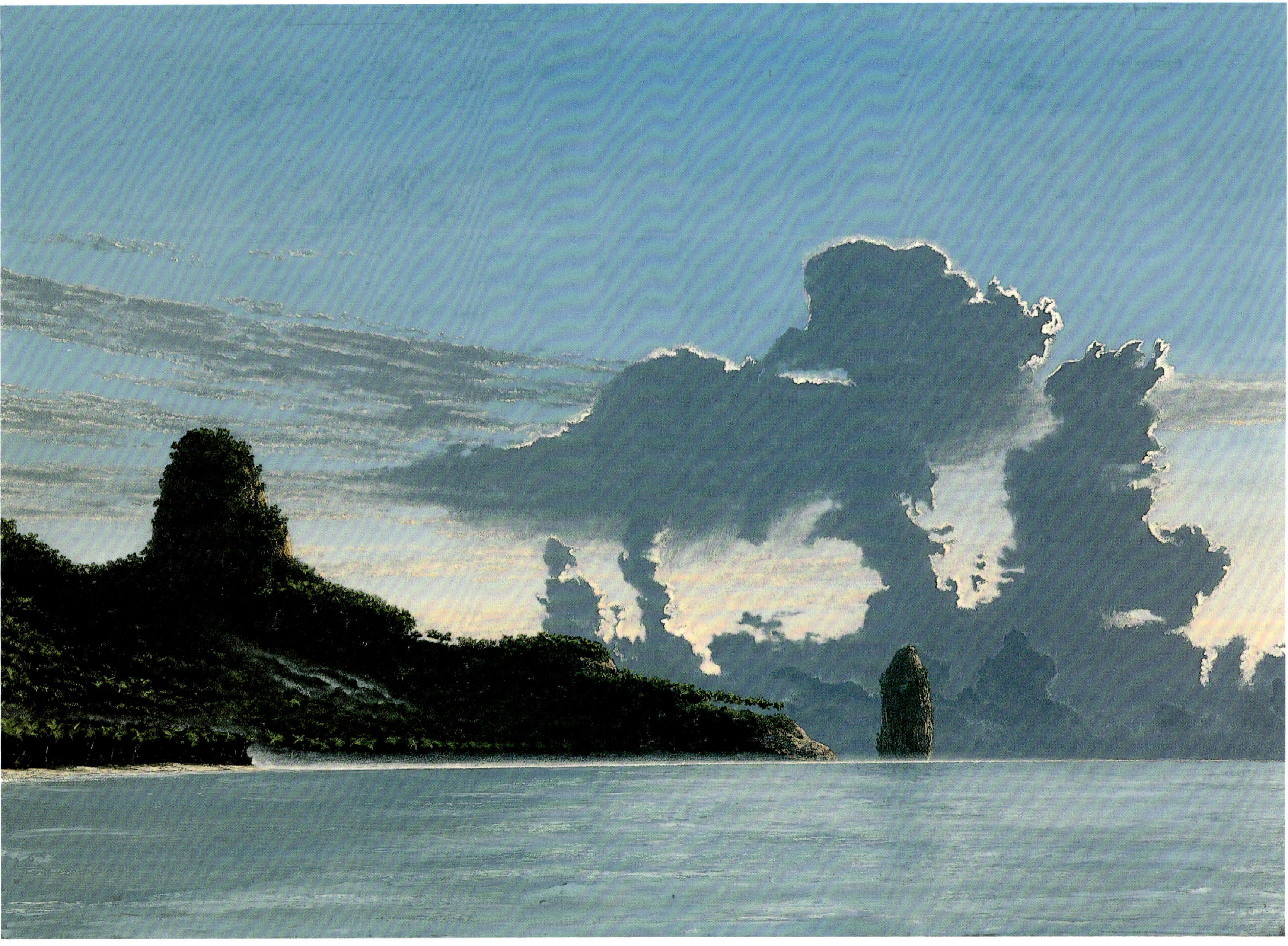

Thai Landform with Dueling Dragons, 1988

Oil on canvas, 18 x 26 inches (46 x 66 cm). Private Collection

NOCTURNE FOR THE RIVER KEEPER: GREEN LIGHT, 2001

Polished oil on canvas, 66 x 60 inches (168 x 152 cm). Albany Institute of History & Art, Albany, New York, Purchase and Gift of the Artist

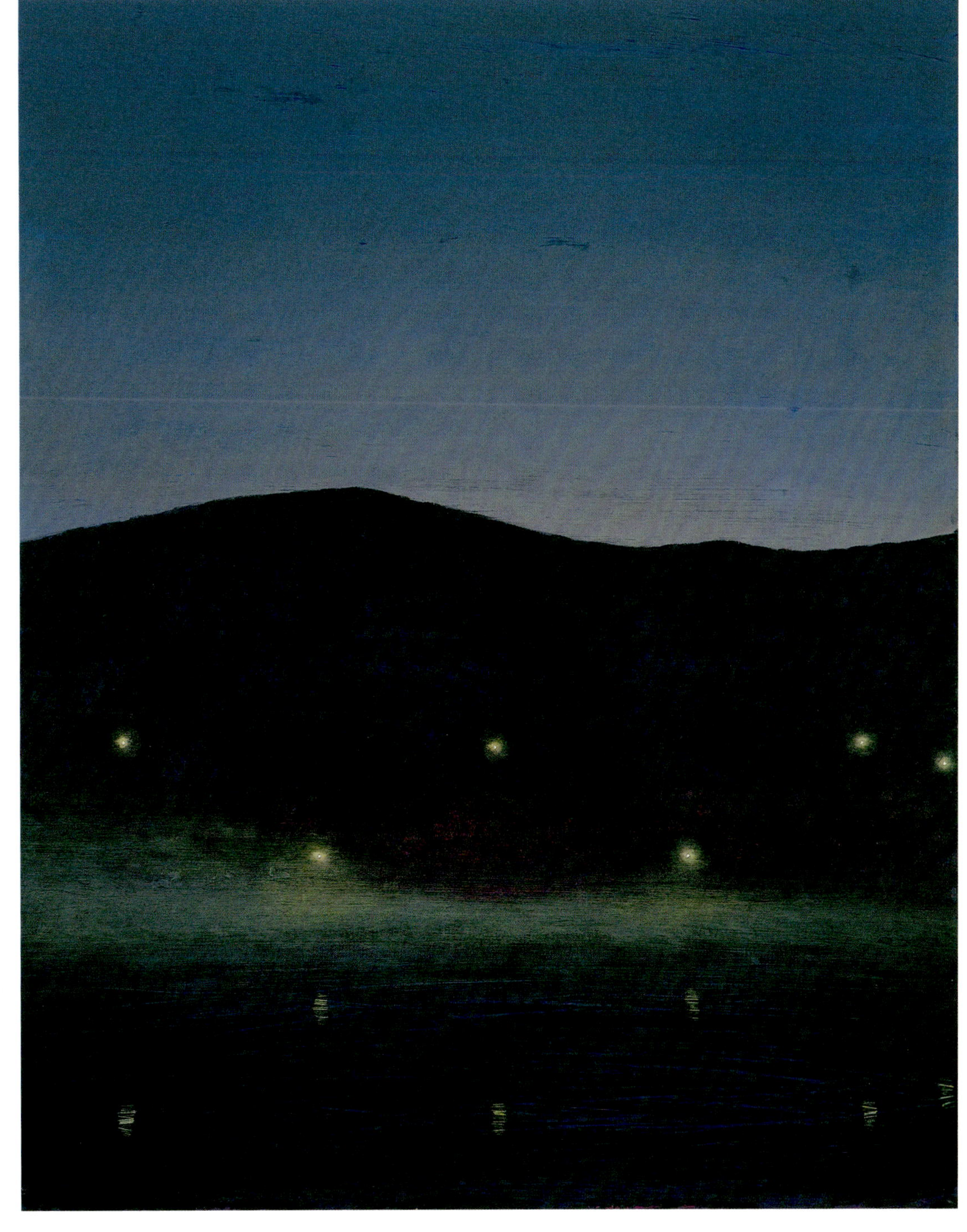

Homage to the River Keeper, 1993
Polished oil on canvas, 30 x 24 inches (76 x 61 cm). Bowdoin College Museum of Art

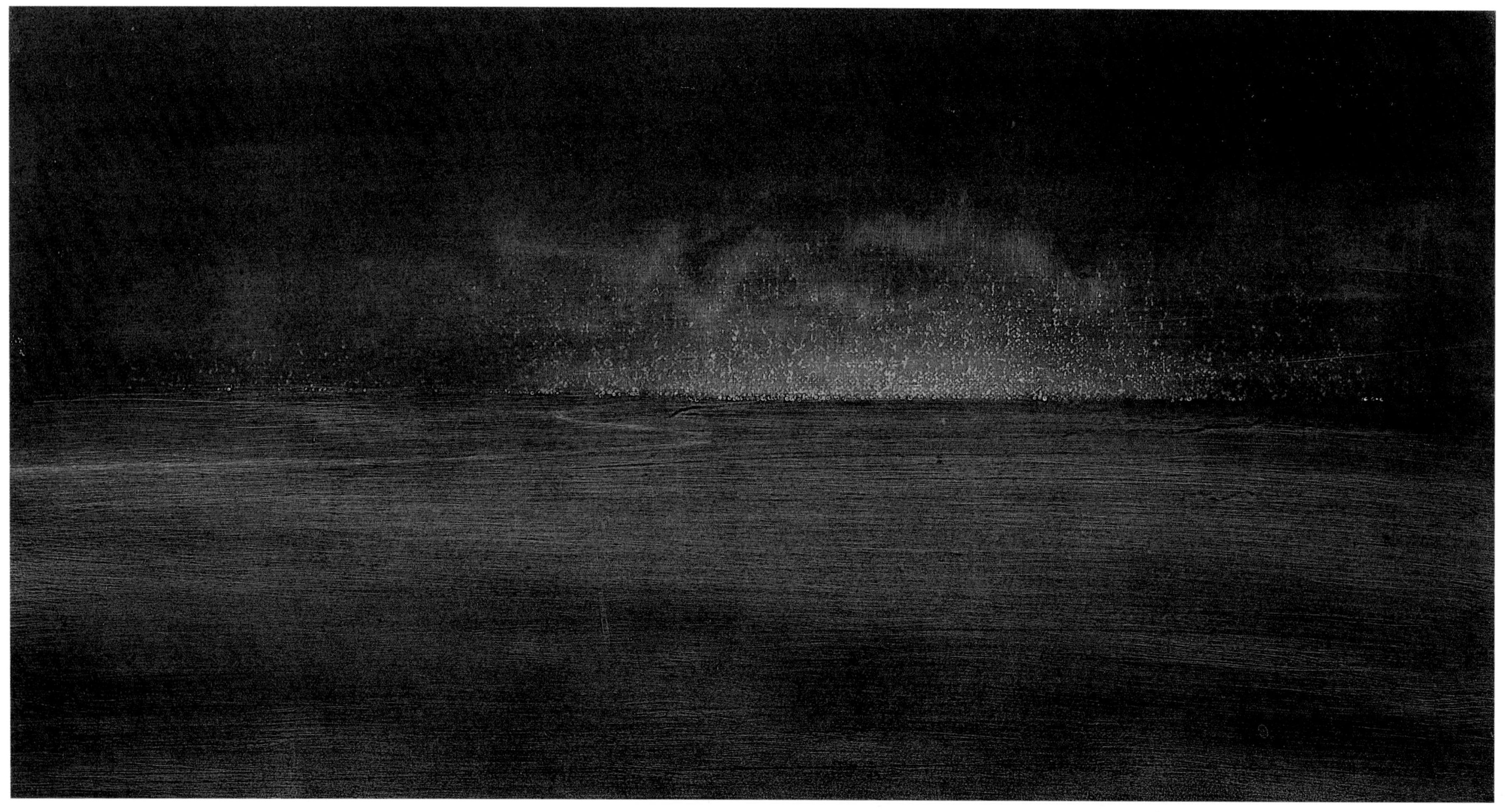

Desert City Nocturne: Evening Storm, 1999

Polished oil on canvas, 8½ x 16 inches (22 x 41 cm). Private Collection

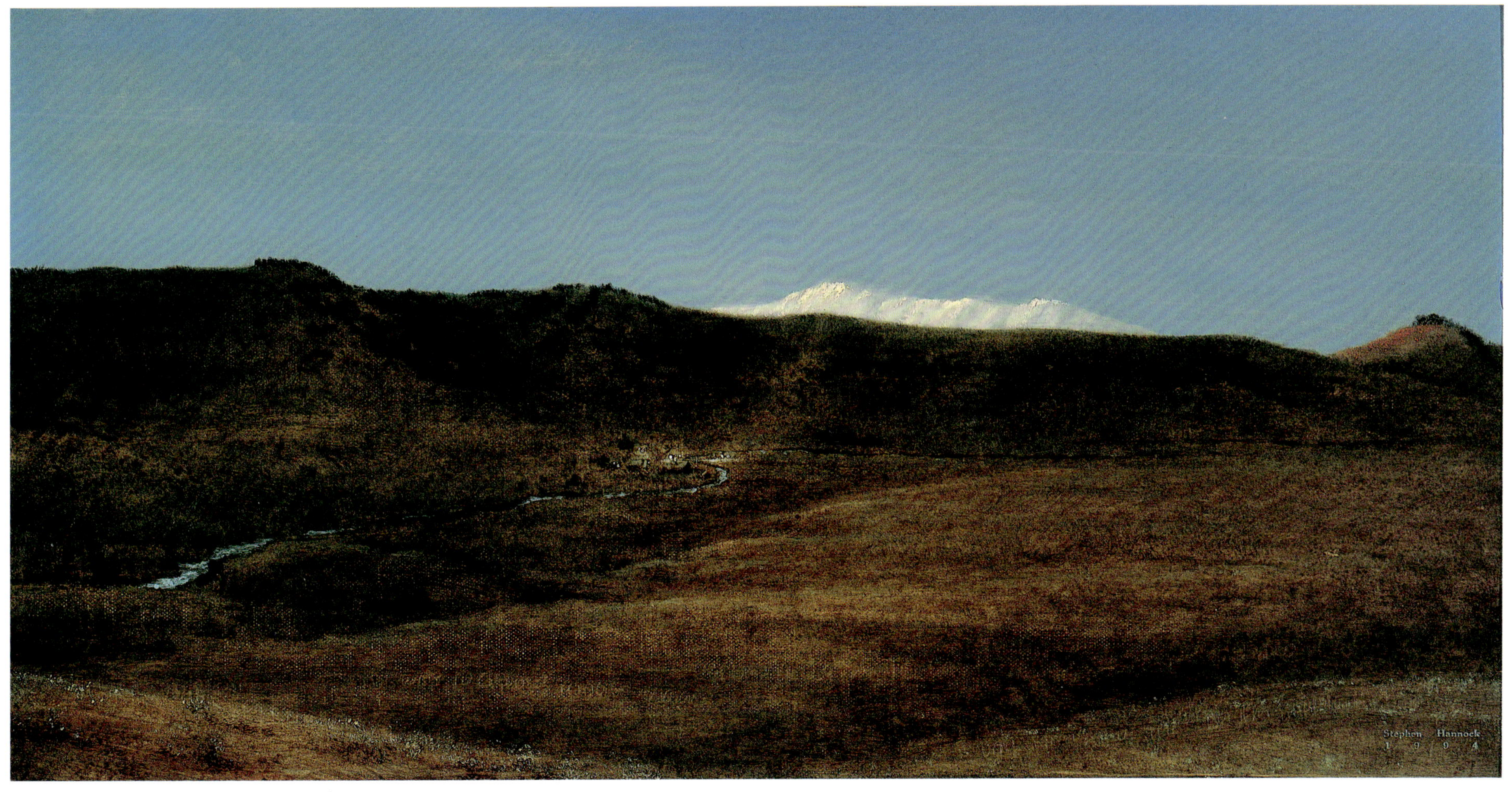

Montana Nocturne with Crazy Mountains, 1994

Polished oil on canvas, 10 x 18 inches (25 x 46 cm). Private Collection

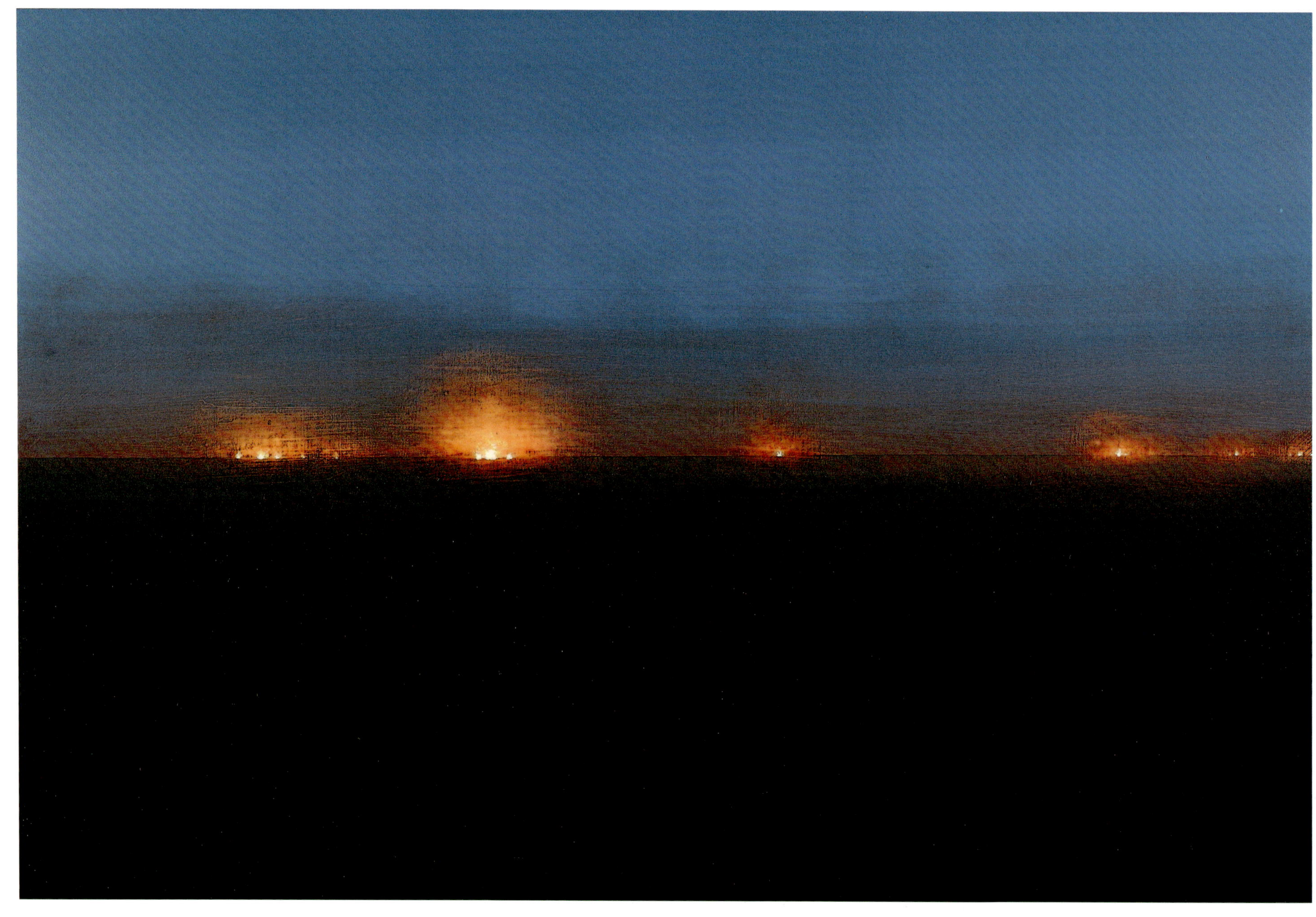

Mediterranean Nocturne: Warm Horizon at Dawn, 1999
Polished oil on canvas, 24 x 36 inches (61 x 91 cm). Private Collection

Mediterranean Nocturne: Approaching Front, 1997

Polished oil on canvas, 28 x 38 inches (71 x 97 cm). Private Collection

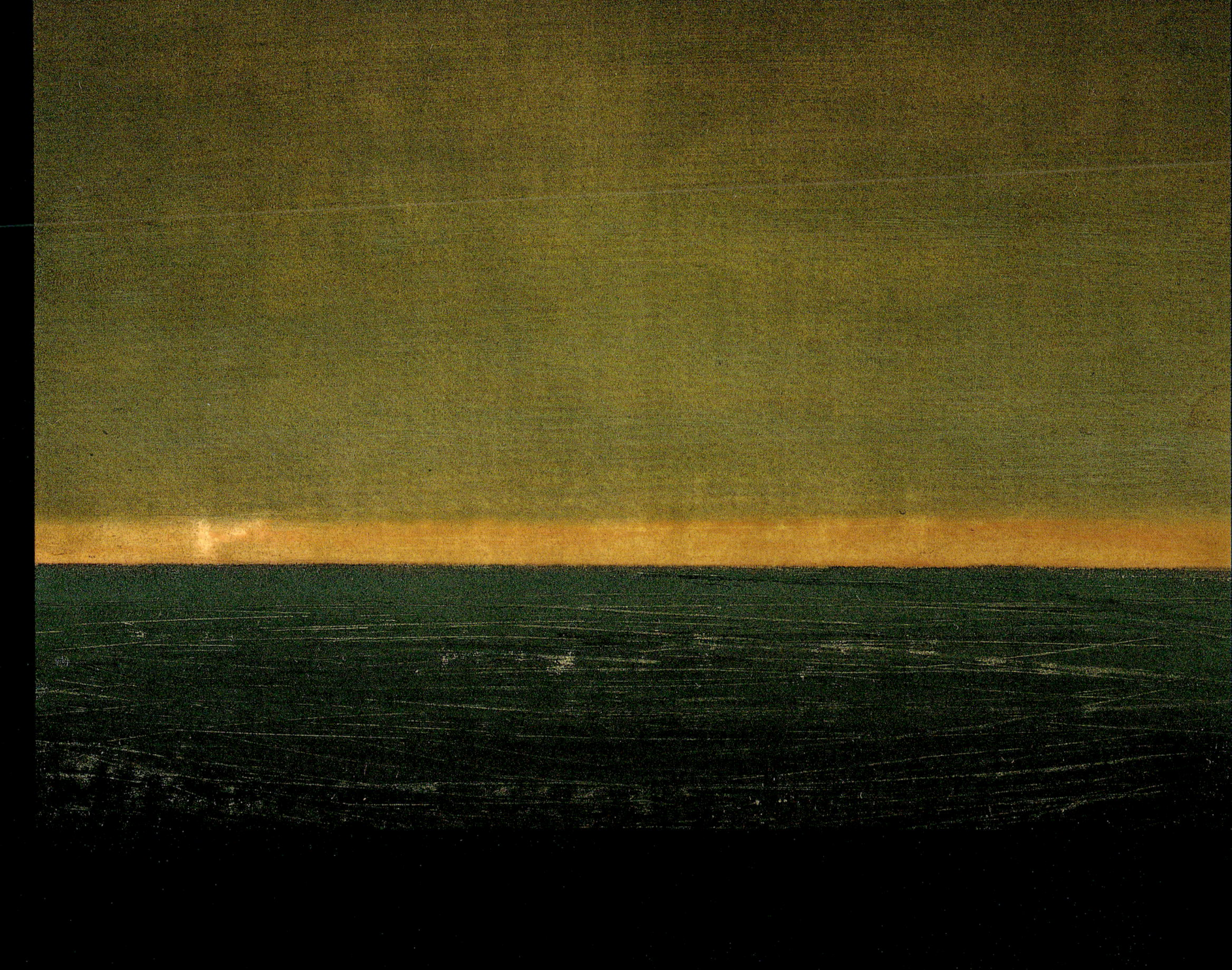

MARINE NOCTURNE: WINTER LIGHT, 1995

Polished oil on canvas, 5¼ x 7³/8 inches (13 x 19 cm). Private Collection

Squid Boats on the Gulf of Siam, 1991

Polished oil on canvas, 12 x 22 inches (31 x 56 cm). Private Collection

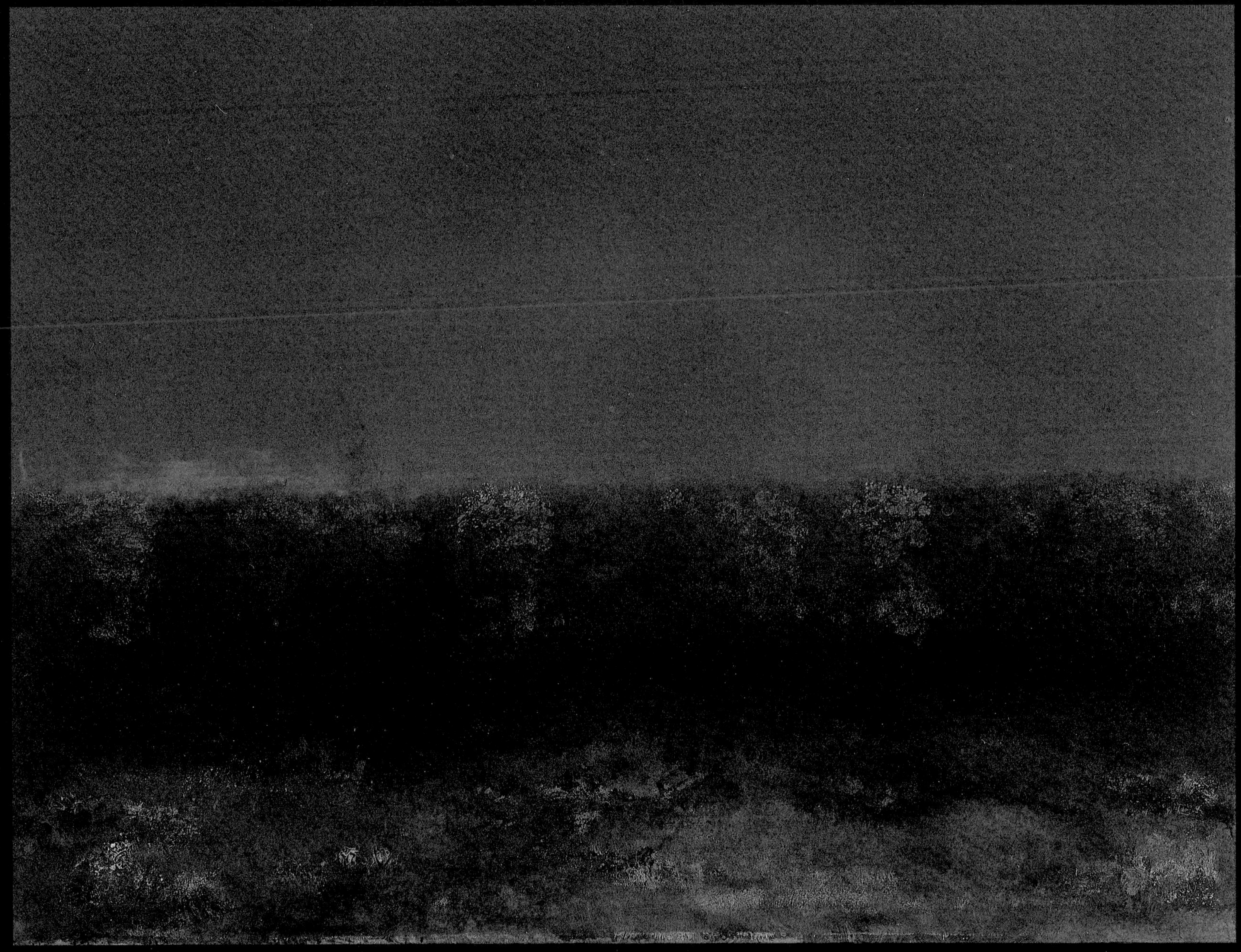

Nocturne with Mauve Orchard, 2002

Polished oil on canvas, 9 x 12 inches (23 x 31 cm). Private Collection

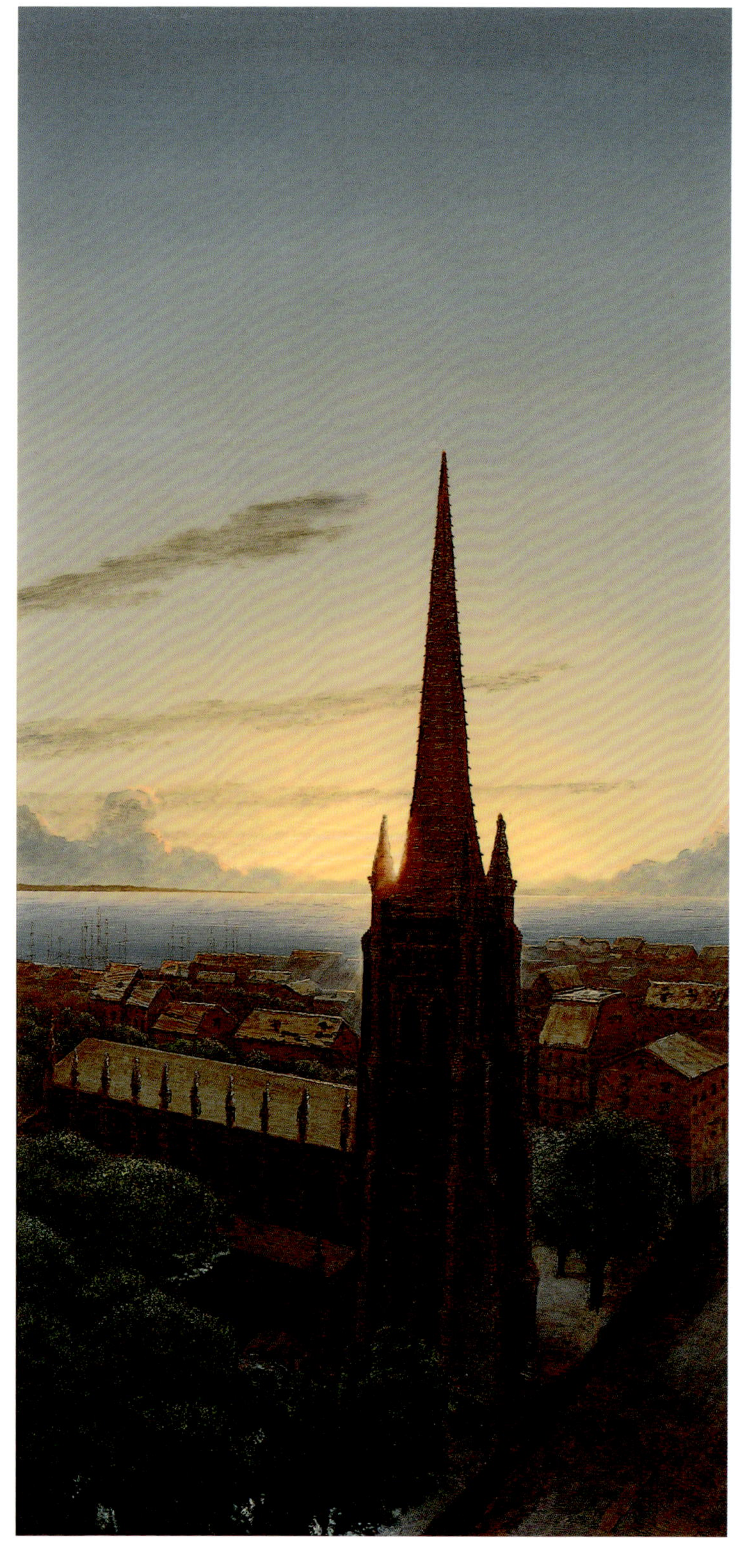

Trinity Church at the Turn of the Century, 1993

Polished oil on canvas, 72 x 36 inches (183 x 91 cm). Knickerbocker Club, New York

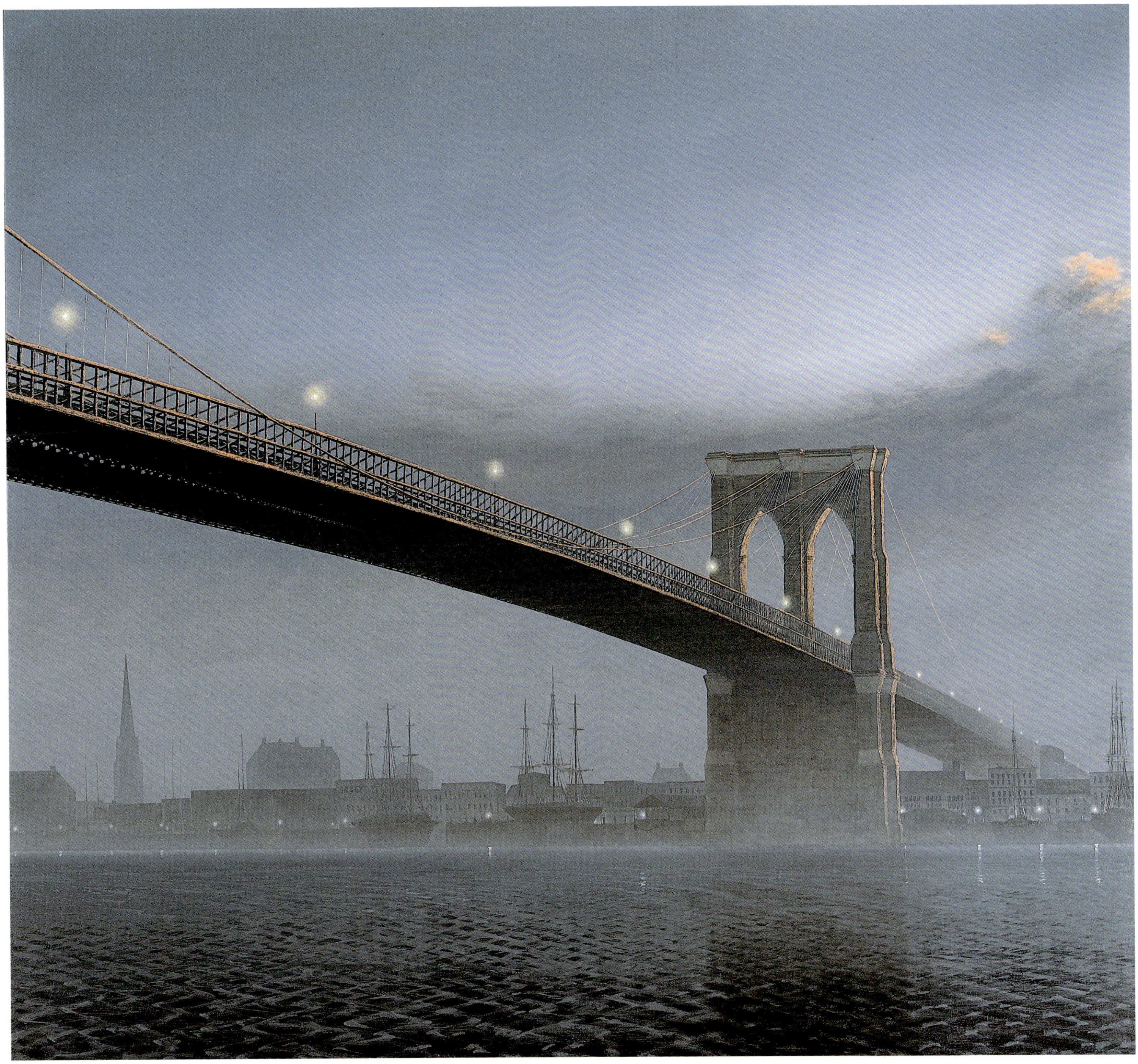

BROOKLYN BRIDGE AT DAWN, 1993
POLISHED OIL ON CANVAS, 72 x 96 INCHES (183 x 244 CM). KNICKERBOCKER CLUB, NEW YORK

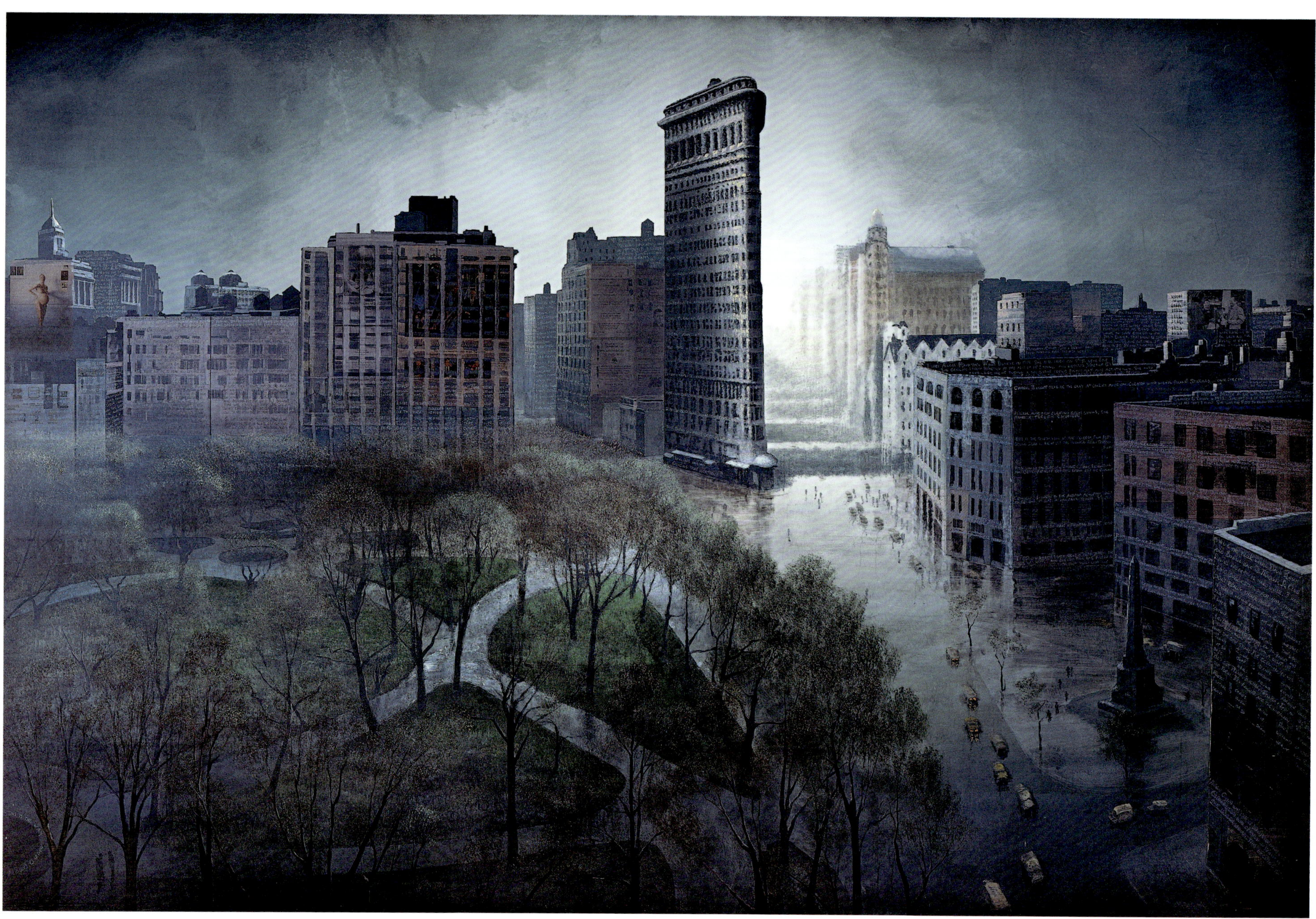

American City with Restored Park (Mass MoCA #10), 2005
Polished mixed media on canvas, 84 x 126 inches (213 x 320 cm). Private Collection

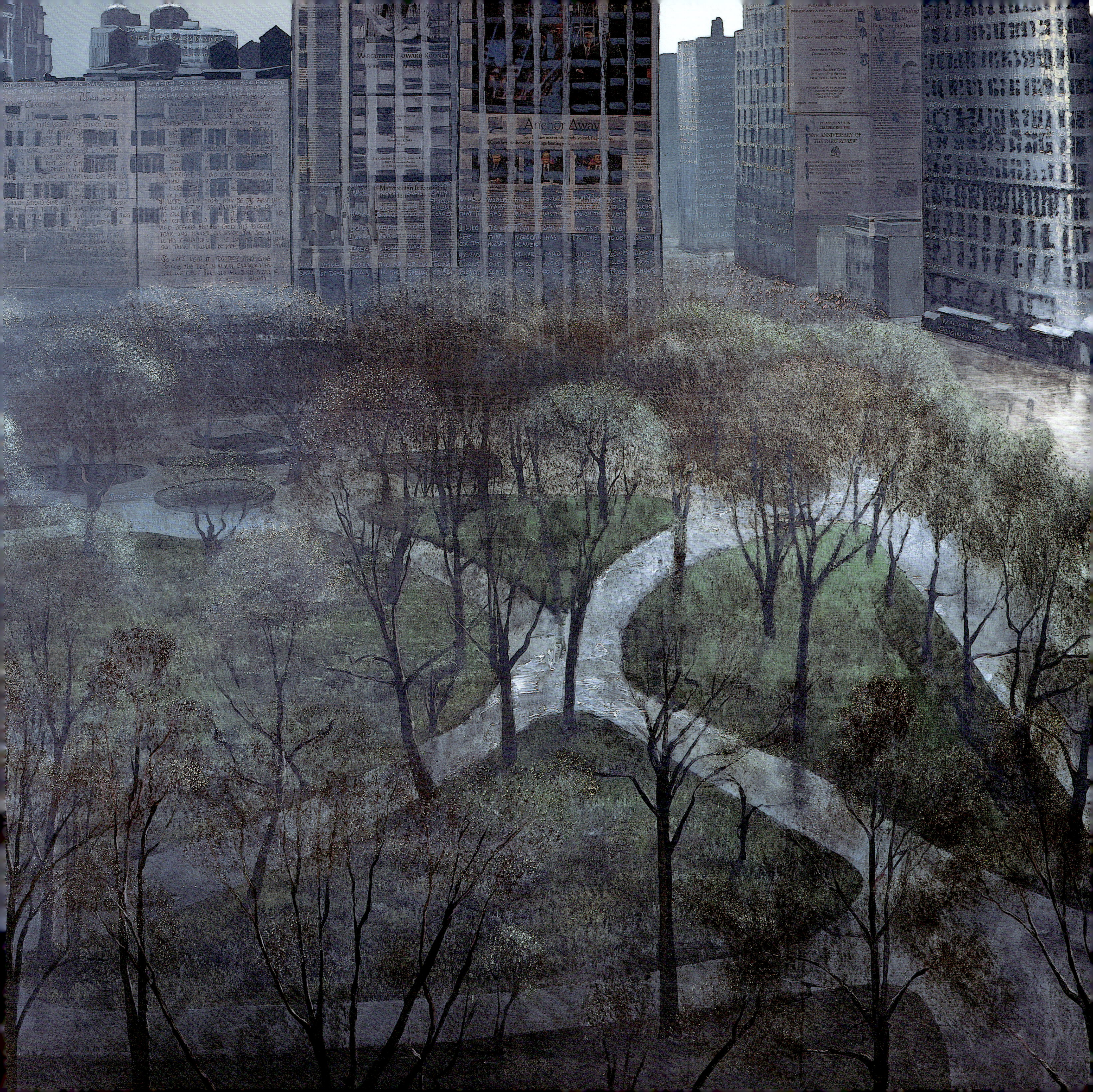

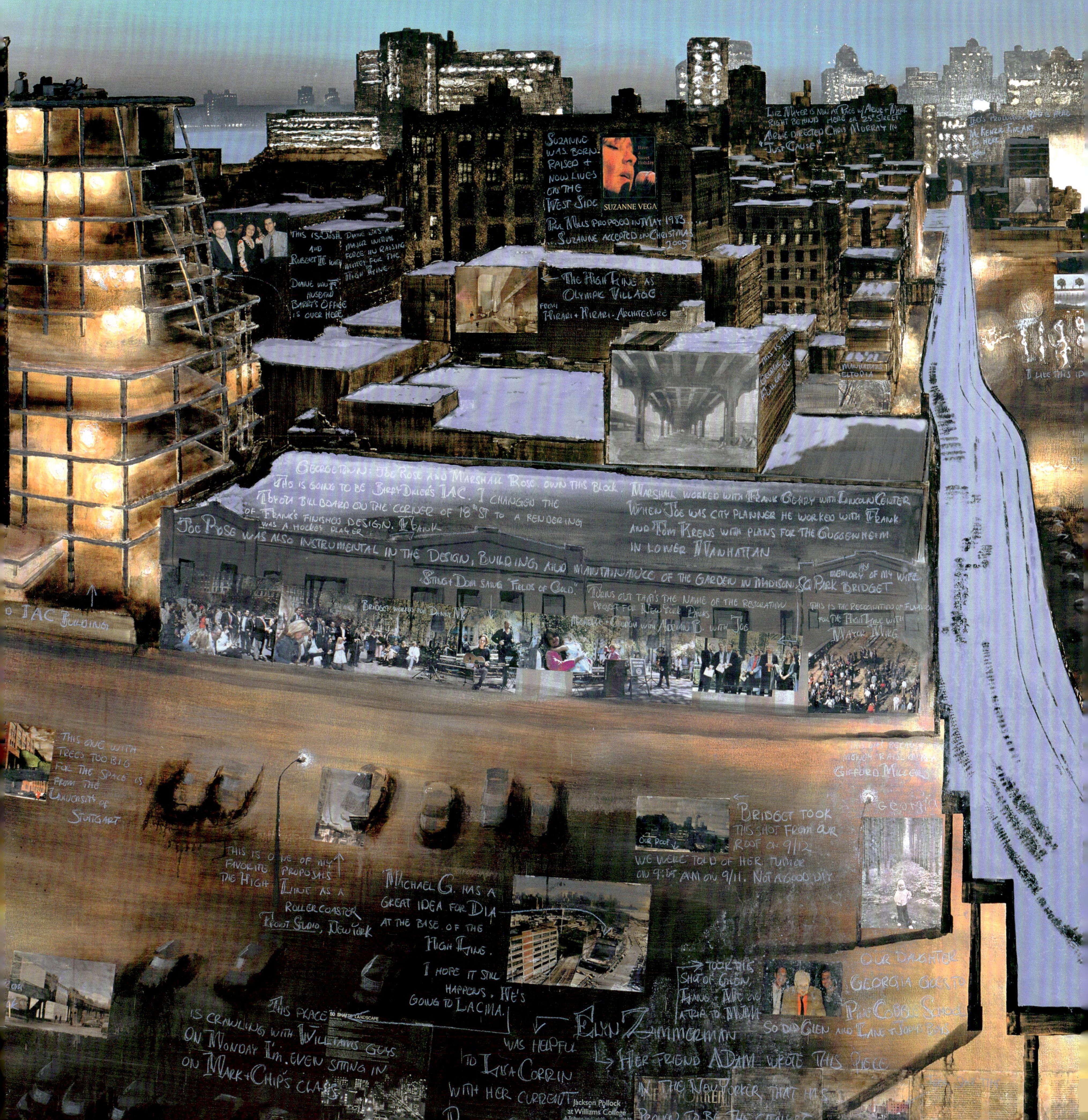

Liz Mayer is now at Pace w/ Arne + Mark right behind here on 25th Street.
Arne directed Chris Murray in "Just Cause"
Suzanne was born, raised + now lives on the West Side
Paul Mills proposed in May 1983... Suzanne accepted on Christmas 2005
SUZANNE VEGA
Have a Sweet Holiday
← The High Line as Olympic Village
from Hariri + Hariri - Architecture
This is Josh. Diane was a major initial force in raising money for the High Line.
and Robert H. with
Diane von F husband Barry's office is over here
I TAC Building
Georgetown: Joe Rose and Marshall Rose own this block
This is going to be Barry Diller's IAC. I changing the Tivoli billboard on the corner of 18th st to a rendering of Frank's finished design. Frank was a hockey player.
Joe Rose was also instrumental in the design, building and maintainance of the garden in Madison Sq Park
Marshall worked with Frank Gehry with Lincoln Center
When Joe was city planner he worked with Frank and Tom Krens with plans for the Guggenheim in lower Manhattan
Sting + Don sang "Fields of Gold"
in memory of my wife Bridget
This one with trees too big for the space is from the University of Stuttgart
This is one of my favorite proposals the High Line as a roller coaster
Front Studio, New York
Michael G. has a great idea for DIA at the base of the High Line. I hope it still happens. He's going to LACMA.
Bridget took this shot from our roof on 9/12
We were told of her tumor on 9:15 AM on 9/11. Not a good day.
Georgia
Our daughter Georgia goes to Pine Cobble School
50 SHAFTS LANDSCAPE
This place is crawling with Williams guys
On Monday I'm even sitting in on Mark + Chip's class
Elyn Zimmerman was helpful to Lisa Corrin
Her friend Adam wrote this piece
Jackson Pollock at Williams College

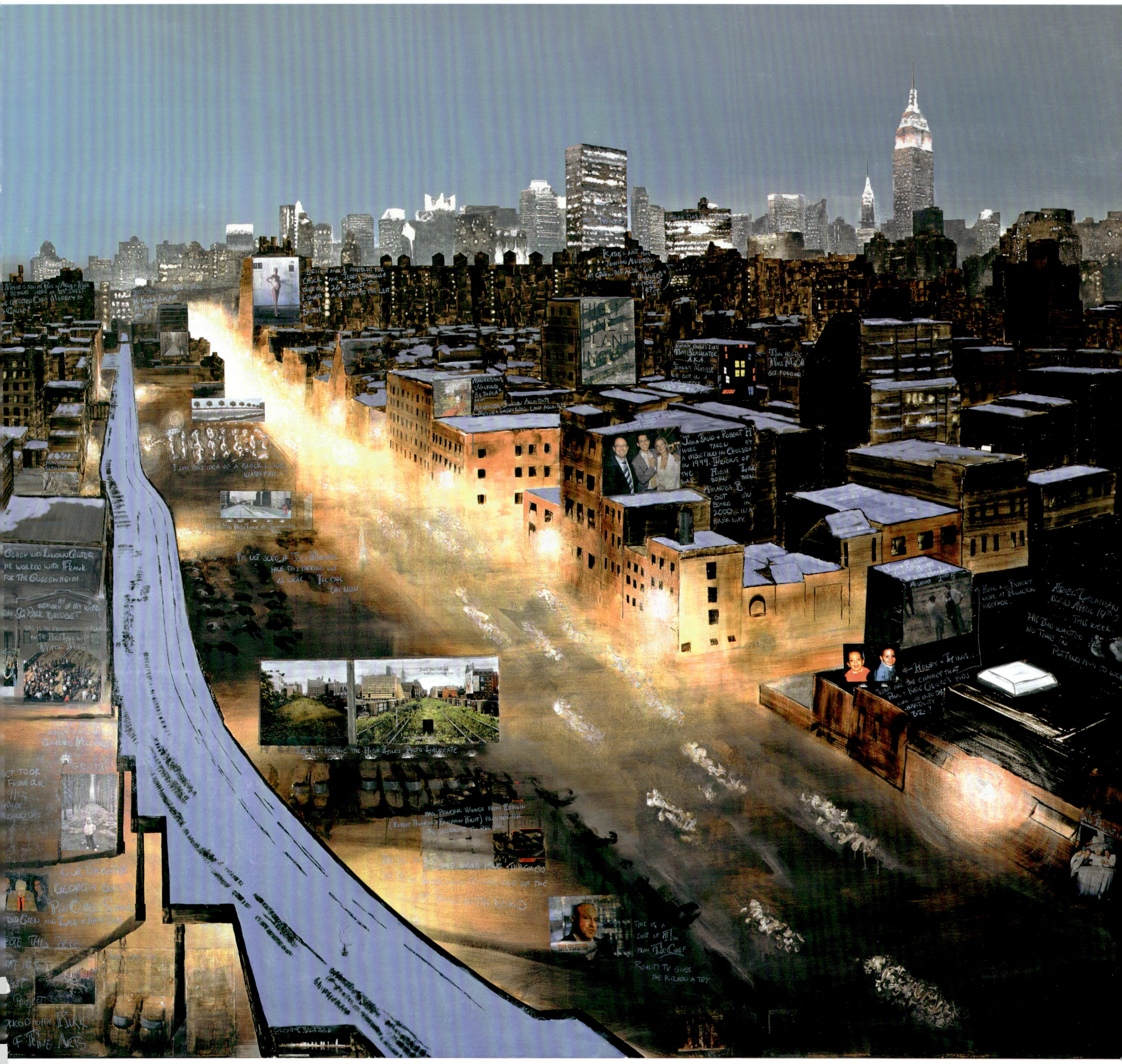

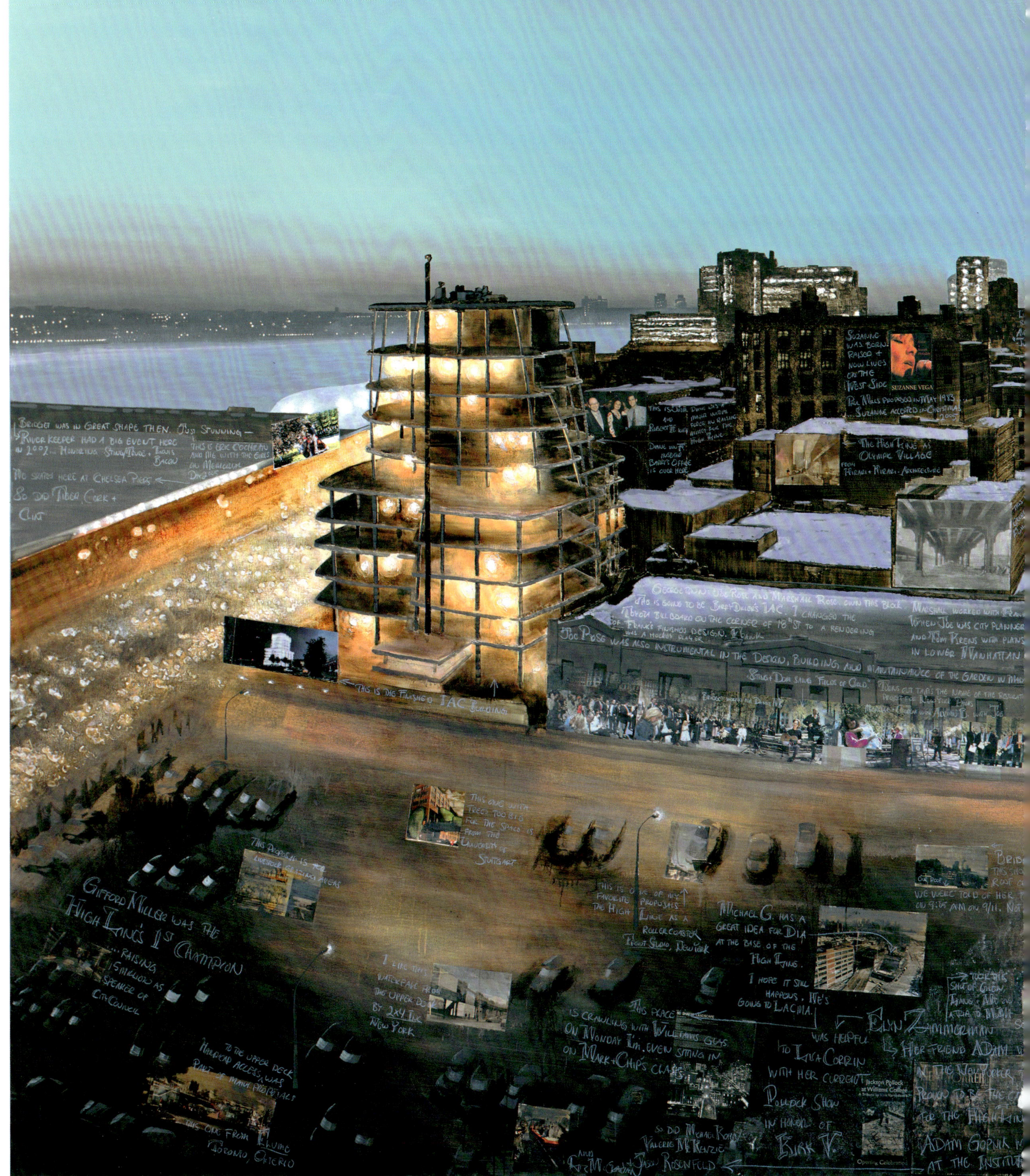

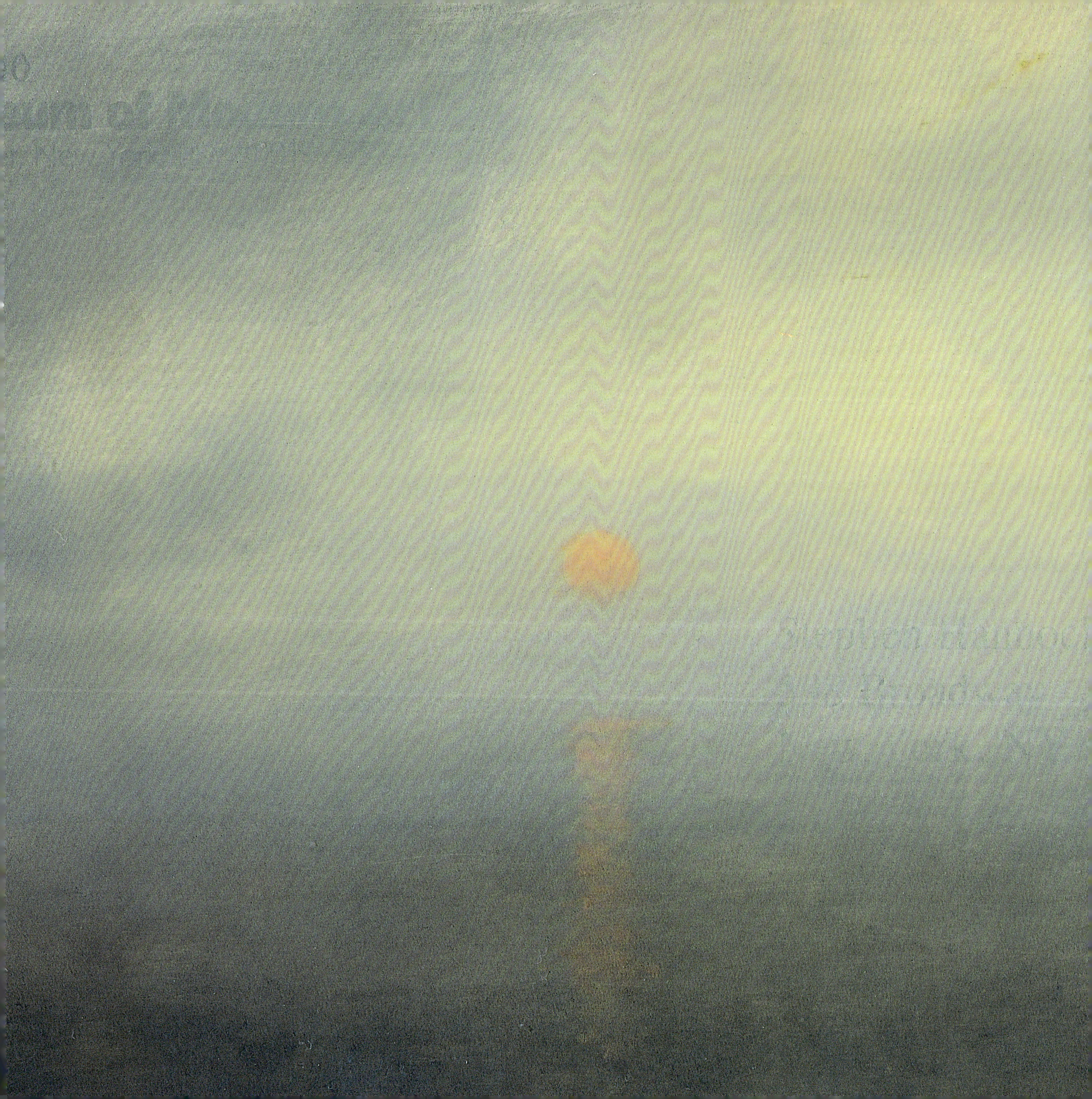

Palimpsests

River at Dawn for Kirk and Elyn, 2002

Polished oil on paper envelope, 4¼ x 9½ inches (11 x 24 cm). Private Cllection

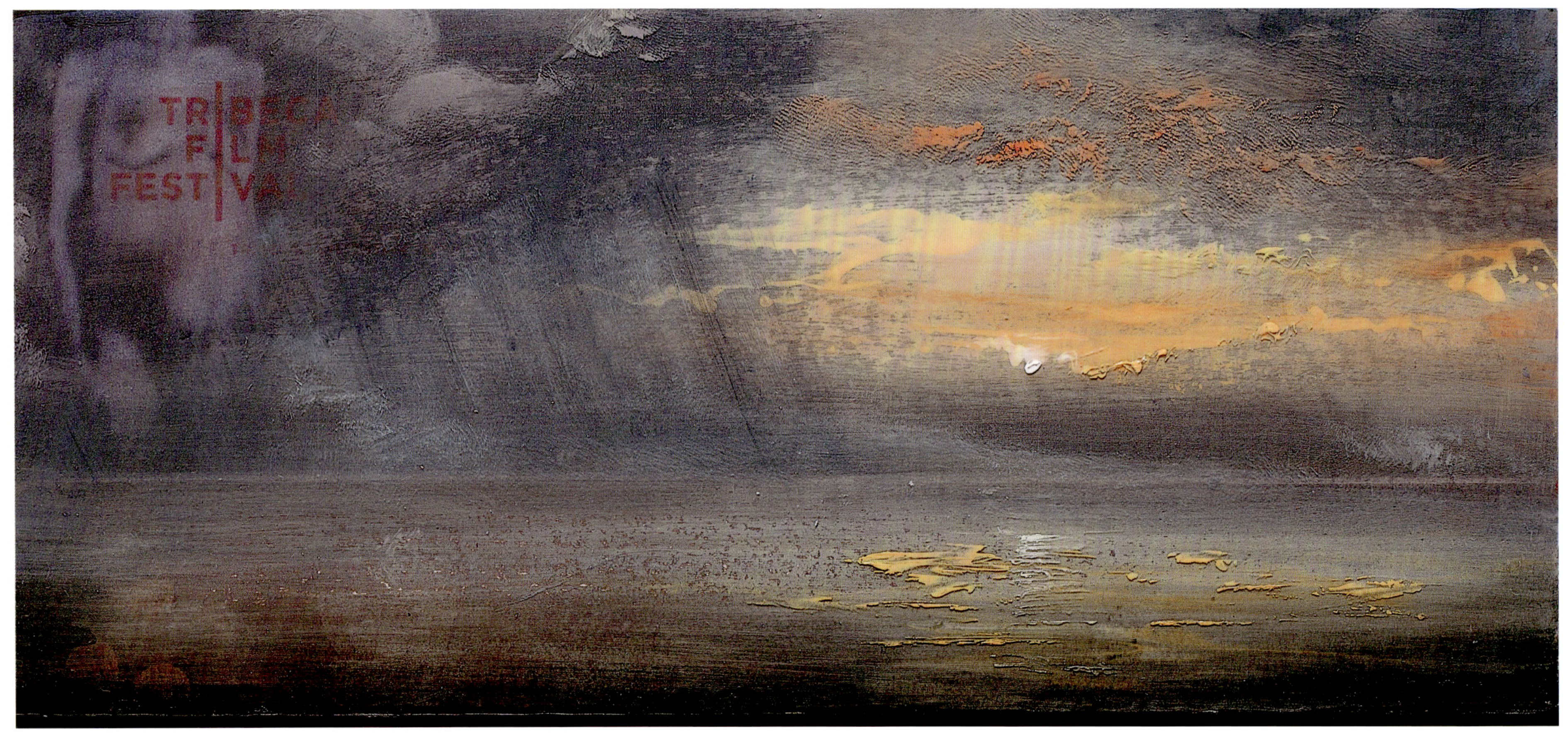

River Glare through Clearing Fog, 2002

Polished oil over Chuck Close daguerreotype on paper envelope, 4¼ x 9½ inches (11 x 24 cm). Whitney Museum of American Art

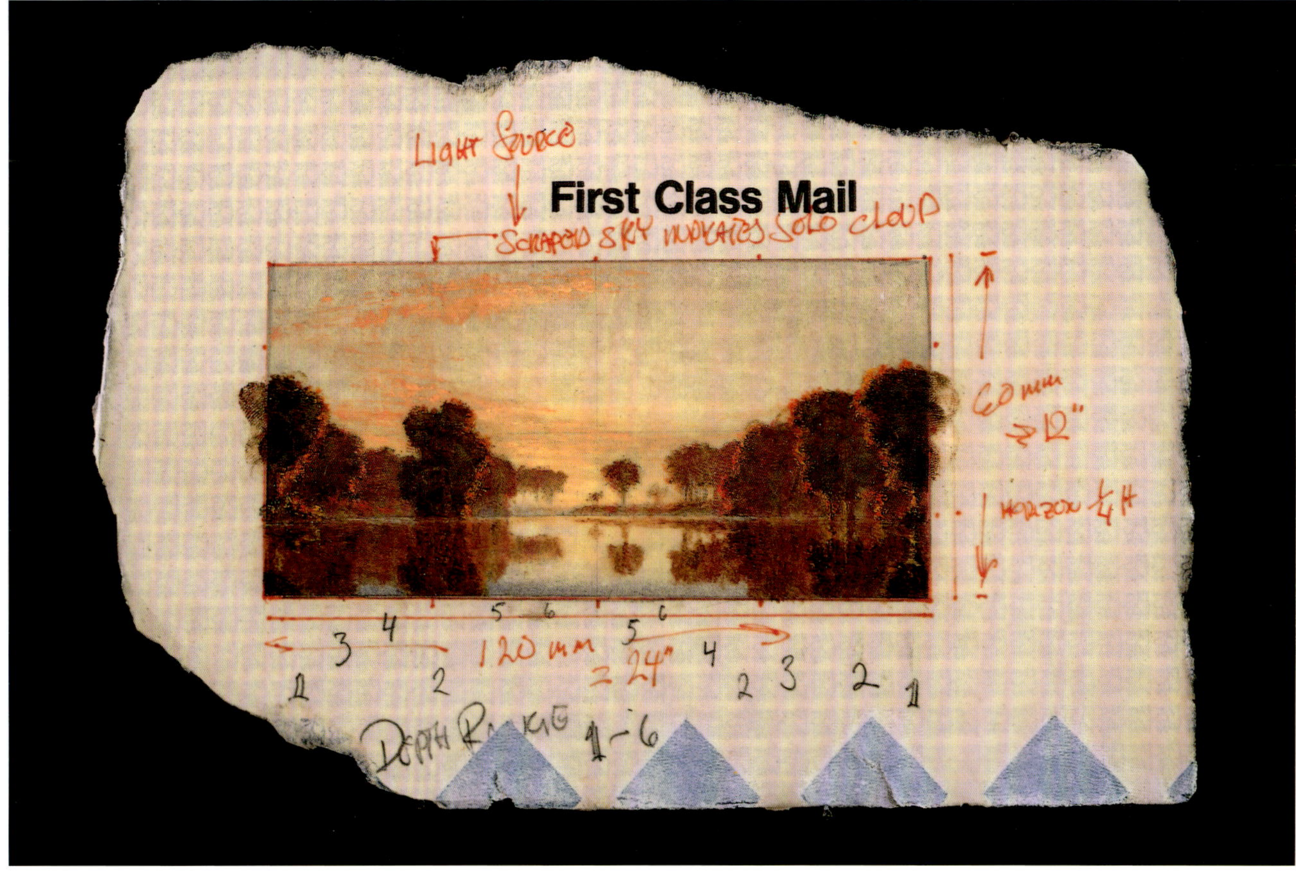

Untitled First Palimpsest, 2003
Oil on paper envelope, 5¼ x 7¾ inches (13 x 20 cm). Private Collection

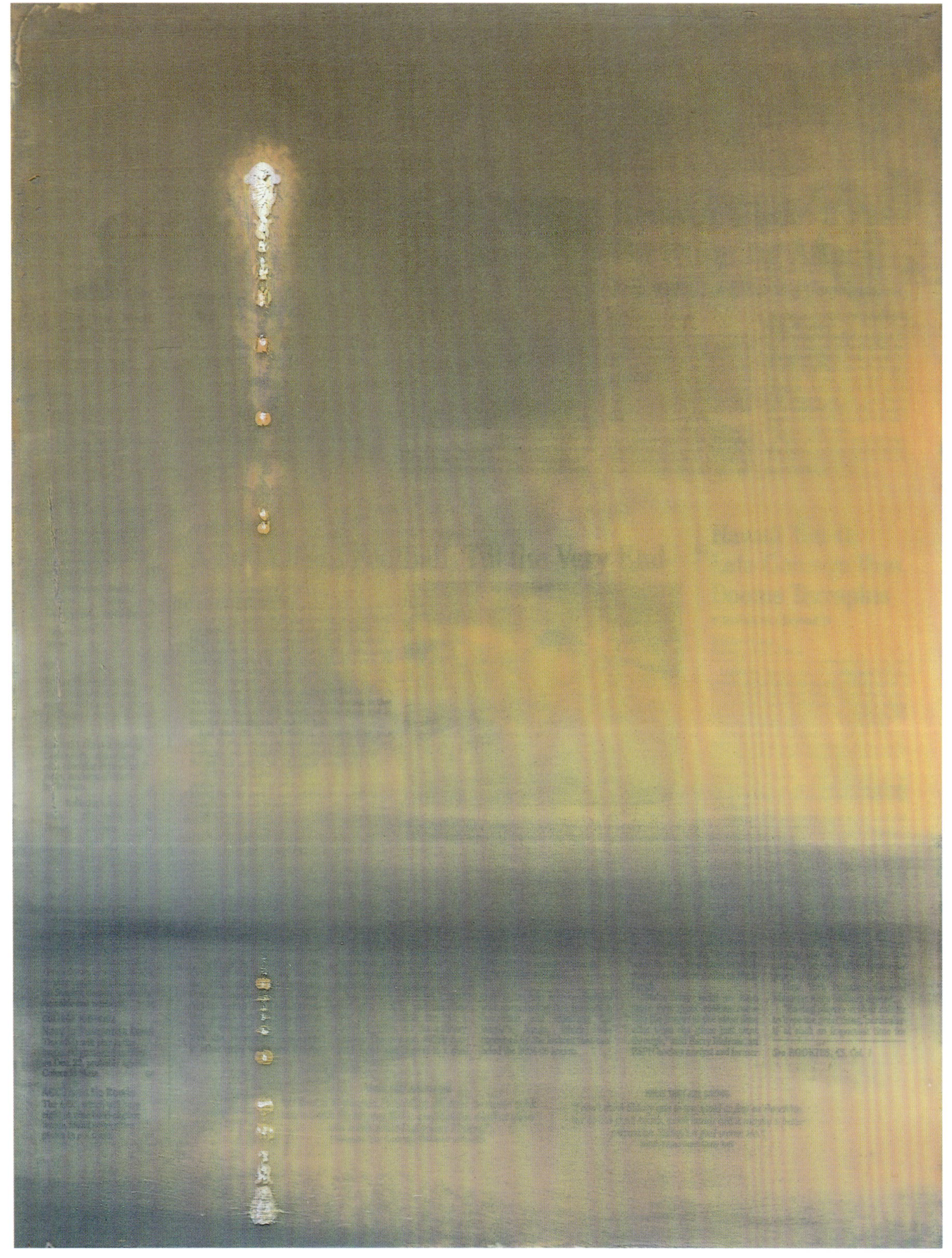

NOCTURNE FOR STEVE BELICHICK, 2006

POLISHED OIL OVER *Washington Post,* 11 X 8½ INCHES (28 X 22 CM). PRIVATE COLLECTION

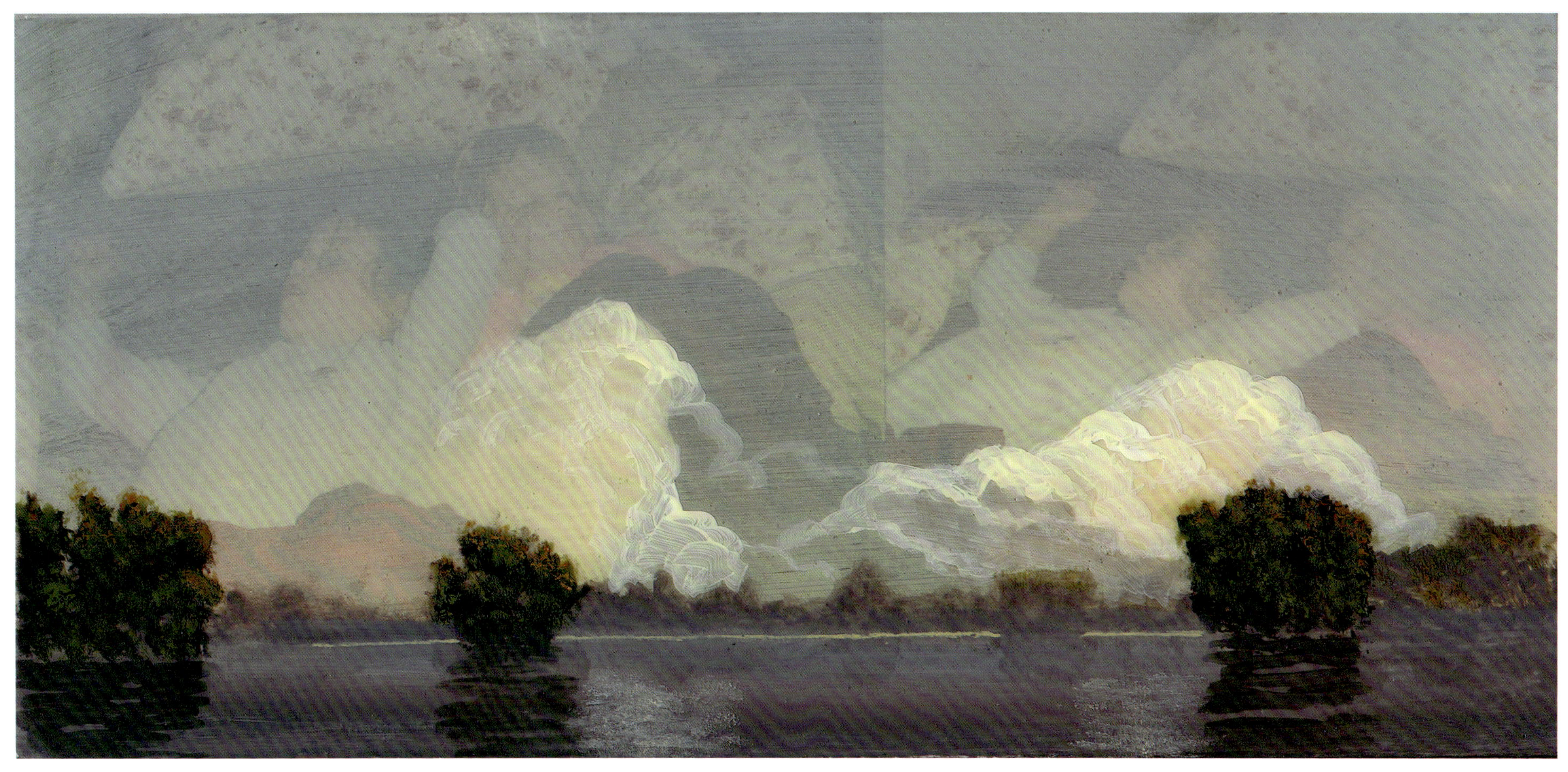

Flooded River on Rachel's Birthday, 2005
Polished oil on paper envelope, 4¼ x 9½ inches (11 x 24 cm). Private Cllection

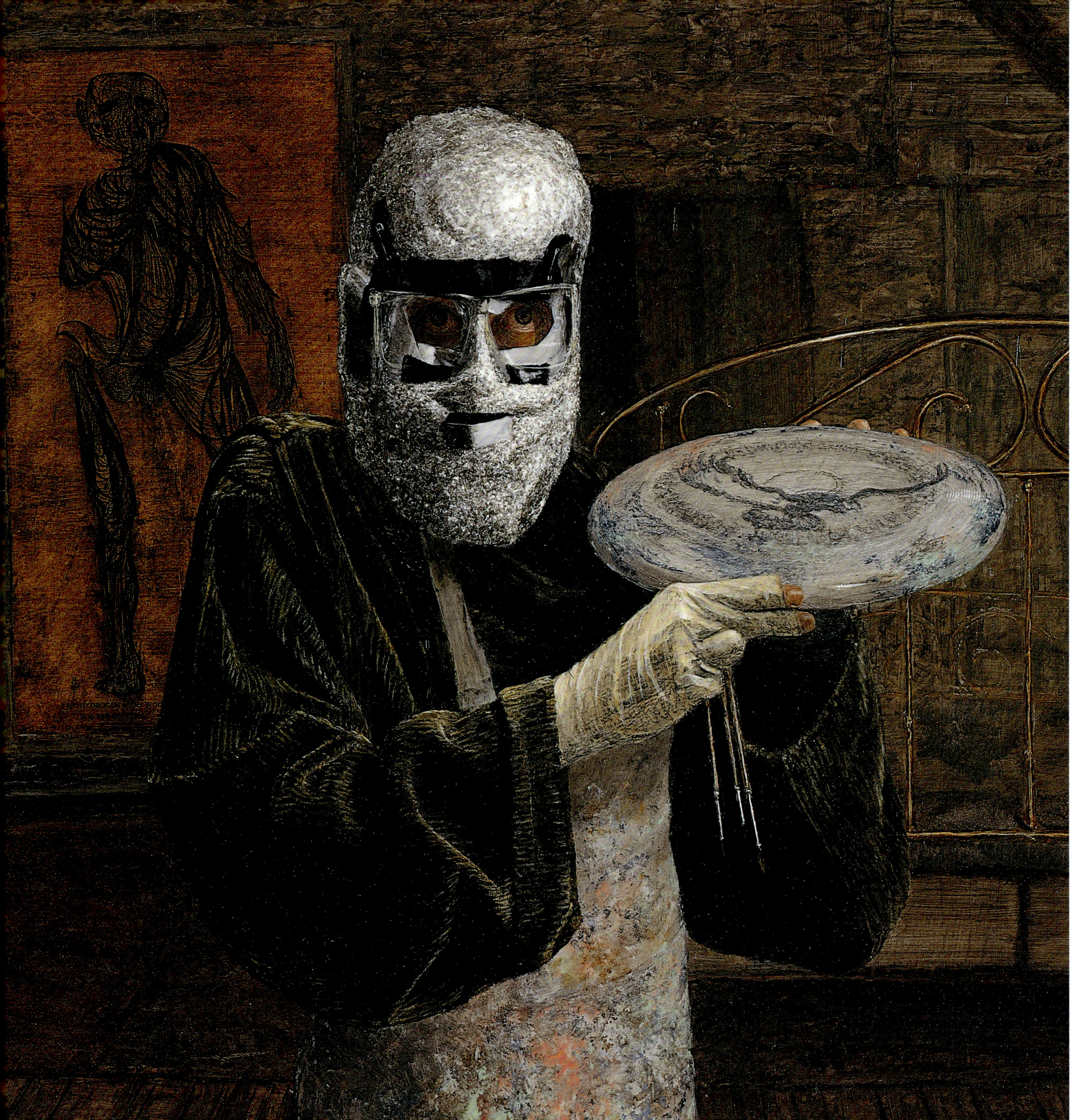

SELF-PORTRAITS

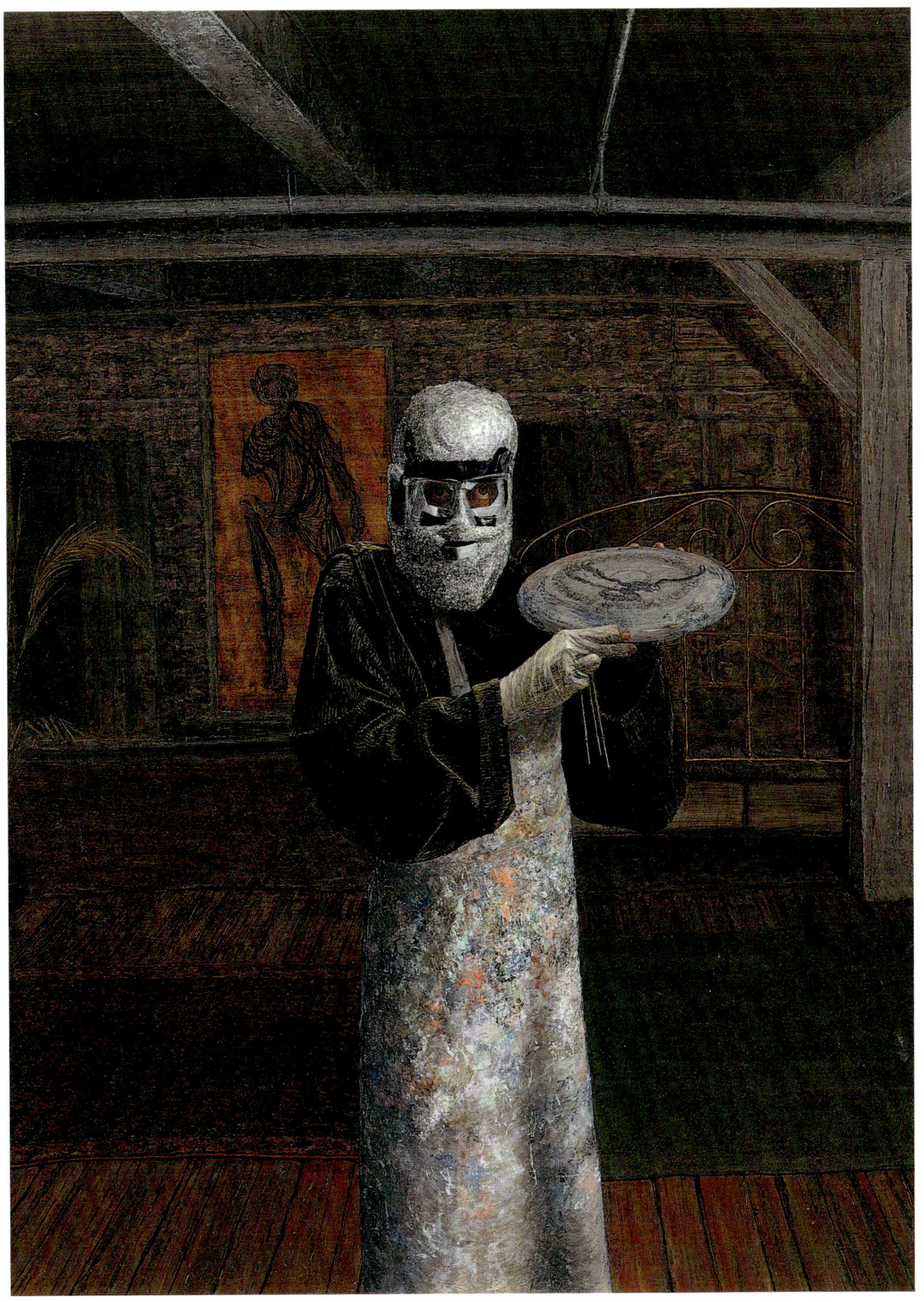

Man of Peace (Child of the Nuclear Age), 1979

Oil on alkyd on panel, 34 x 28 inches (86 x 71 cm). Private Collection

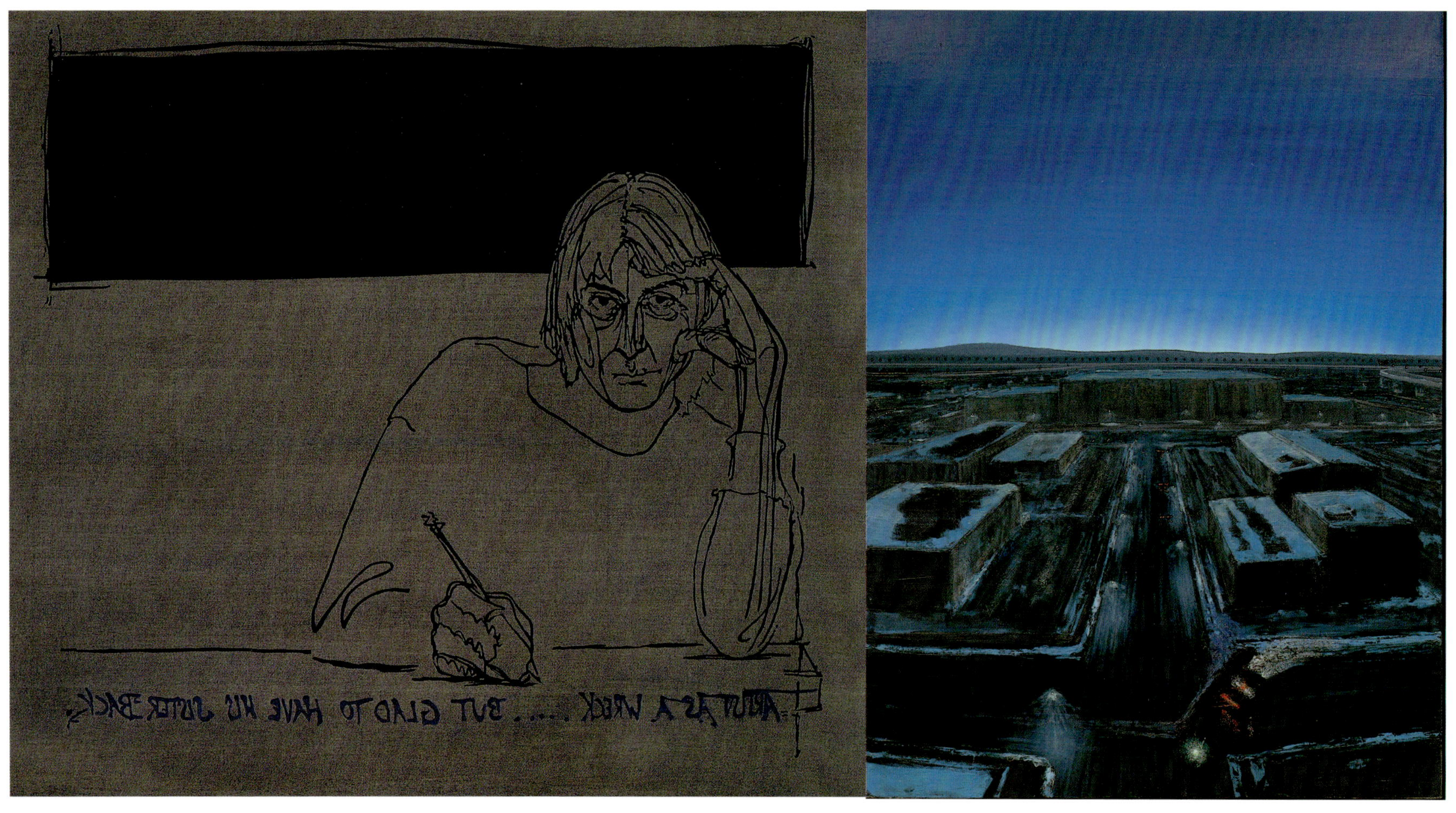

ARTIST AS A WRECK, 1986

Polished oil on canvas, 48 x 96 inches (122 x 244 cm). Collection of the Artist

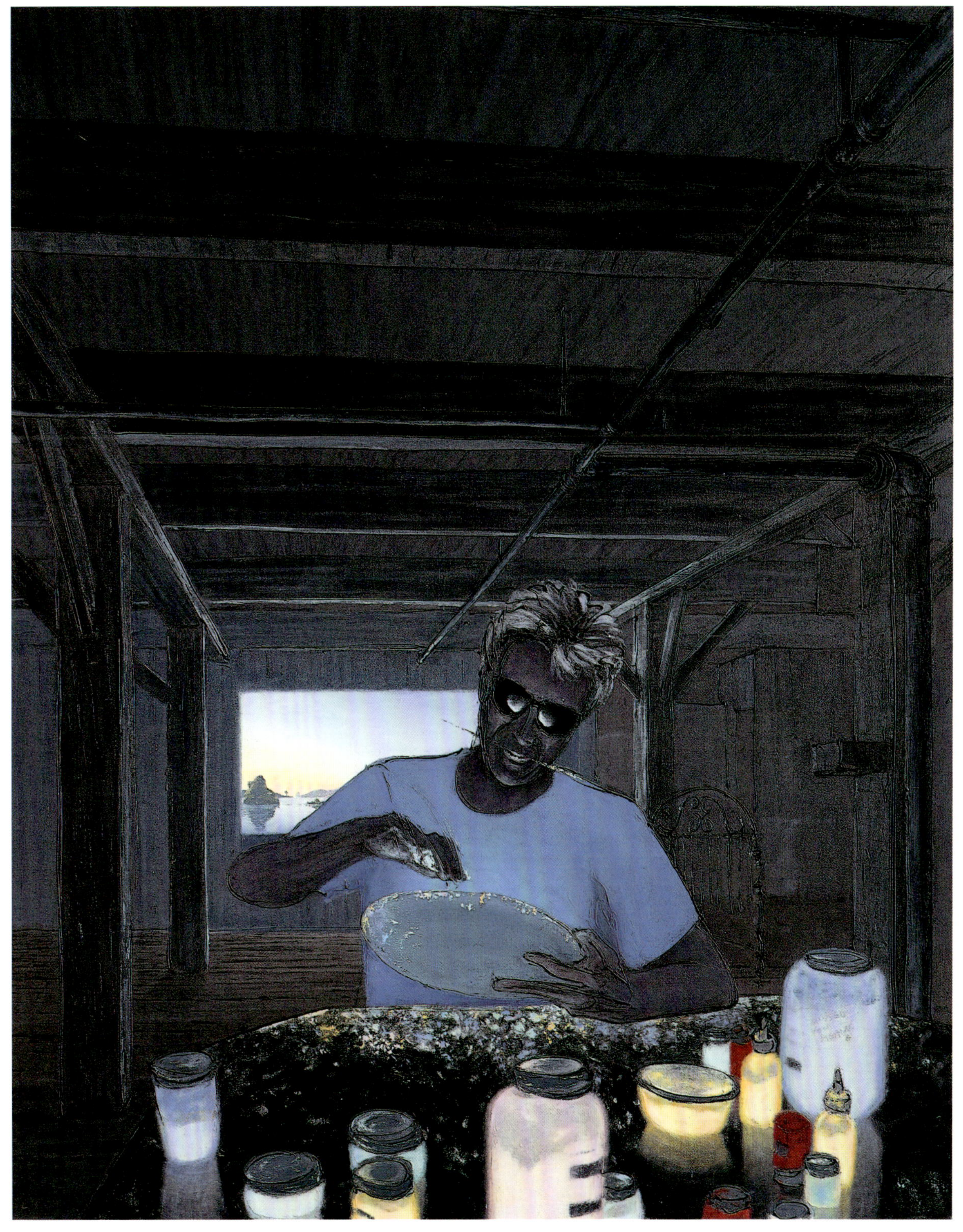

Portrait of the Artist in the Dark, 1986

Polished oil on canvas, 72 x 48 inches (183 x 122 cm). Collection of the Artist

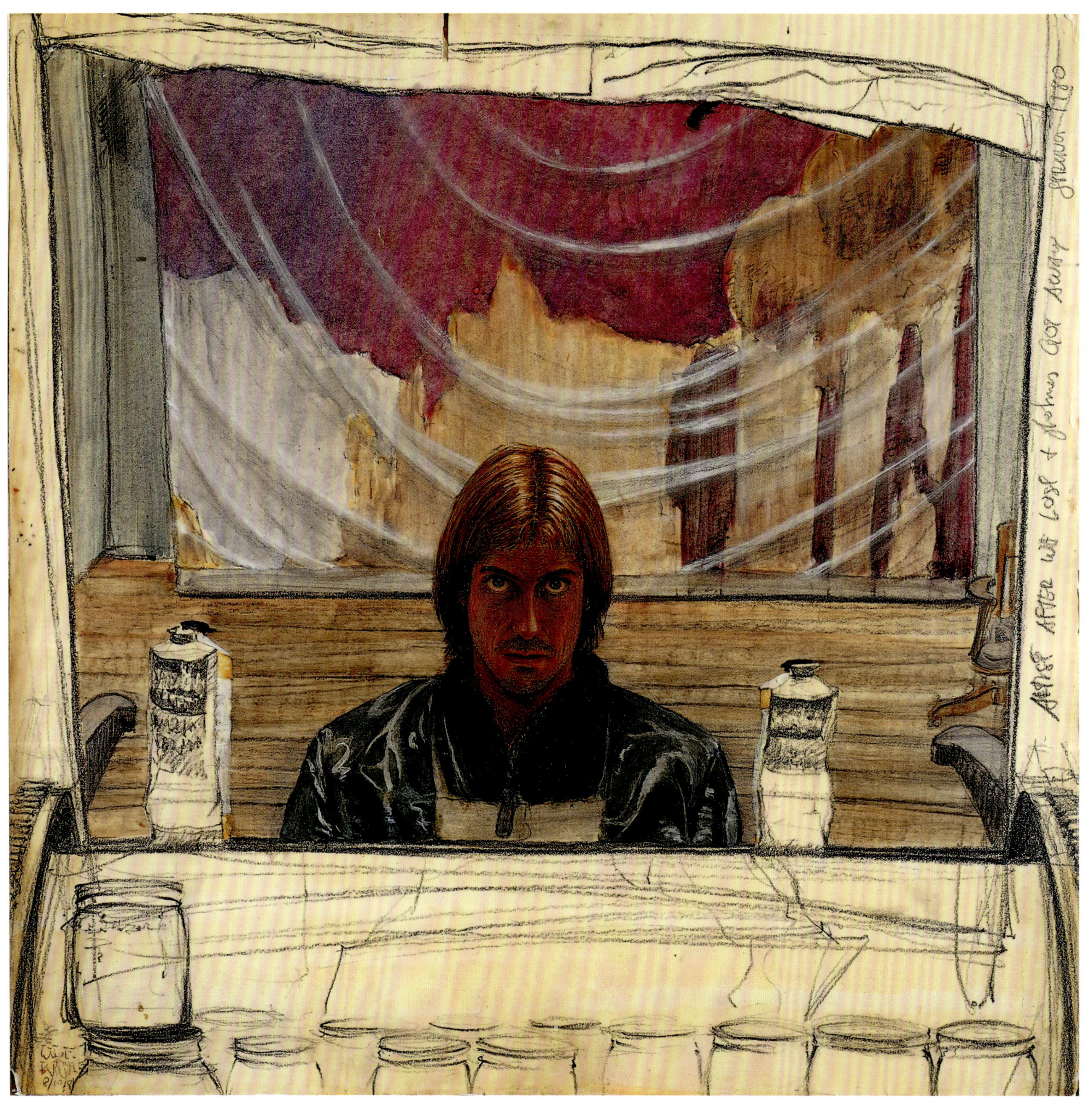

Artist After We Lost, and Holmes Got Away, 1980

Oil on board, 21 x 21½ inches (53 x 55 cm). Collection of the Artist

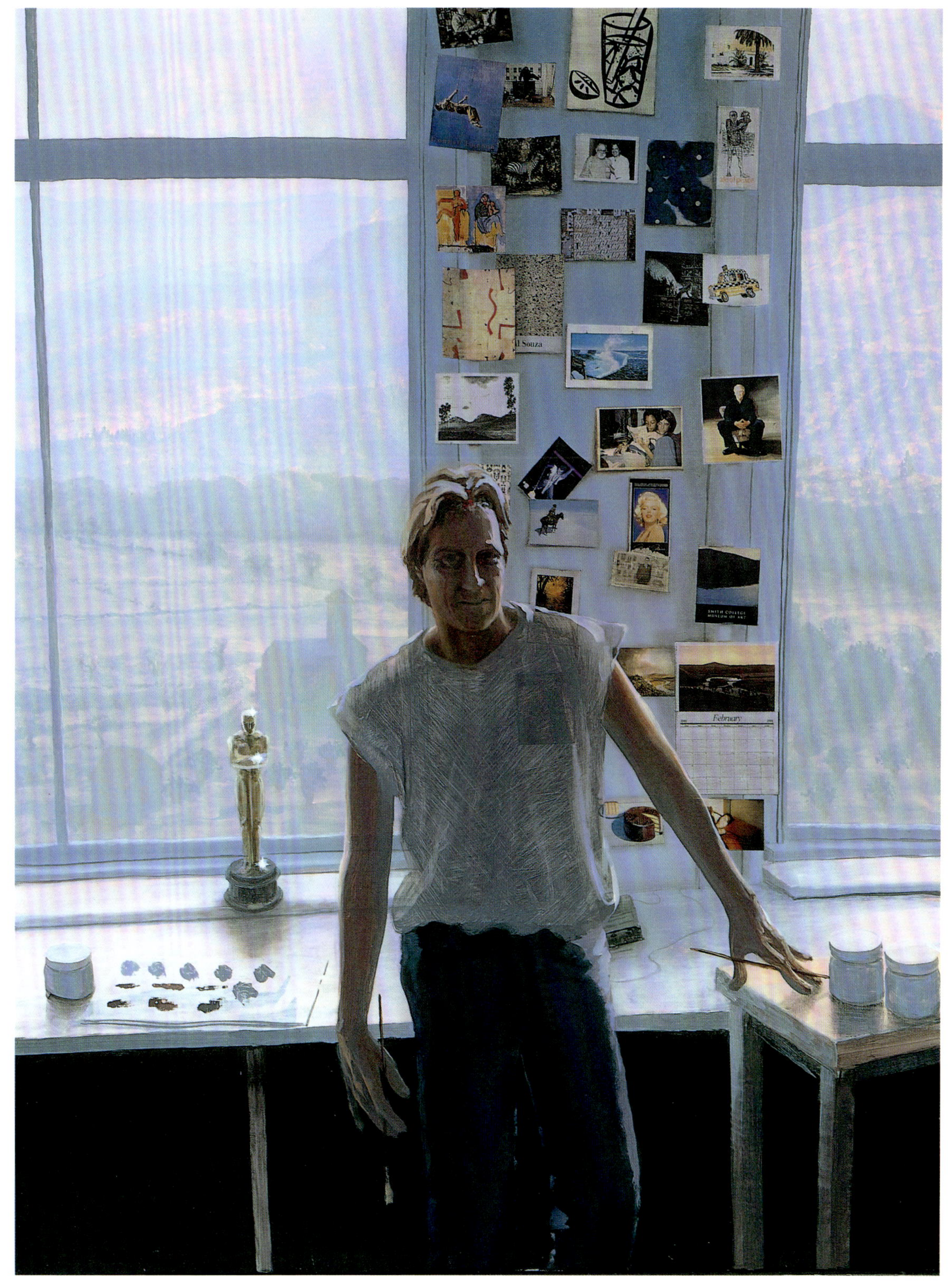

Self-Portrait with Oscar and Skin Cancer, 2000–2001

Mixed media on canvas, 72 x 54 inches (183 x 137 cm). Collection of the Artist

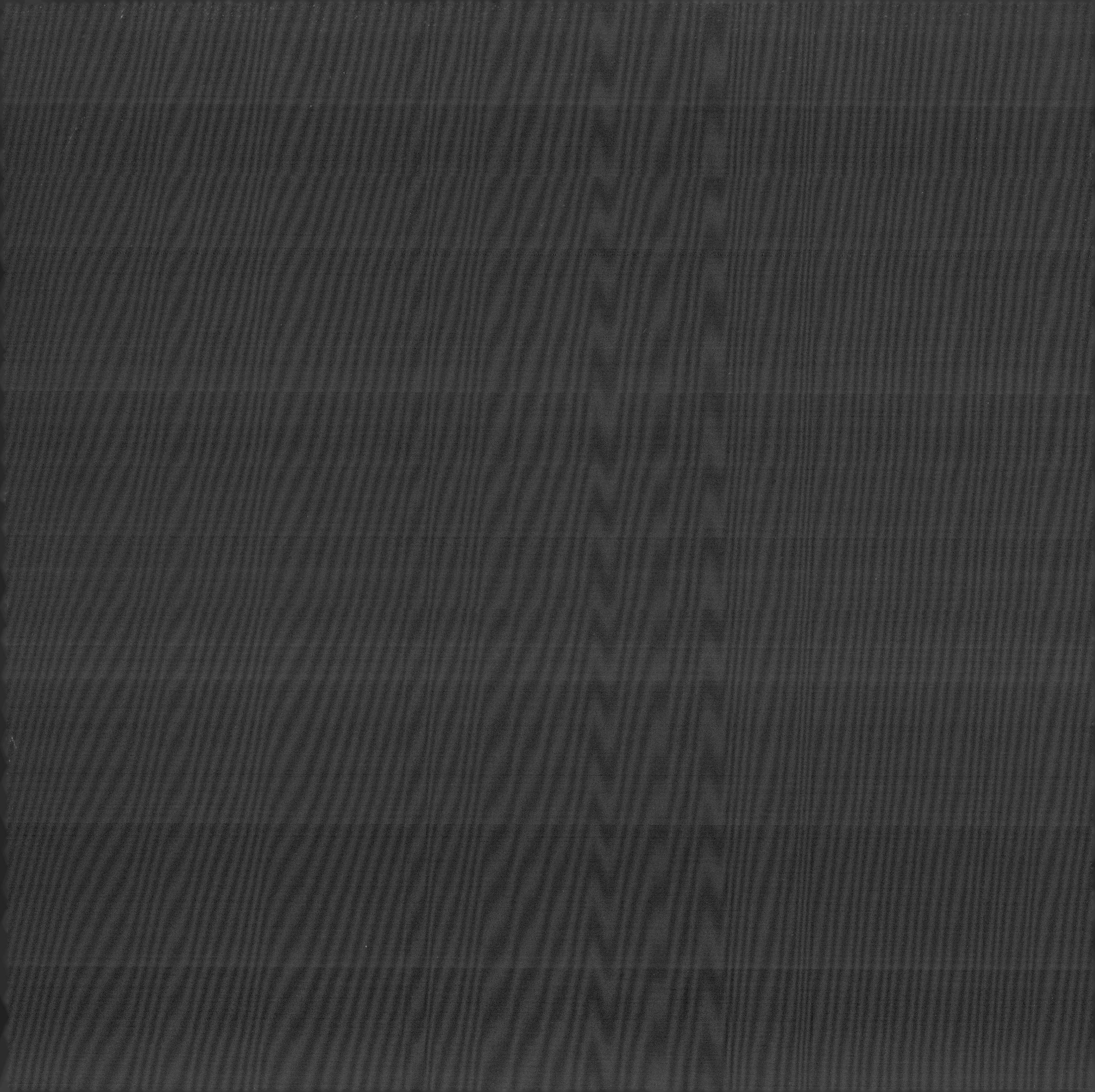

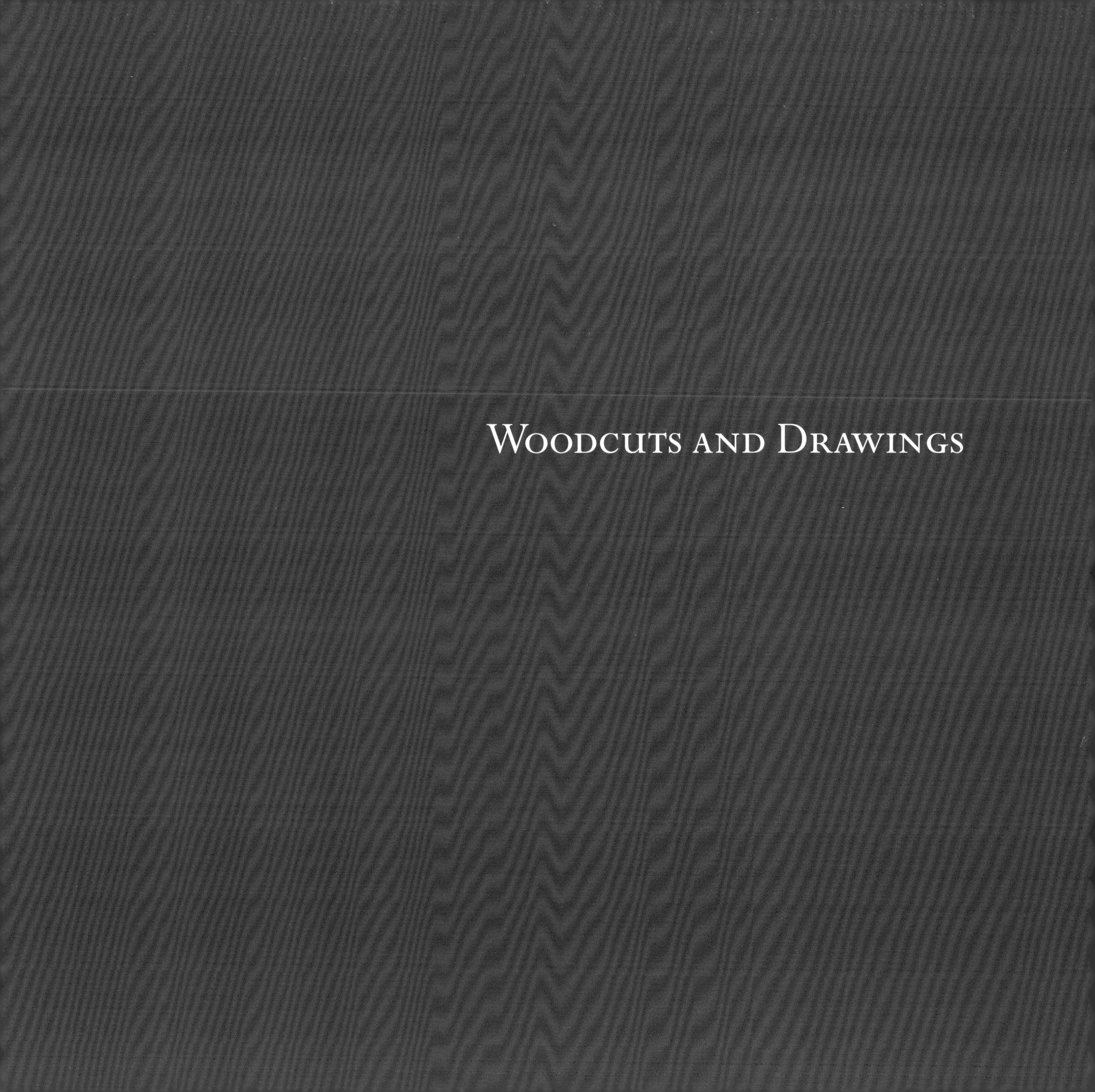
Woodcuts and Drawings

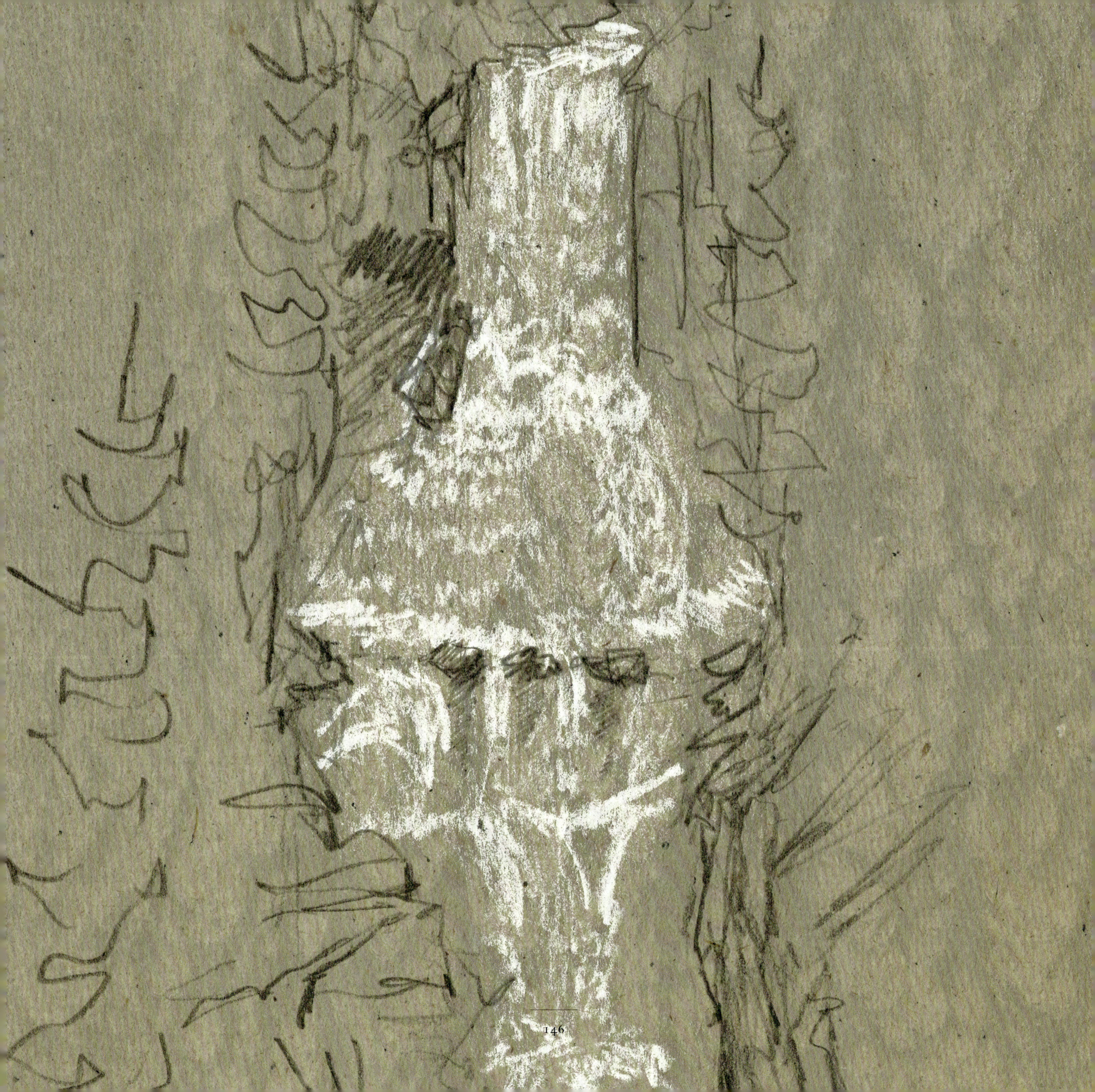

Mountain Water

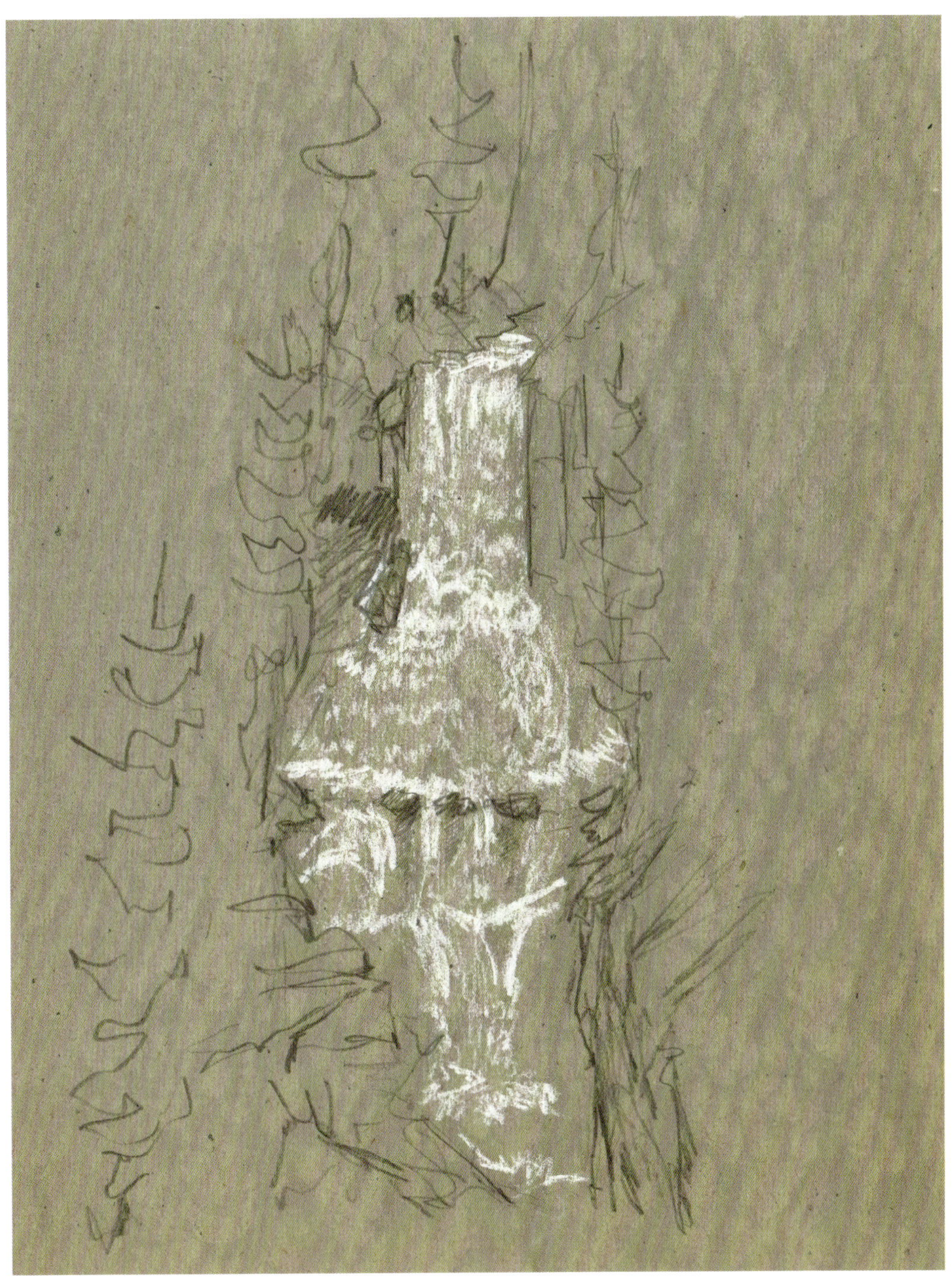

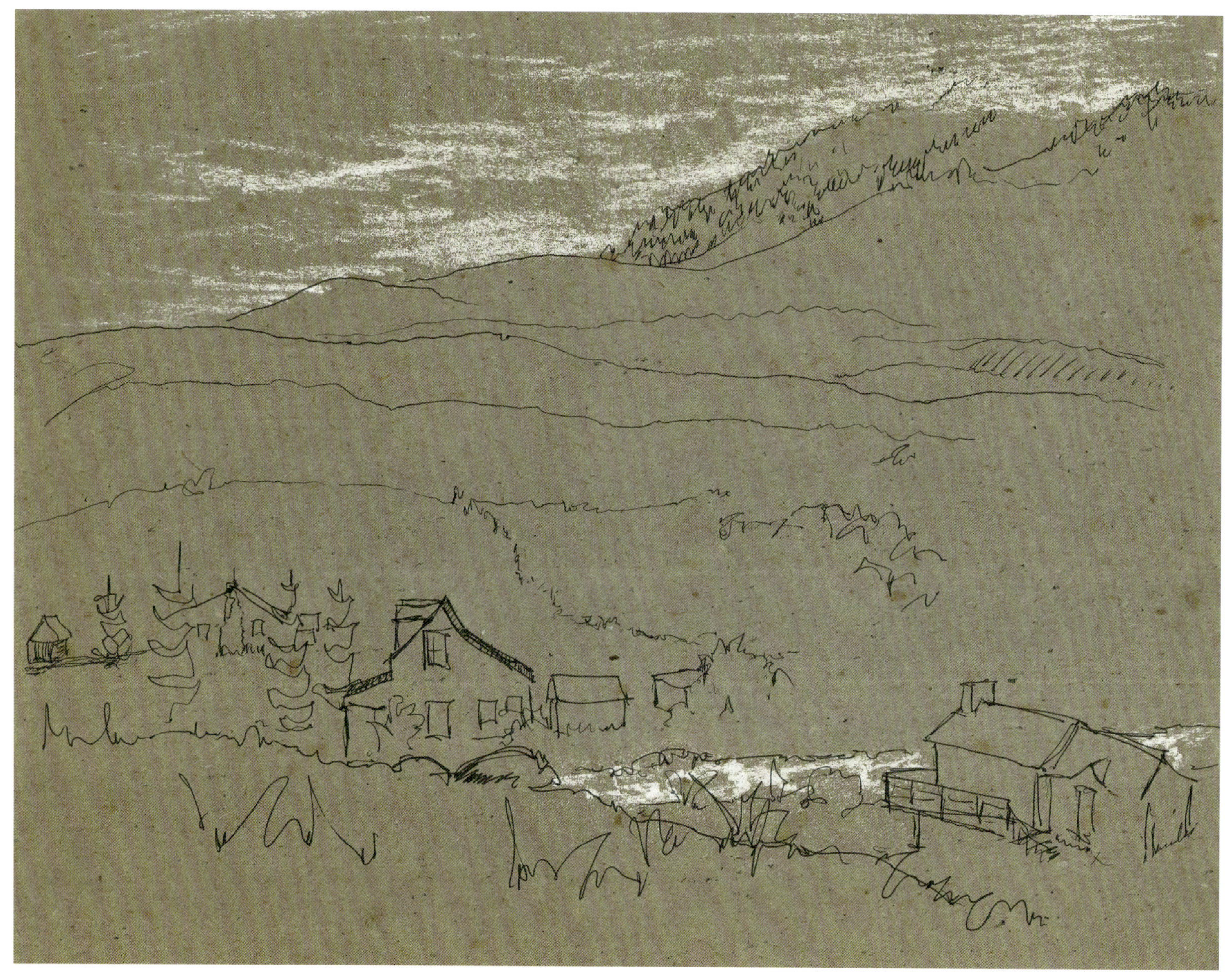

West Boulder Homestead, 1991

Ink and crayon on gray paper, 8½ x 11 inches (22 x 28 cm). Collection of the Artist

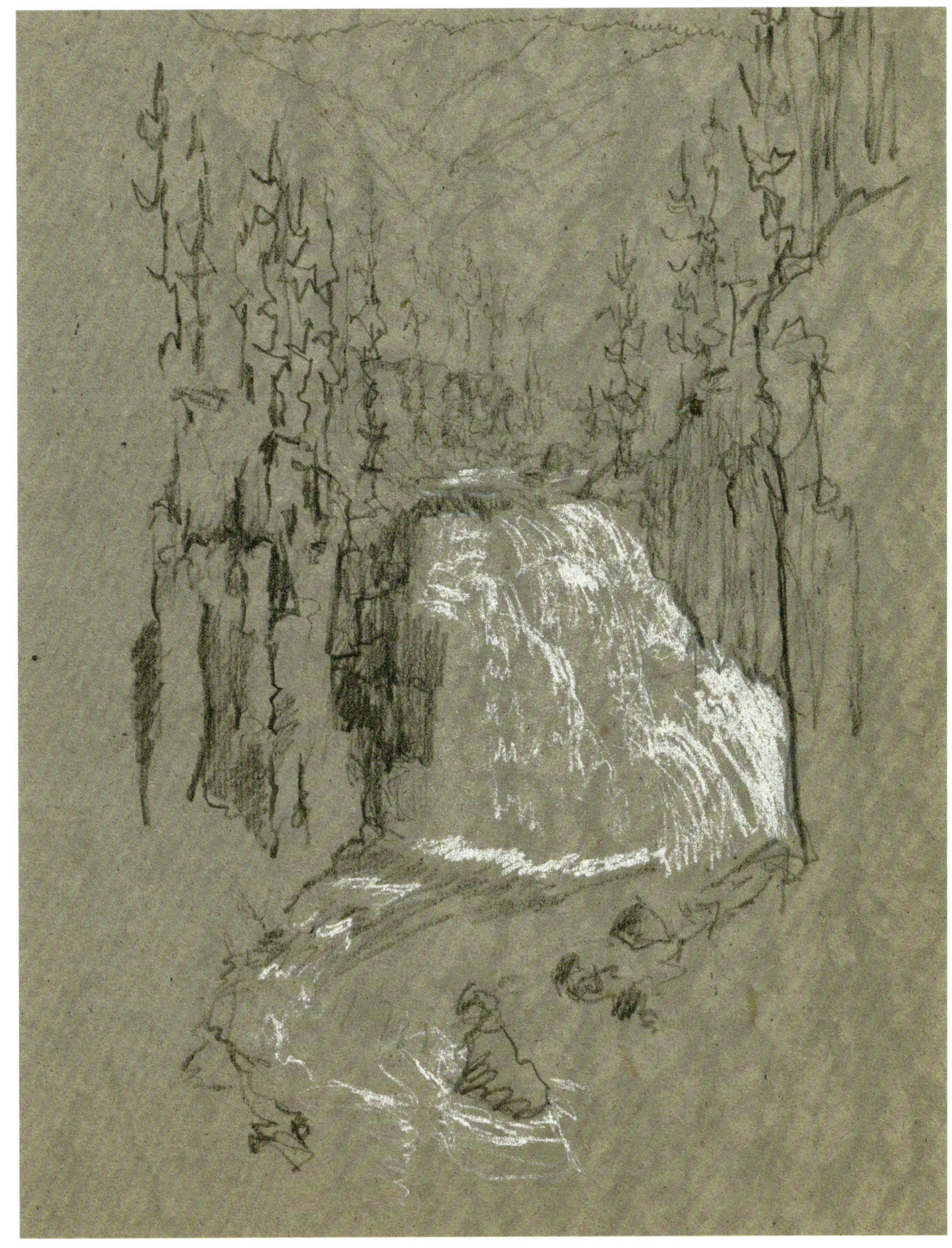

Yellowstone Cascade with Close Wall, 1991
Colored pencil on gray paper, 11 x 8½ inches (28 x 22 cm). Collection of the Artist

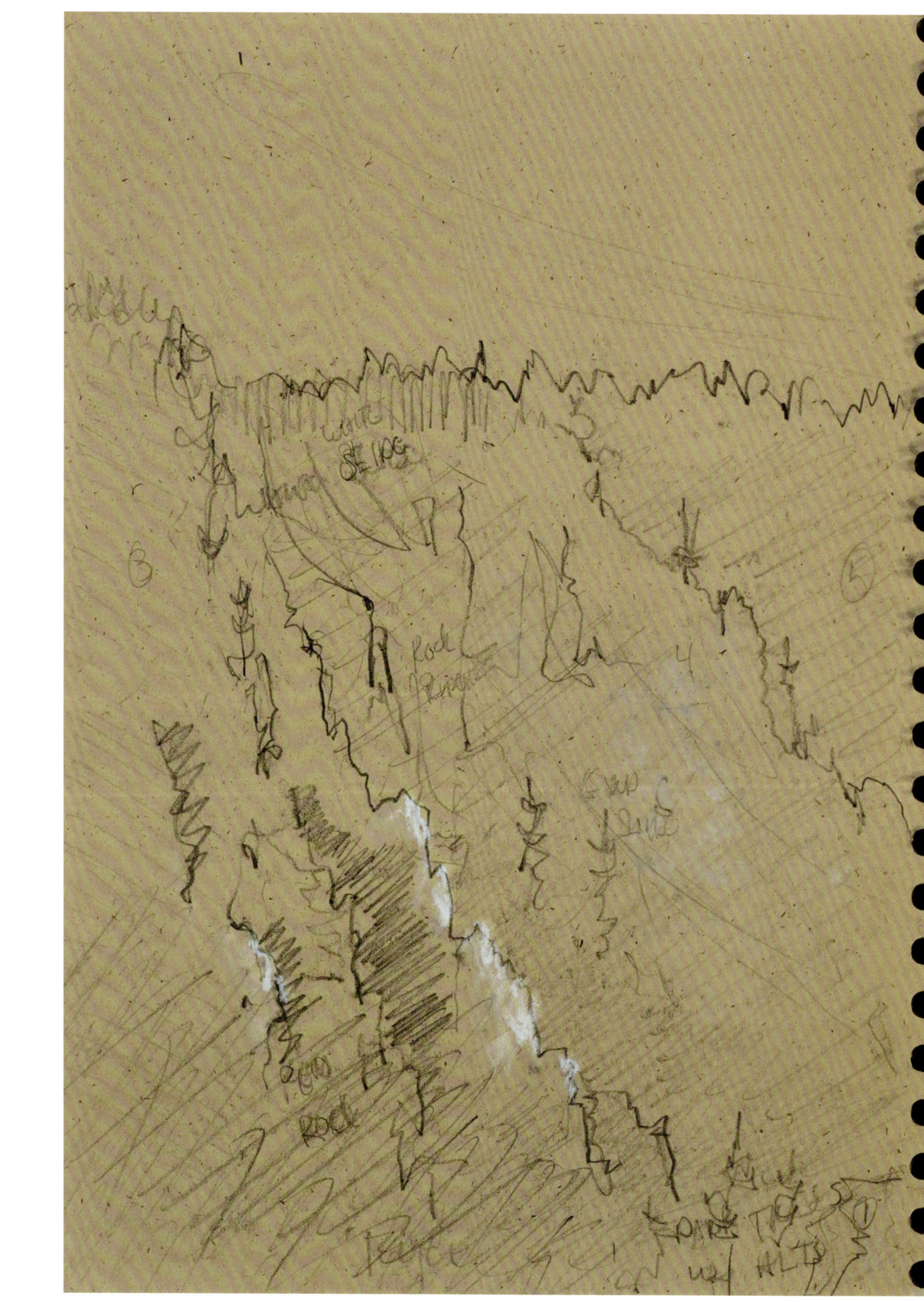

GREAT FALLS AT DAWN, YELLOWSTONE PARK, 1996
Pencil and chalk on gray paper, 12 x 17½ inches (31 x 45 cm).
Collection of the Artist

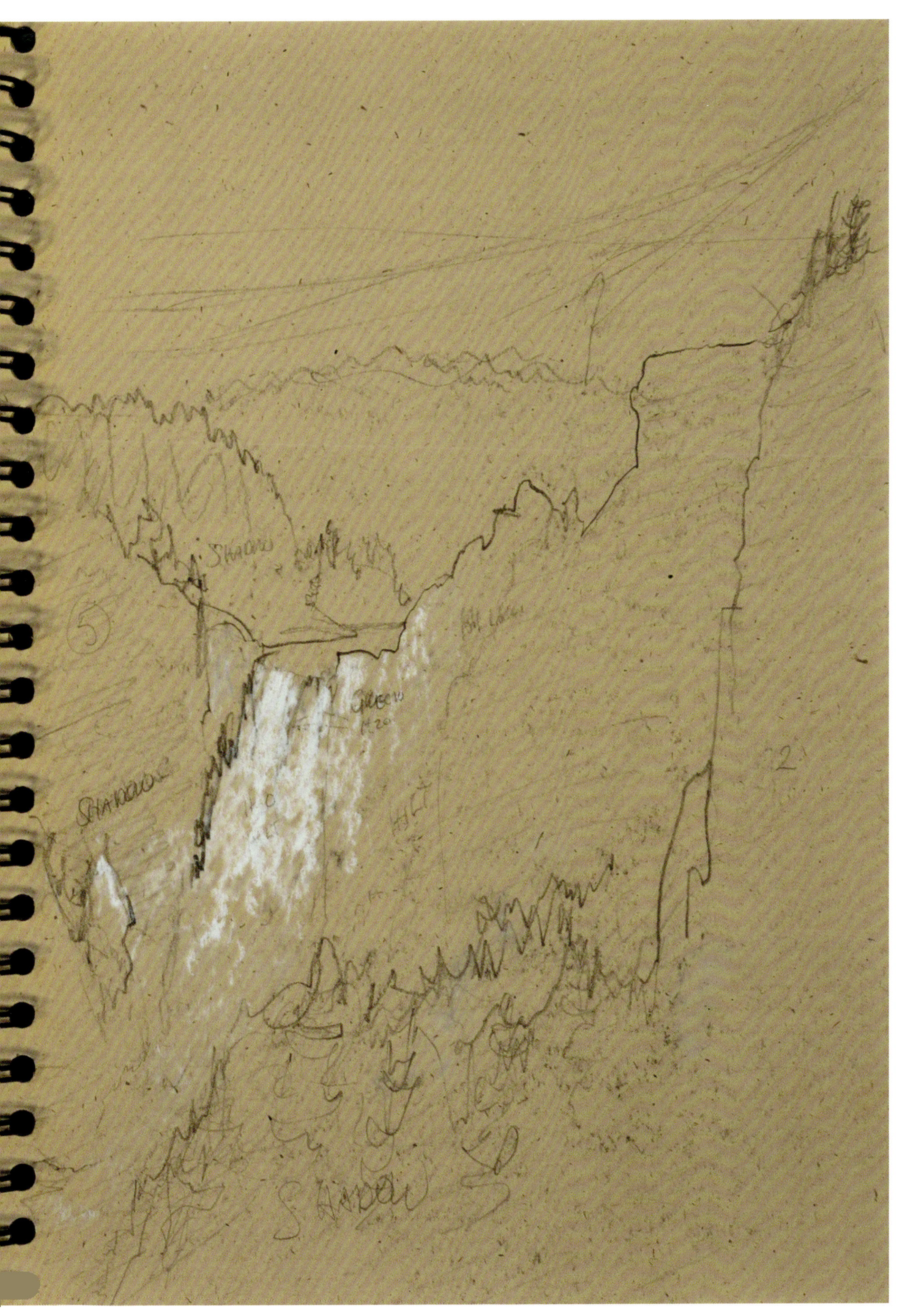

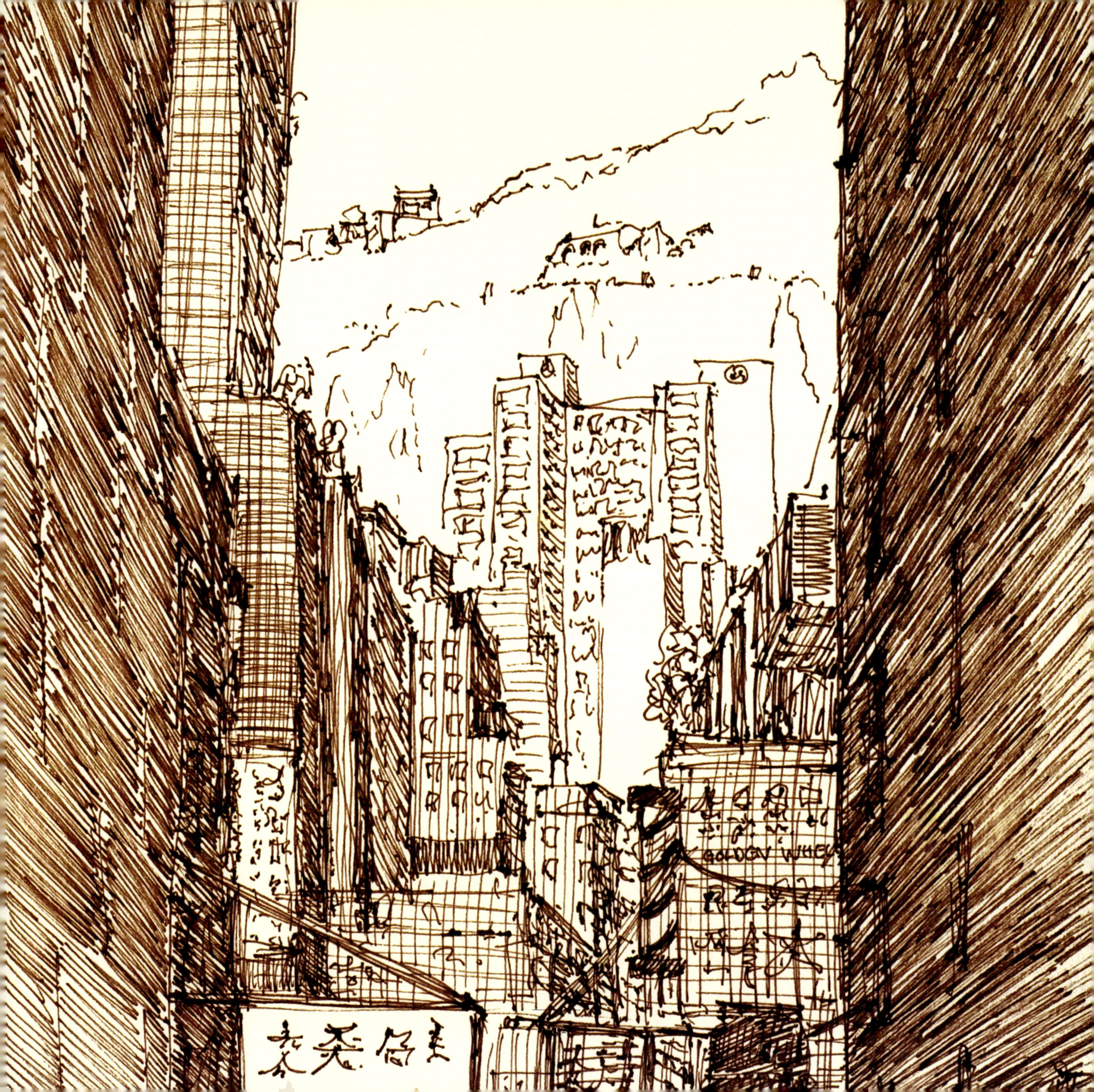

GOLDEN WHEEL

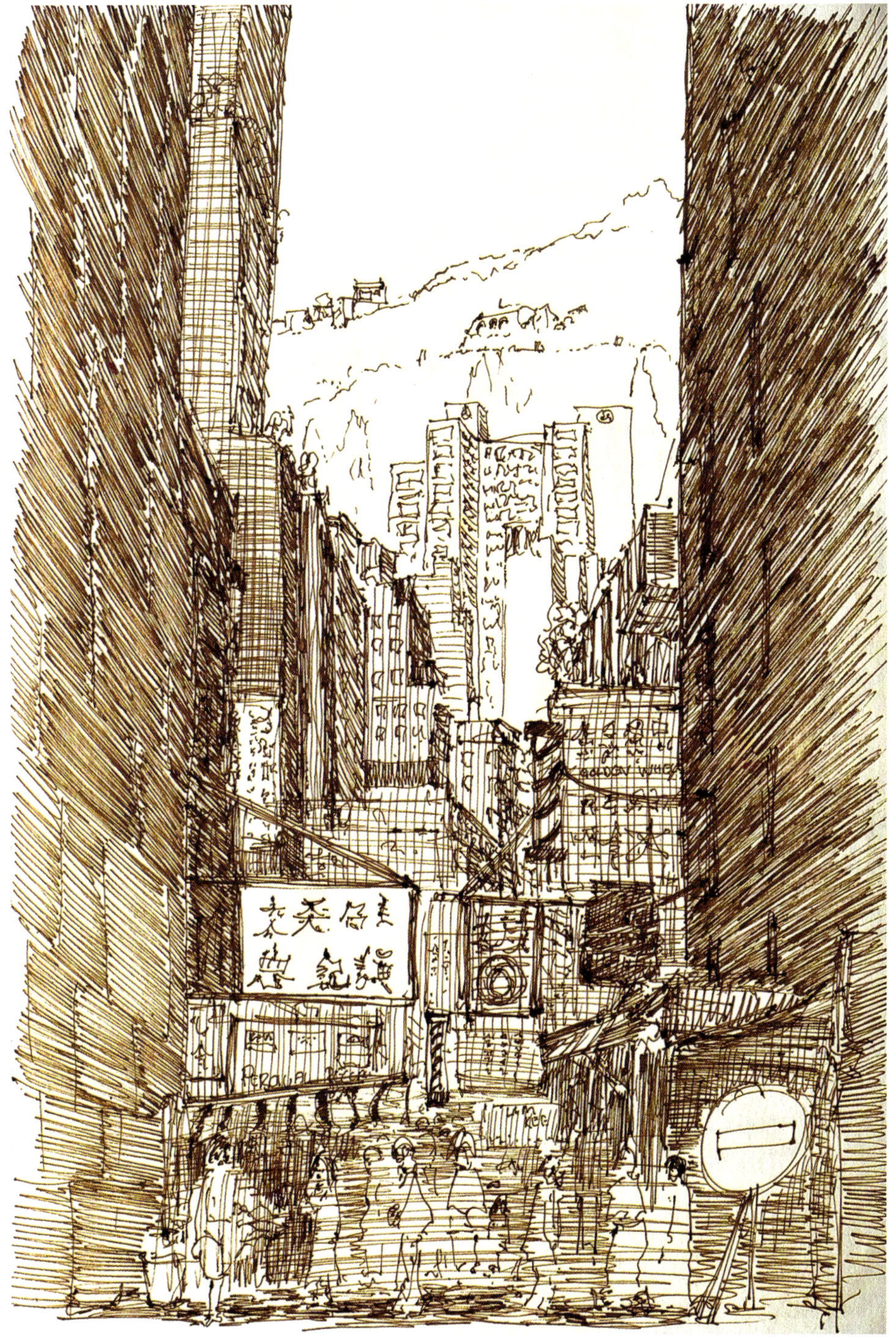

Victoria Peak from the Street, 1987

Ink on paper, 11¾ x 8¼ inches (30 x 21 cm). Collection of the Artist

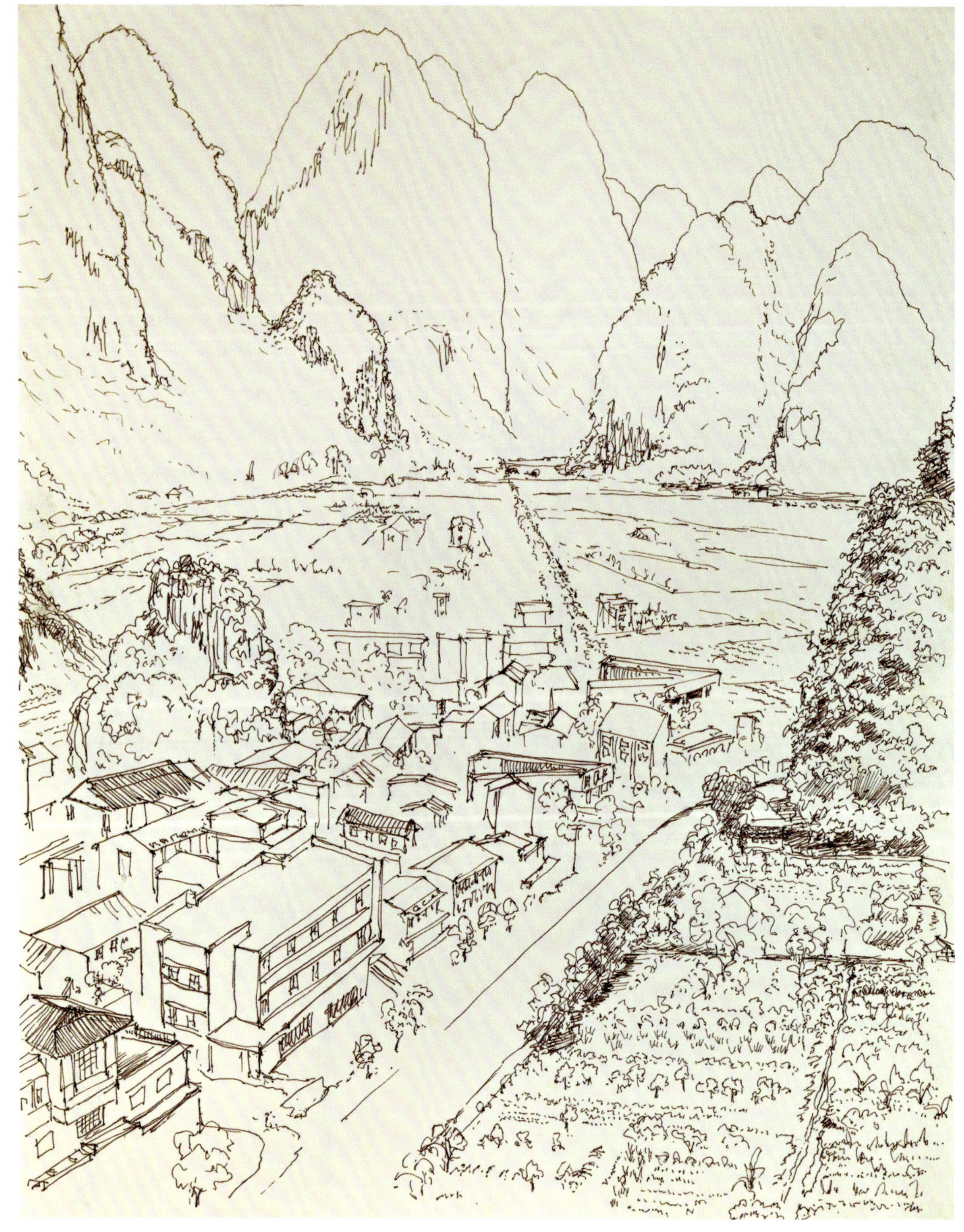

Li River Village, 1987

Ink on paper, 16 x 12½ inches (41 x 32 cm). Collection of the Artist

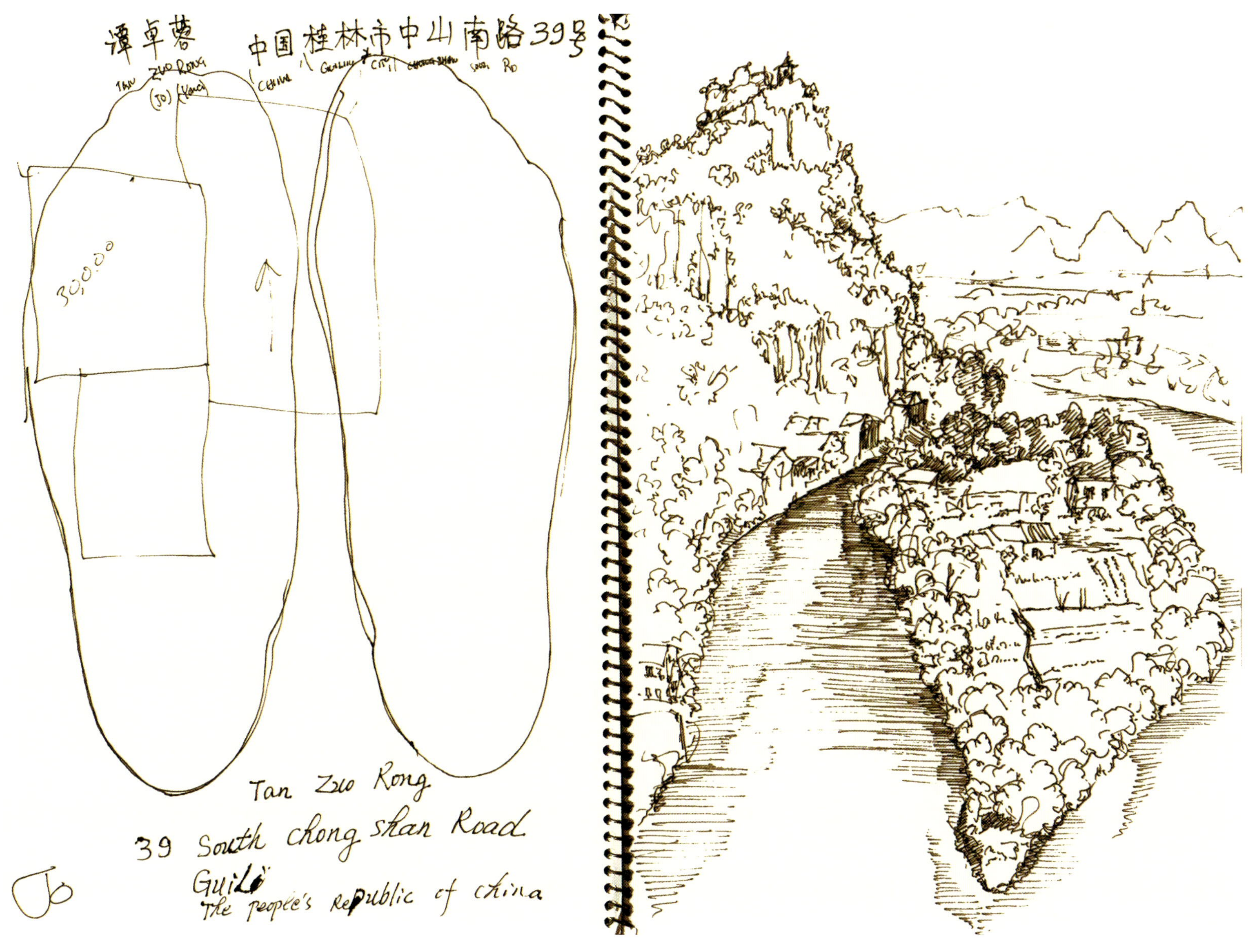

CHINA SKETCHBOOK, 1987

Ink on paper, 11¾ x 16½ inches (30 x 42 cm). Collection of the Artist

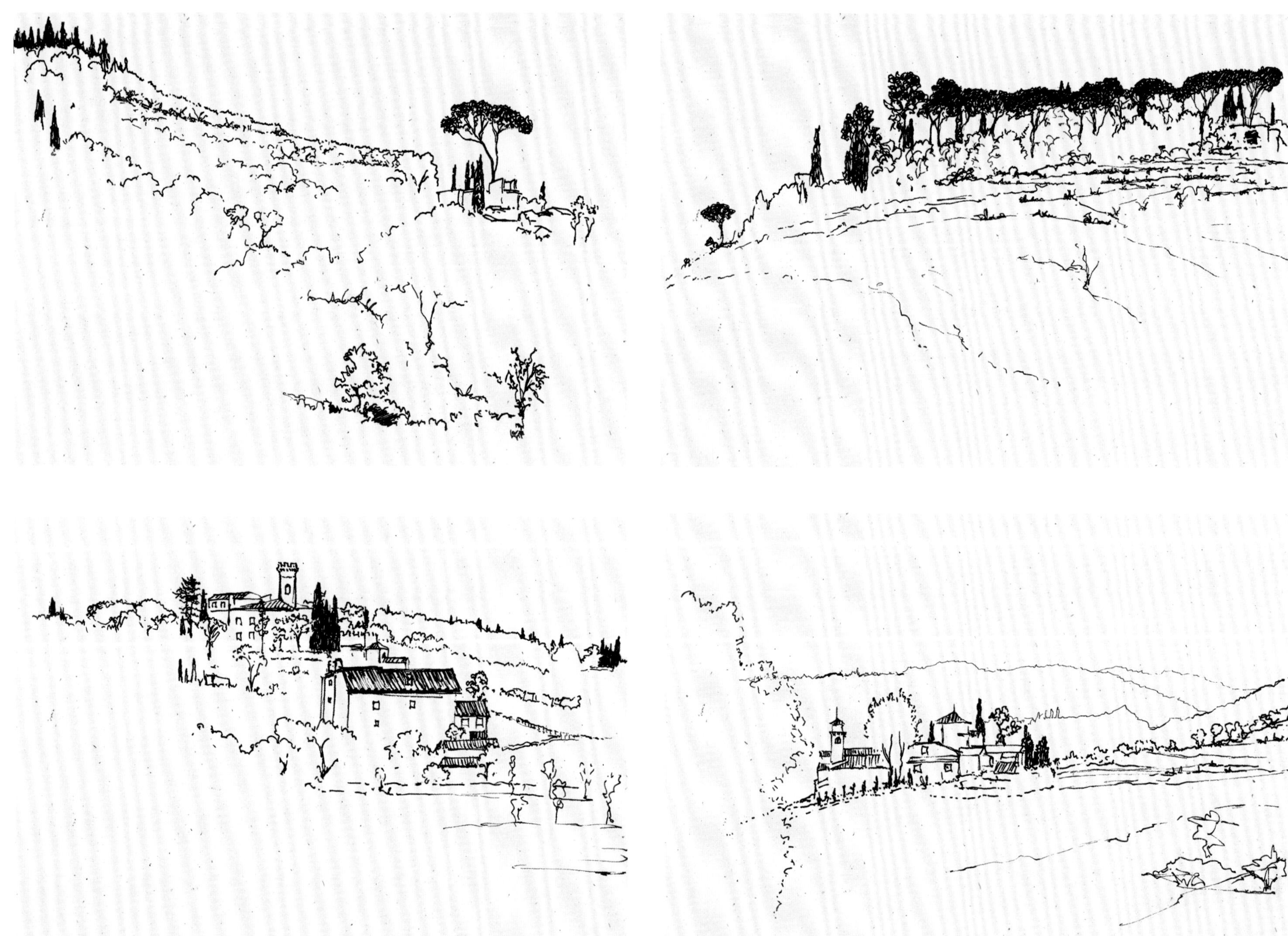

Four Views from Villa I Tatti, Tuscany, 1993

Ink on paper, each 8½ x 12 inches (22 x 31 cm). Collection of the Artist

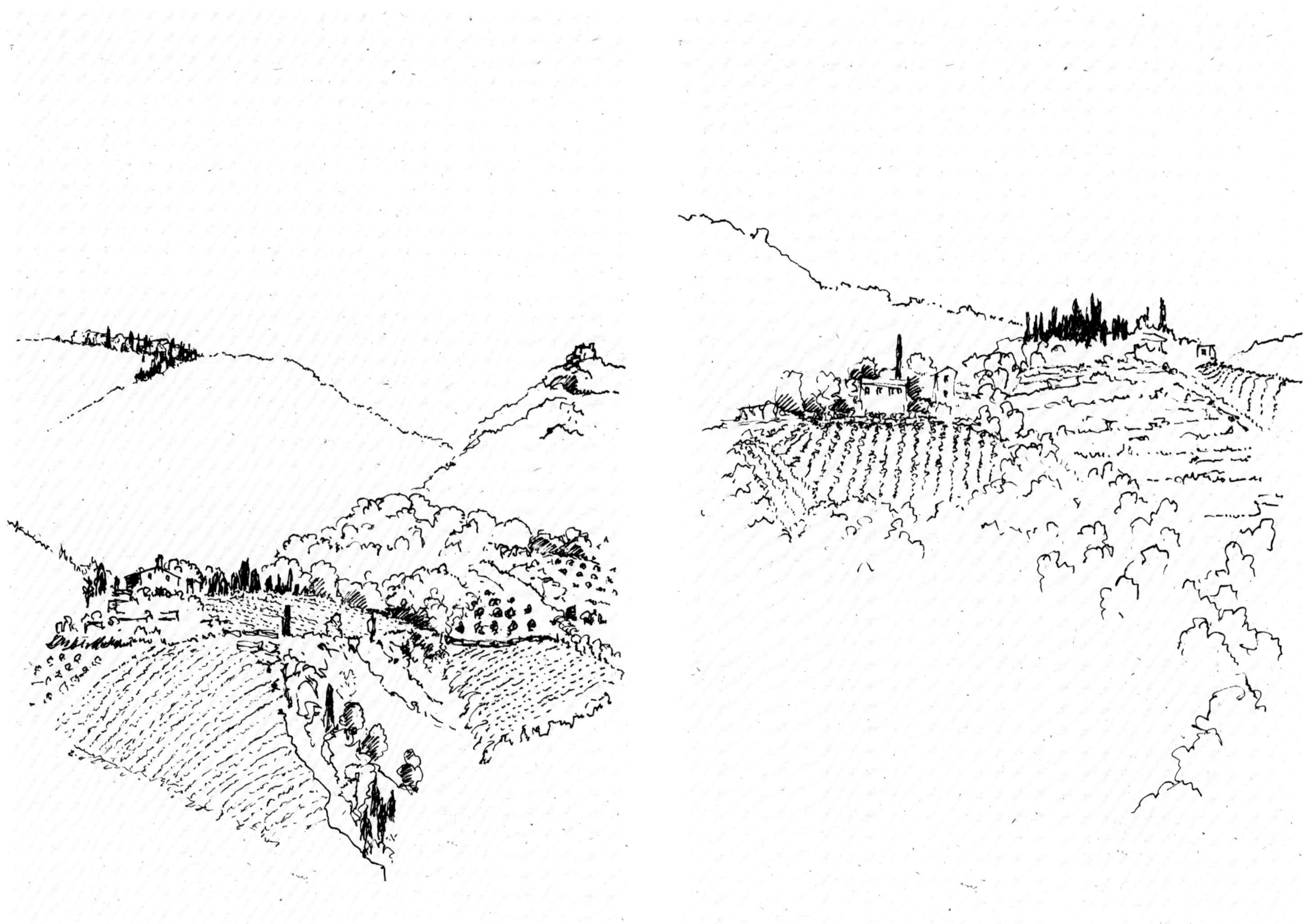

Two Views of Tuscan Vineyard, 1993

Ink on paper, each 12 x 8½ inches (31 x 22 cm). Collection of the Artist

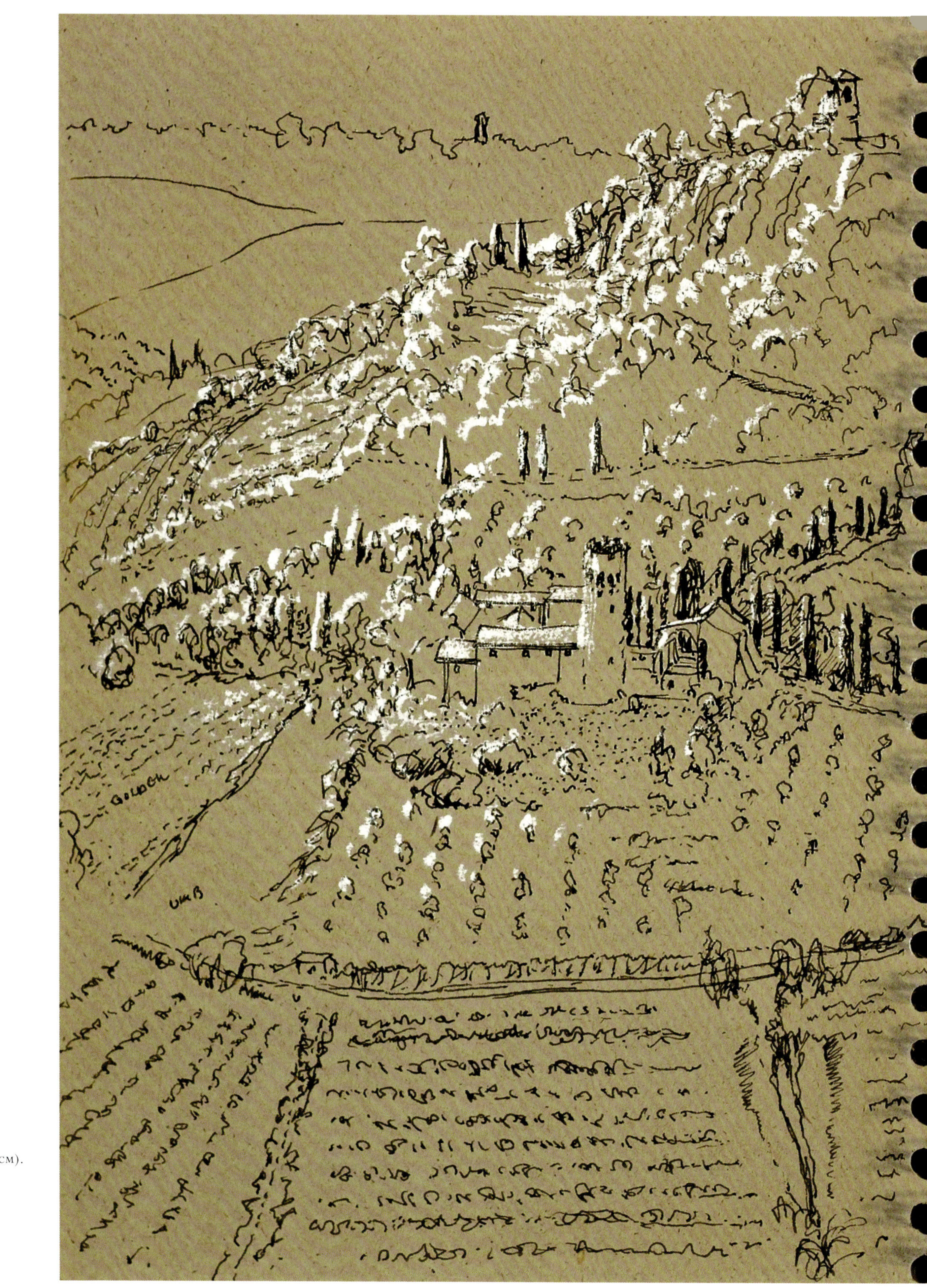

View from Orvieto, 1998
Ink and chalk on wheat paper, 12 x 17½ inches (30 x 44 cm).
Collection of the Artist

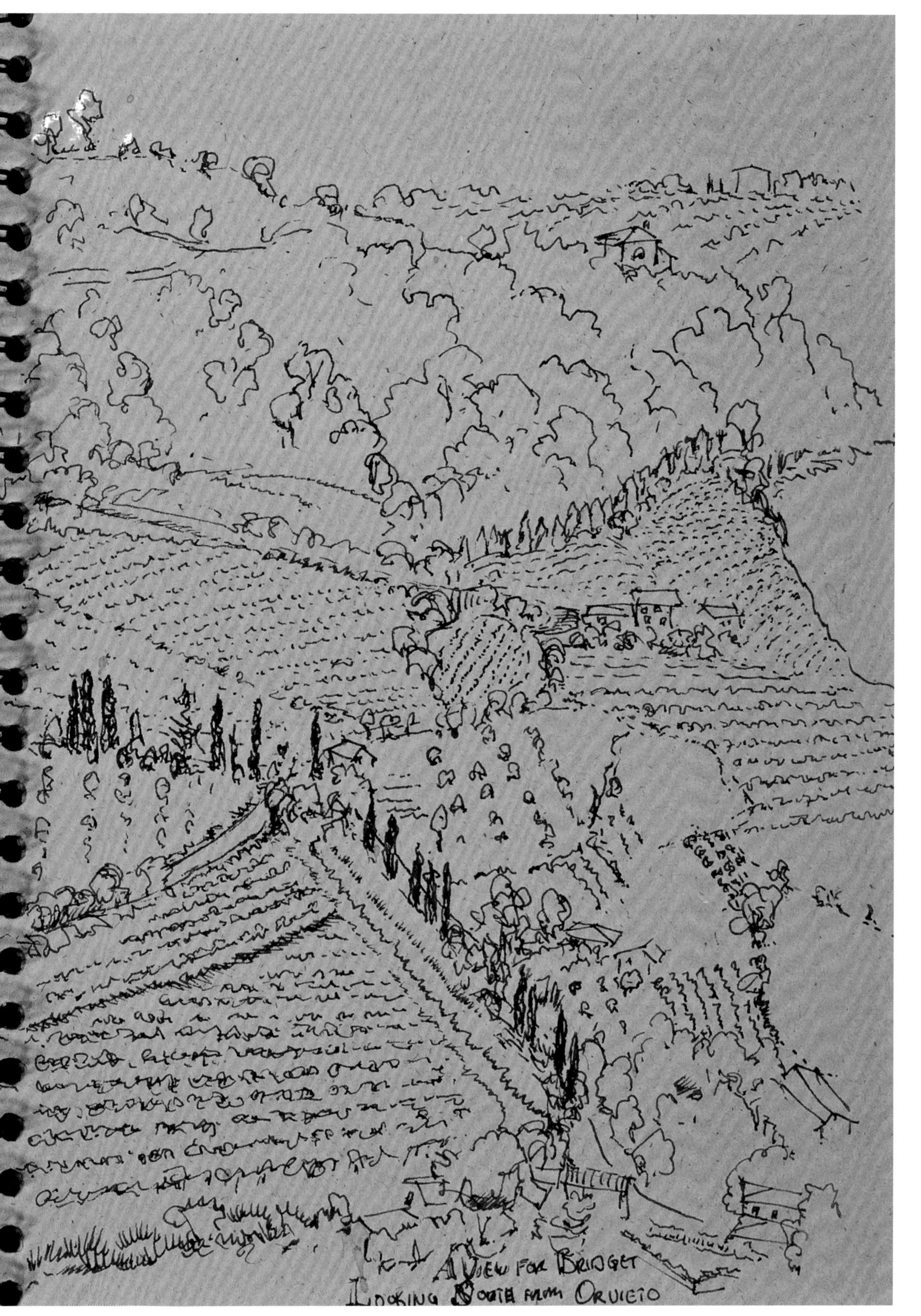

A View For Bridget
Looking South from Orvieto

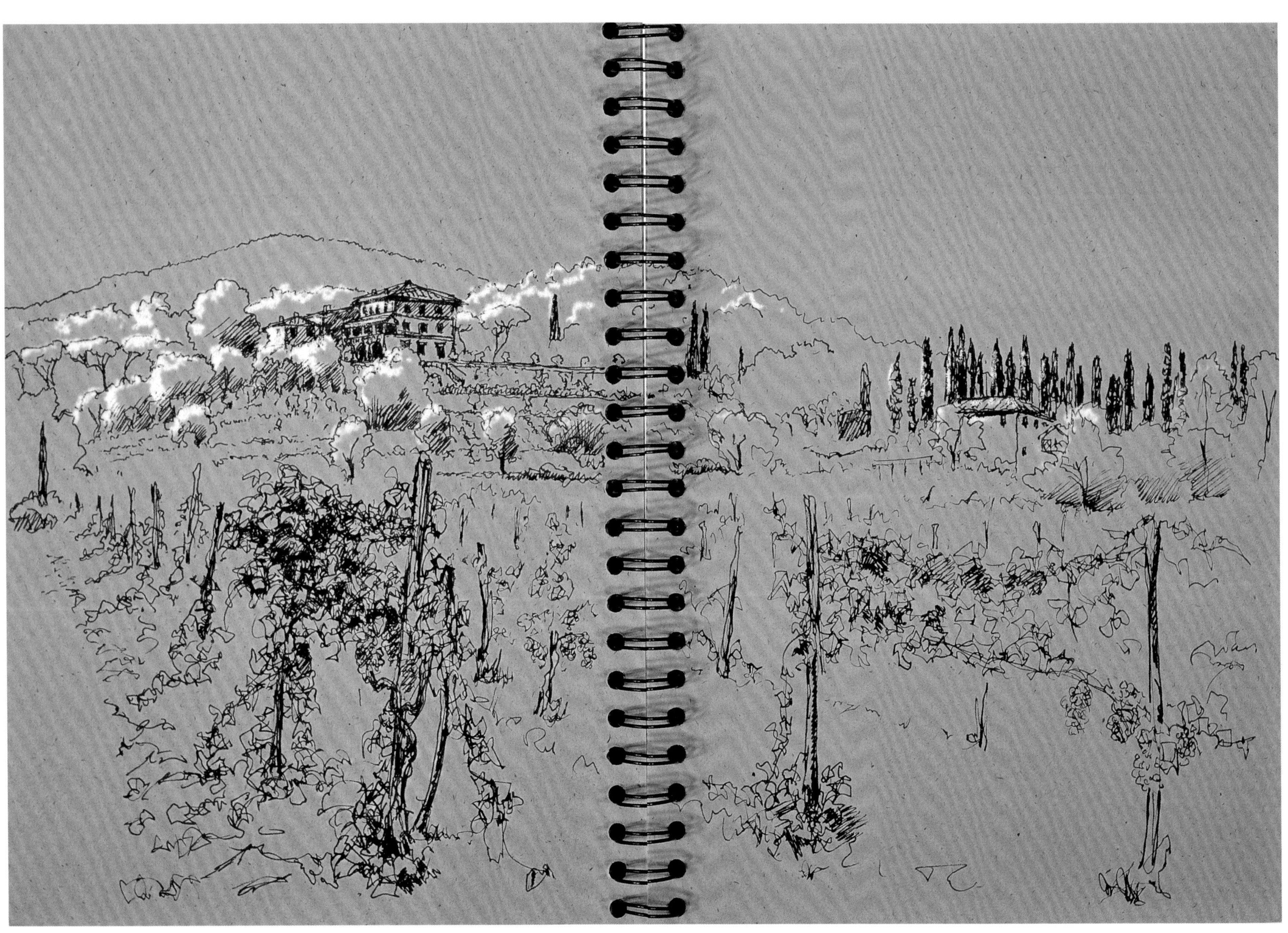

IL PALAGIO, 1998

Ink and chalk on wheat paper, 12 x 17½ inches (31 x 45 cm). Collection of the Artist

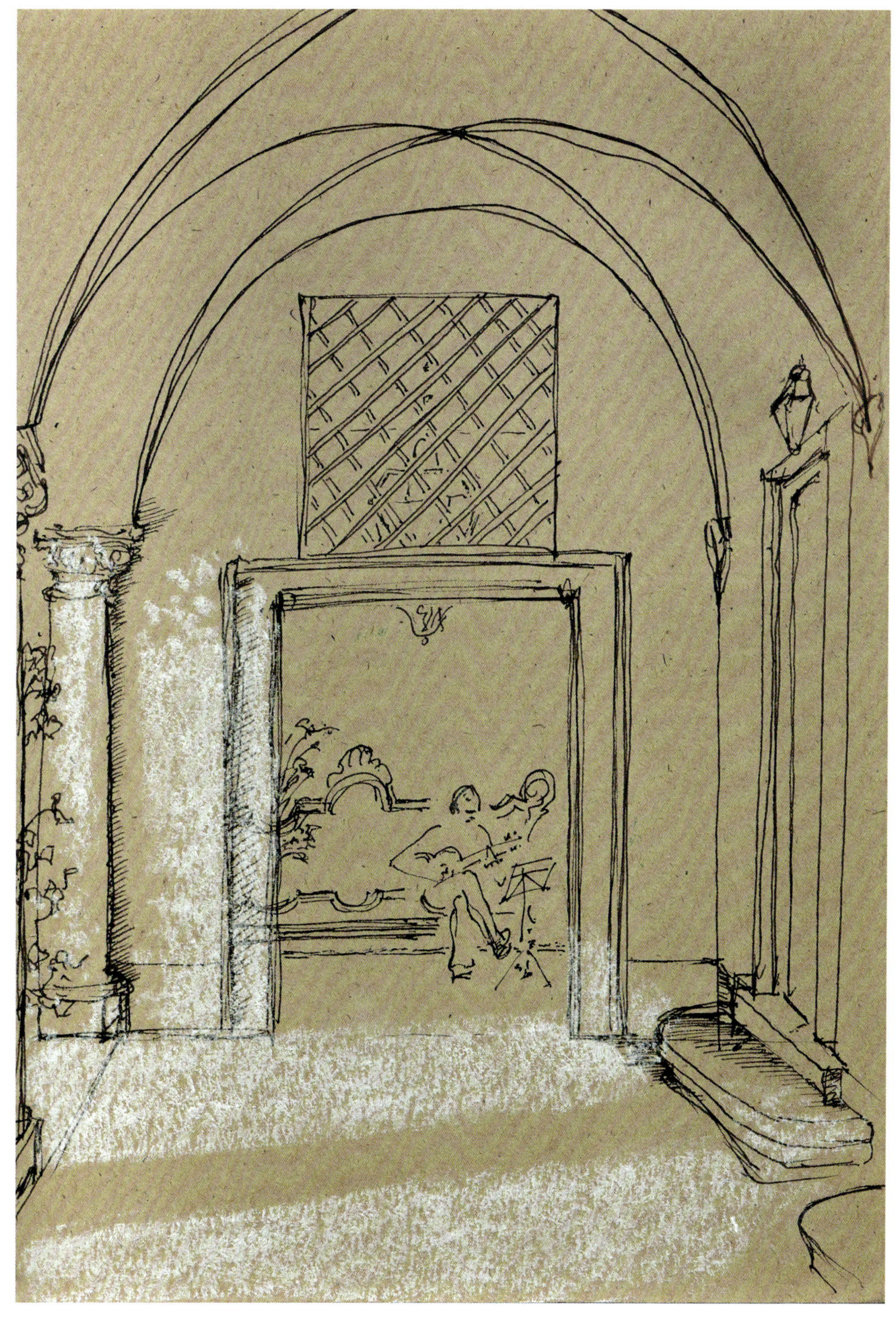

BACH FUGUES IN THE MORNING, TUSCANY, 2000
Ink on wheat paper, 12 x 8½ inches (31 x 22 cm). Collection of the Artist

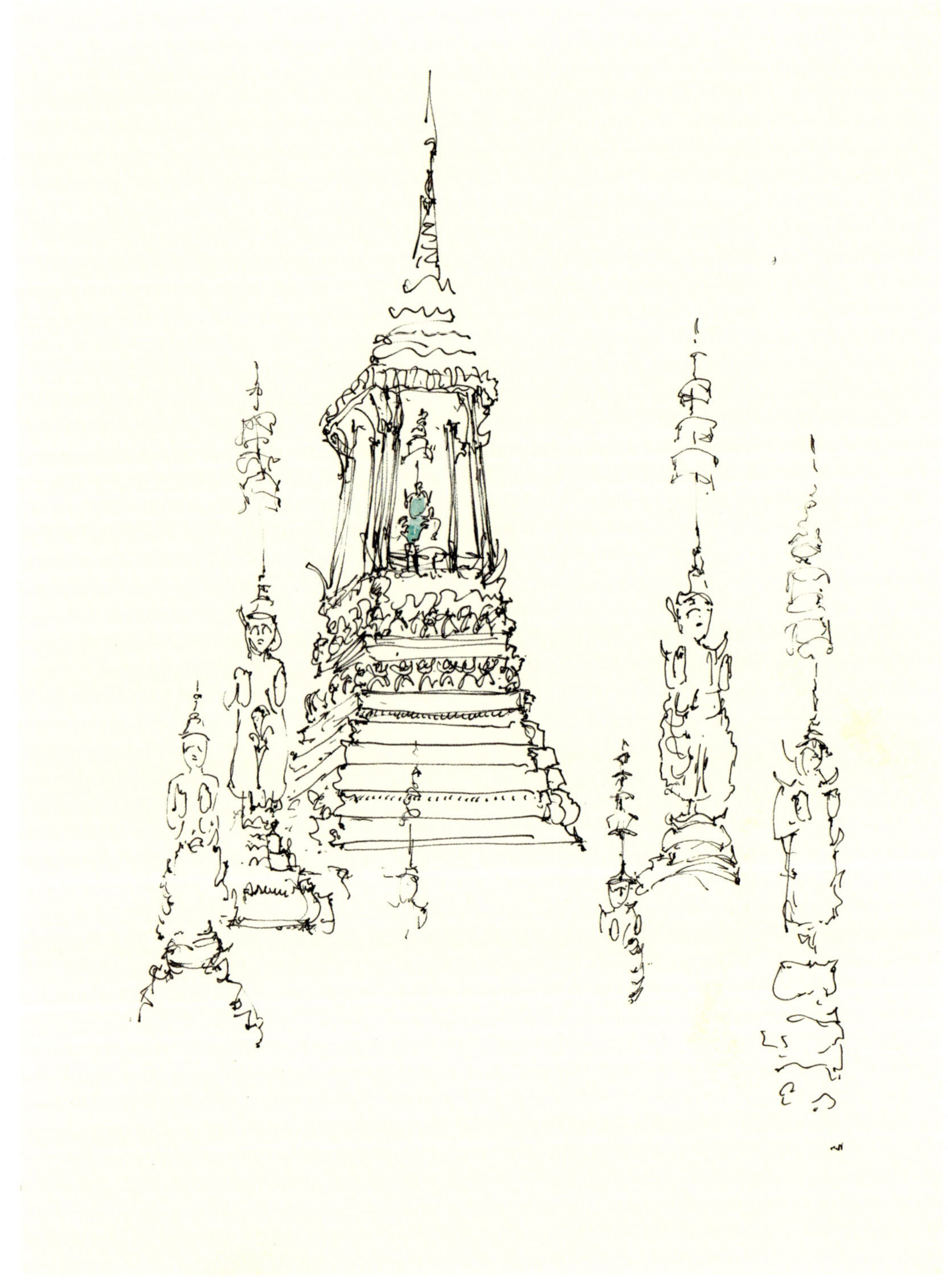

Emerald Buddha, Bangkok, 1987

Ink and watercolor on paper, 12 x 9 inches (31 x 23 cm). Collection of the Artist

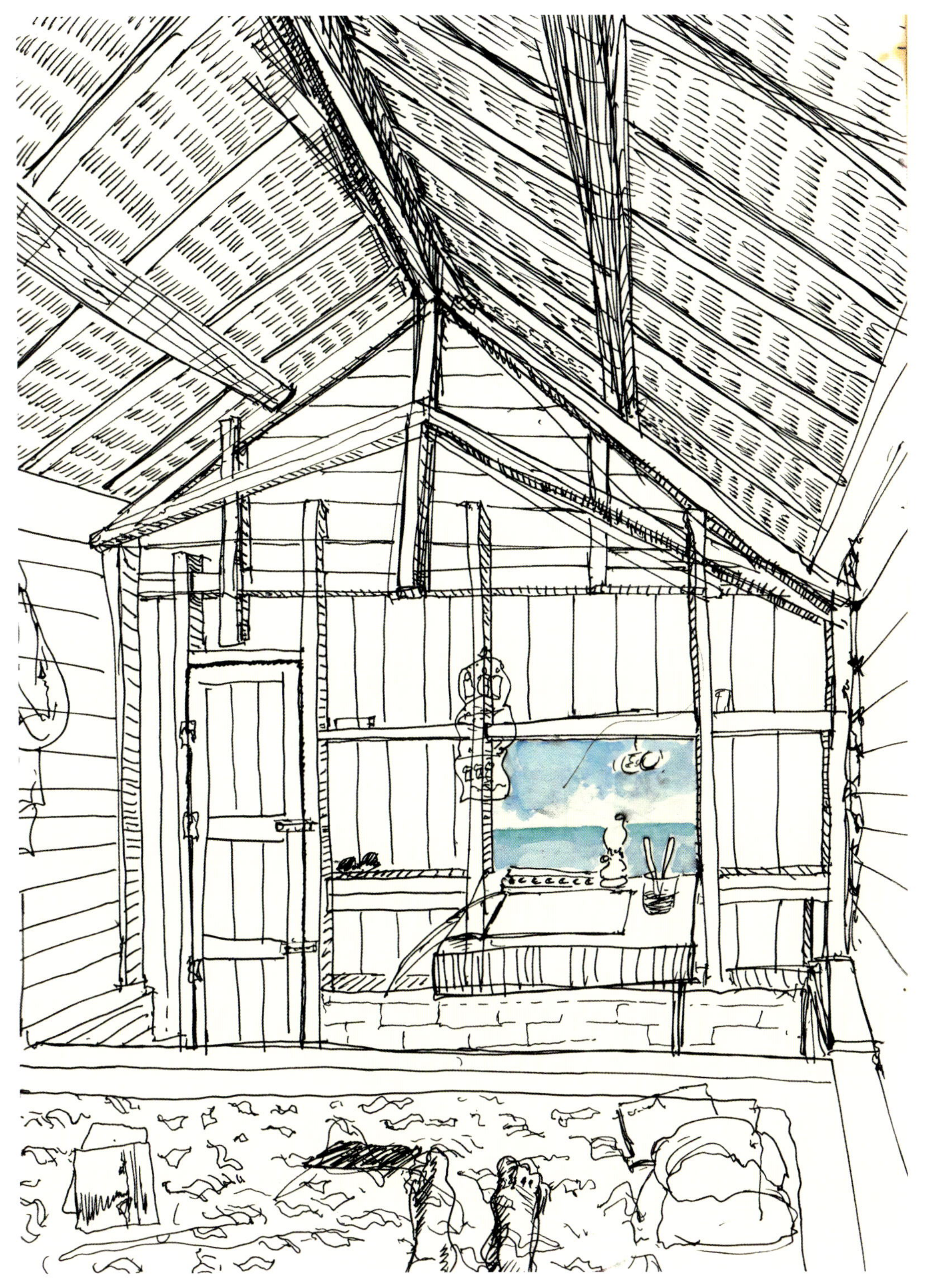

Bungalow on the Gulf of Siam, 1987
Ink and watercolor on paper, 12 x 9 inches (31 x 23 cm). Collection of the Artist

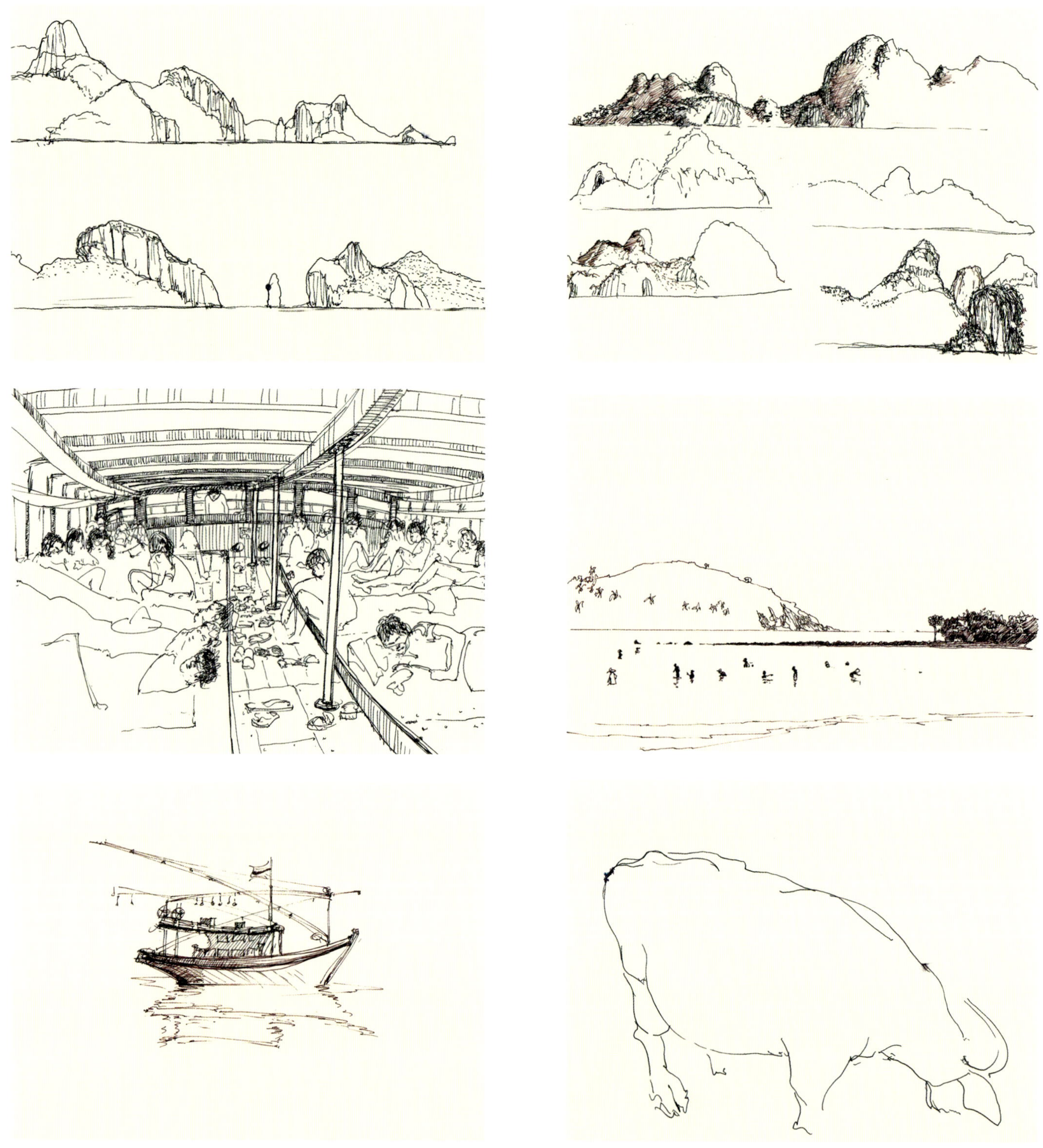

UNTITLED DRAWINGS FROM THAI SKETCHBOOK, 1987

INK ON PAPER, EACH 9 X 12 INCHES (23 X 31 CM). COLLECTION OF THE ARTIST

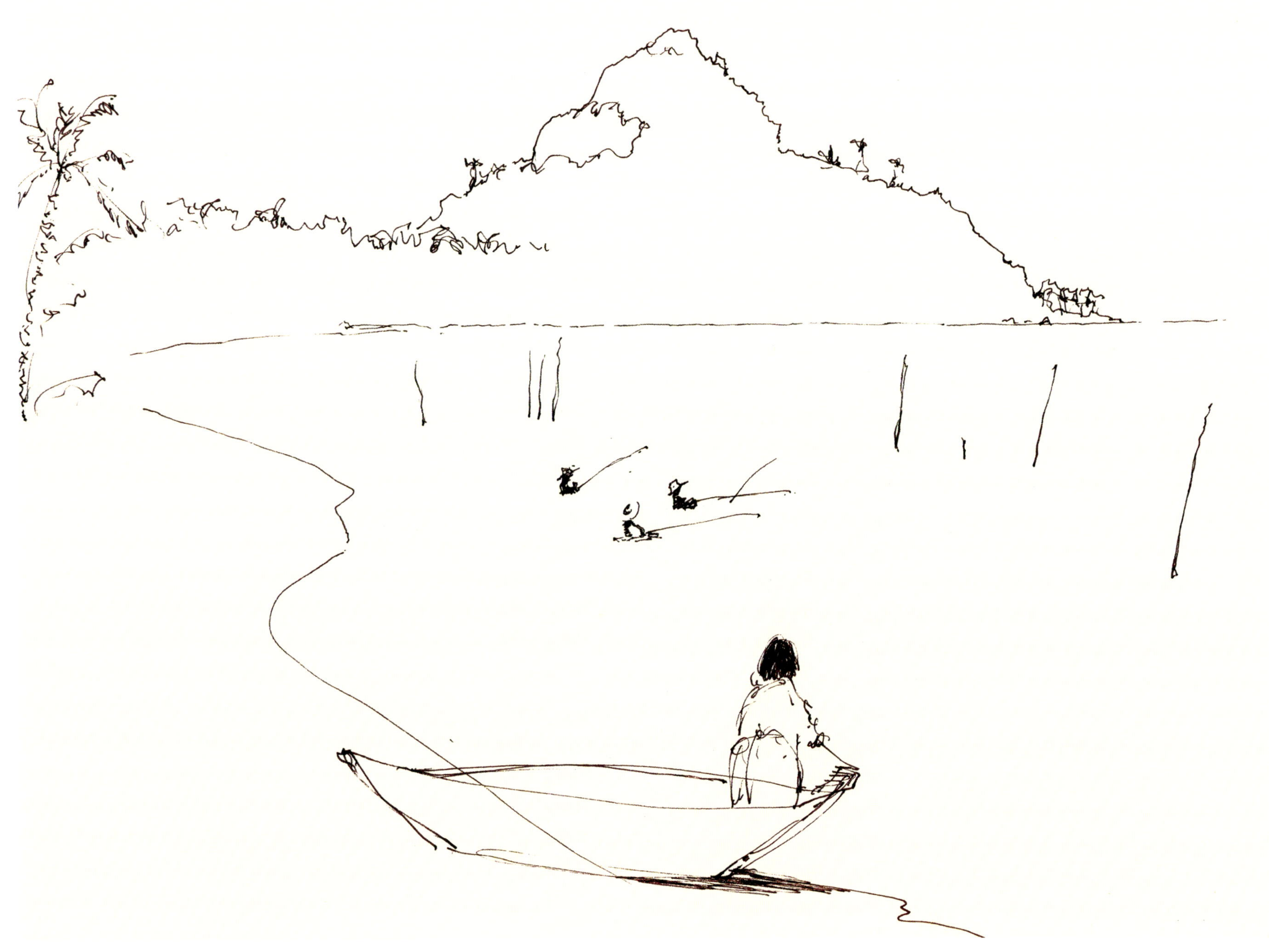

Fishing Cove on the Gulf of Siam, 1987
Ink on paper, 9 x 12 inches (23 x 31 cm). Collection of the Artist

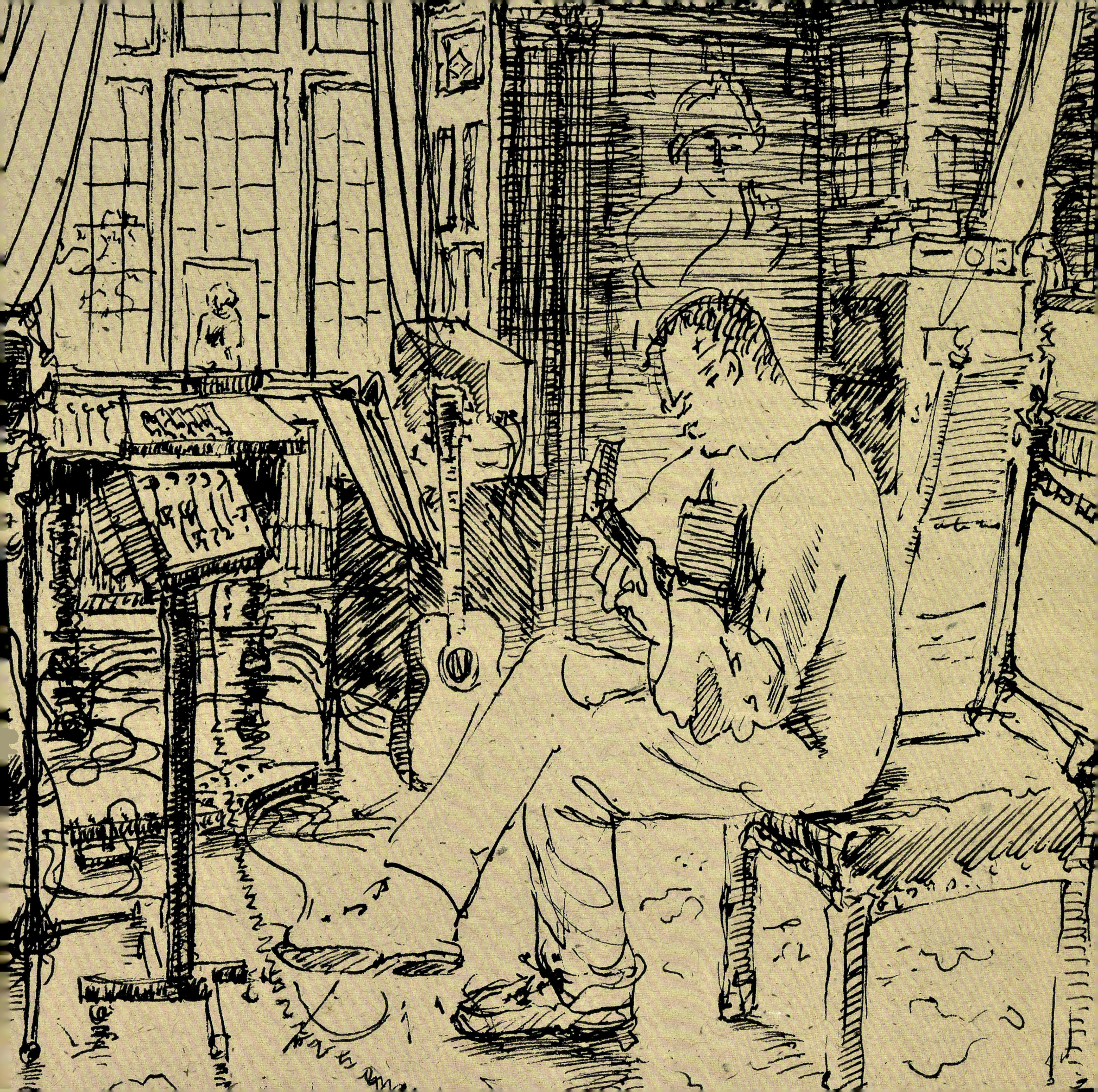

Figures and Friends

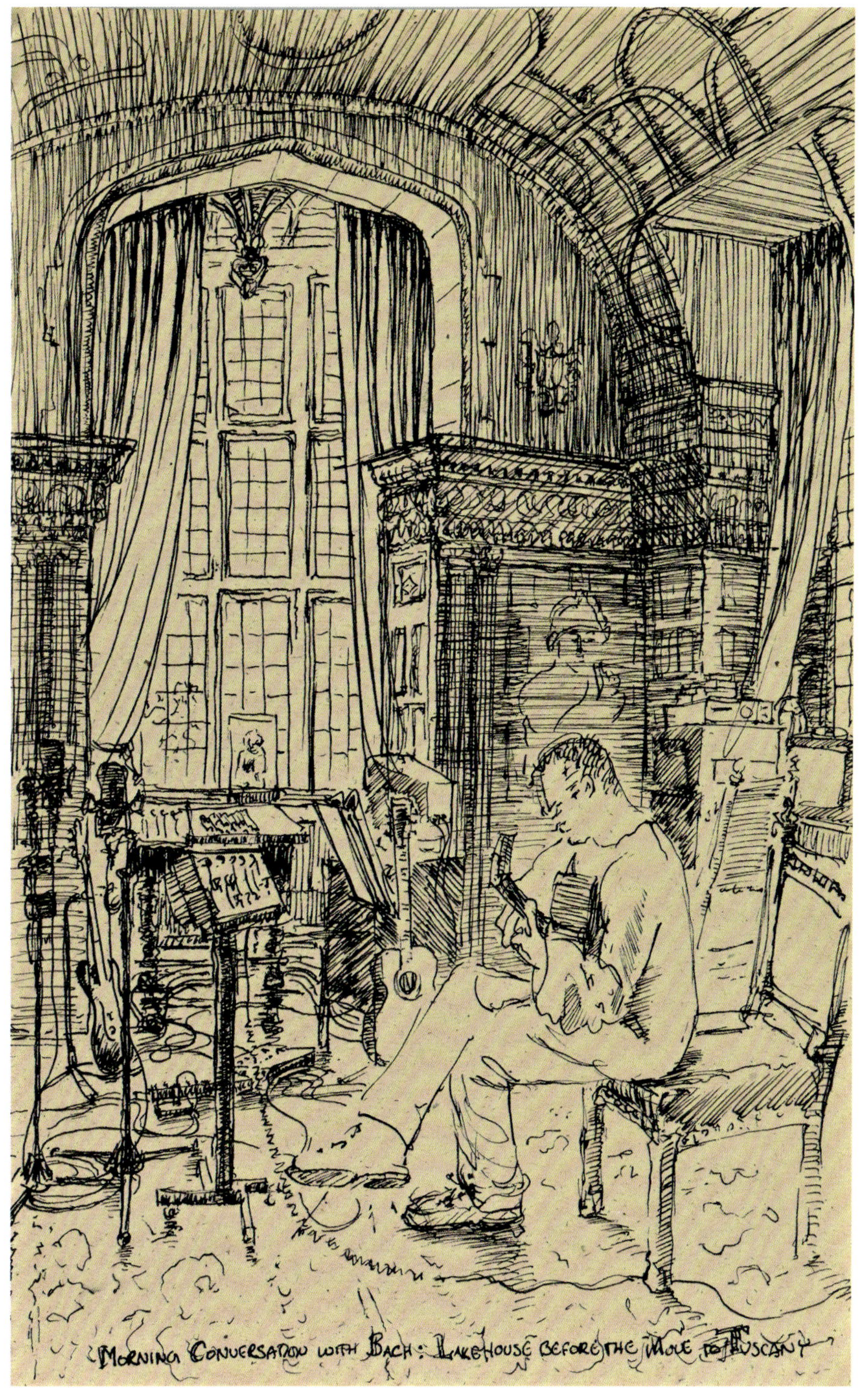

Morning Conversation with Bach, Lake House, 1998

Ink on wheat paper, 12 x 8½ inches (31 x 22 cm). Collection of the Artist

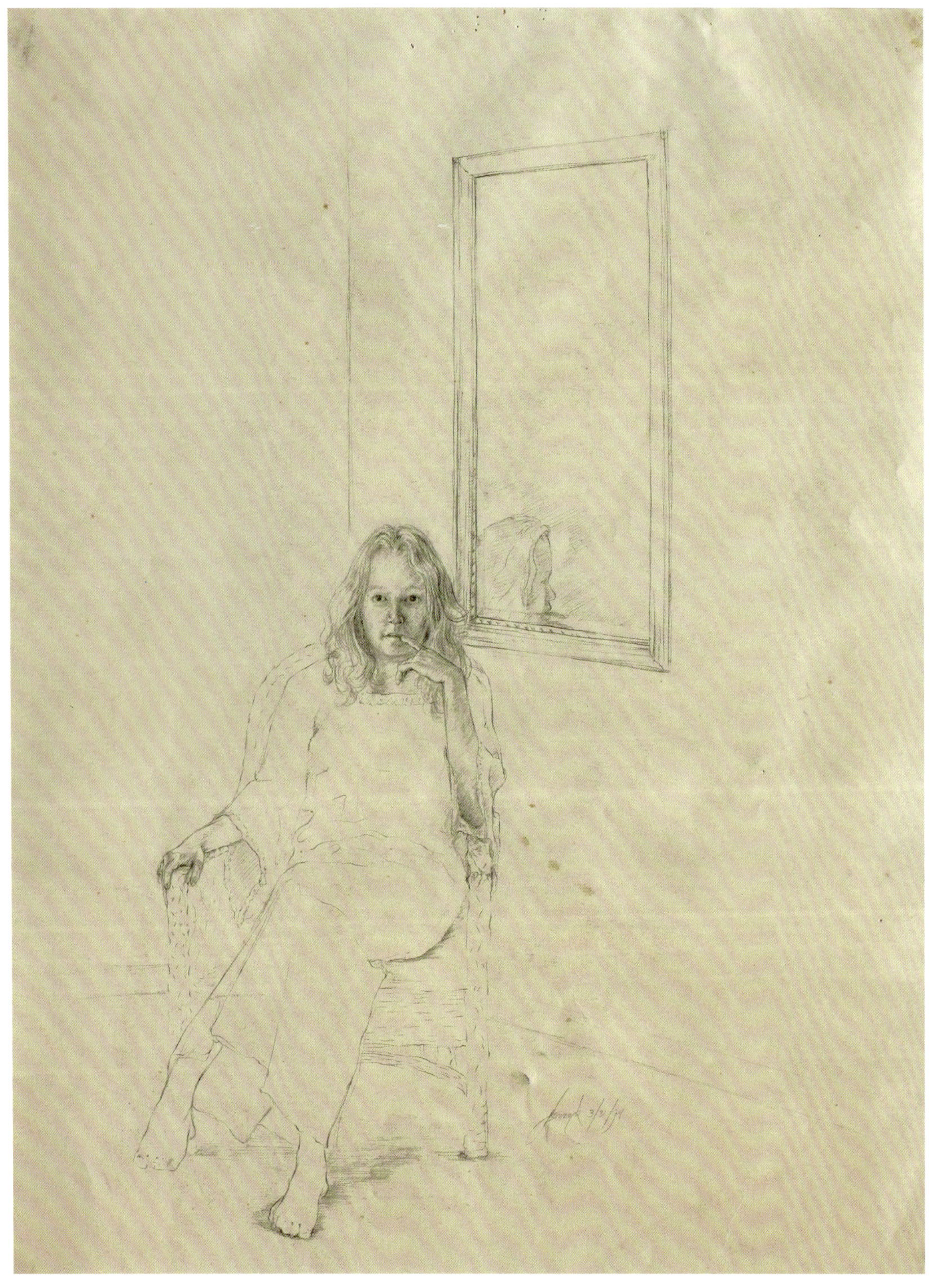

LAURIE, 1973

PENCIL ON PAPER, 23 X 18 INCHES (58 X 46 CM). COLLECTION OF THE ARTIST

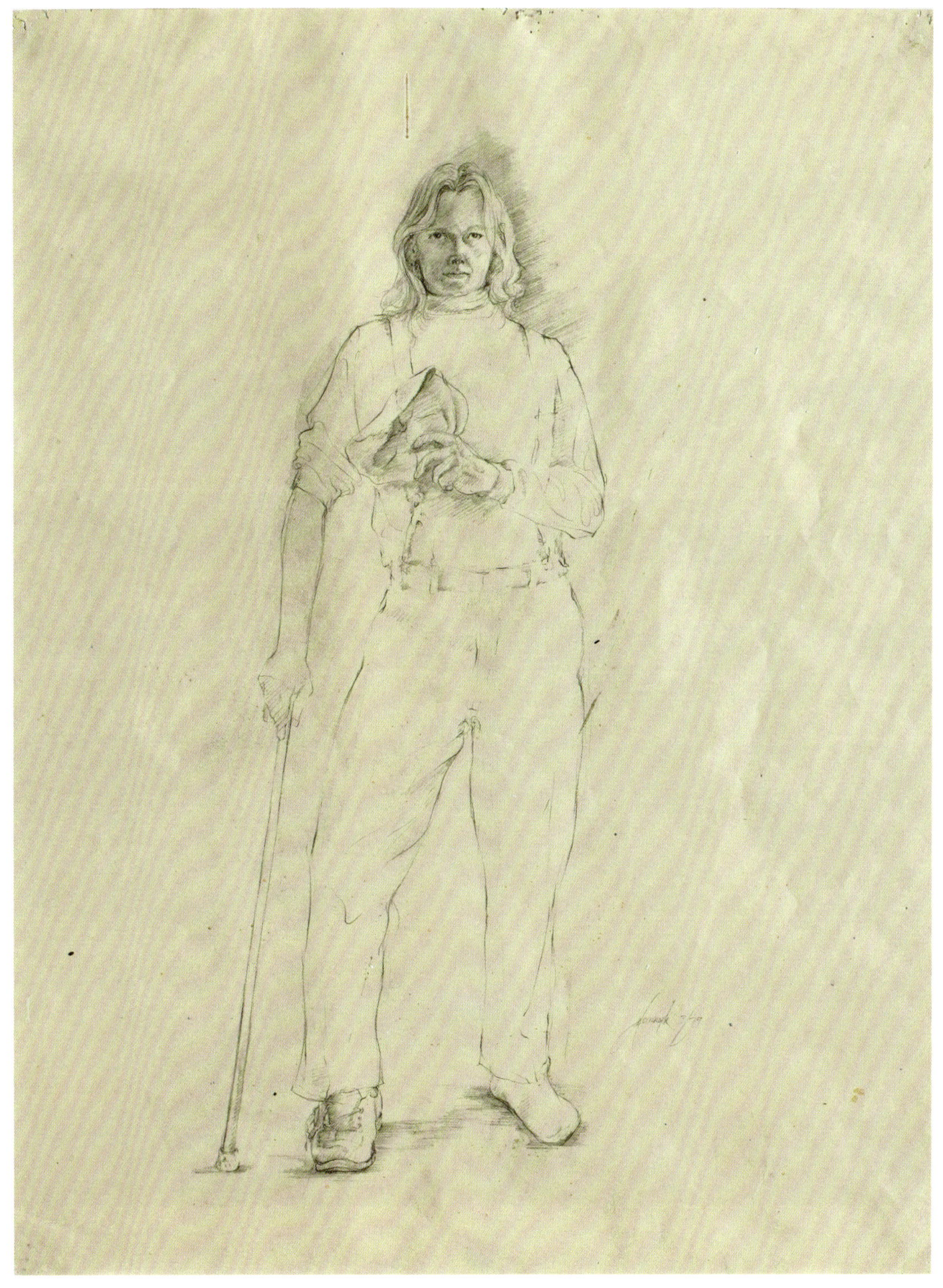

Buz, 1973

Pencil on paper, 23 x 18 inches (58 x 46 cm). Collection of the Artist

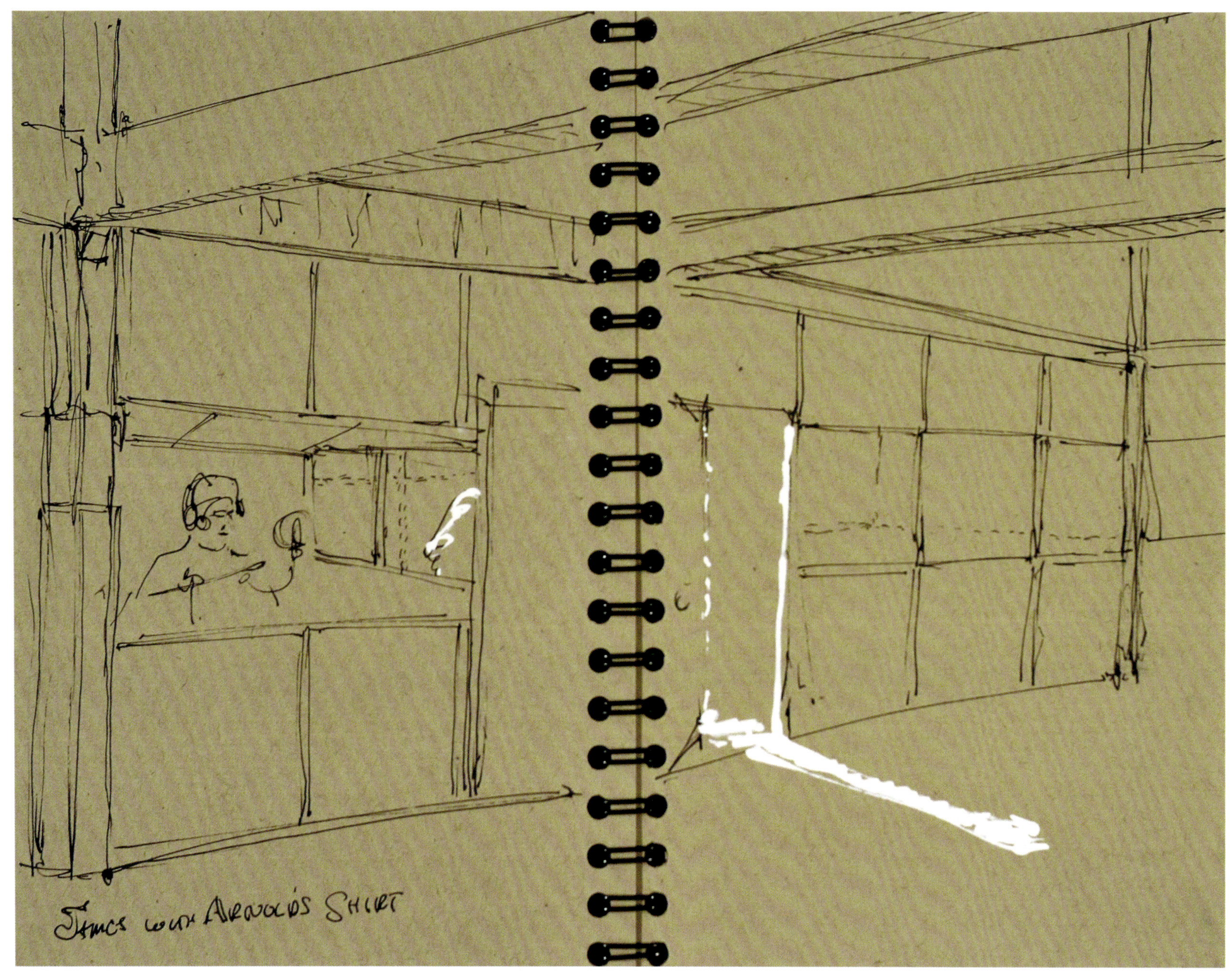

James with Arnold's Shirt, 2008

Ink and Wite-Out® on wheat paper, 12 x 17½ inches (31 x 45 cm). Collection of the Artist

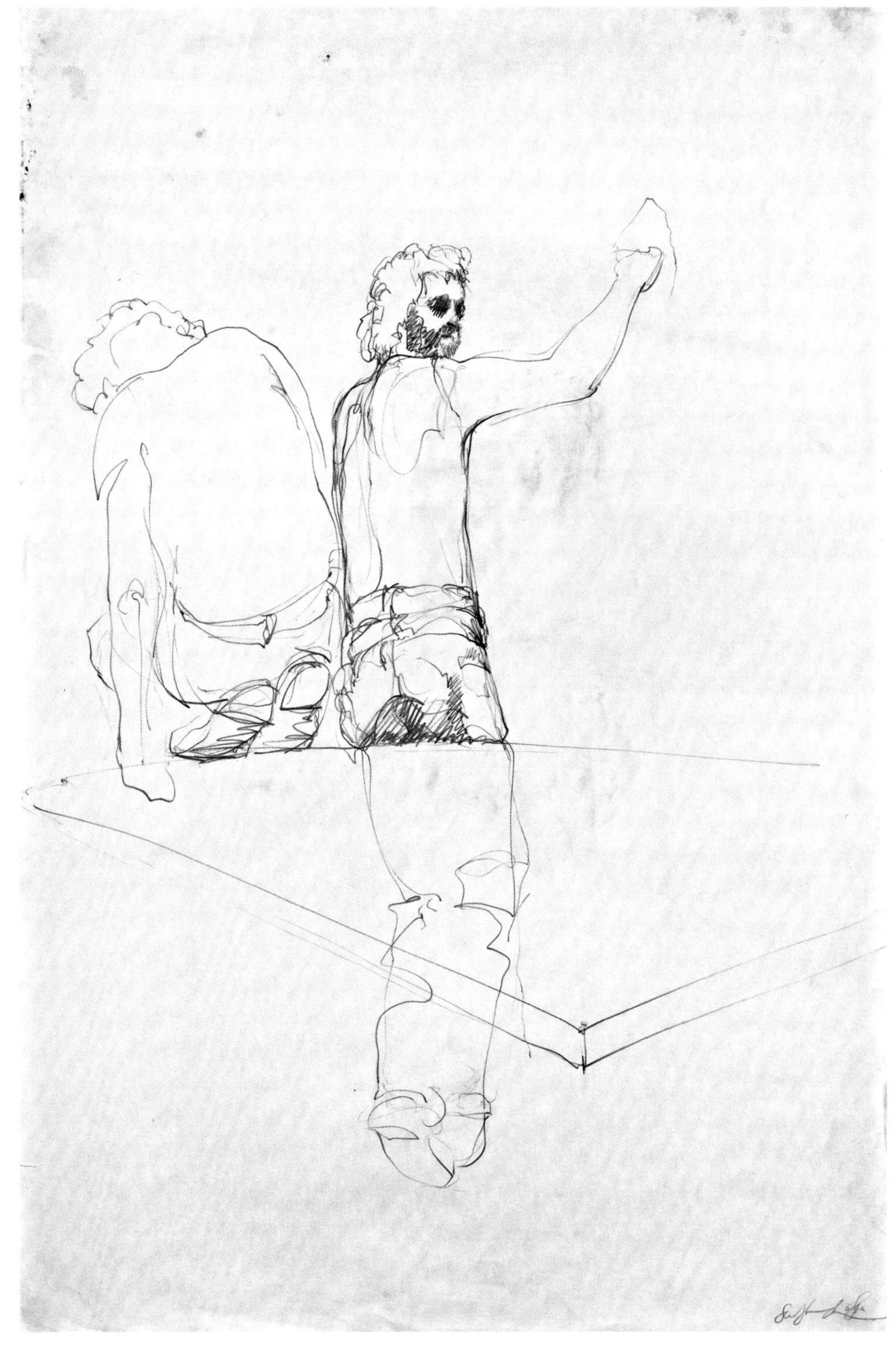

Paul Putting in the New Window at Jake's, 1981
Pencil on paper, 35½ x 24 inches (90 x 61 cm). Collection of the Artist

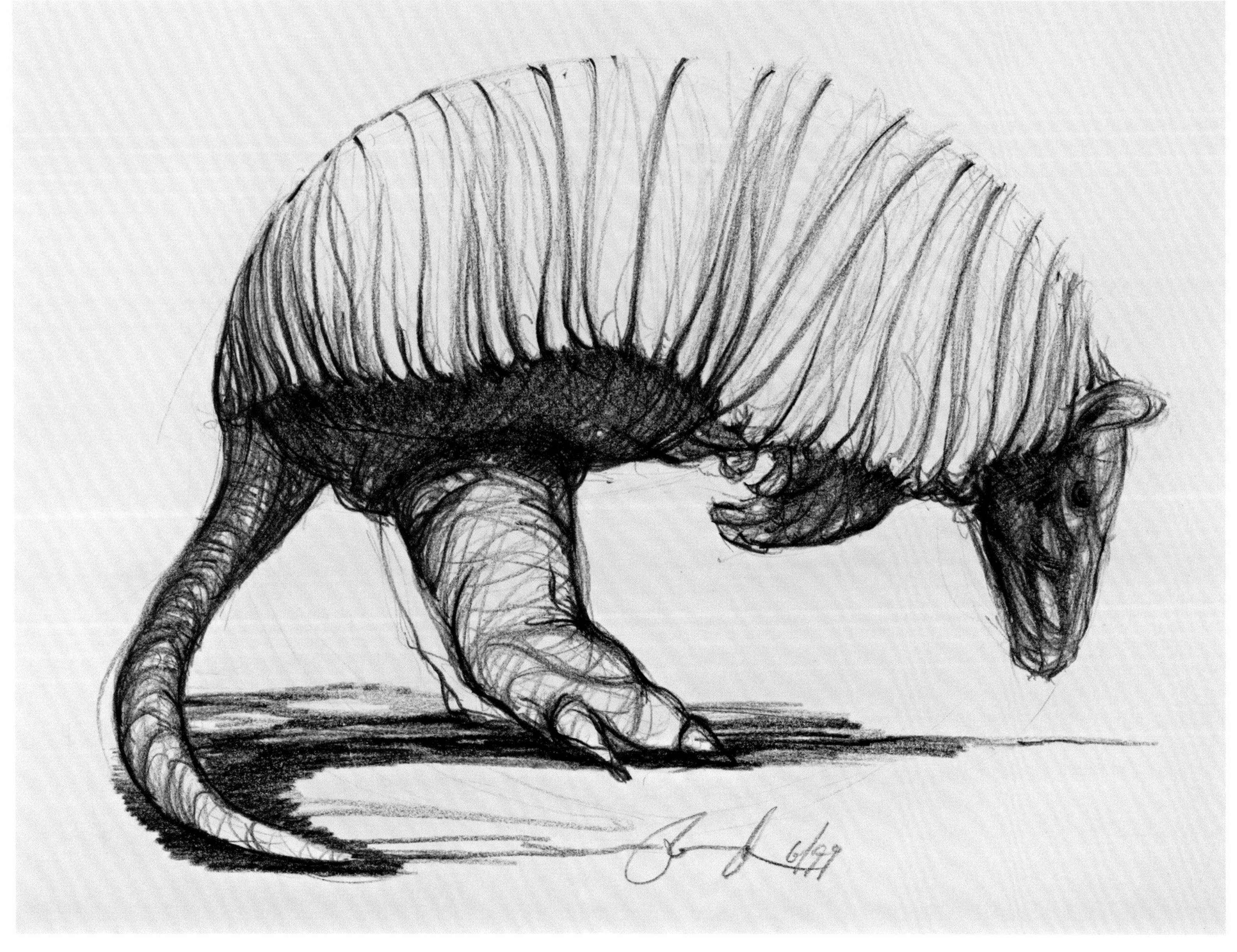

Armadillo, 1979

Grease pencil on paper, 18 x 23 inches (46 x 58 cm). Private Collection

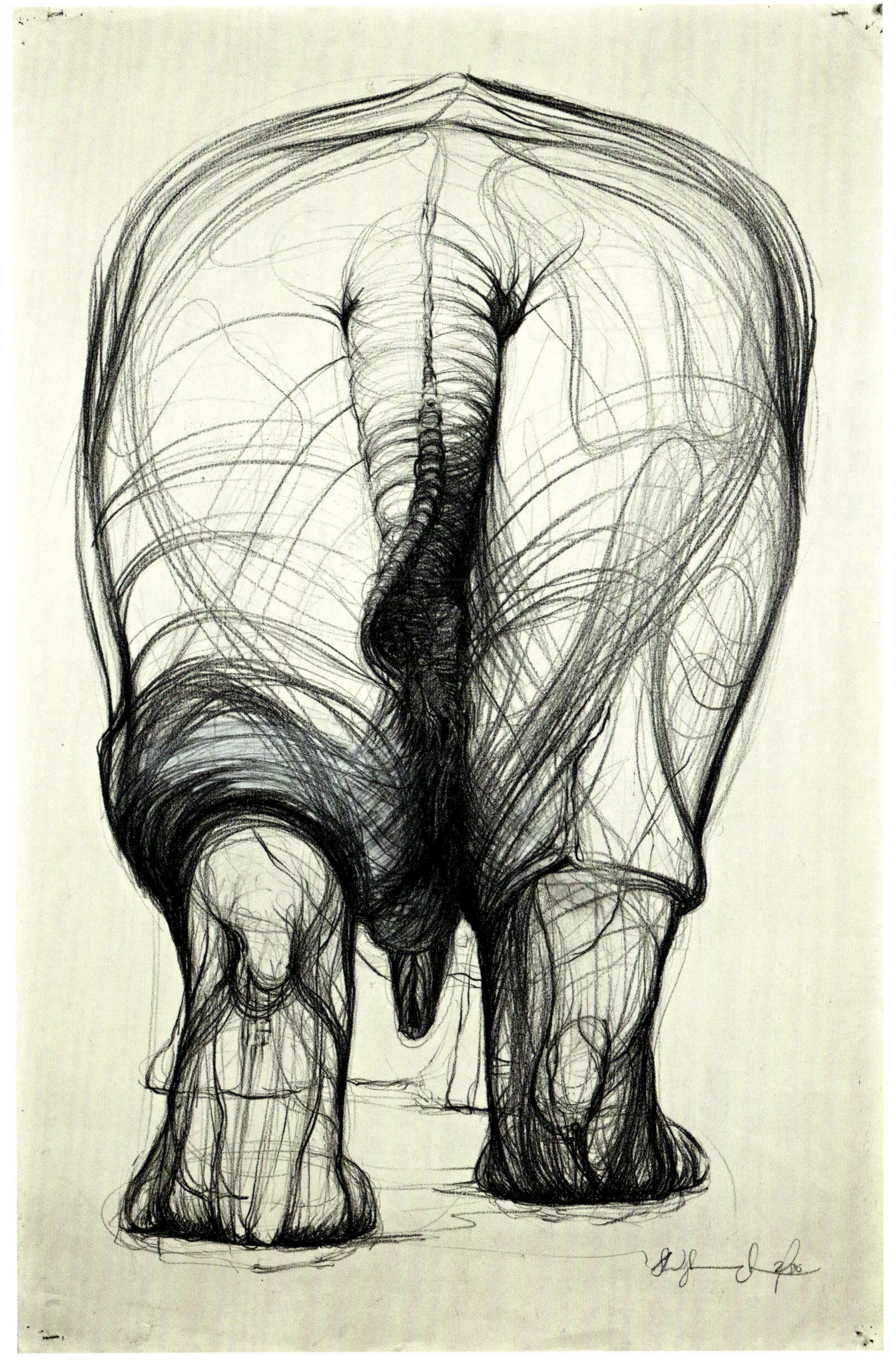

GREAT HIPPO, 1980

GREASE PENCIL ON PAPER, 40 X 26½ INCHES (102 X 67 CM). COLLECTION OF THE ARTIST

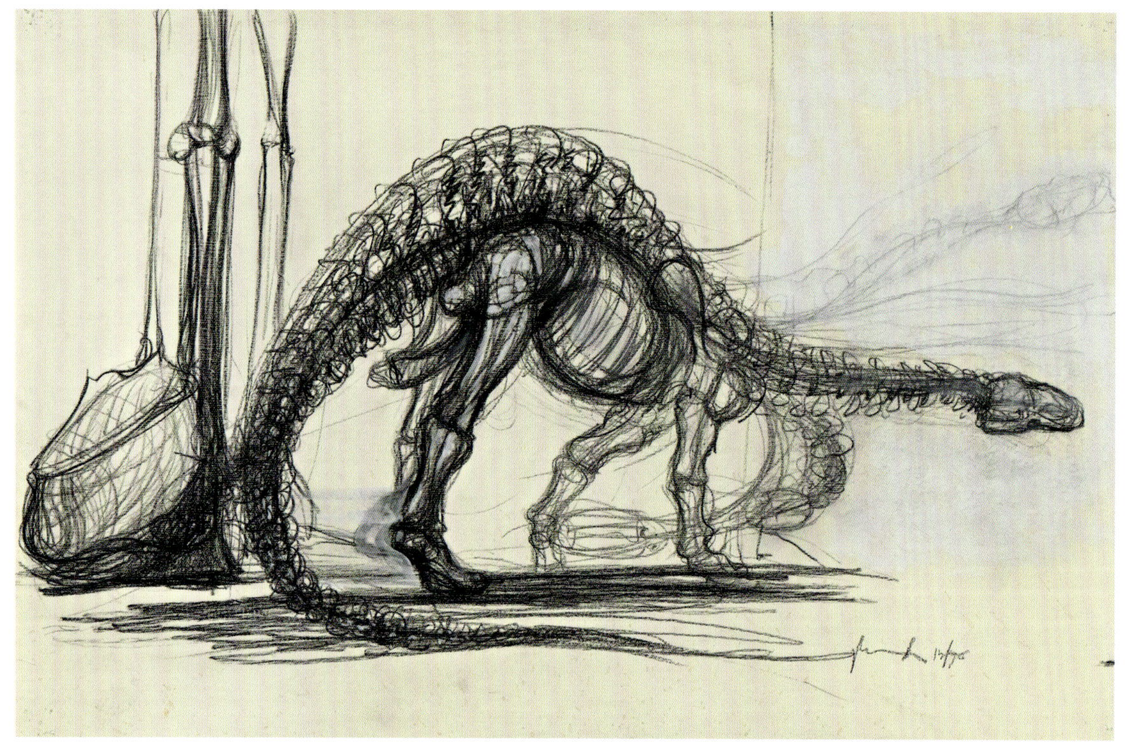

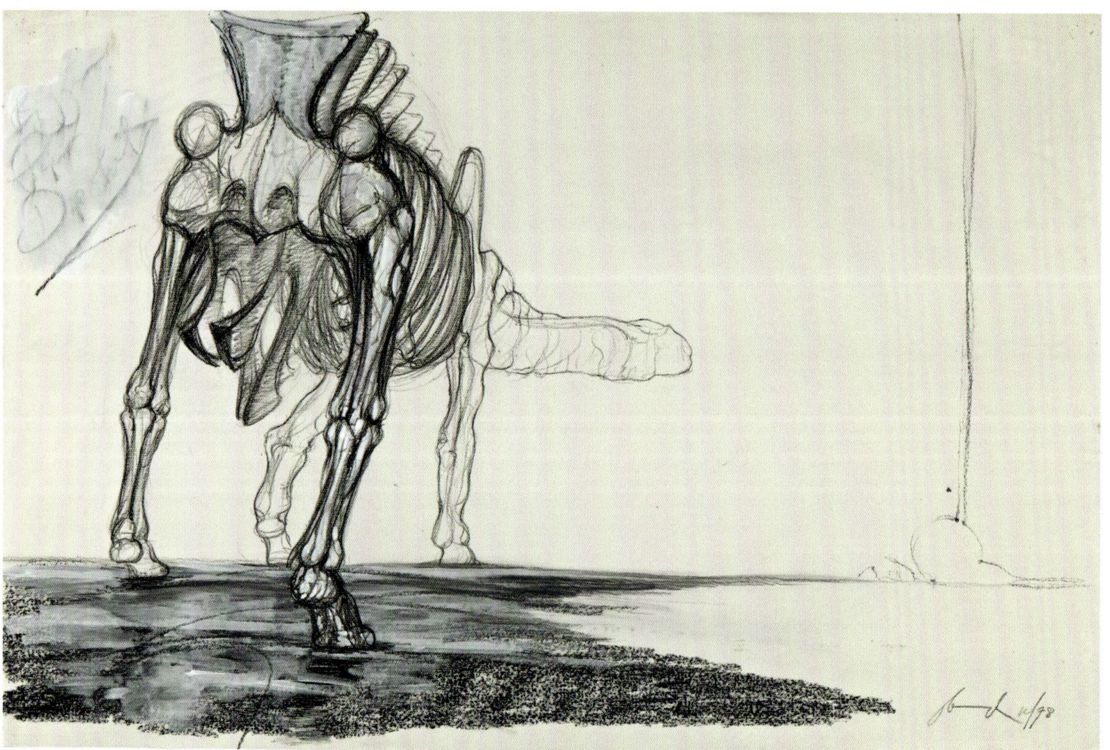

(top) Dinosaur Model from the Side, 1978
Grease pencil on paper, 22 x 34 inches (56 x 86 cm). Collection of the Artist

(bottom) Dinosaur Model from the Rear, 1978
Grease pencil on paper, 22 x 34 inches (56 x 86 cm). Collection of the Artist

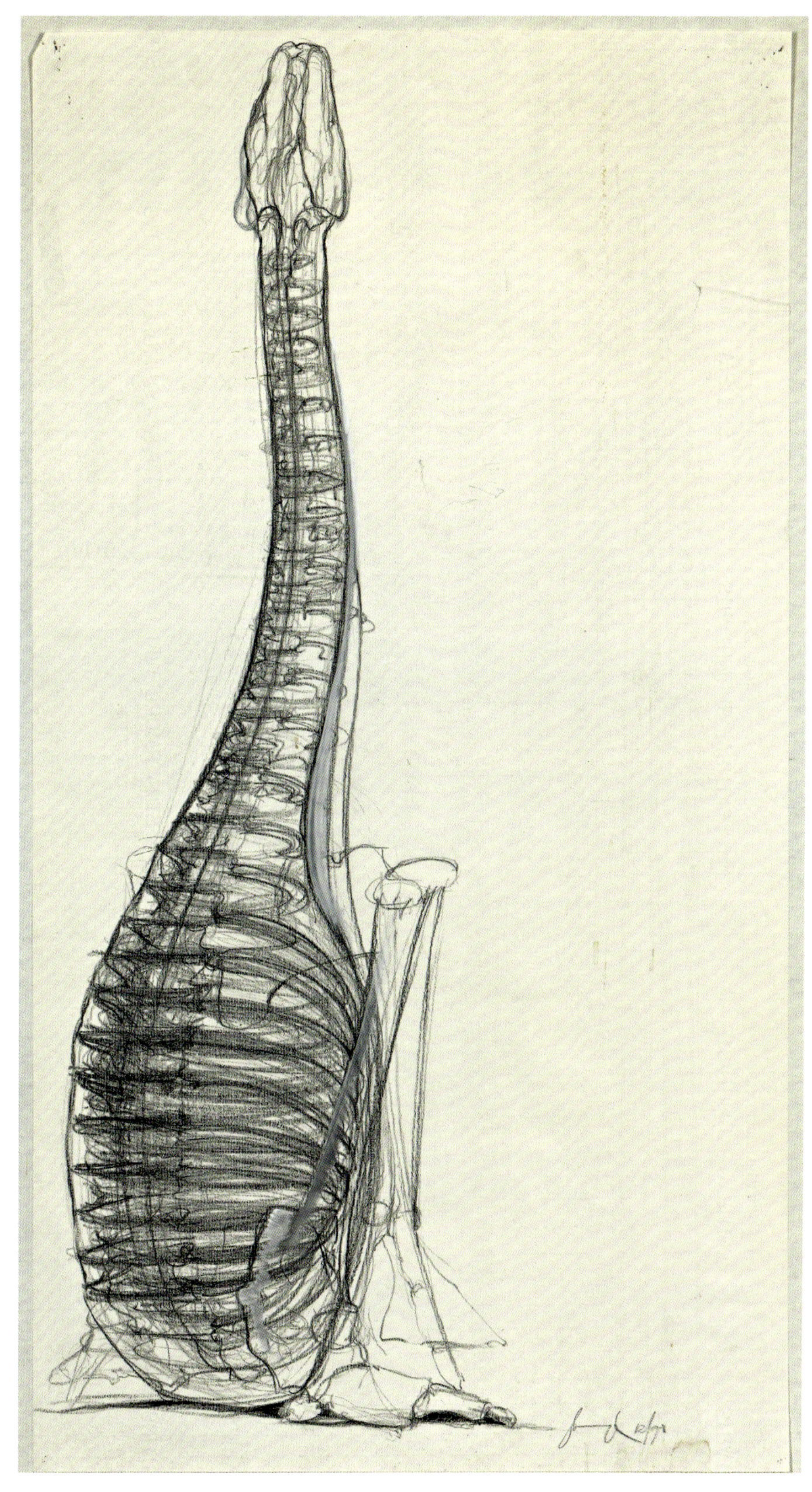

Dinosaur Model on End with Invented Feet, 1978
Grease pencil on paper, 34 x 22 inches (86 x 56 cm). Collection of the Artist

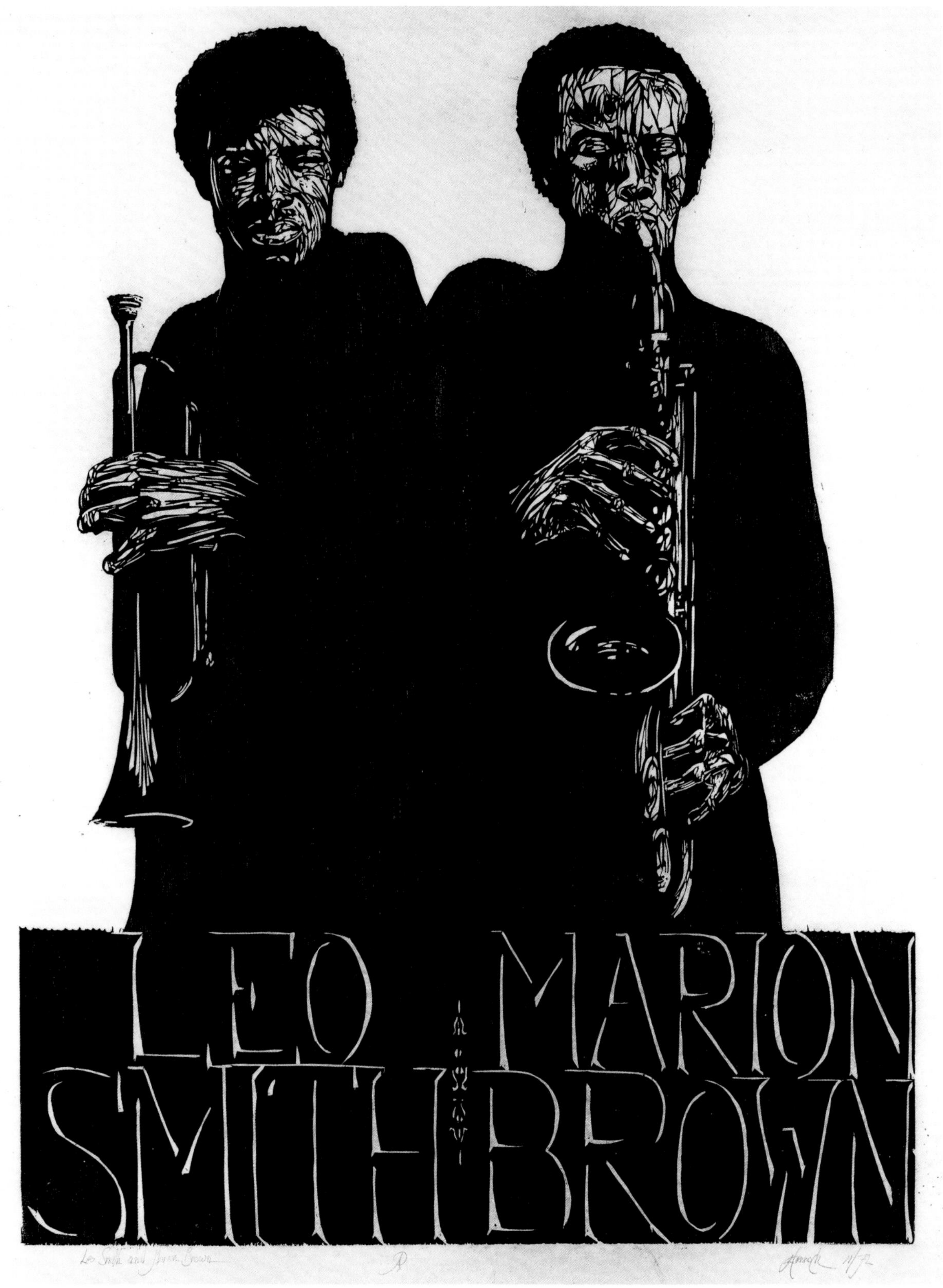

Leo Smith and Marion Brown, 1972

Woodcut, 31 x 24 inches (79 x 61 cm). Collection of the Artist

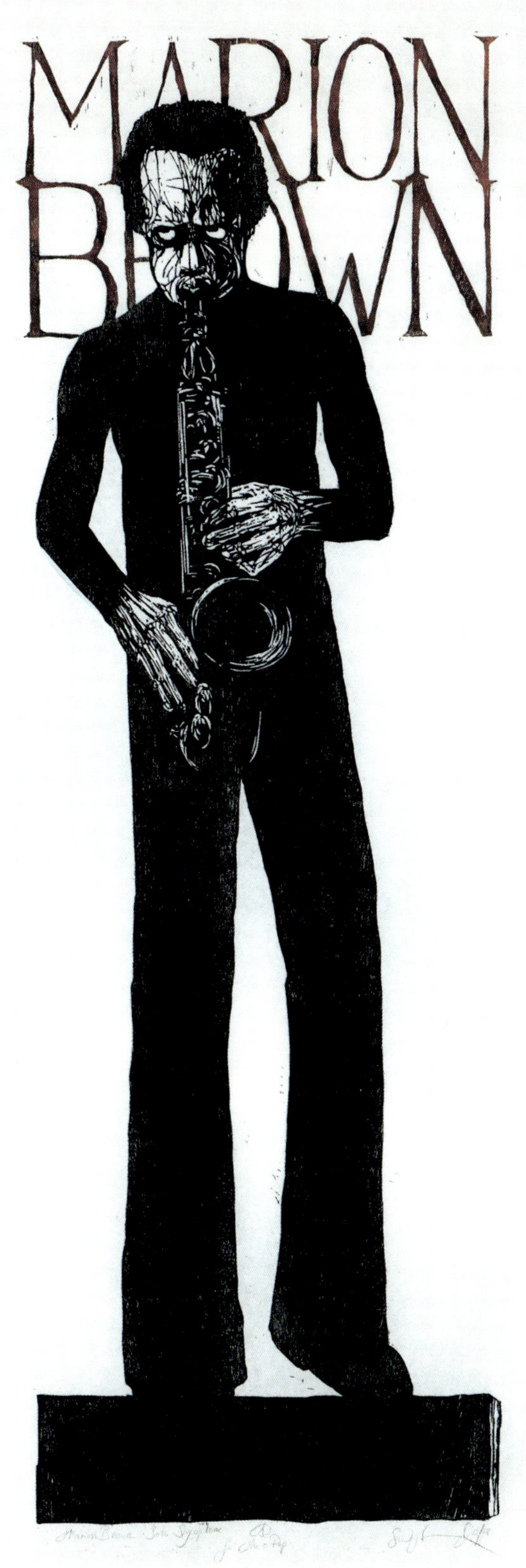

MARION BROWN, 1976

WOODCUT, 55 x 18 INCHES (140 x 46 CM). COLLECTION OF THE ARTIST

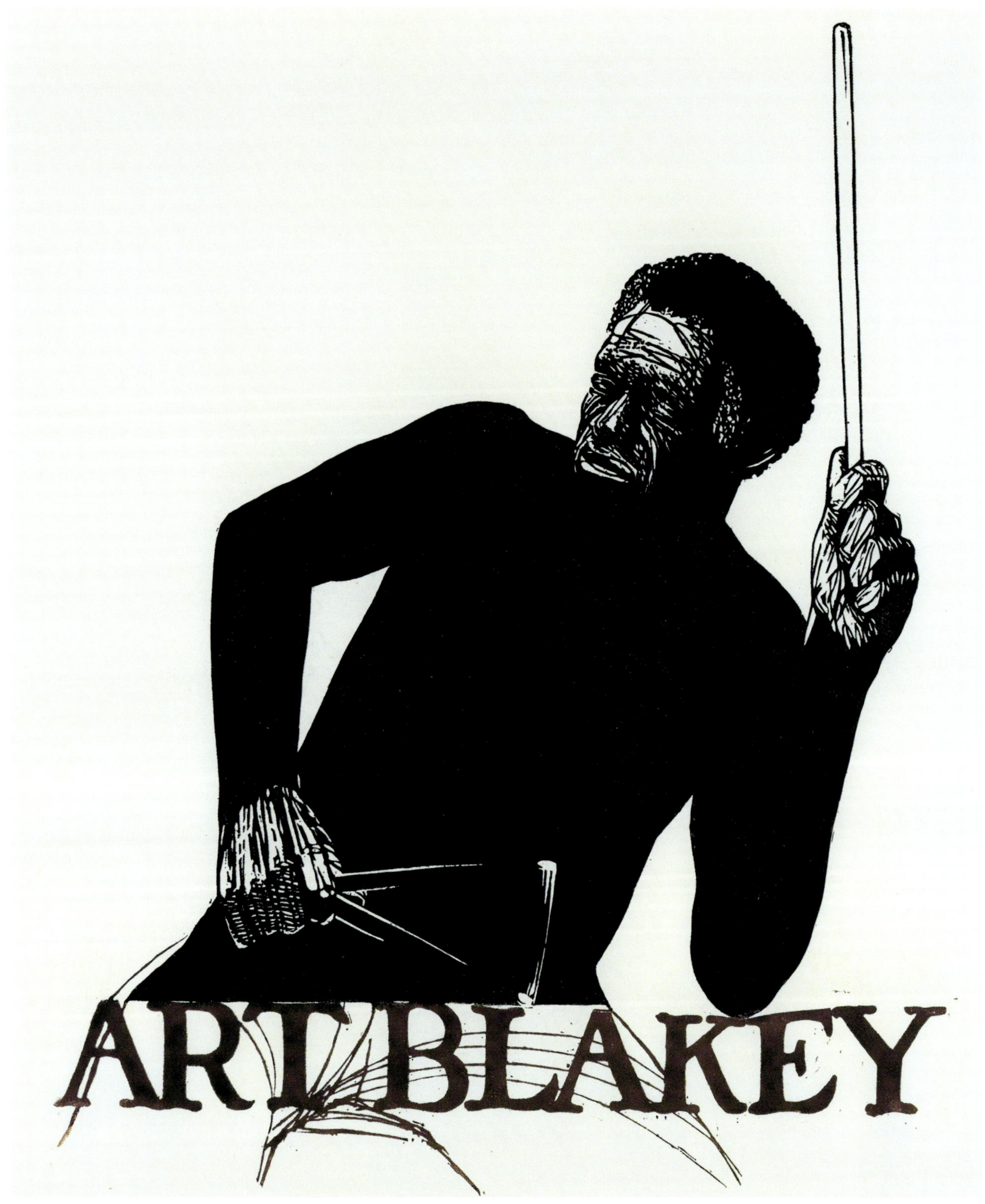

Art Blakey, 1978

Woodcut, 31 x 24 inches (79 x 61 cm). Collection of the Artist

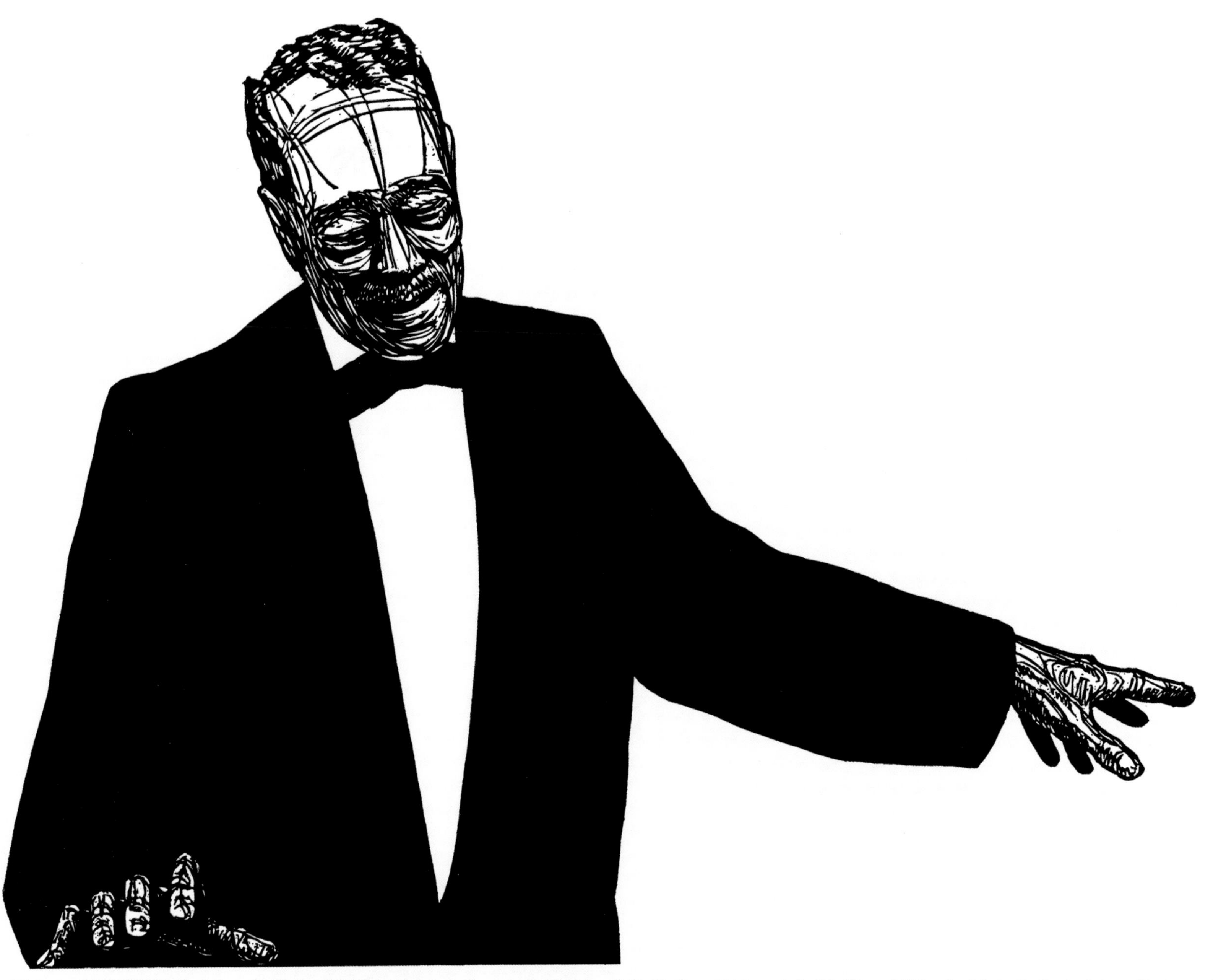

Ellington (poster for Lincoln Center, 1999), 1979
Silkscreen from woodcut, 21 x 29 inches (53 x 74 cm). Collection of the Artist

179

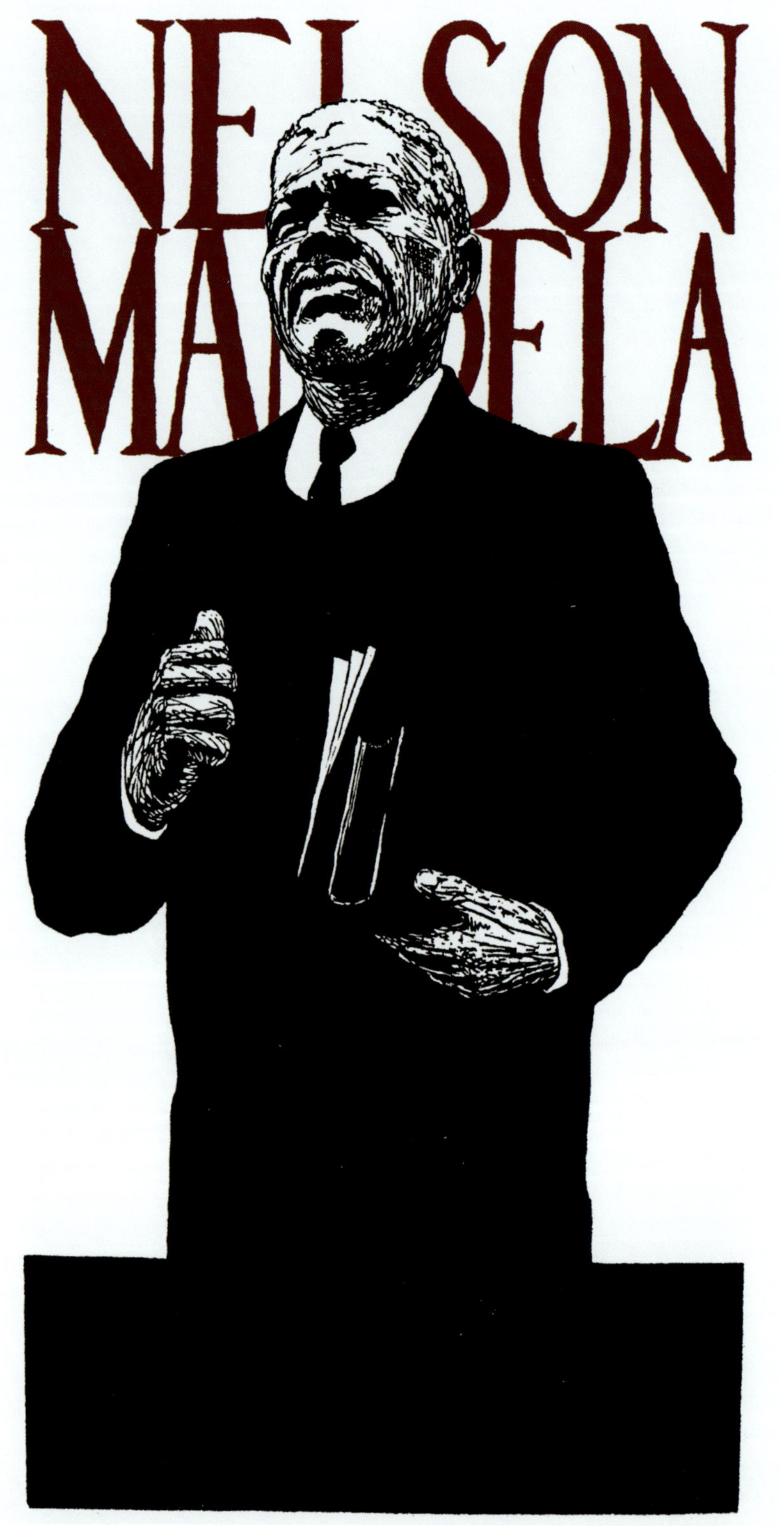

Nelson Mandela, 1989

Woodcut, 48 x 24 inches (122 x 61 cm). Collection of the Artist

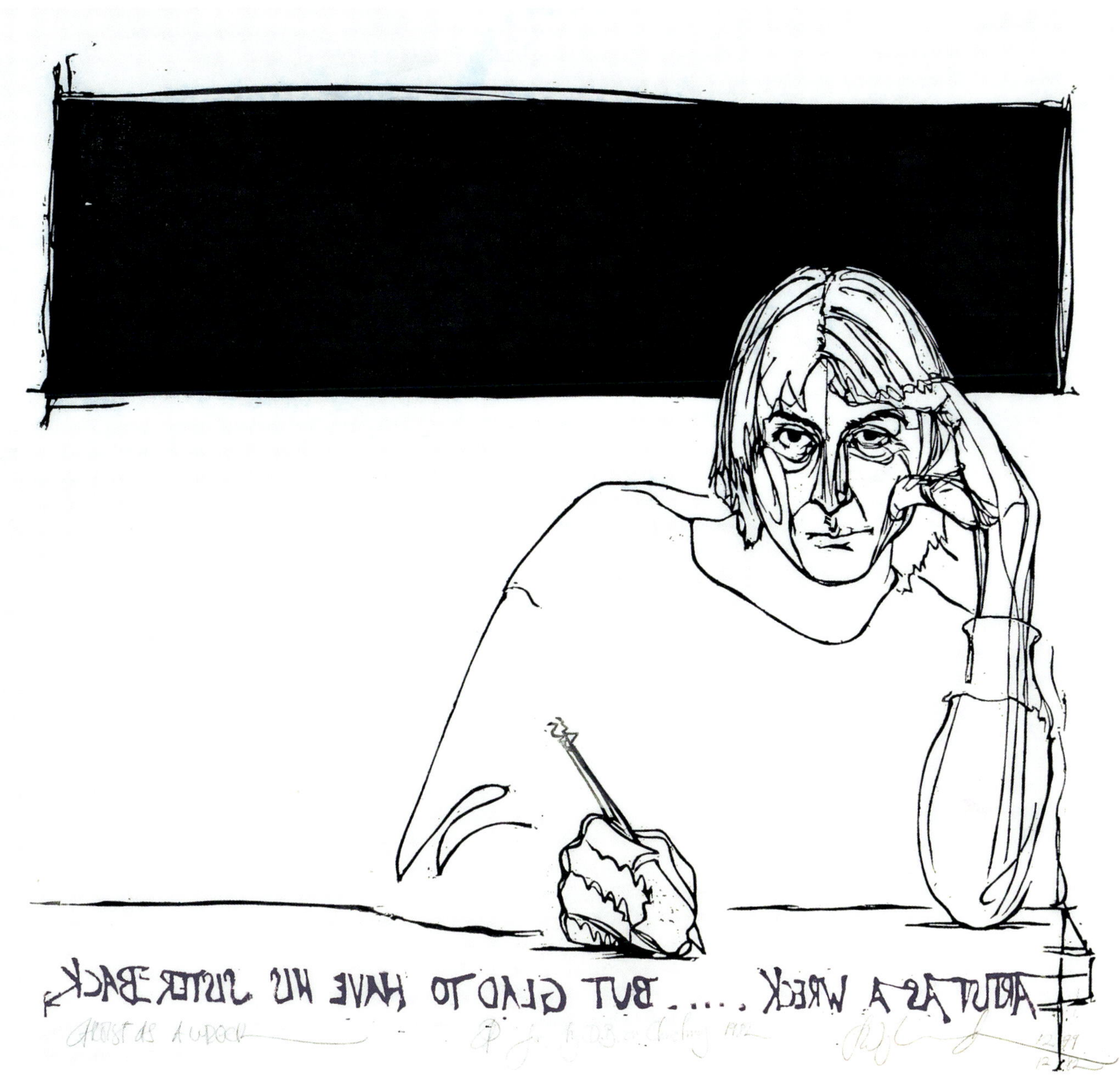

ARTIST AS A WRECK, 1979

WOODCUT, 19 x 20 INCHES (48 x 51 CM). COLLECTION OF THE ARTIST

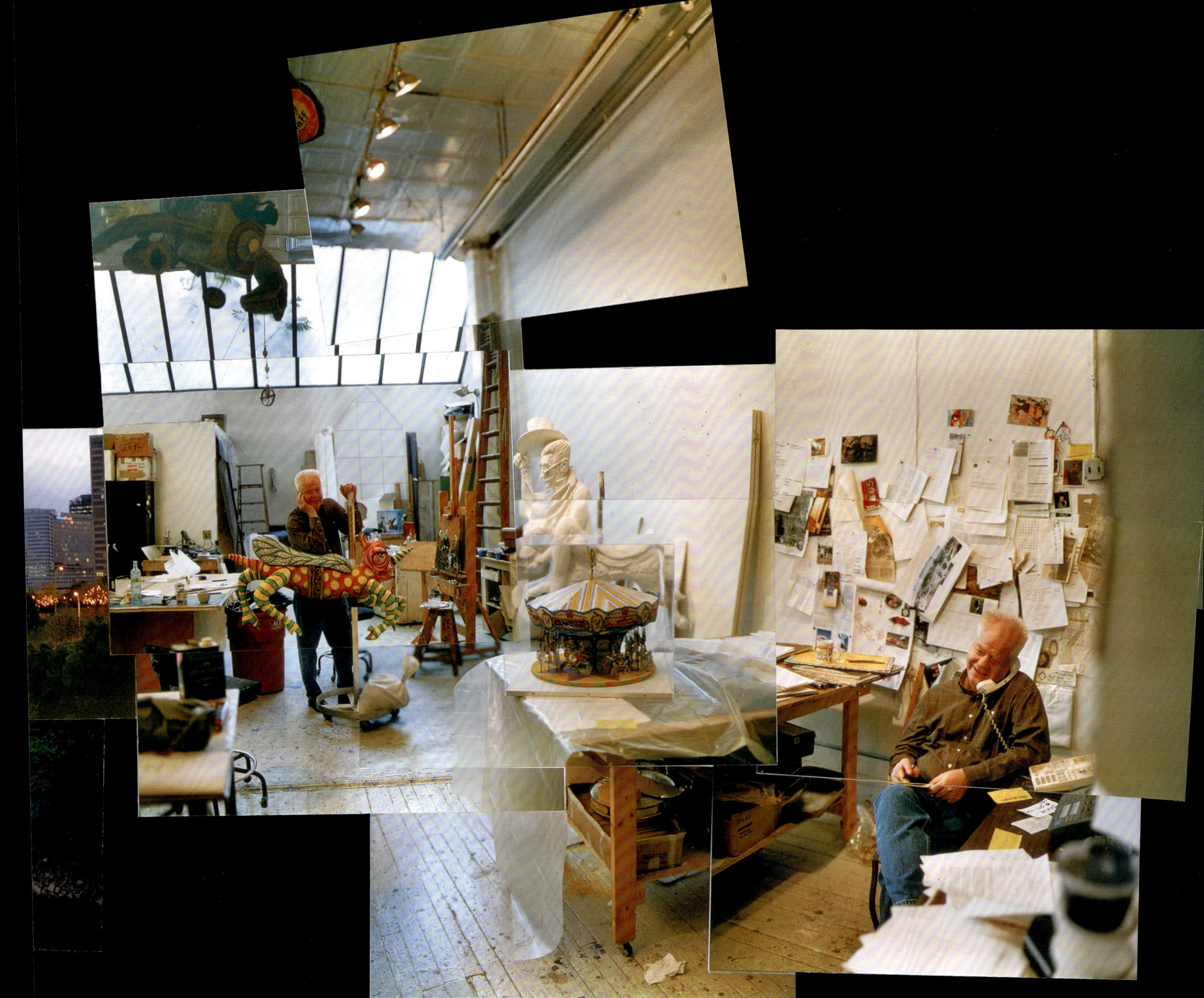

Photo Assemblages

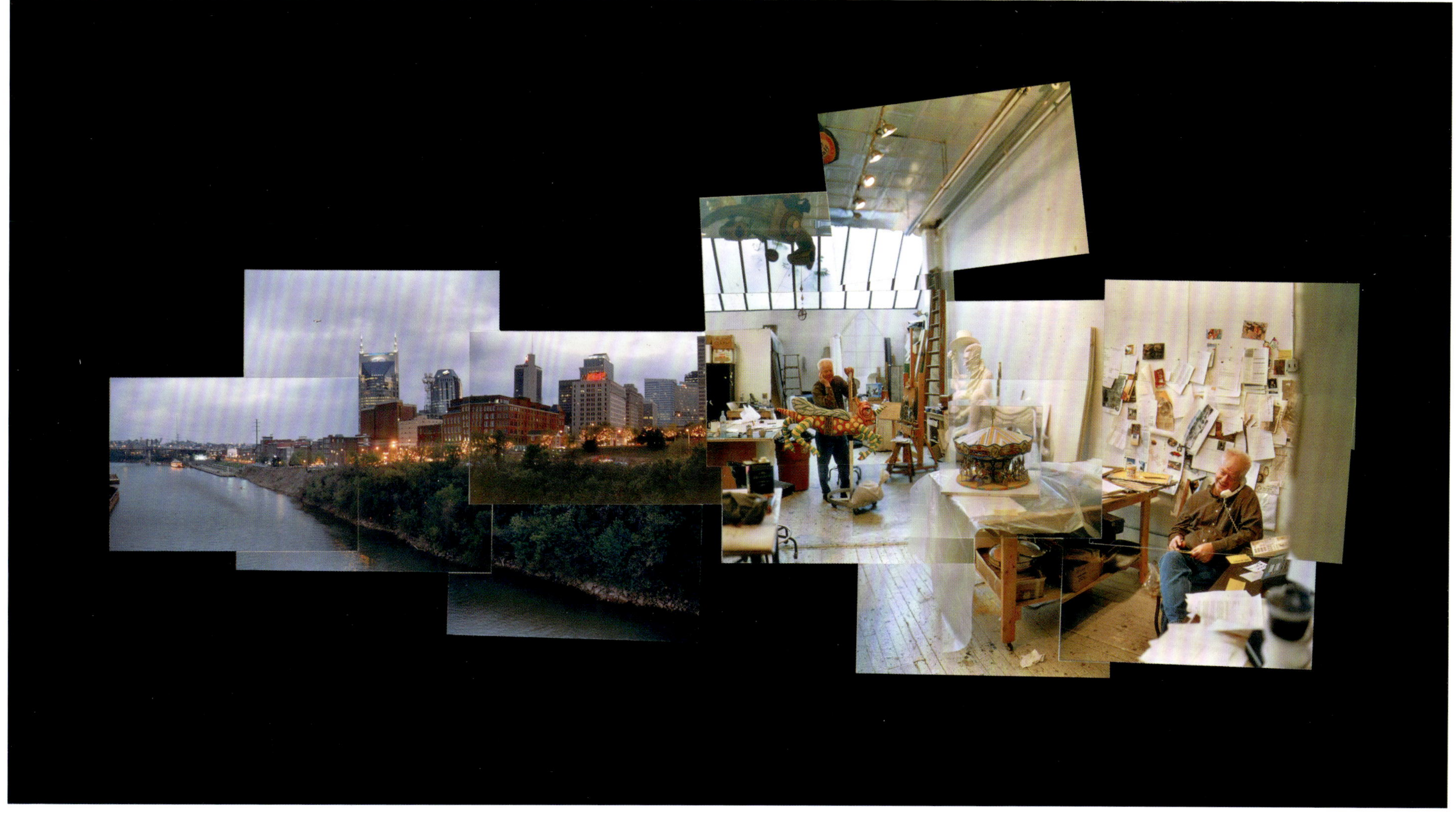

Red Grooms, 1997
Digital ink on paper, 20 x 50 inches (51 x 127 cm). Collection of the Artist

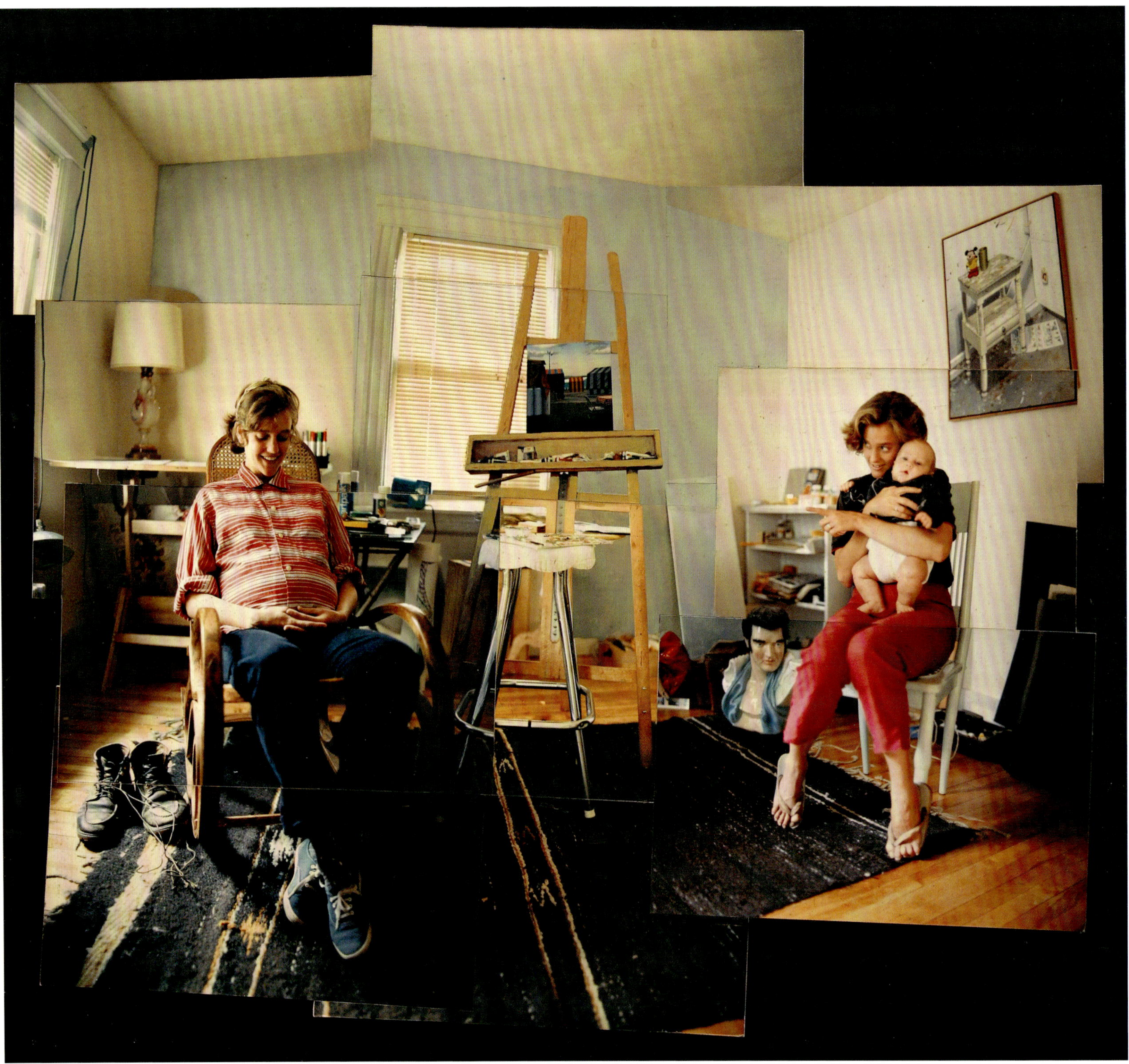

Nanny and Max before and after Birth (Nanny Vonnegut and Max Prior), 1984
Oil on c-type print assemblage, 25¾ x 28 inches. (65 x 71 cm) Private Collection

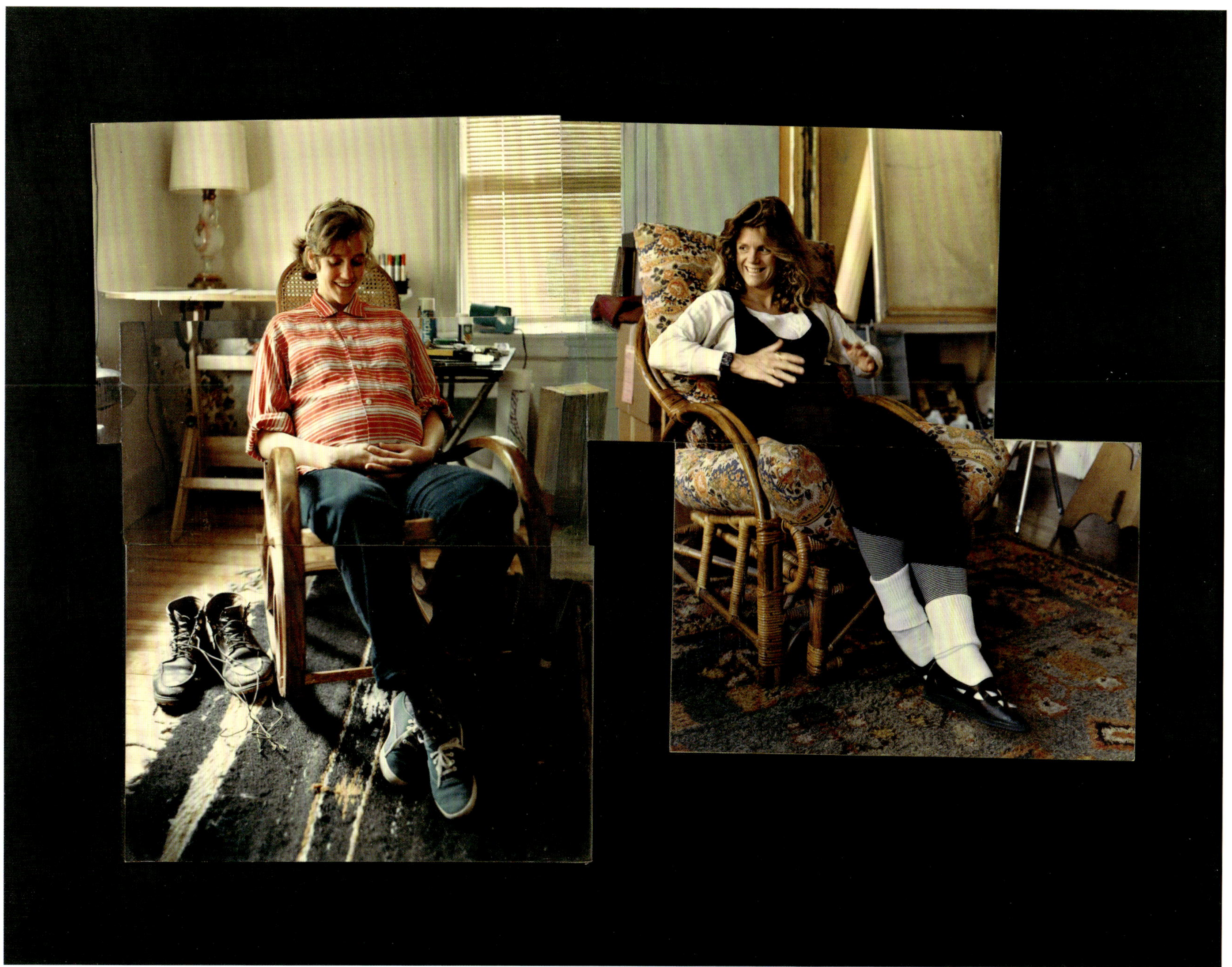

American Artists, Expectant Sisters (Nanny Vonnegut and Edie Vonnegut), 1988
Oil on c-type print assemblage, 20¼ x 26¾ inches (51 x 68 cm). Private Collection

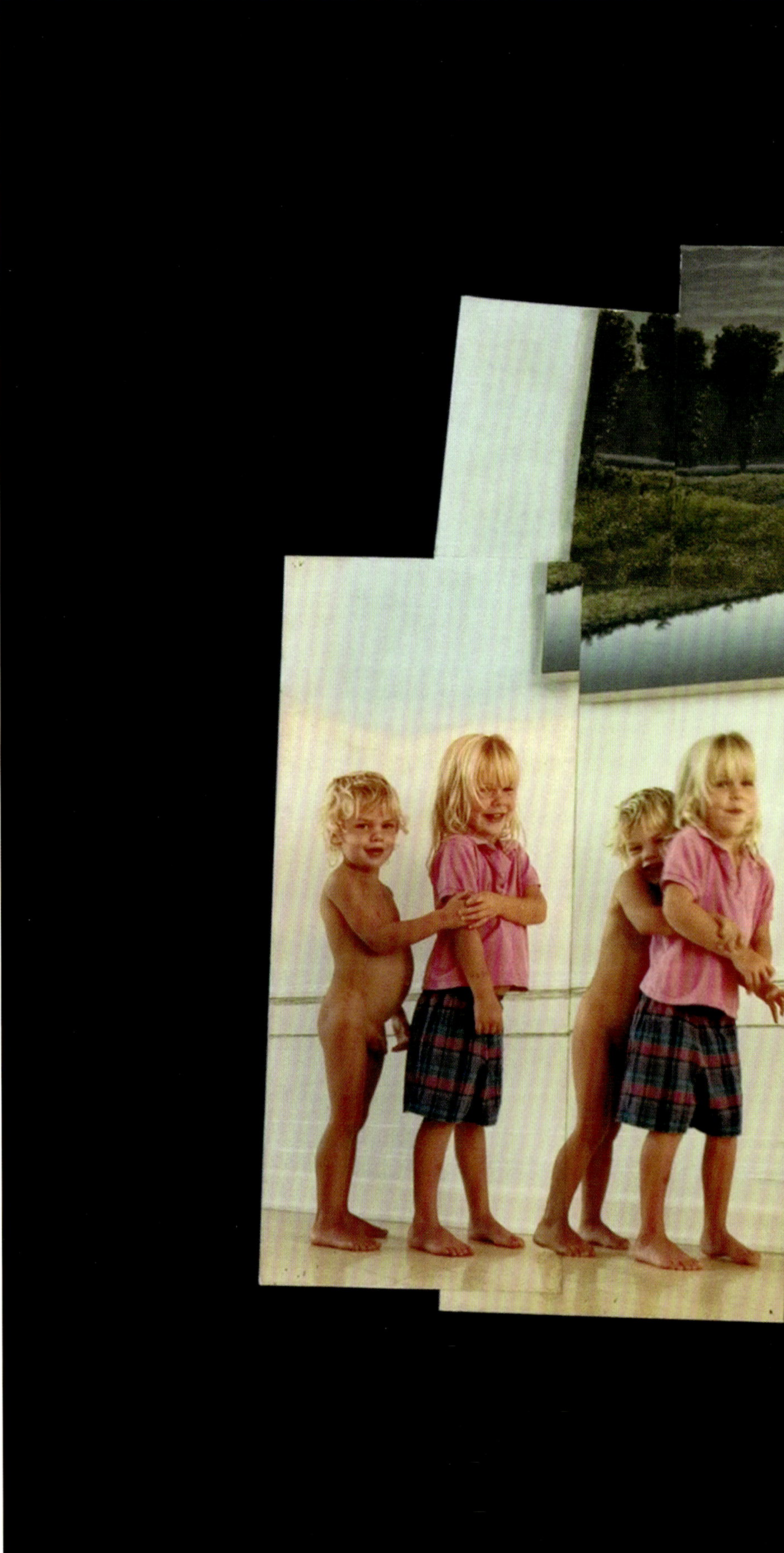

MICKEY AND JAKE SUMNER
(WHAT A DIFFERENCE A TOUR MAKES), 1987–1991
ALKYD ON C-TYPE PRINT ASSEMBLAGE, 18 X 34 INCHES (46 X 86 CM). PRIVATE COLLECTION

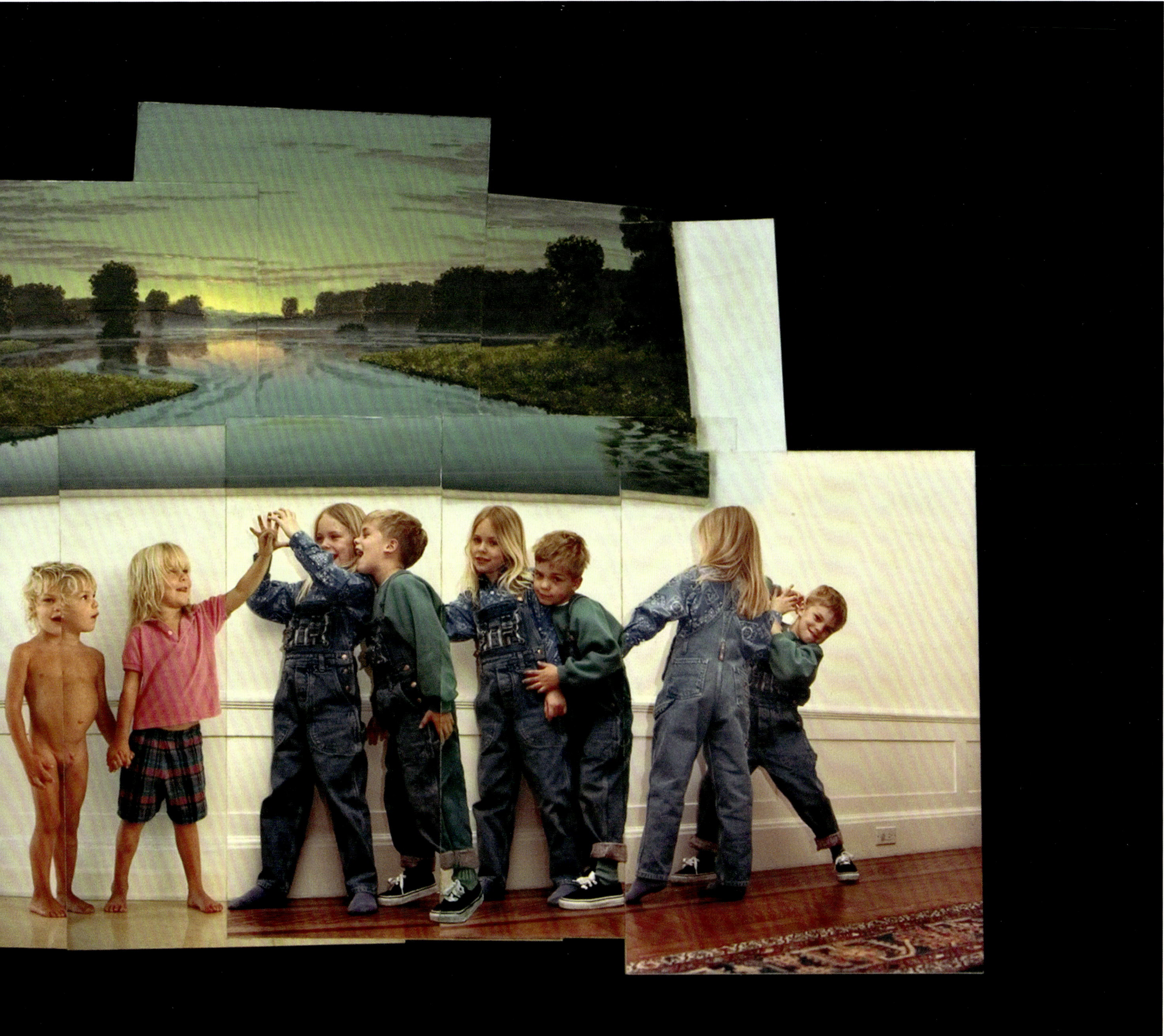

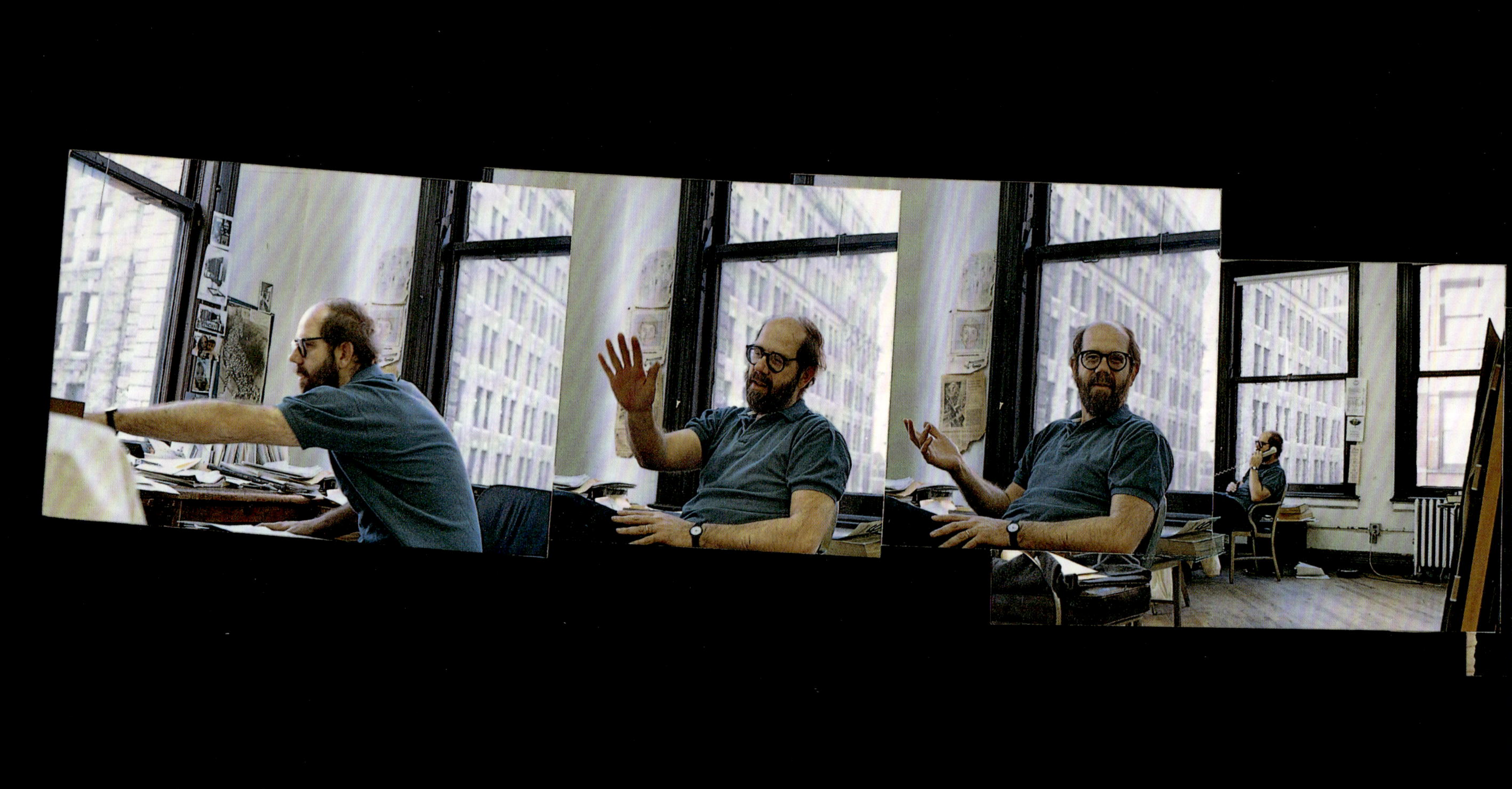

Chuck Close, 1986

Alkyd on c-type print assemblage, 23 x 59 inches (58 x 150 cm). Collection of the Artist

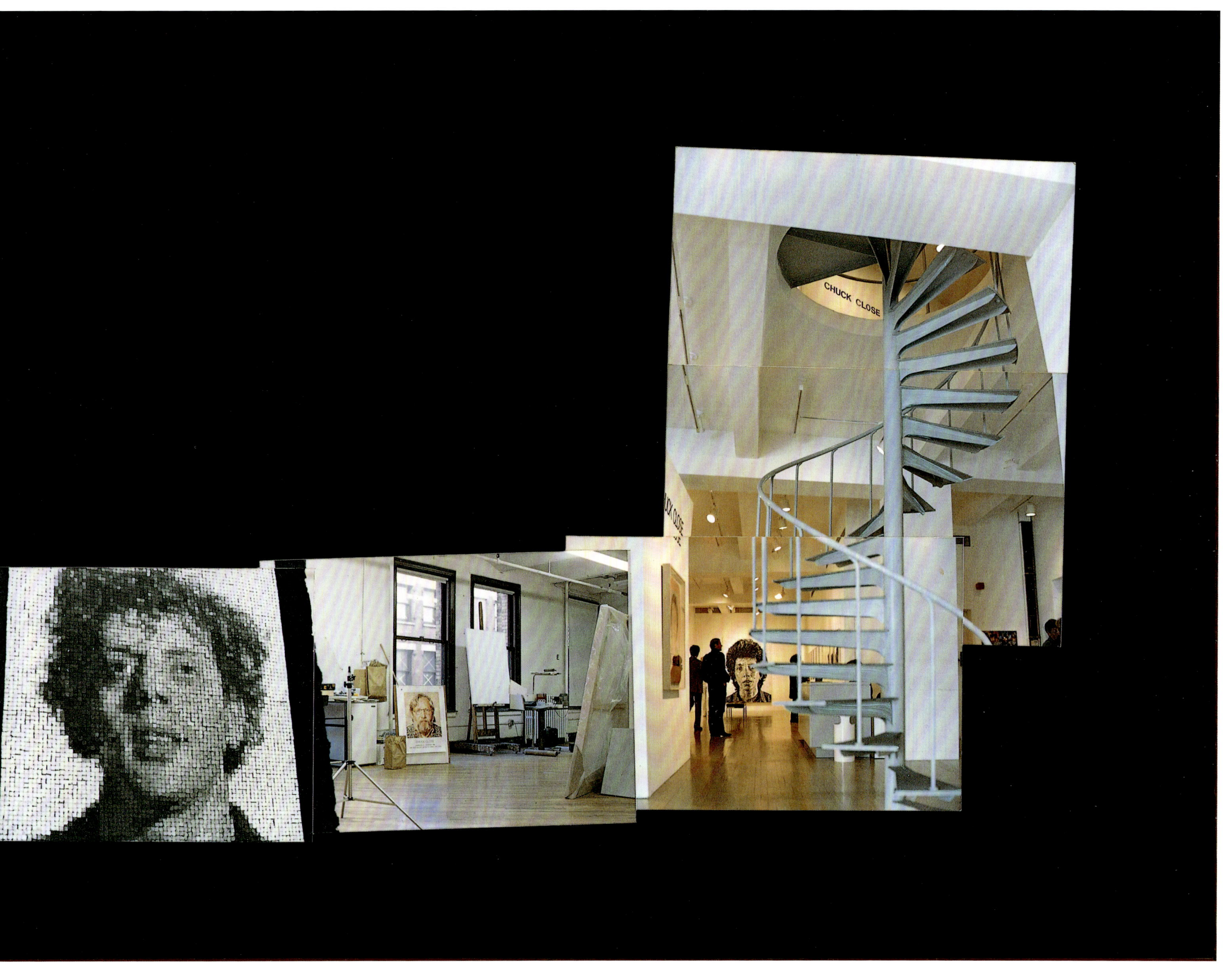

CHUCK CLOSE

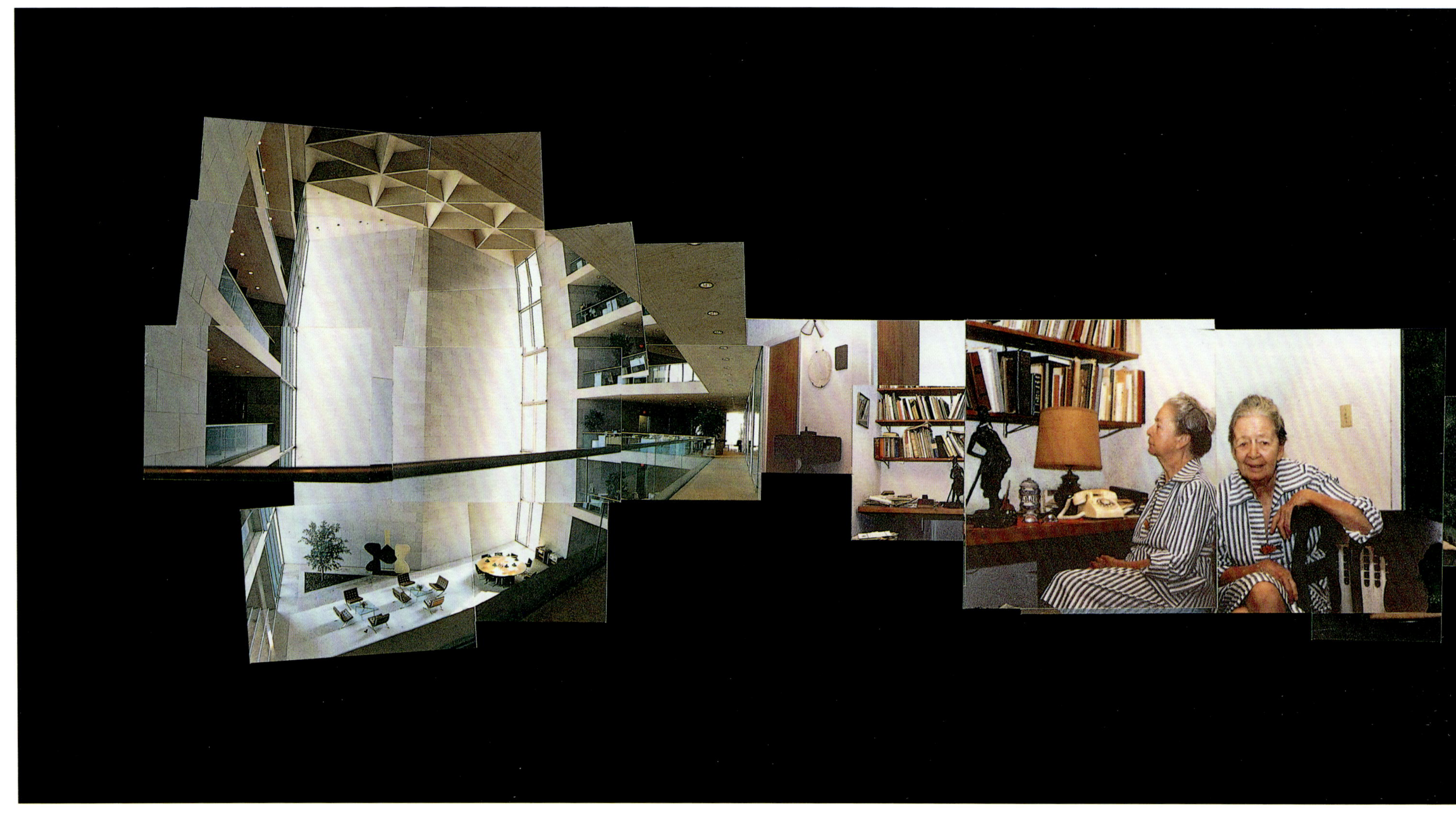

Digital ink-jet print on paper, mounted on stretched black fabric, 20½ x 73 inches (52 x 185 cm). Museum of Fine Arts, Boston, Gift of Nash Editions, 1998

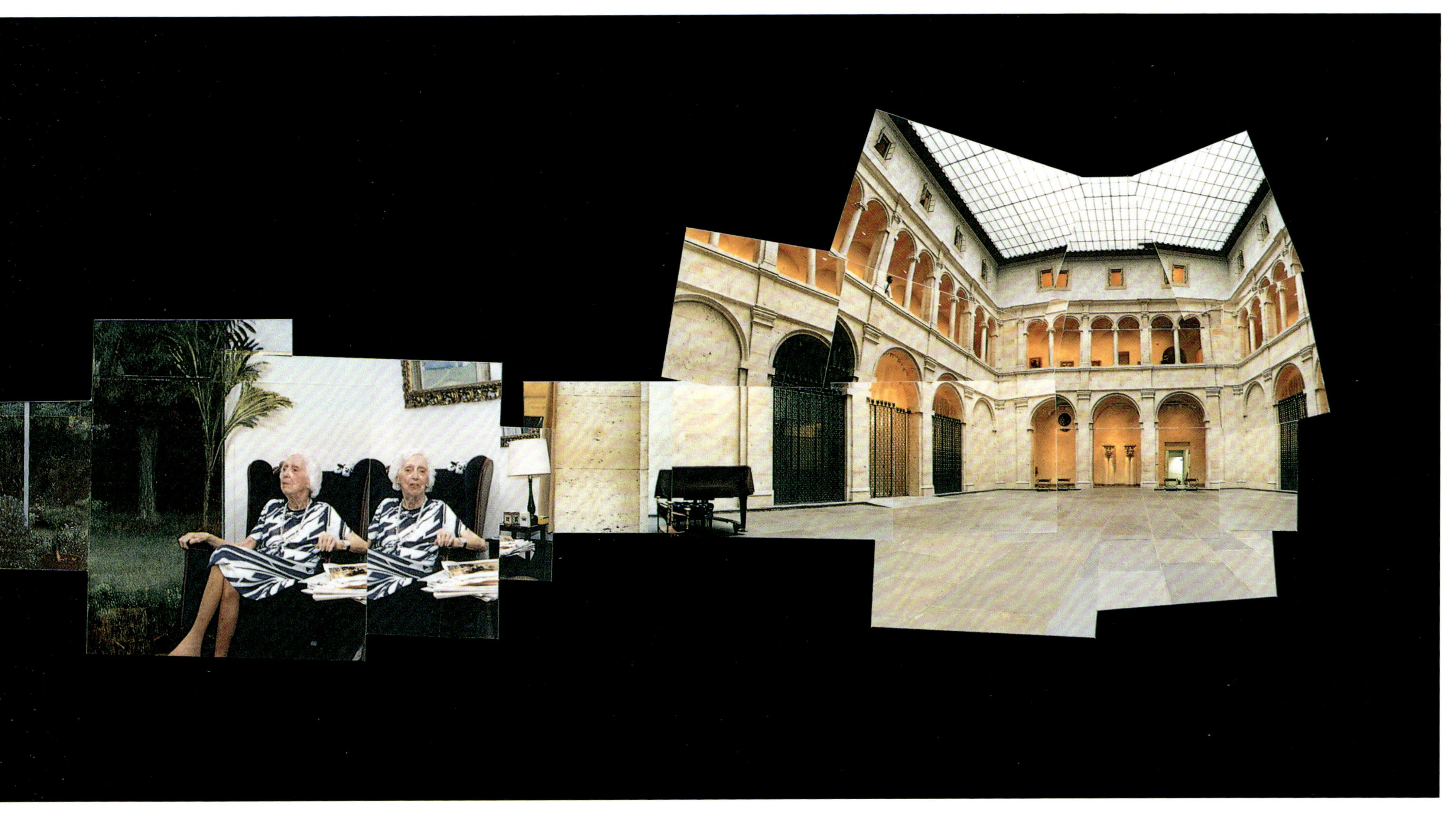

I MET FRAN AND GREGORY GILLESPIE THE DAY THEY DECIDED TO SPLIT UP IN 1978. THEY CAME OVER FOR A STUDIO VISIT AND ANNOUNCED THIS AS THEY ENTERED MY CONVERTED FACTORY SPACE IN NORTHAMPTON. THEY WERE TERRIFIC ARTISTS....AND PROMINENT IN THE CREATIVE COMMUNITY OF WESTERN MASSACHUSETTS. THEY ALSO ROAMED RATHER REMOTE PSYCHIC PRECINCTS. THEIR ONLY REAL TETHER TO PLANET EARTH WAS HUGH DAVIES, THEN THE DIRECTOR OF THE U. MASS MUSEUM. WHEN HE LEFT TO DIRECT THE CONTEMPORARY MUSEUM IN SAN DIEGO, A RELIABLE RUDDER WAS REMOVED FROM THIS ART COMMUNITY. (AFTER THAT, MAKING ART IN THE NORTHAMPTON/AMHERST AREA DIDN'T SEEM TO BE AS MUCH FUN.) NONE THE LESS, WE ALL STILL REFERRED TO "FRAN + GREGORY" IN THE SAME BREATH.... NOT ONLY AFTER THEIR SPLIT, BUT EVEN NOW AFTER THEIR DEATHS. ALTHOUGH THEY LEFT SOME WONDERFUL ART, I MISS THEM BOTH TERRIBLY.

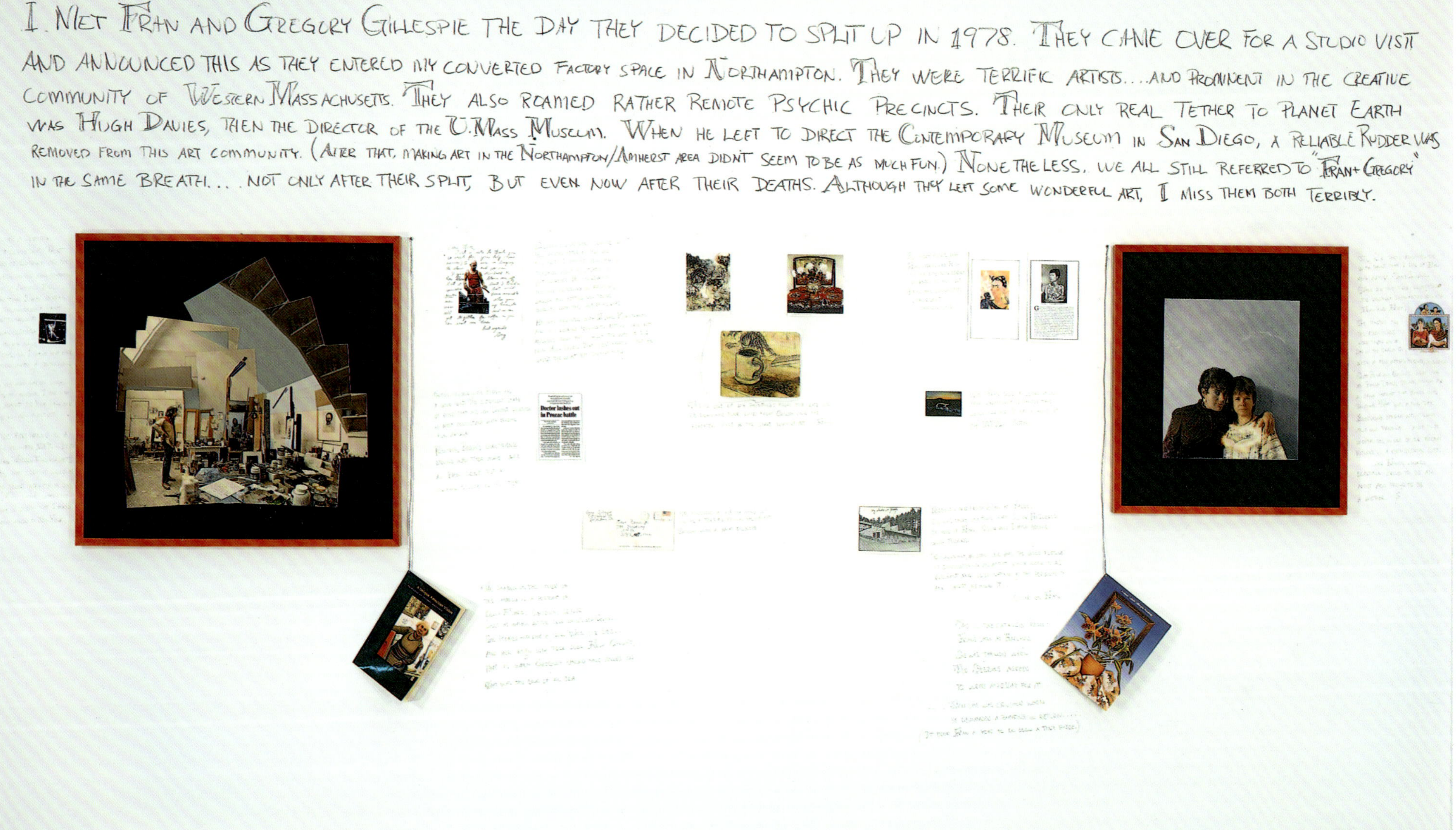

I Miss My Friends: Memorial for Fran and Gregory Gillespie, 2002

Installation of photo assemblages with mixed media, 108 x 192 inches (274 x 488 cm). Museum of Contemporary Art, San Diego, California, Gift of the Artist

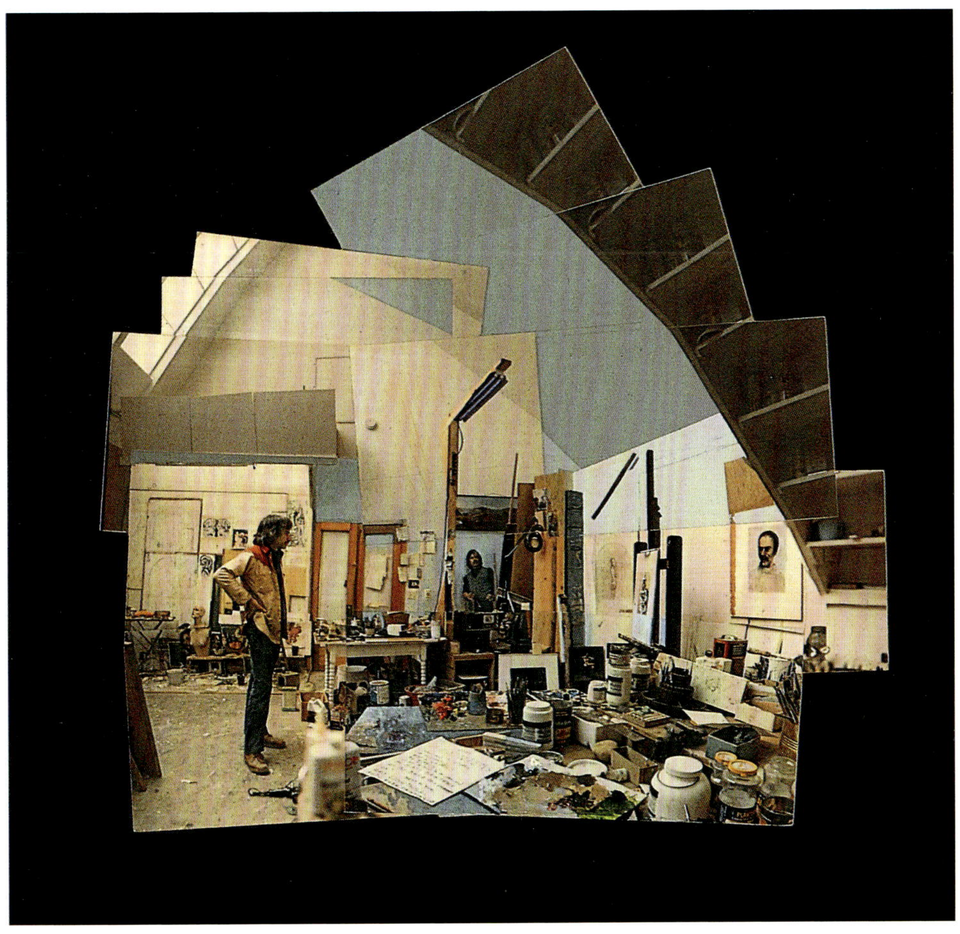

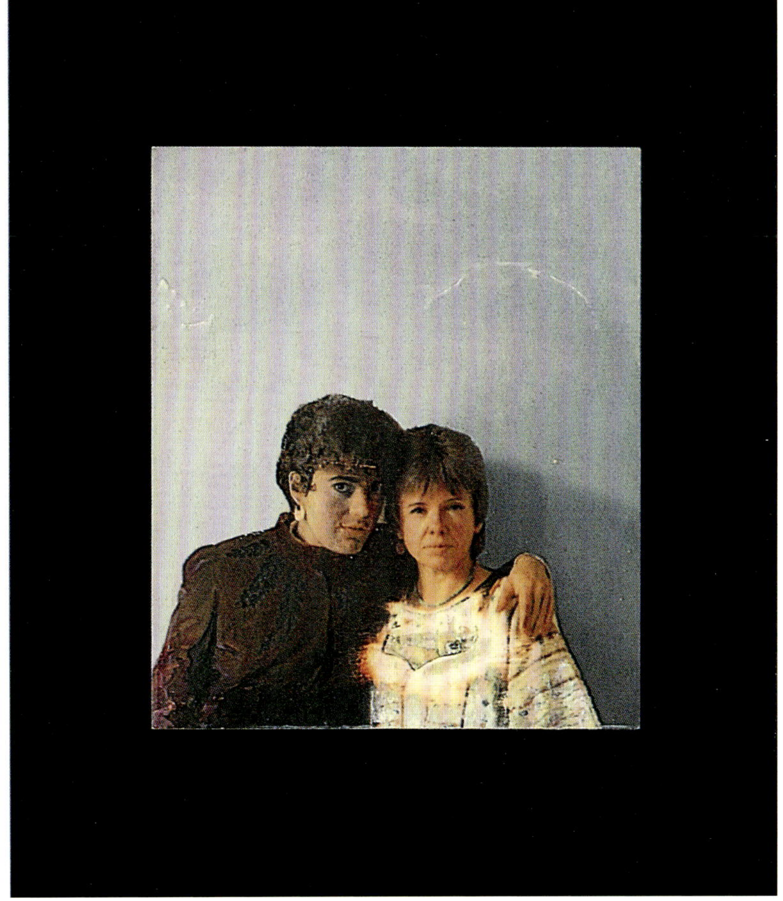

(LEFT) DETAIL OF INSTALLATION: GREGORY GILLESPIE, 1983
ALKYD ON C-TYPE PRINT ASSEMBLAGE

(RIGHT) DETAIL OF INSTALLATION: FRAN GILLESPIE AND JANE LUND, 1983
ALKYD ON C-TYPE PRINT ASSEMBLAGE

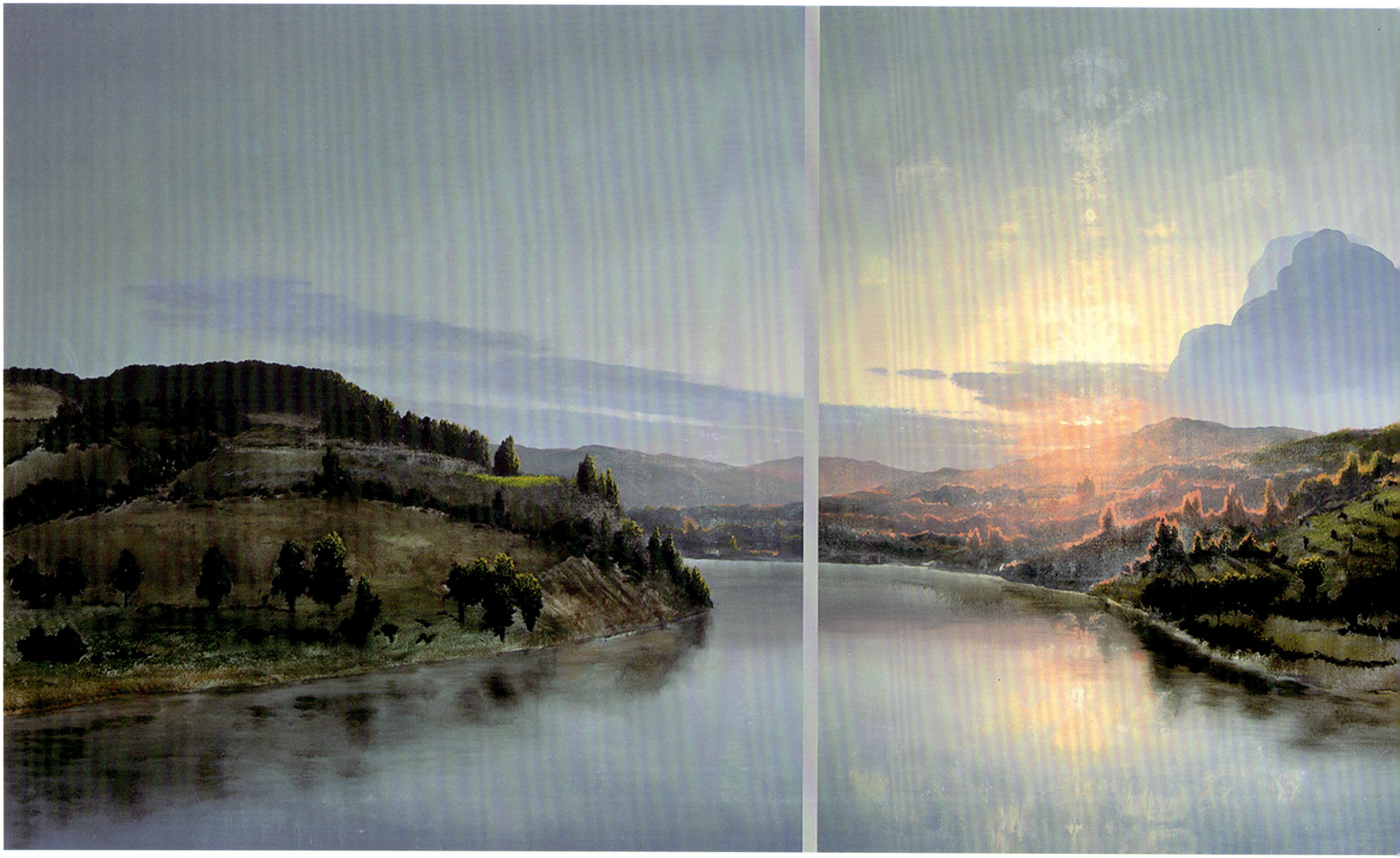

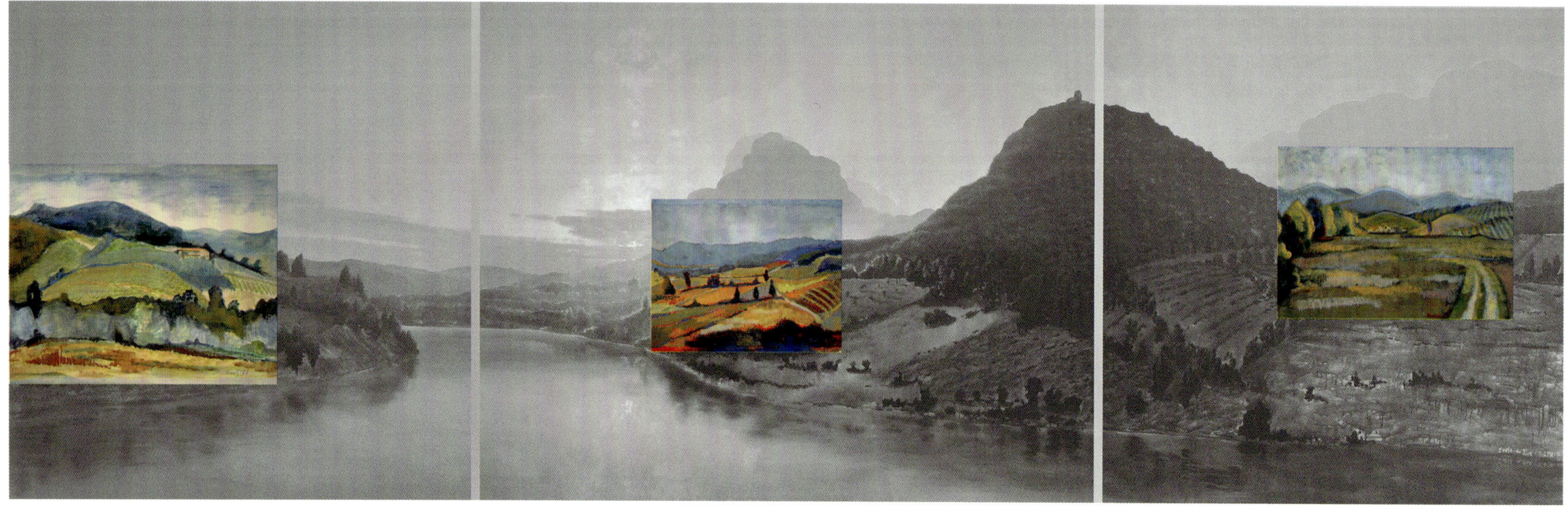

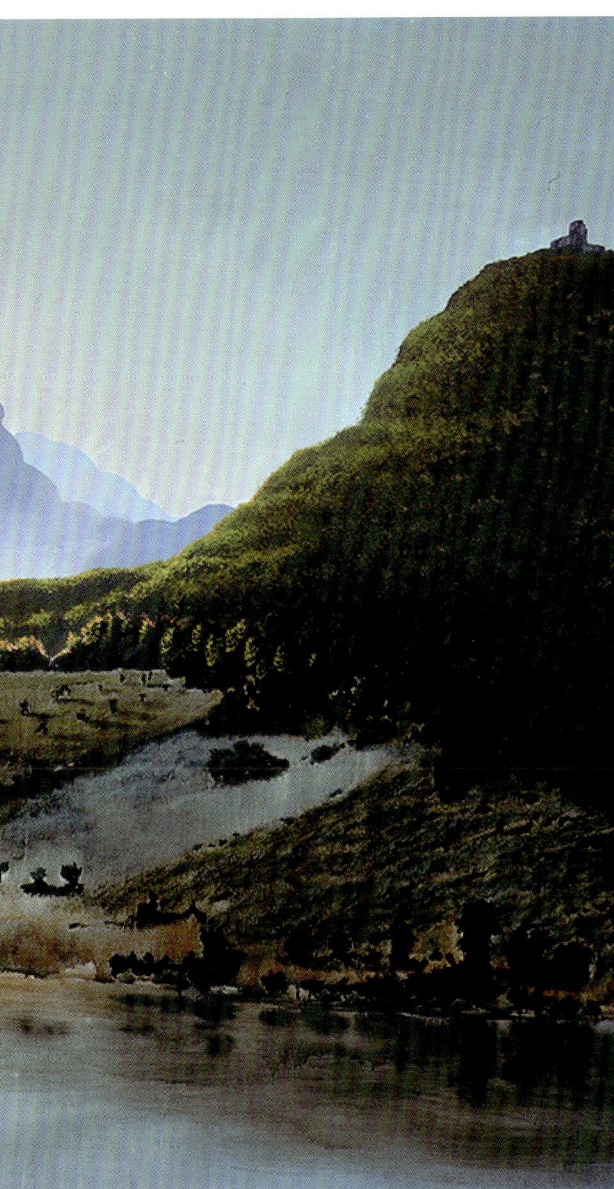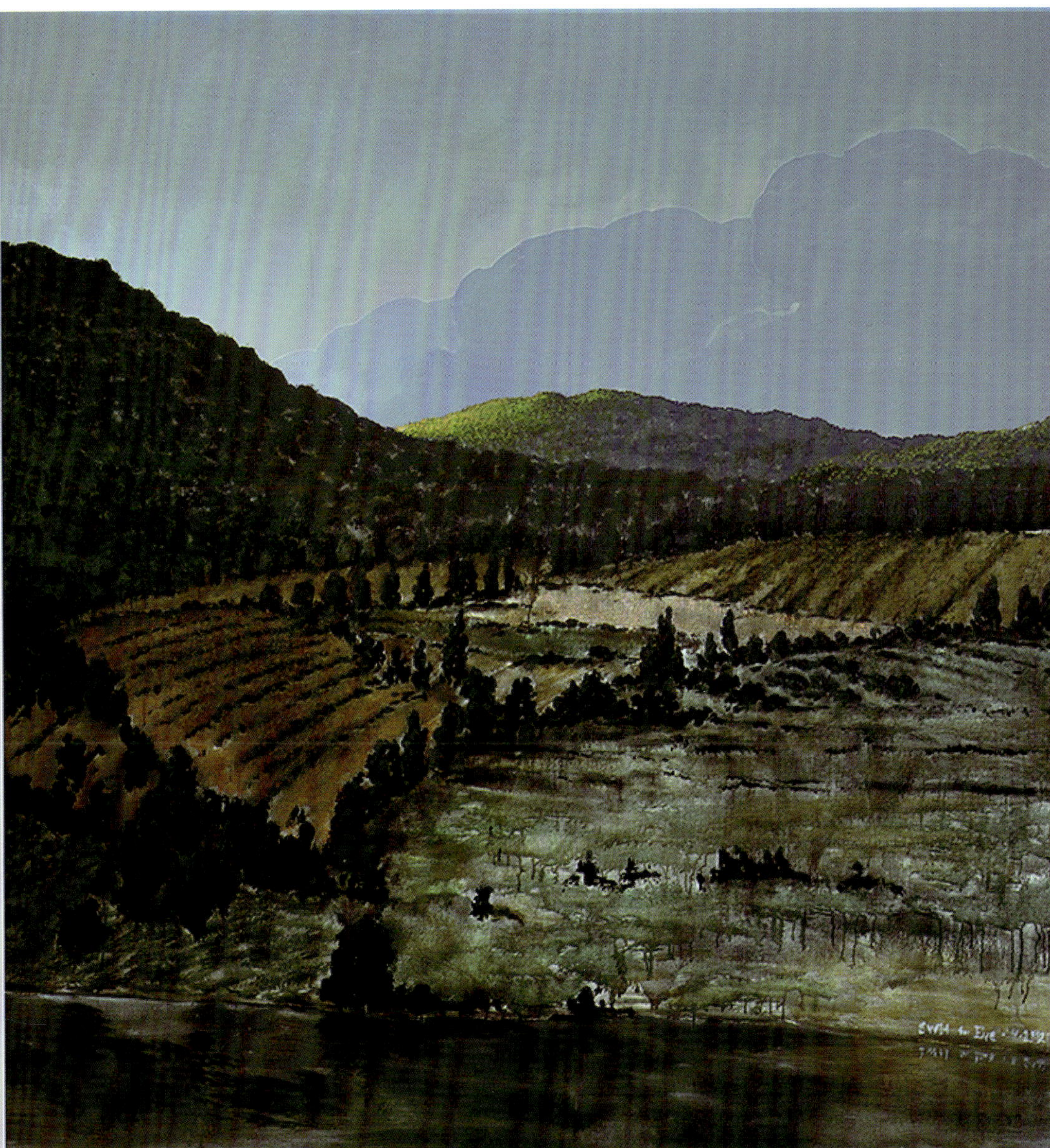

FLOODED RIVER TUSCANY FOR EVE, 2001
Tribute to aunt and artist Evelyn Jordan
ACRYLIC ON CANVAS (TRIPTYCH), 84 X 288 INCHES (213 X 732 CM). PRIVATE COLLECTION

STUDY FOR FLOODED RIVER TUSCANY FOR EVE INCORPORATING PAINTINGS BY EVELYN JORDAN, 2001
DIGITAL INK ON PAPER, 6 X 16 INCHES (15 X 41 CM). COLLECTION OF THE ARTIST

EVELYN JORDAN: DA FRISO, 1977, OIL ON PAPER, 13¾ X 18 INCHES (35 X 46 CM). PRIVATE COLLECTION
ROAD TO LORENZANA (FOR JOHN), 1976, OIL ON PAPER, 13¾ X 18 INCHES (35 X 46 CM). PRIVATE COLLECTION
ROAD TO LORENZANA, 1978, OIL ON PAPER, 15¾ X 23½ INCHES (40 X 60 CM). PRIVATE COLLECTION

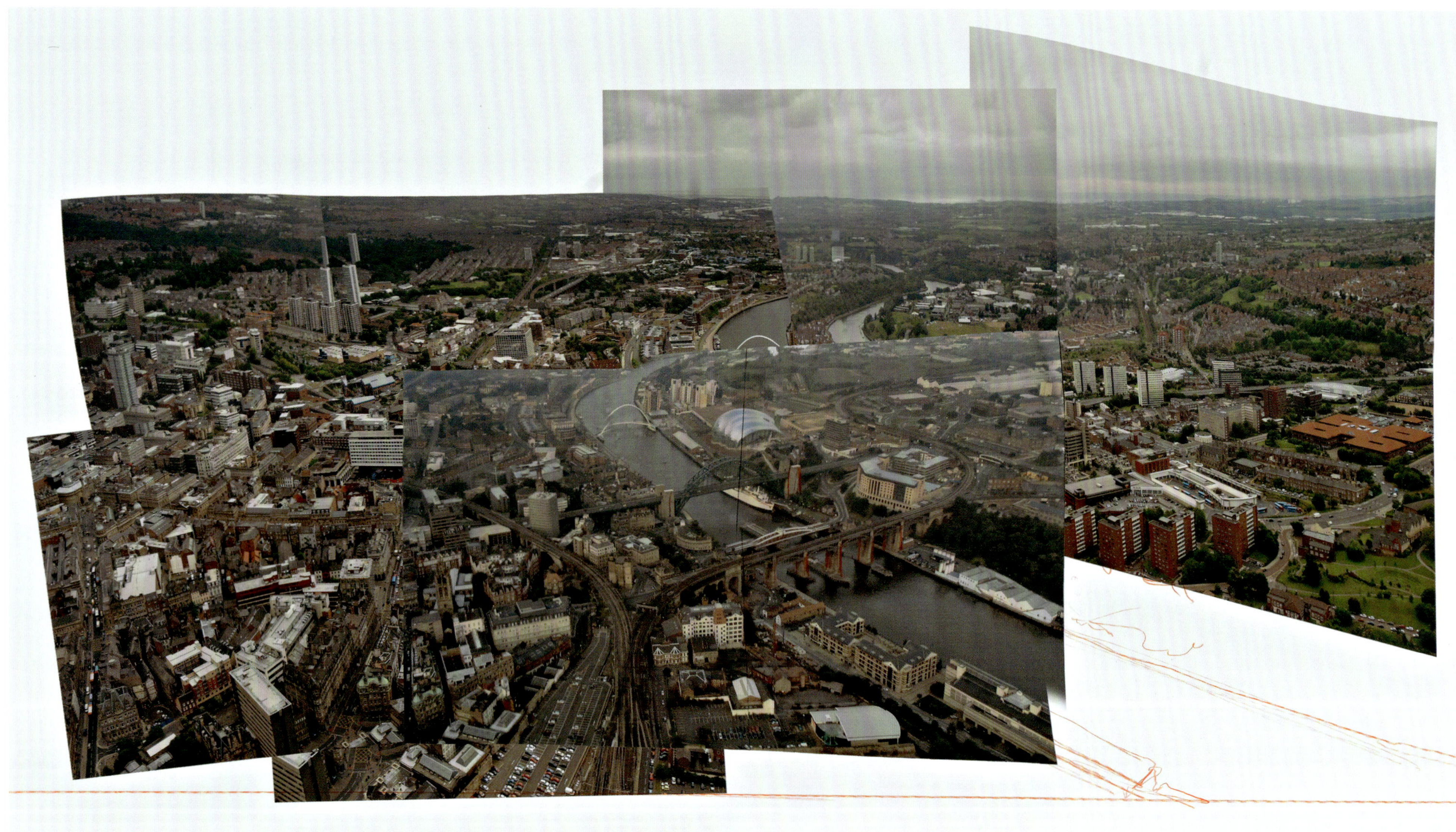

Study for Northern City Renaissance, 2005
Digital ink on paper, 22 x 34 inches (56 x 86 cm). Collection of the Artist

Beneath the Light:
Digital Imaging in the Art of Stephen Hannock

Garrett White

THE BASIC OUTLINE OF STEPHEN HANNOCK'S EVOLUTION AS AN artist is well known: his education in his native Northeast; his apprenticeship with Leonard Baskin in Northampton, Massachusetts; the early experiments with phosphorescent paint; and his gradual movement toward the subjects of landscape and light that would bring comparisons of his work to the Hudson River School and the nineteenth-century landscape painters of the Northeast. Hannock's untiring pursuit of a figurative vision when Minimalism and Conceptualism were still ascendant eventually earned him his current reputation as one of the preeminent American landscape painters.

The quality of the light in Hannock's landscapes, and the art-historical references he has often cited in relation to them, has led some to refer to him as a latter-day Luminist.[1] The phantasmagorical character of much of the work—from the early invented landscapes to the more recent nocturnal "rocket" paintings—has prompted others to call him an Imaginary Realist.[2] At mid-career, however, even the label *landscape painter* seems inadequate to describe the scope of his art. Hannock's mature style developed from his discovery in the 1980s of the technique of power sanding successive layers of resin and paint. The final unvarnished effect eliminates surface glare, laying bare the subtle play of light that has always been his primary obsession. (Topography, he has said, is mainly "an excuse to hang the light."[3]) The resulting seamless beauty Hannock achieves in his finished canvases accounts in large measure for his dedicated following (along with the occasional note of snooty disapproval, given that beauty remains suspect in a critical discourse steeped

in irony and contradiction). But the casual accessibility of Hannock's painting belies a process that is both technically and imaginatively complex. At first glance a typical Hannock painting may appear to be a traditional, if slightly etherealized, landscape or cityscape. Closer inspection reveals a multimedia approach that draws upon a rich practice of collage, photo assemblage, and appropriation that runs through all of Hannock's work. By these methods, which include painting passages of text into his canvases, along with the traditional panoply of painterly effects, Hannock combines history and personal experience to tell stories that transform and overwhelm the realistic rendering of setting or topography.

The deceptive simplicity of a Hannock tableau has been as frequently noted as the laborious reworking of the canvas by which he achieves his effects. Less known is the fact that the flowering of his signature style was made possible by an equally painstaking and labor-intensive process of experimentation with digital imaging. For more than fifteen years, Hannock has collaborated on the creation of his most complex paintings with R. Mac Holbert, cofounder with artist and musician Graham Nash, of Nash Editions, the world's first fine-art digital printmaking studio.[4] Opened in 1990 in Manhattan Beach, California, and directed by Holbert, Nash Editions began at a time when digital image making was still struggling for legitimacy, and when ink sets were still extremely fugitive. It was Nash, Holbert, and the team they assembled who first adapted the Iris 3047 digital ink-jet printer—a proofing machine used by commercial printers—for the purpose of printing fine-art photographs. The Iris 3047 was the backbone of the medium through the 1990s, before being overtaken by products from Epson and other makers of increasingly affordable and varied printers and ink sets for the photography market.

When Hannock first came to Nash Editions in 1992, however, he wasn't interested in making prints. Recommended to Nash and Holbert by their mutual friend Jackson Browne, Hannock was drawn to the studio by his restless search for new techniques through which to realize his eclectic and highly personal vision. ("I think it's impossible," he once said, "to express oneself as an artist in this day and age in one medium."⁵) He had long been painting on photographs and making photo-assemblage pieces. By his own admission he didn't like working with computers but was intrigued by Holbert's expertise. A photographer himself, Holbert was formerly the road manager for Crosby, Stills, and Nash. In the 1980s, he devoted much of his free time to researching new computer technologies, both for streamlining his tour management responsibilities and, in concert with Nash—also a lifelong photographer—for scanning and manipulating photographs. An early Photoshop initiate, Holbert was already a leading expert on the software when Hannock met him, and he continues to teach and lecture widely on its now ubiquitous uses in photography.

On his first visit to Nash Editions, Hannock wanted to see how he might incorporate drawing and painting into a picture Jackson Browne had given him of Browne holding a surfboard skag he had found on the beach. It was as an informal adventure at that point, but he was pleased with the results. Nash and Holbert brought the free-spirited attitude of rock 'n' roll experimentation into their pioneering work in digital imaging, and Hannock was attracted as much to the atmosphere at Nash Editions as to the new technology. Hannock himself has the amiable, low-key affect of a successful rock musician whose talent speaks for itself, and it's easy to see why he attracted the celebrity friends and clients—his close friends Sting and his wife Trudie Styler were early and avid supporters—who collected his work before it

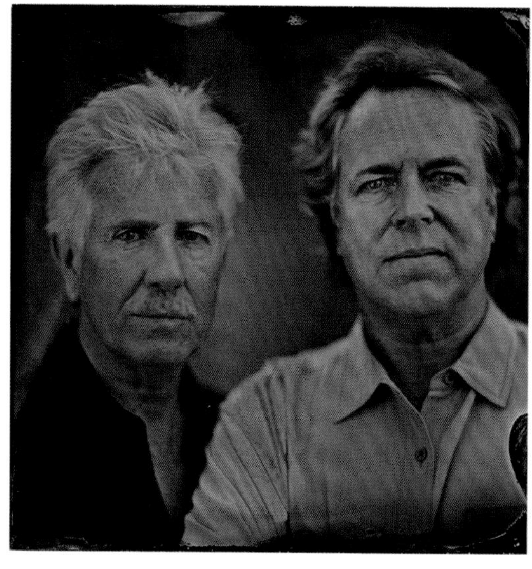

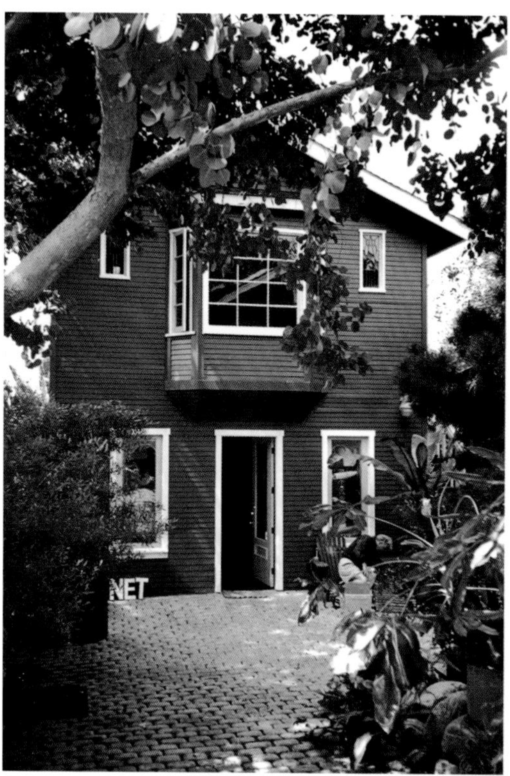

(TOP) PHOTOGRAPH OF GRAHAM NASH (LEFT) AND MAC HOLBERT
(BOTTOM) PHOTOGRAPH OF NASH EDITIONS ON OAK AVENUE,
MANHATTAN BEACH, CALIFORNIA, 1989

drew broader critical and public attention.

"Mac and Graham were so generous and easy to hang out with," Hannock recalls of his first visits to Nash Editions. "Mac's digital expertise was already prodigious. When he was on the road, he found whatever was out there and tampered with it. By the time these tools became available for commercial consumption, he was able to hit the ground running." [6] Although, to some extent, Hannock was still finding his voice as a painter when he began working at Nash Editions, he already had the impulse to incorporate an ever-wider range of elements into his art, along with an intuition that the new digital tools could enhance and quicken the process. Photography features prominently in his work, but painting directly from a photograph or a realistic sketch of a particular view never suited his purpose. "I have no problem with the tradition of working from a photograph," he says. "Thomas Eakins worked from photographs, and he was one of the greatest draftsmen ever. The end result speaks for itself."

More to the point perhaps is the fact that Hannock finds realism boring. The ideas behind the nineteenth-century landscapes his work references, whether spiritual, social, or personal, were always as important as fidelity to color and light. What he shares with Thomas Cole or Frederic Edwin Church or George Inness isn't technique or subject matter so much as a Romantic emphasis on the primacy of emotion and personal experience—mood. (There is a little-remarked Symbolist strain in Hannock's work; Odilon Redon was another early influence.) Yet for all their beauty, Hannock's paintings do not idealize nature. There is often a strangeness to the light in his landscapes, but nature isn't mystified—the Romantic idea of nature as eternal and possessed of an autonomous spiritual presence outside of human agency is long gone—nor is there more than a small dose of awe at nature's remaining beauty. If there is mystery in the work, it is about the power of human imagination; ultimately, Hannock's work is the expression of an interior reality. He shies away from total abstraction, but

he's happy to allow figuration to evaporate when the spirit moves him, hence his reverence for Turner and Whistler. A good deal of the light in his work is threadbare canvas.

Contrary to what might be imagined on viewing his serene, large-scale compositions, especially since many bear specific place names, Hannock does not have a complete graphic image in mind when he begins a project, though at the outset he might be inspired by a particular locale. His eventual goal at Nash Editions, after making a few archival prints from earlier painted photo-assemblage pieces in which the photographs had begun to fade, was to see if he could use the new digital tools to develop a vision and create an image on paper that would serve as an artist sketch or study—not as an exact reference for the finished painting, but as the starting point for creative elaboration and revision in the studio. The first large-scale painting Hannock and Holbert worked on together was *Madison Square Park at the Turn of the Century, Looking North* (1997). The 16 x 12-foot canvas hangs in Eleven Madison Park, Danny Meyer's award-winning New York restaurant.

In the course of their work, Holbert and Hannock developed a method that became the model for subsequent collaborations. Hannock starts with a small painted sketch, often executed on a postcard or an envelope. The sketch is scanned, then Holbert and Hannock work on the image in the computer. Hannock says, "I describe what I want—and that could be anything—and Mac goes through his arsenal of tools, sometimes researching new ones, until we find a solution. We've worked together for so long, we have a language now, so we move very quickly through what works and what doesn't."

Once they have an iteration that they like, a digital pigment print of the image is made on archival paper. Hannock then reworks the print with paint, pen, crayon, or chalk, and the image is scanned again. Depending on the complexity of the tableau, it may go through a half dozen or more generations before the study is finished to Hannock's satisfaction. It's a process of obsessive refinement and subtraction as well as of layering and addition. "It's laborious, it takes time," Hannock says, "but it's still a fraction of the time it would take if I were to start painting right away. Neither the studies nor the finished pieces would come out nearly as well. When I get that final state, the finished study that answers my questions, I'm still going to take it to a different place on canvas in the studio."

Most photographers, even those shooting and printing digitally, still aim for an image that approximates the real world—fidelity to color and shadow and light. As a non-realist painter, Hannock has limitless choices, presenting challenges that often go beyond what Holbert and his staff face with most Nash Editions clients. Still, the techniques employed will be generally familiar to anyone with experience in Photoshop: regional selections to change the shape or color values of specific areas; the use of gradient effects for making smooth merges; compositing and scaling to bring in new elements and blend them seamlessly into the existing piece. Hannock considers Holbert a true collaborator and artist in his own right, not only in his mastery of digital imaging and printing, but in his graphic sense and keen understanding of Hannock's aesthetic.

"There have been numerous occasions," Holbert says, "when Stephen will ask me to do something, and I'll do it but perhaps I didn't quite understand the request. So I'm doing what I think he asked me to do, and he'll say, no, no—wait a second, that works! We end up finding the right thing, something we wouldn't have seen otherwise, through miscommunication. Or we'll cycle through a whole series of color relationships that you couldn't achieve if you were painting on canvas—it would just be impossible without endless scraping and remixing. This approach allows you to move through many different possibilities and to sort and refine them very quickly. It's not making the art for you. There's still the Crest Jewel of Discrimination of the artist constantly watching over the process."[7]

Hannock's cityscapes can seem calmer and less threatening than his landscapes. Pared down to an almost Precisionist purity, and with a wry nod to photorealism, they display a belief in human endeavor and community that seems to come naturally to Hannock. But, like the landscapes, they are only apparently innocent and also require an elaborate process of composition by hand and computer. The vista *American City with Restored Park* (Mass MoCA #10), 2005, began with a clipping from the *New York Times* of a 1908 Brown Brothers photograph of New York's Flatiron Building. Hannock placed the clipping on the right-hand side of piece of drawing paper and completed the composition with a pencil drawing of the eastern half of Madison Square Park and a row of buildings to the south. This rudimentary sketch was given to Holbert for scanning, while Hannock went to the location and photographed it close up with a variety of lenses. Eventually there were four major phases of the study that involved scaling and compositing Hannock's photographs; altering and, in some cases, removing buildings and other artifacts; adjusting light and shadow; and painting and drawing on the successive prints.

"I remember when Stephen was working on the sky in that piece," Holbert recalls. "I said, 'Why don't we try that in the computer?' He said, 'You don't have the control that you do with a crayon or a piece of chalk.' So I brought out a Wacom tablet, which allows you to work on the screen with a pen, and he ended up doing amazing work on the sky that I learned a lot from. He was able to make it look incredibly realistic with just a few smooth movements of the pen." Despite this proficiency, however, Hannock dislikes painting digitally and prefers painting and drawing on the prints or altering them directly by scraping the pigment, something that can't be done with a traditional dot pattern: "Obviously there are smudges and exaggerations and accidents that happen with knives and paint that you can't get in the computer."

Nevertheless, it would be a mistake to think of the role of digital imaging in Hannock's work as related only to expediency.

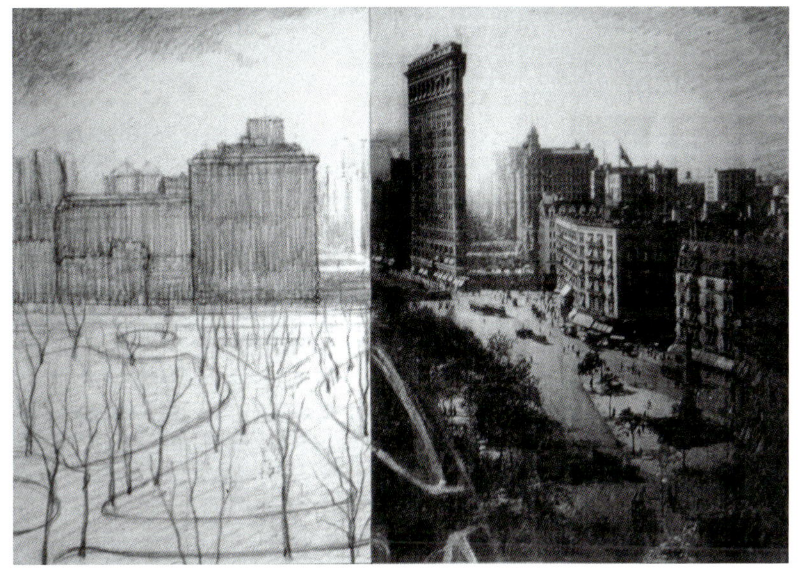

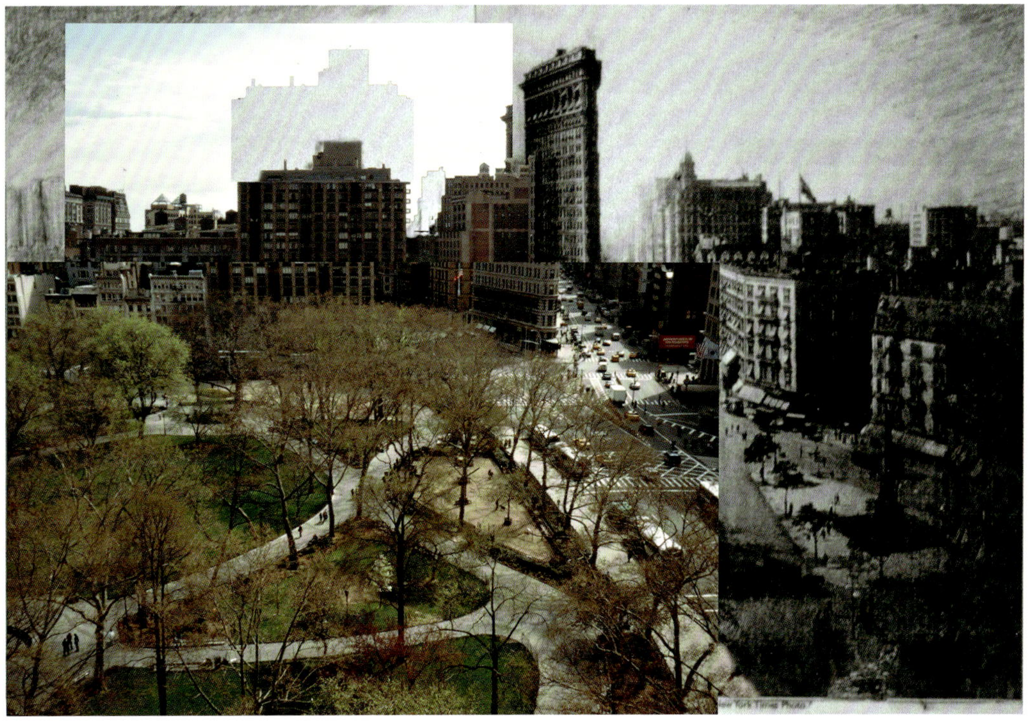

(TOP) AMERICAN CITY WITH RESTORED PARK, STUDY #1, 2005
Pencil on paper and newspaper clipping on paper, 6 x 9 inches (15 x 23 cm). Collection of the Artist

(BOTTOM) AMERICAN CITY WITH RESTORED PARK, STUDY #2, 2005
Digital ink on paper, 10 x 15 inches (25 x 38 cm). Collection of the Artist

Asked what he is able to do digitally that couldn't be achieved in the studio, albeit at a vastly slower pace, his response is immediate: "There is also serendipity, accident, and chance with Photoshop."

Holbert adds, "I've learned more from Stephen about imaging than from almost any other artist. Bringing the aesthetics of a painter into what I do with photographs has been absolutely invaluable in terms of adding to my skill set. It's given me an understanding of light and shadow that I didn't have on the level that he sees it. When you're a painter, you are god in terms of light and shadow, so you learn how important direction is, you see the relationship between light and shadow differently. Working with Stephen on his paintings gave me insight into my own work that I wouldn't have found any other way." Hannock especially enjoys discovering color on the screen, printing it as faithfully as possible, then re-creating it in the studio. Finding color through the dialogue of painting, scanning, alteration, and printing is as important as his search for composition.

Of course, not everything works, and they frequently stumble upon effects that may not be appropriate for the task at hand, but which they want to preserve. "These ideas go through a metamorphosis that really nurtures the concept," Hannock says, "so by the time I'm ready to paint, it's really come to fruition or it has died. Some things just haven't been worth taking to the next step, and some of it's completely off the mark, but we might use it later, so it's all stored. That's exactly why I use paper palettes; when I'm mixing something and it comes out great, or there's a mark from a knife or even an elbow, I tear that piece off and put it on the wall. It's not what I'm looking for, but I don't want to lose it."

Hannock's work at Nash Editions is generally reserved for large-scale paintings that require extensive research and that will eventually include collaged elements and painted text that would be prohibitive to rework if the color palette and composition had not been developed in detail in advance. In the case of *Madison Square Park*, the result was a palimpsest with a surface nostalgia that masks elements of homage, self-portrait, and reminiscence. Hannock's late wife, Bridget Watkins Hannock, who died in 2004, was a champion of the restoration of Madison Square Park. Painted into the final canvas is a nude photographic portrait of her, along with a letter Hannock wrote to their daughter, Georgia, when his wife was in the hospital. "When I paint with an actual place in mind," Hannock says, "I start thinking about people and events as a natural course. It gets to the point where those acts and those people mean more to me than the rendering of the topography, so I want to tell about them. What started as a helpful tool to achieve this end result has now become crucial because it allows me to create a finished painting that renders more of these stories. As with the texts, you don't notice the collaged elements built into the rhythm of the composition until you're right on top of them. And I couldn't begin to do that until I had the fundamentals of color and drawing and composition solved."

Hannock's most ambitious painting to date is *Northern City Renaissance (Newcastle, England, Mass MoCA #53)*, 2008 (p. 215). Commissioned originally by Sting, who was born in Newcastle, the 8 x 12-foot painting was more than four years in the making, including completion of the final study at Nash Editions. The study—a painted digital pigment print and one of the rare studies Hannock has displayed as a unique work of art, which he donated to the Berkshire Museum in Pittsfield, Massachusetts— was itself a monumental undertaking. Newcastle, in Hannock's words, is "the everyman of postindustrial cities" and is currently experiencing a cultural and economic rebirth. As Hannock researched the city's history since Roman times, he realized that a sweeping aerial view would provide opportunities for epic storytelling.

The work began with two different helicopter shoots over Newcastle from different heights and using three different lenses. Hannock and Holbert began with an impossible composite of the aerial photographs, fitting them together like incompatible puzzle pieces through scaling and blending. A months-long process of layering and reworking by hand and in Photoshop included the addition of a medieval bridge (from a photograph Hannock took of a museum model) destroyed in 1400 and a nineteenth-century bridge captured in period photographs. As always, Hannock's goal was a compelling rhythm and feeling rather than a realistic depiction of the landscape—a search for a contemporary image that despite its many layers of history and reverie would nevertheless feel whole and convey its own reality.

Hannock's palette of earth tones and celestial blues in *Northern City Renaissance* is evocative of the work of another Newcastle native, the English Romantic painter John Martin (1789–1854), whose fantastic scenes of imagined events outside of time have an echo in the sometimes eerie coexistence of overlapping eras and events in Hannock's work. (In the finished painting, an image of a closed coal mine viewed from close up is revealed to be a reproduction of a John Martin image.) "What I've done in this vista looking east over the city of Newcastle," Hannock says, "is to appreciate the history of the closed shipyards; and instead of keeping them there as abandoned slag-heaps, I represent them as an array of ethereal swimming-pool blue-green ghost villages. The river Tyne winds its way toward the sea through these glowing, majestic illuminations."

This ethereal effect—the result of an epiphany on Holbert's part—reveals Hannock's paintings for what they are: works of imagination. Hannock often uses Rorschach designs on a vertical seam in the creation of his rocket paintings. "Mac put a horizontal seam in the composition halfway down the page," Hannock recalls, "about a third of the height of the piece from the horizon. I told him not to do it, as a matter of fact, and he did it anyway. That became the basis of the composition. It formed the illumination at the bottom so that the whole thing appears like an illuminated chalice hovering in space that celebrates the renaissance

that this previously burned-out industrial city in northern England is enjoying now."

As the filmmaker Luis Buñuel once said, when you make a work of art, "you must put in whatever you want."[8] Hannock has described his large-scale works as "two-dimensional movies"—accessible yet layered with history and memory and multiple meanings. But he never tells the whole story; that, as with any great, transforming work of art, is left to the mind of the viewer. Beneath the skin of perfection in his most accomplished paintings lies a thoroughly modern network of informed allusion and free association. His success is a measure of an intuitive balance of craft, using every tool at his disposal, and the courage to put into his art only what his own imagination requires.

Notes

1. Gerrit Henry, "Reclaiming Luminism," in *Stephen Hannock: Rockets and Flooded Rivers* (New York: Tibor de Nagy Gallery, 1990).

2. Jason Rosenfeld, *Stephen Hannock*, 2002, p. 5.

3. Timothy Cahill, "July Portfolio: Stephen Hannock," *Chronogram*, July 2007, p. 44.

4. For a complete history of Nash Editions, see Garrett White, ed., *Nash Editions: Photography and the Art of Digital Printing* (Berkeley: New Riders, 2007).

5. Gerrit Henry, "Reclaiming Luminism," p. 3.

6. Unless otherwise noted, this and the subsequent quotes are from a taped interview of Stephen Hannock with Garrett White, New York, NY, May 20, 2008.

7. This and the subsequent quotes are from a taped interview of R. Mac Holbert with Garrett White on June 27, 2008.

8. José de la Colina and Tomás Pérez Turrent, *Objects of Desire: Conversations with Luis Buñuel*, ed. and trans. by Paul Lenti (New York: Marsilio Publishers, 1992), xiii.

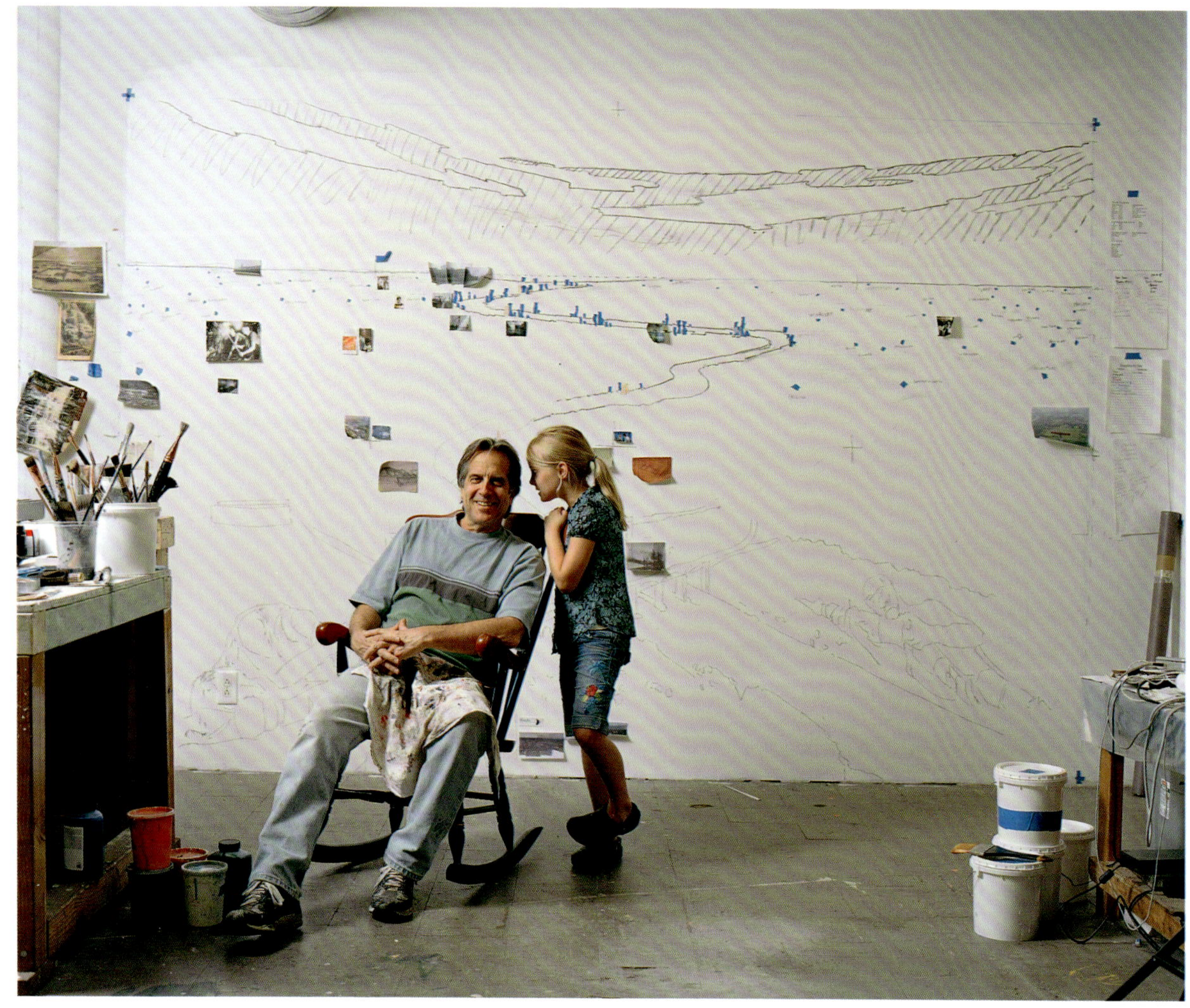

STEPHEN AND DAUGHTER GEORGIA IN STUDIO, 2008

1969   The marvel of drawing was first demonstrated by Daniel Hodermarsky, my larger-than-life influence, who proved there was life beyond the hockey rink. The Kaaterskill Falls piece at The Metropolitan Museum of Art is in honor of Dan and his nephew, the artist Frank Moore.

1971   The most profound influence imaginable came from sisters Betty and Agnes Mongan. I met Betty my first week at Smith College during a print study at the art museum. Shortly afterward she sent me to Cambridge, Massachusetts, to meet her sister, Agnes, who was at the Fogg Art Museum. Betty and Agnes demonstrated the necessity of knowing art history and introduced me to original work from the masters' hands. Betty left me in the print room at the Smith College Museum with several Rembrandt etchings. A few months later at the Fogg, Agnes sat me down with a stack of drawings by Ingres. This privilege went on for two decades. My *Oxbow* series through 2001 was dedicated to the Mongan sisters.

And it was from Agnes and Betty that I first heard of Lane and Jodie Faison who lived in Williamstown, Massachusetts. I met the Faisons a few years before Jodie's passing. Lane became one of my closest friends until his passing in 2006. The vista at the National Gallery of Art in Washington, D.C., was painted in his honor.

1972   I dreaded the days when Leonard Baskin would relegate me to the library in the main house to draw from anatomy books. The library was magnificent, right out of a scene from *My Fair Lady,* with the spiral staircase that wound up to a balcony. And the books! First-edition works of William Blake, *The Anatomy of the Horse* by George Stubbs, printed from the original plates…two copies! And then the prints: Odilon Redon, Rodolphe Bresdin, Käthe Kolwitz…. But I couldn't stand the tedious anatomy drawing.

Then, several weeks into these labors everything clicked. I remember the day it happened. The lines became effortless. The rhythm just happened. I remember drawing the figure without even looking at the page. "Once you can draw," Leonard would say as he stared me down, "you can do anything."

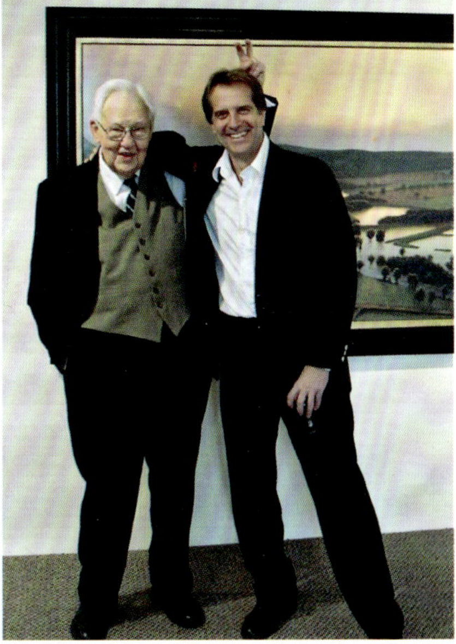

WITH S. LANE FAISON JR., 2003

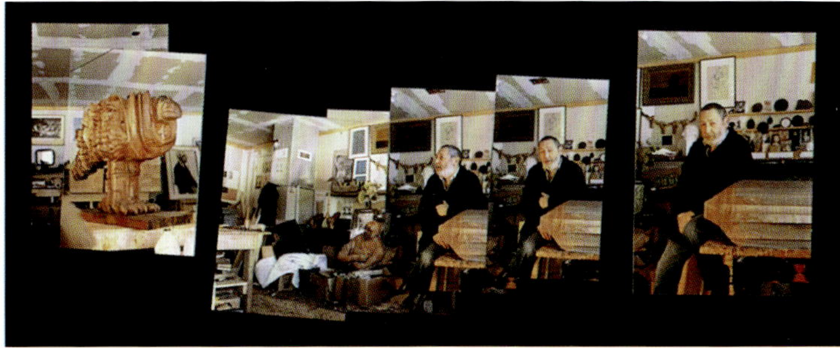

LEONARD BASKIN, 1986

1976   In Northampton, Massachusetts, during the years after college we would frequently take to the Connecticut River— usually north of the Oxbow—in a rubber boat with a silent electric motor. We would move through the flooded forests while sitting right at the water's surface. The light on the river at water level was uncanny. And the relationship of the trees to one another

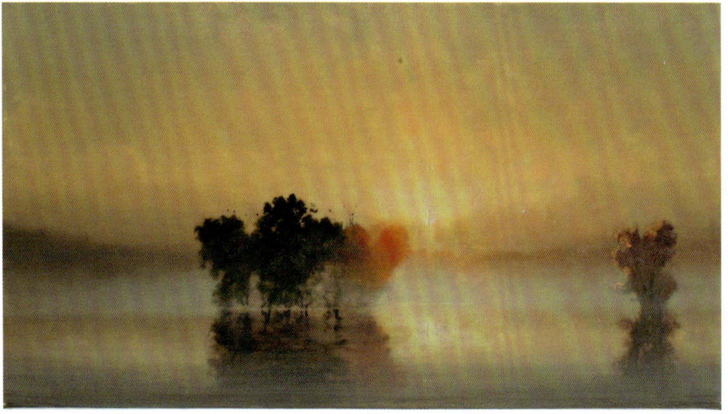

would change as we moved through. The vistas were cinematic; the trees were like people in the compositions of Hitchcock or David Lean.

From the top of Skinner Park on the Holyoke Range, the river becomes a light-engraving carved right out of the flood plain. It was most notably Thomas Cole who was first inspired by the primordial nature of the omega shape. But in any case, the river seemed to be constantly generating stories. And from my first attempts to paint the river, these stories were as interesting to me as the topography.

1983 Moving full time to New York was so different from the routine two-to-three-day visits from Massachusetts. It was taking in the art world without a safety net. My first studio in the city

was 8 x 12 feet—with curtains for two of the walls. But life changed dramatically once the daily trips to this Crosby Street studio began. Equally seismic was the shift from mentors Betty and Agnes Mongan, sisters in their 90s at Smith and Harvard, to a man several years my junior. I met Maurice Berger shortly after my arrival in New York. He was a professor at Hunter College and curator of their galleries at the ripe old age of 27. Maurice and I could not have been more different as people. But his every breath was in celebration of art. He took me to waves of openings in the East Village. (Maurice went to grade school at the East Side Hebrew Institute on 8th Street between Avenues B and C.) On

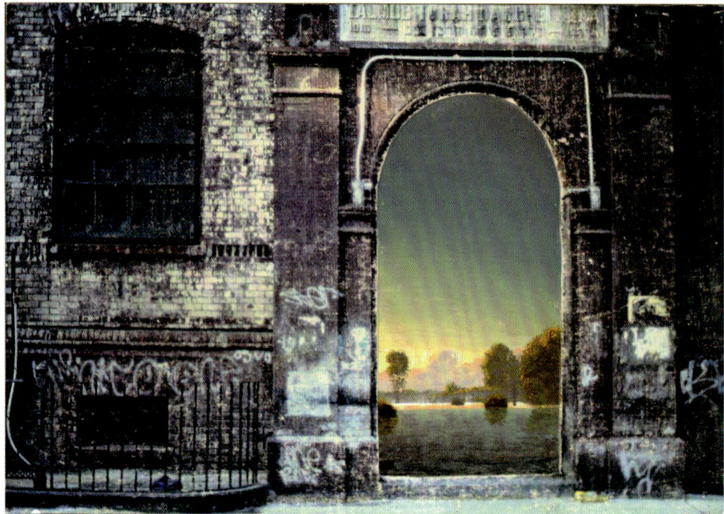

one of these junkets he introduced me to Sherrie Levine. One of the most invigorating things about Sherrie was the way her pre–New York life became part of the art she was being recognized for in the contemporary arena. The magazines that an artist tends to devour from the provinces were a source for many of her images as well as surface. This appreciation of surface was reminiscent of my interest in polished canvas. And as she was borrowing images for her works, I was inspired to recycle previous works of my own into current ideas.

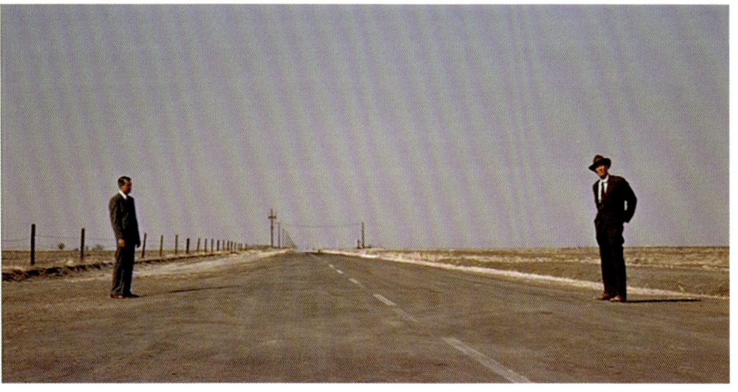

(TOP) FLOODED RIVER WITH DAWN FLARE
(BOTTOM) STILL FROM MOVIE NORTH BY NORTHWEST

THE SCHOLAR FROM 8 BC, 1985

1988   Early on, I used old envelopes to soak up excess paint from the canvas. Rather than wait for the brush-applied paint to set before I ripped into it (with the random orbital sander), an envelope would absorb just enough paint to quicken the drying time and still leave an even film that would respond to the polishing. Working with already-used envelopes was obvious. Then one day, after pressing an envelope into the wet canvas, I tossed it into the wastebasket…but missed. And what was lying on the floor was more interesting than the painting I was making. I put the envelope on the windowsill, where it sat for weeks. After this time the paint marks on the envelope were still interesting, but so was the travel documentation: canceled stamp, intended destination, place of origin. When I eventually began to make paintings on these surfaces, this documentation made the painting process considerably more engaging than working on the inert surface of the canvas. While the painting was being made, it was impossible not to think of the people/places/events that were somehow connected to the document.

1992   Starting with *The Oxbow* and including the recent *Northern City Renaissance,* the locations of the large vistas exist as a real place. The process of learning about these places is as interesting as studying what to paint. Interest in a location for a painting usually begins visually, but sometimes learning of events that have happened in a given place can inspire the work.

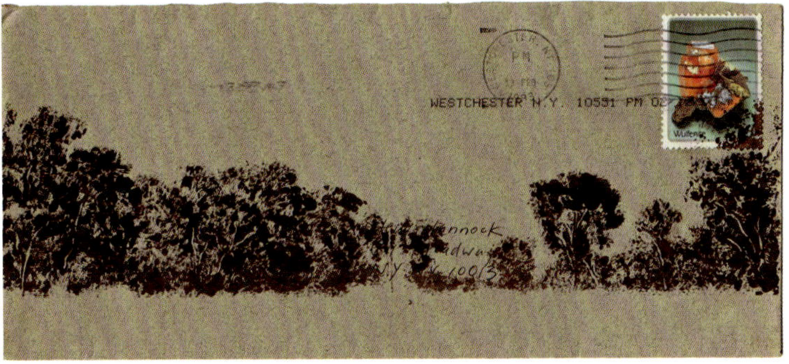

MONOTYPE ON ENVELOPE, 1993

OIL ON PAPER ENVELOPE, 4¼ X 9½ INCHES (11 X 24 CM). COLLECTION OF THE ARTIST

And during the months and sometimes years that I may study a place visually *and* historically, a third element is introduced: the diary. The events and adventures I experience as the work process unfolds become part of the tapestry of the final painting. An accomplished dealer once encouraged me to hire research assistants to more efficiently gather information about the place I was painting. But the people and situations encountered during the learning process itself become an important part of the art. This work must be done by me.

Weaving these elements into a finished idea can be a painful process, one that often has more in common with what I've learned about filmmaking than making a "traditional" painting. As whimsy is crucial to the success of the painting, one becomes more of a curator of accidents than an applier of paint. And in that role, one must accept that strong visual ideas as well as interesting facts may wind up "on the cutting-room floor."

2002   The *Northern City Renaissance* project, which began as a simple though immense backdrop, evolved into a smaller canvas but more complex vista with text and collage. The city of Newcastle-upon-Tyne won a countrywide lottery for a performing arts center called the Sage Gateshead, designed by Sir Norman Foster. The grand opening was scheduled for 2004. My friend, a native son, was asked to perform with the Newcastle Symphony. There were many other events in the works including a wire-walk by Philip Petit from the north bank of the Tyne to the top of the Sage. "Do you think there is a painting there?" Sting asked in 2002, regarding the event that was to be one of the most celebrated in northern England in years.

My first idea was a 24 x 36-foot painting that would be unfurled inside the vast Sage lobby during the opening ceremonies. Then I began studying the region's history: Hadrian's Wall in AD 170; shipbuilding and the hundreds of companies that had thrived along the Tyne; the centuries of collieries ("…coals to

Newcastle"); then the tradition of artists who went *into* the mines to paint the working miners. I discovered that Alfred William Hunt, the pre–Raphaelite painter, was my great (times three) uncle. (And his most famous work was *The Lighting of the Lamps on the Tynemouth Pier* in 1868.) This painting had to be made and these stories had to be told.

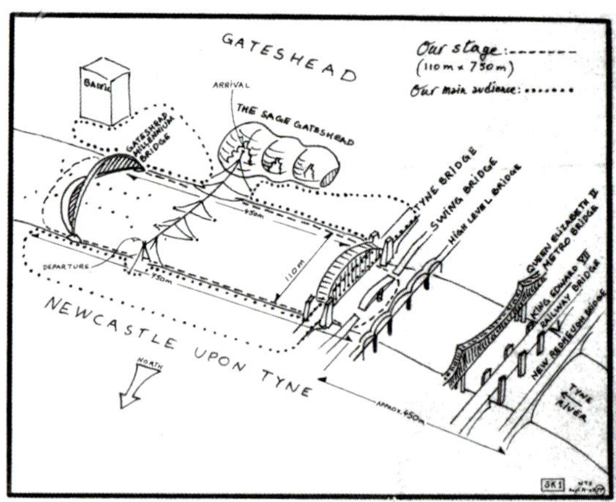

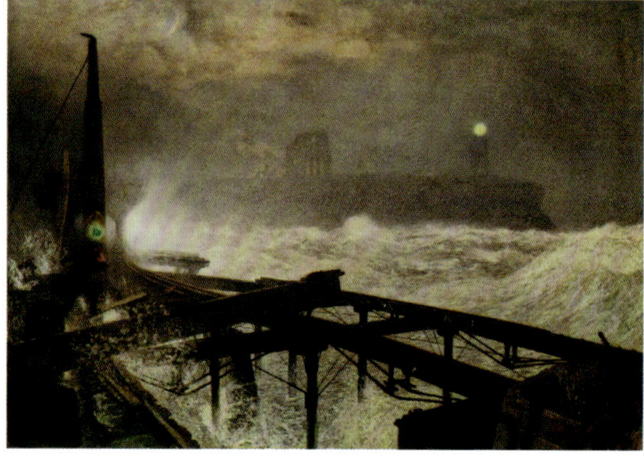

(top) Petite blueprint for Tyne Wire Walk, 2002
(bottom) Alfred William Hunt, The Lighting of the Lamps
on the Tynemouth Pier, 1868
Oil on paper envelope, 4¼ x 9½ inches (11 x 24 cm).
Collection of the Artist

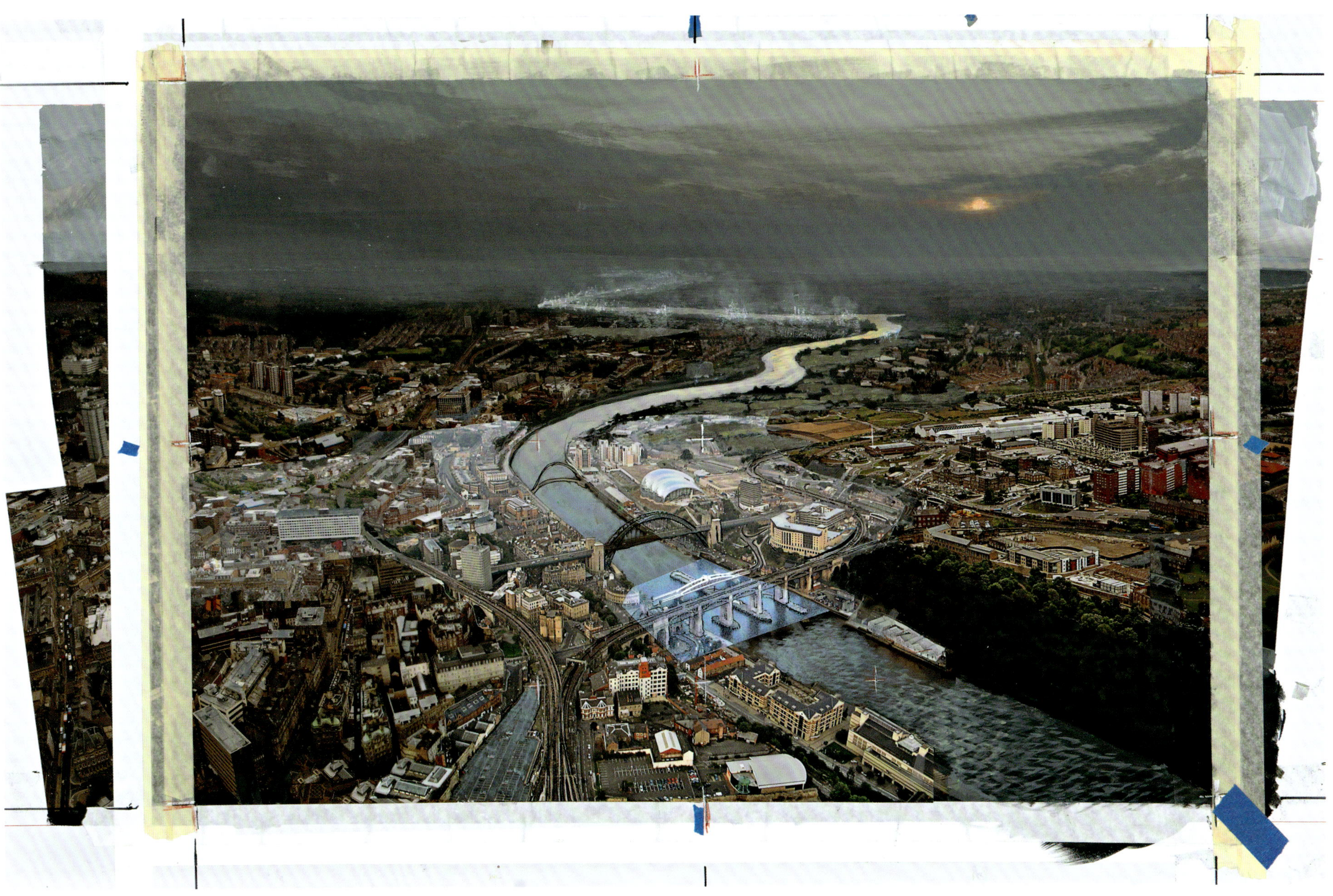

STUDY FOR NORTHERN CITY RENAISSANCE, 2005

Acrylic on digital print assemblage, 19 x 36 inches (48 x 91 cm). Collection of the Artist

Northern City Renaissance (Newcastle, England, Mass MoCA #53), 2008
Polished mixed media on canvas, 96 x 144 inches (244 x 366 cm).
Collection of Sting, on Loan to the Laing Art Gallery, Newcastle

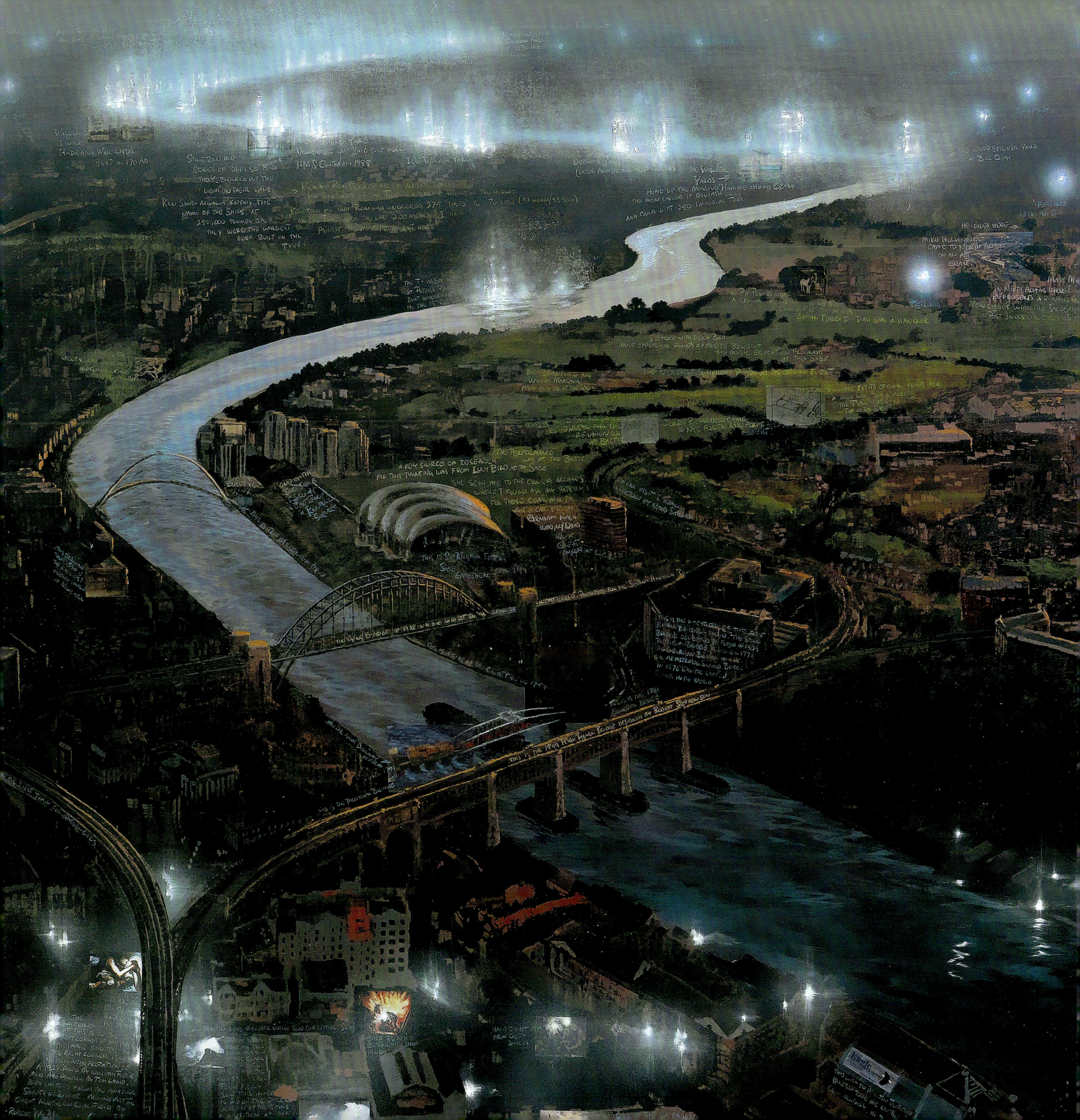

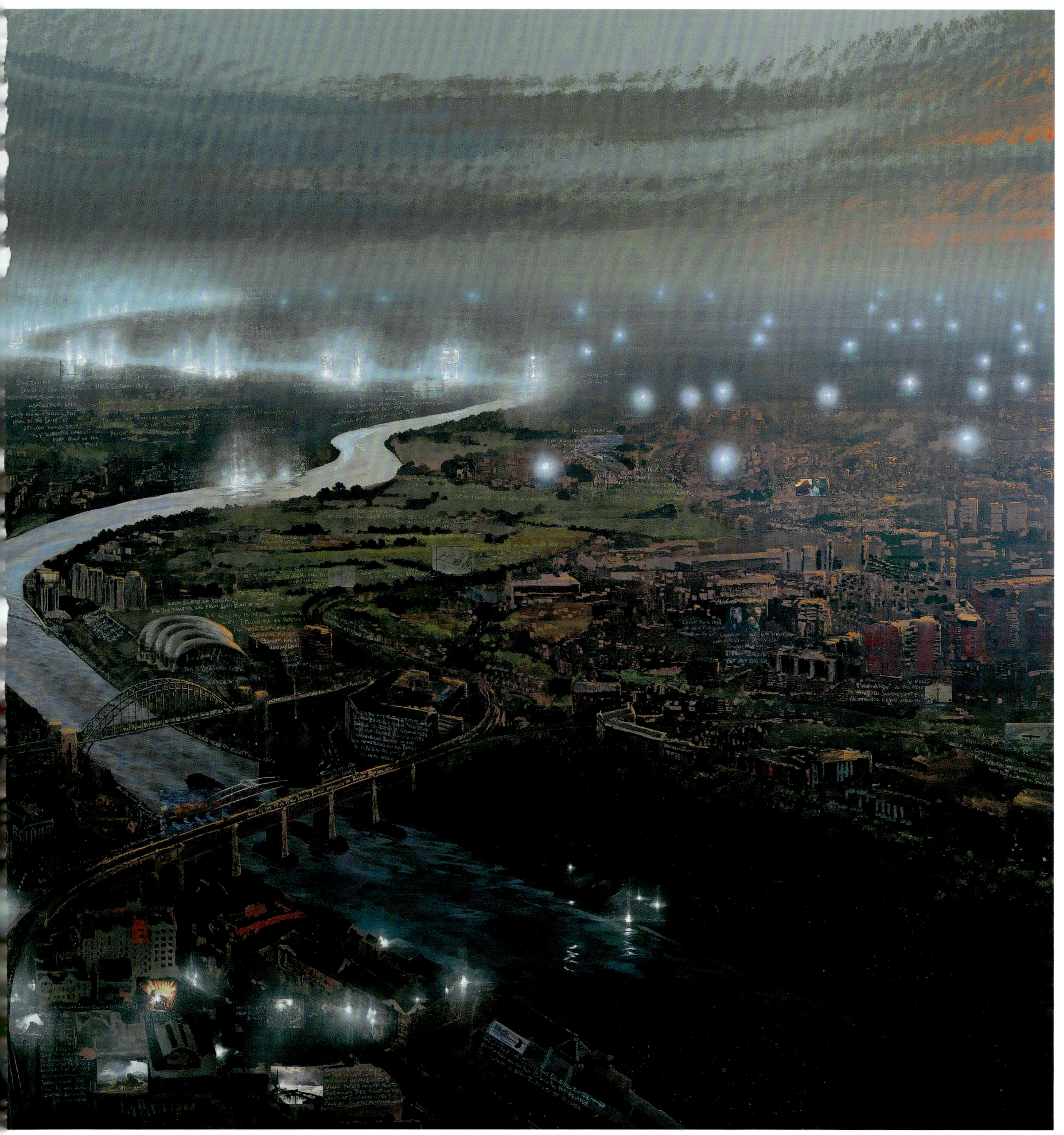

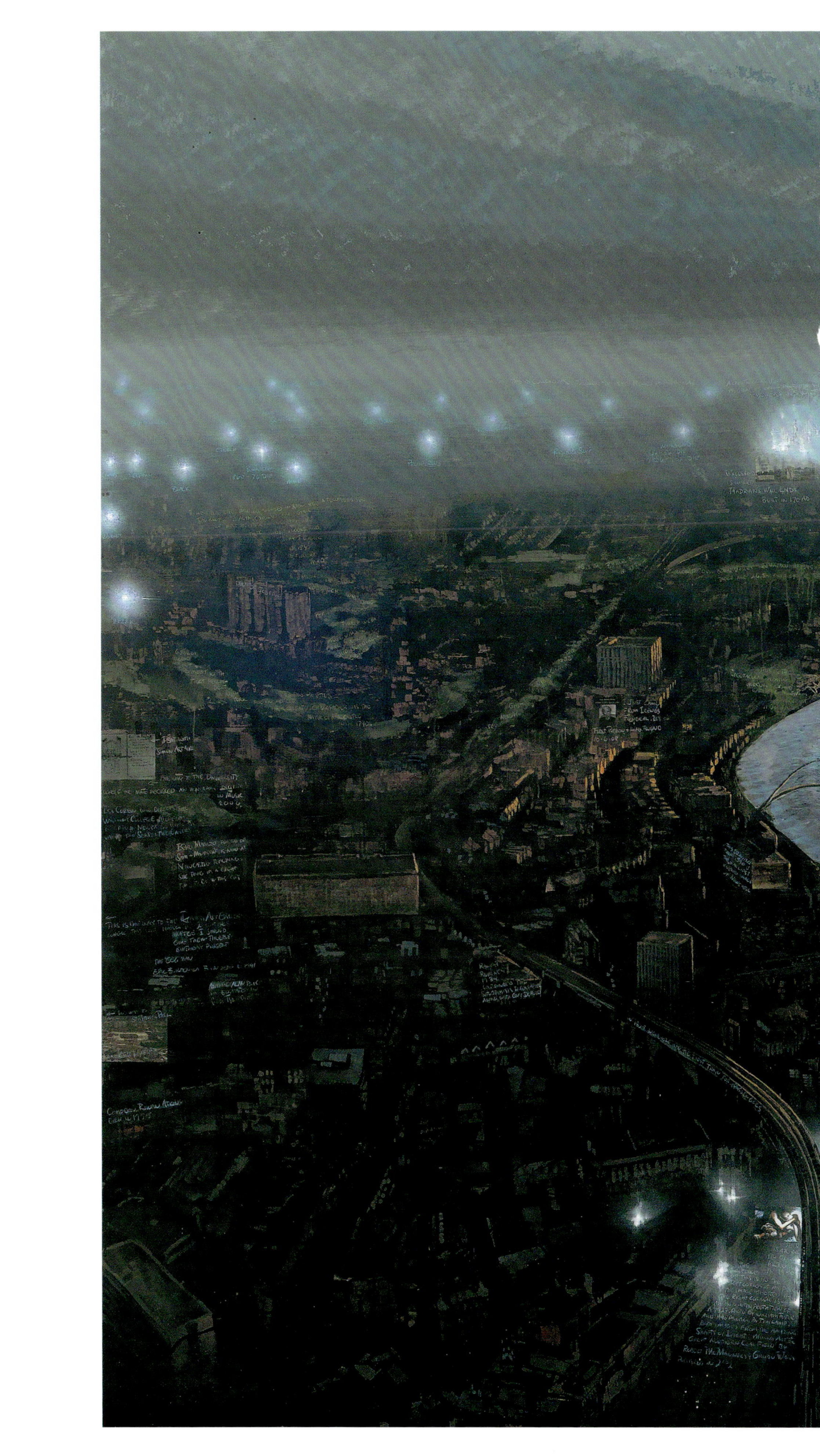

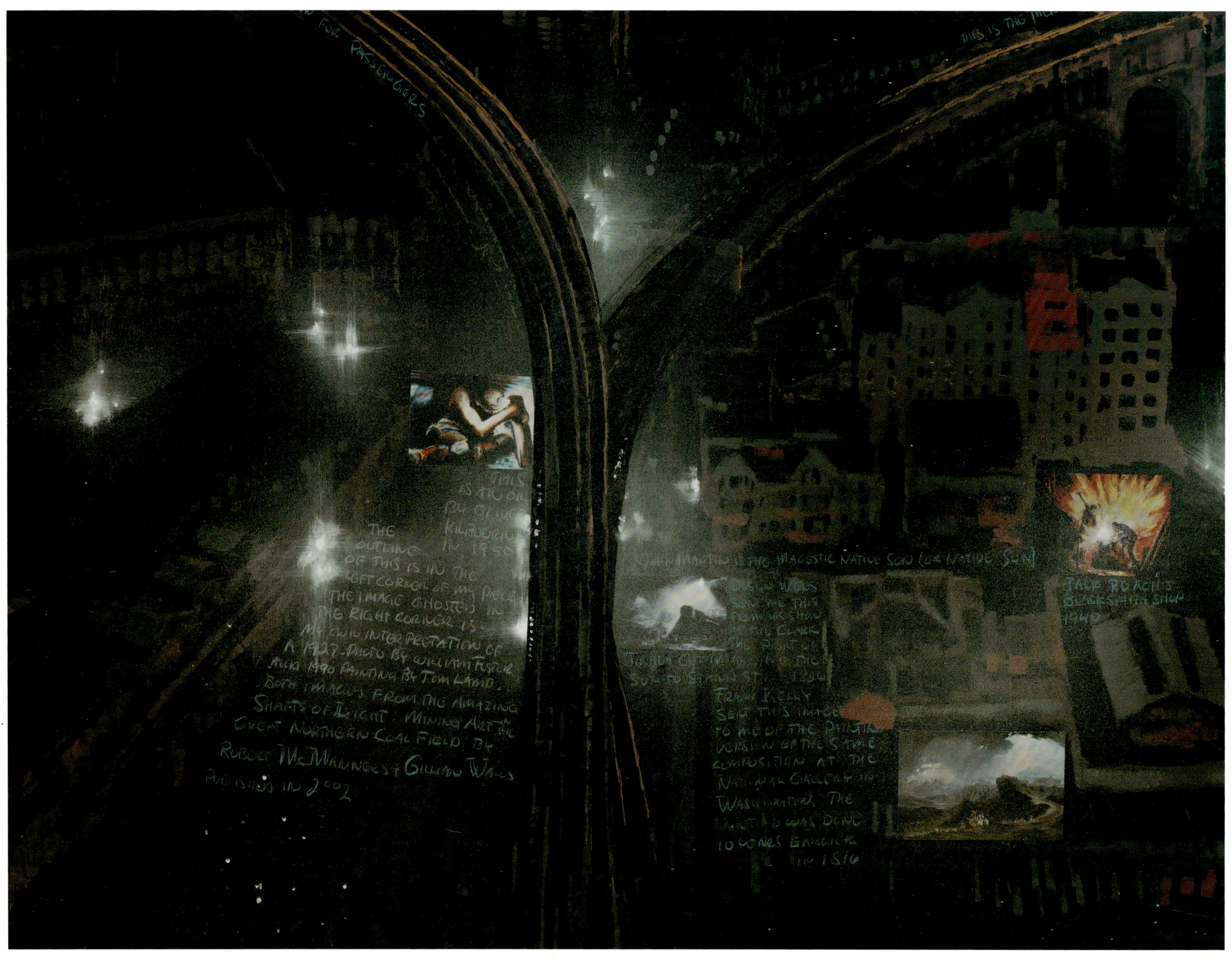

detail: Northern City Renaissance (Newcastle, England, Mass MoCA #53), 2008

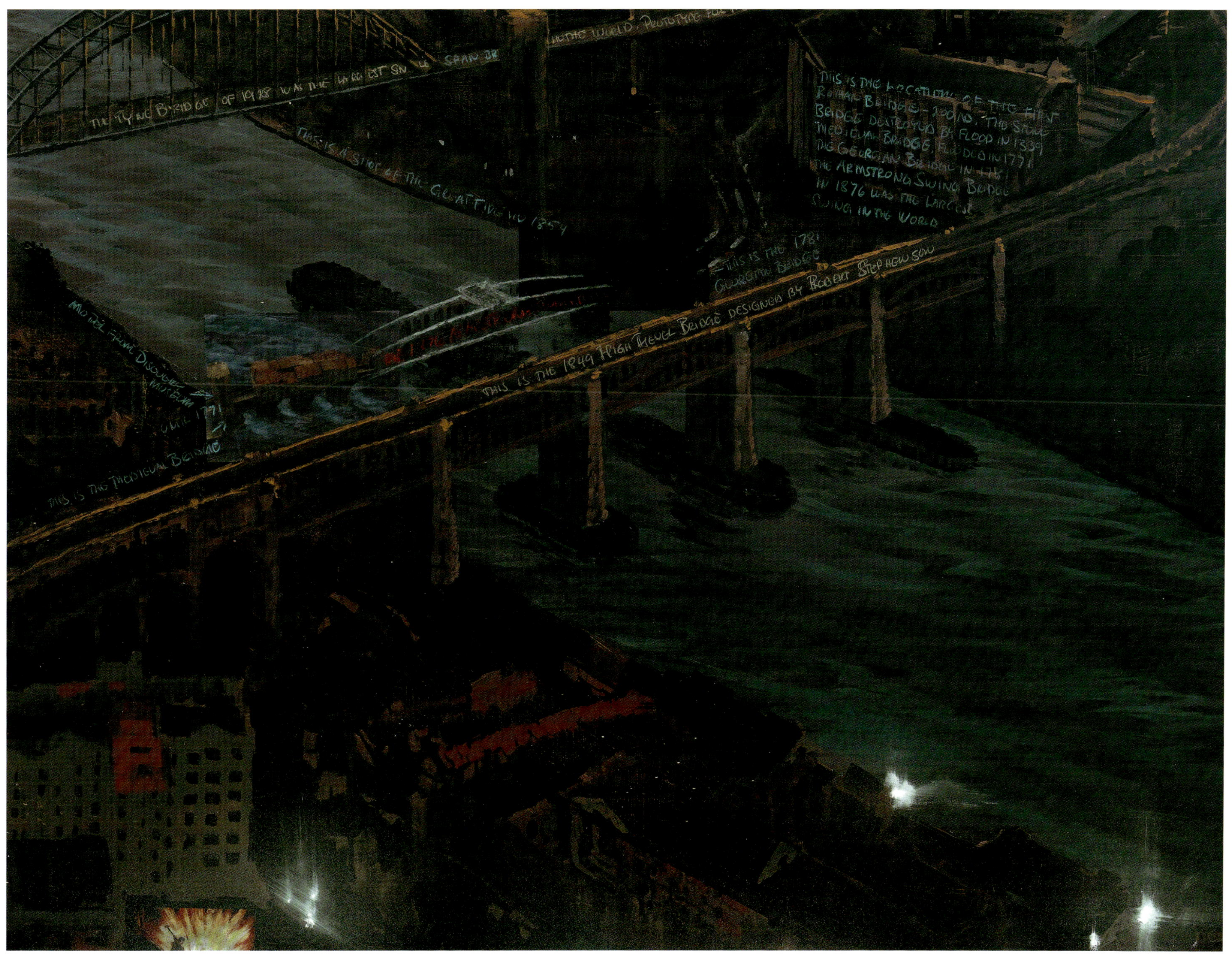

detail: Northern City Renaissance (Newcastle, England, Mass MoCA #53), 2008

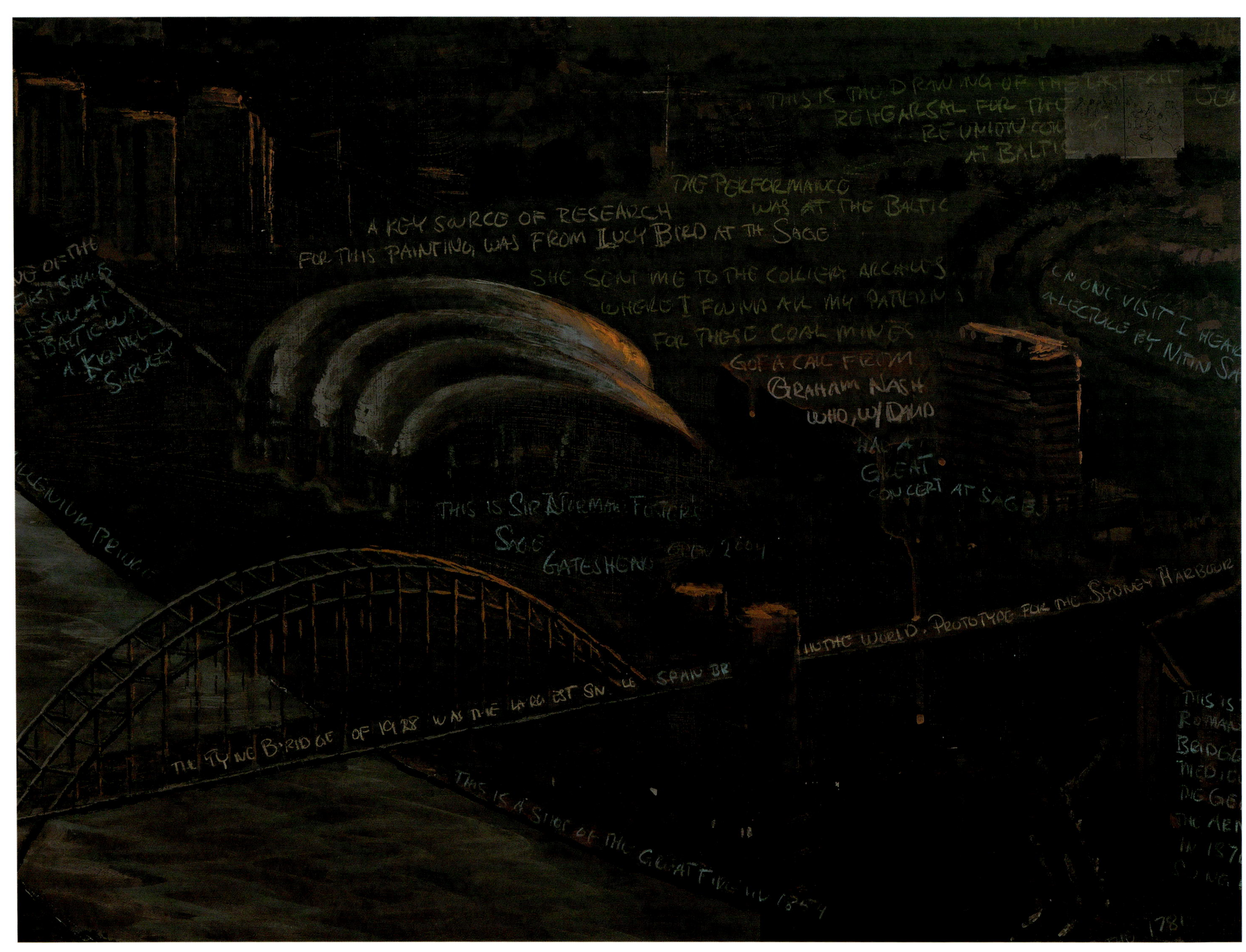

DETAIL: NORTHERN CITY RENAISSANCE (NEWCASTLE, ENGLAND, MASS MoCA #53), 2008

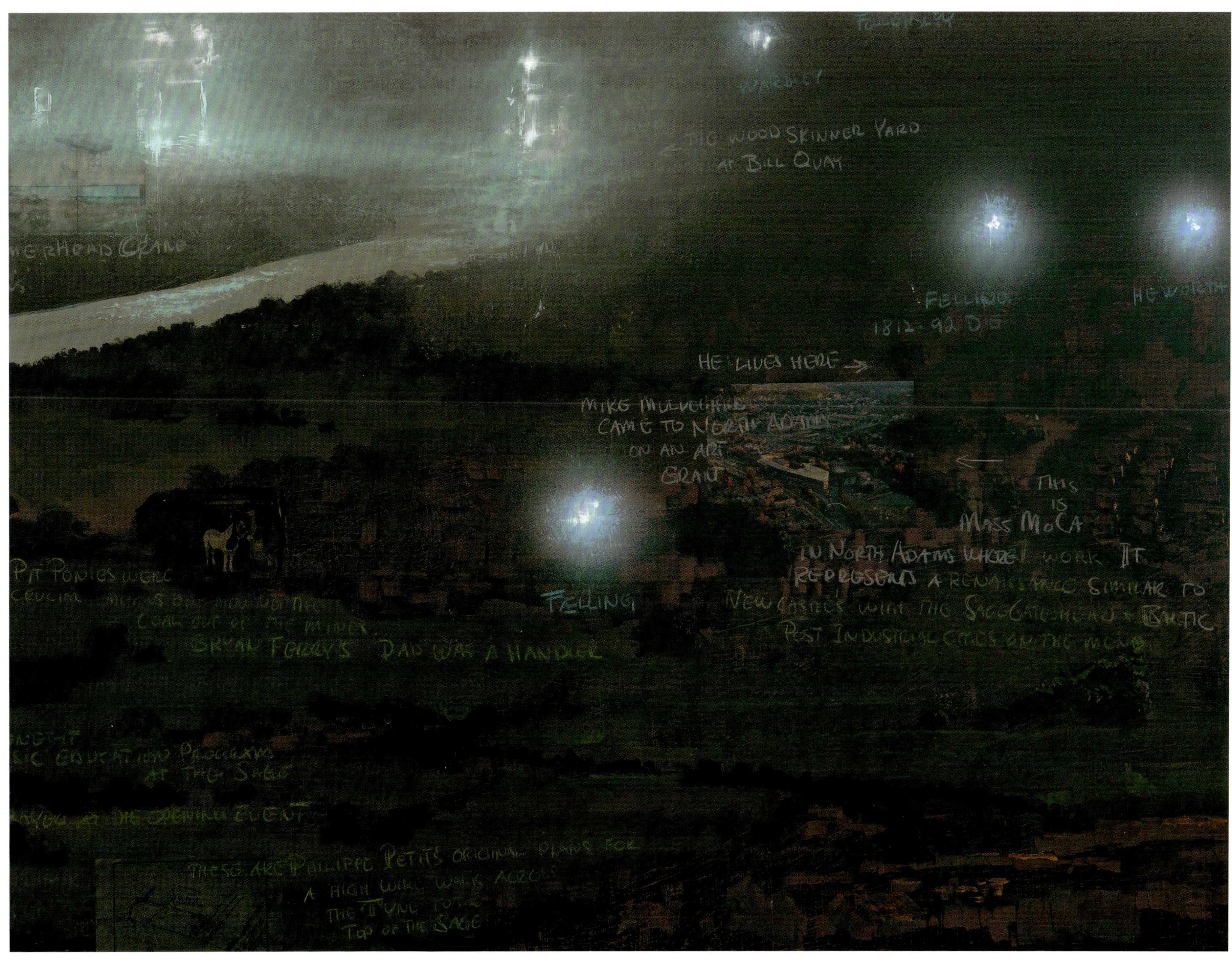

detail: Northern City Renaissance (Newcastle, England, Mass MoCA #53), 2008

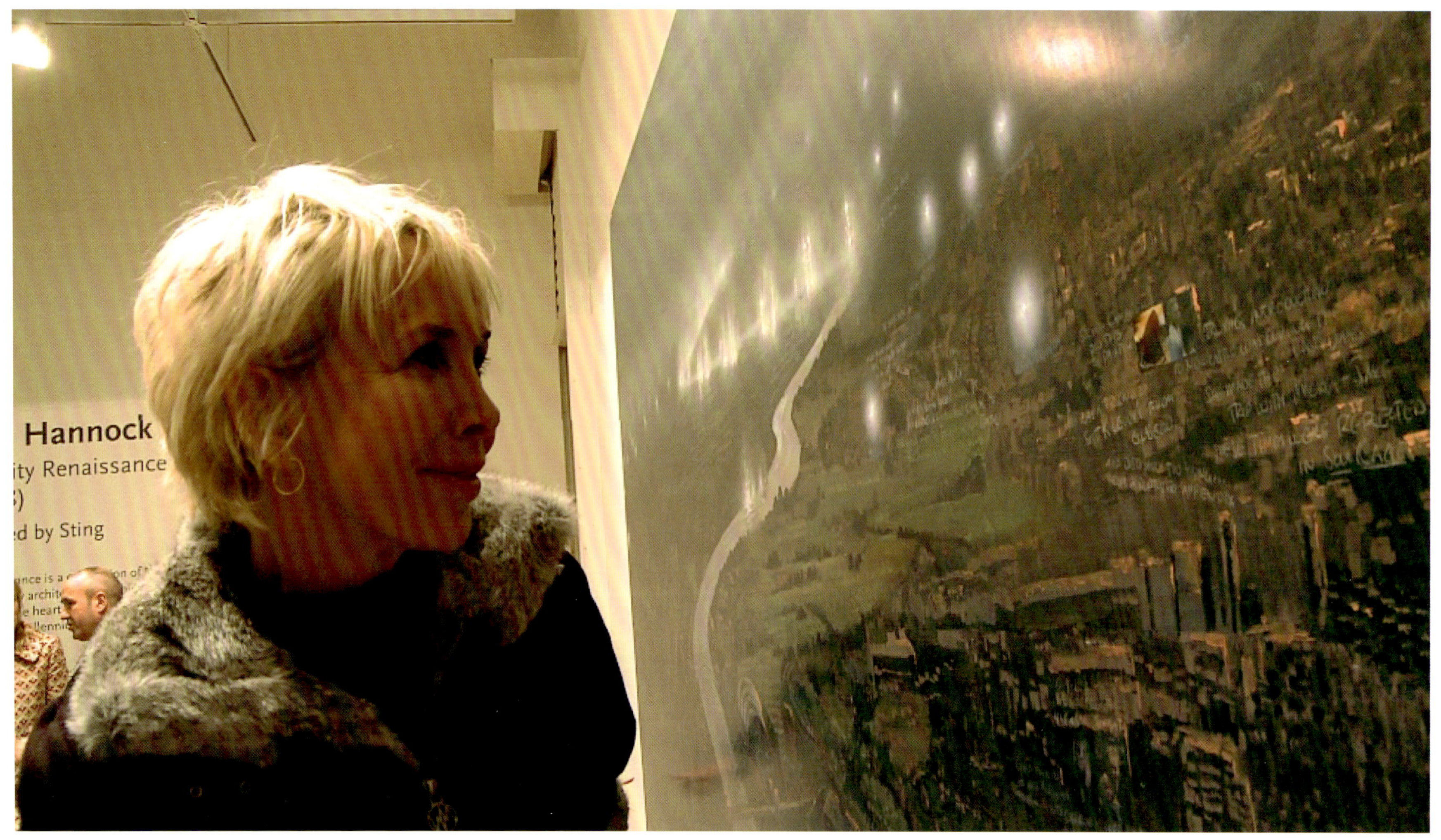

Trudie Styler at the Sumner Clan Reception, Laing Art Gallery, Newcastle, England, November, 2008

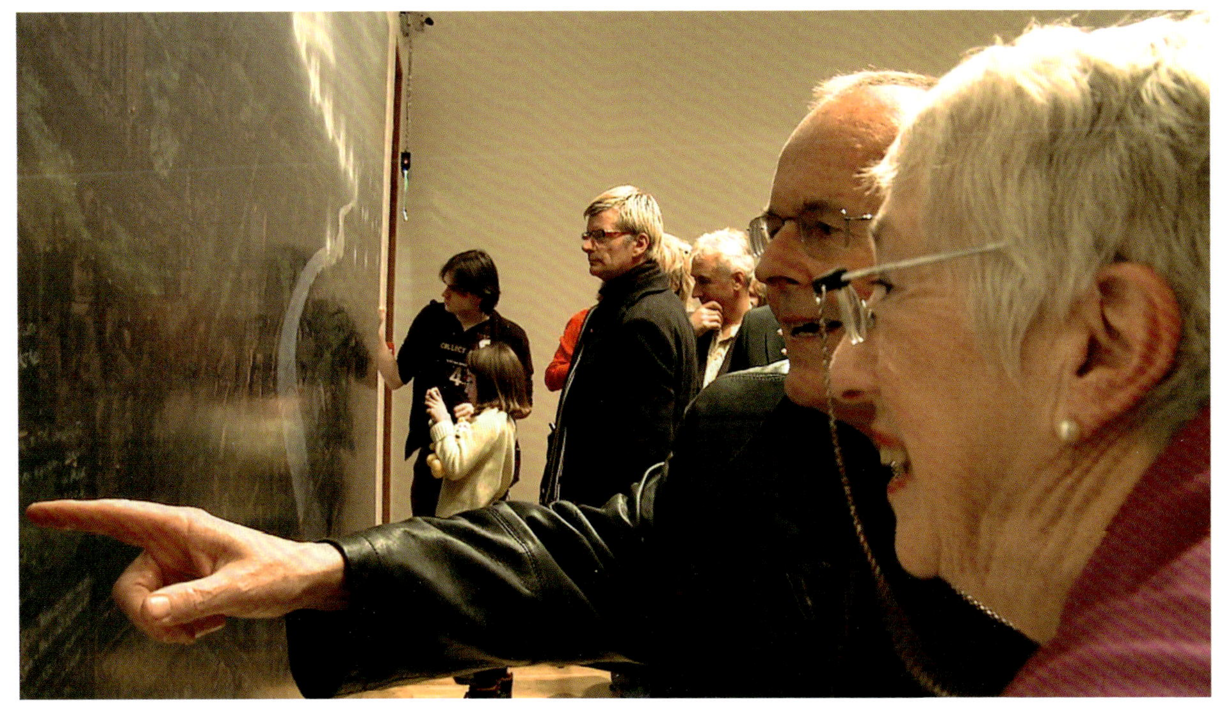

Sumner Clan Reception, Laing Art Gallery, Newcastle, England, November, 2008

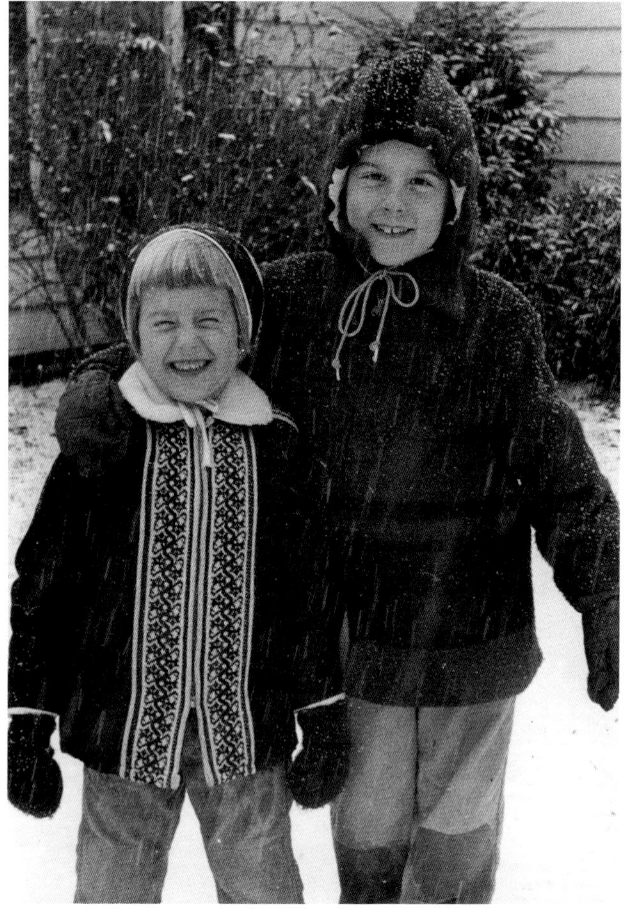

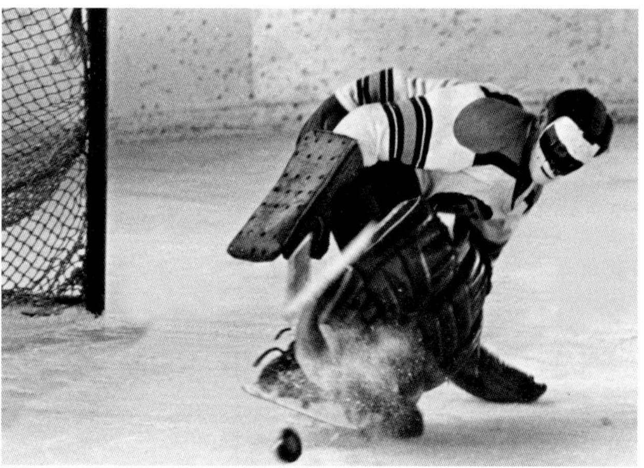

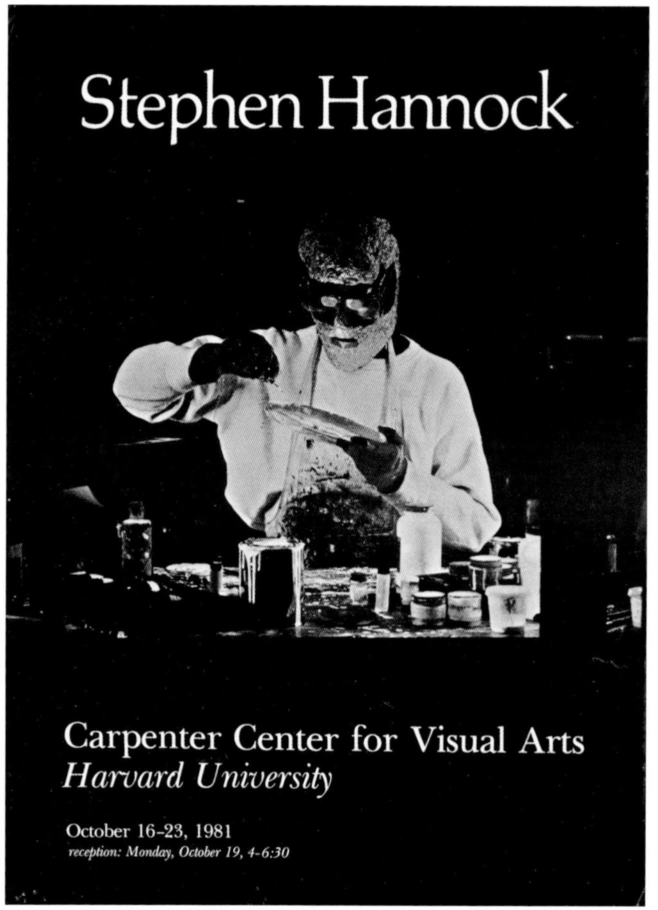

(TOP) STEPHEN AND SISTER SALLY, 1958
(BOTTOM) TENDING HOCKEY GOAL, 1969
(RIGHT) POSTER FOR HARVARD EXHIBITION, 1981

Born March 31, 1951

1963–1971   Attended The Albany Academy, Trinity-Pawling School, Deerfield Academy, and Bowdoin College.

1970   During a postgraduate year at Deerfield Academy, met artist Daniel Hodermarsky.

1971   On exchange to Smith College from Bowdoin College, became apprenticed to Leonard Baskin.

First documentary with Florentine Films, produced by Buddy Squires and Roger Sherman.

Met Elizabeth Mongan at Smith College, Northampton, Massachusetts.

Met Agnes Mongan at Harvard University, Cambridge, Massachusetts.

1975   Competed in the World Frisbee Championships in the Rose Bowl.

1976   First museum show at the Smith College Museum of Art, organized by Elizabeth Mongan and Charles Chetham.

Show at the Fine Arts Center Gallery at University of Massachusetts, organized by Hugh Davies.

Irene Hunter first saw work at the Hatch Shell, Charles River Esplanade, Boston, Massachusetts.

1981   Show at Carpenter Center, Harvard University, organized by Agnes Mongan and Robert Gardener.

1982   Visiting artist at Williams College, Williamstown, Massachusetts, organized by Thomas Krens.

Moved to New York City. First studio at Staley Gretzinger on Crosby Street.

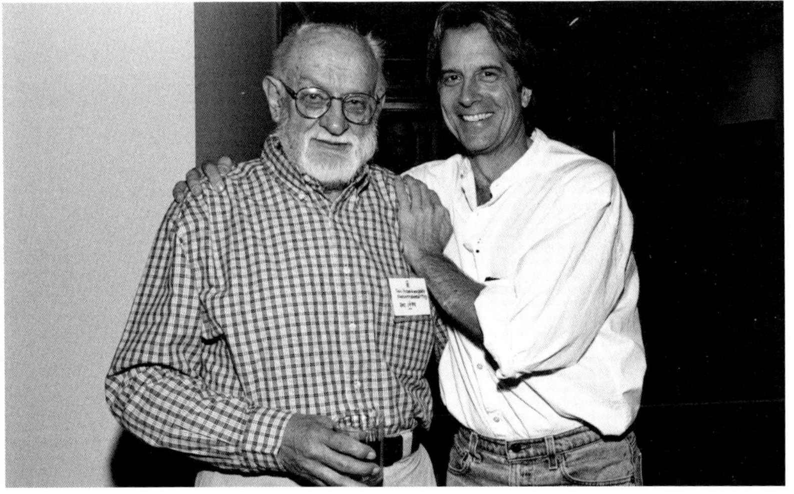

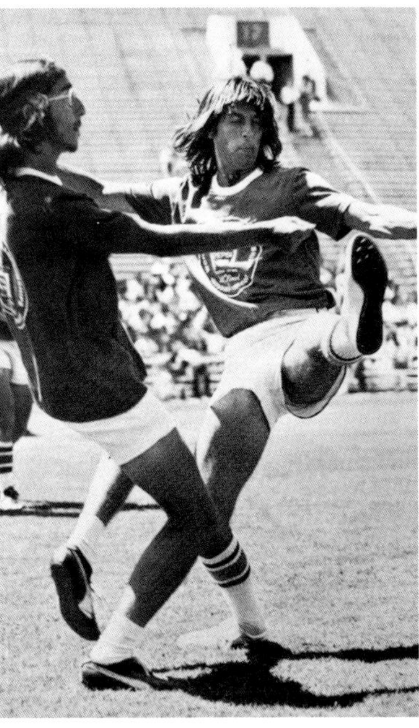

(TOP) DAN HODERMARSKY AND STEPHEN 1998
(BOTTOM) WORLD FRISBEE CHAMPIONSHIPS, 1975

1983 Met Maurice Berger, cultural historian, curator, and art critic.

1984 Had first New York gallery show at Frank Bernarducci Gallery. First show at a New York nightclub, The Pyramid Club.

1985 Met Ashton Hawkins. He introduced Hannock to Andy Warhol, who wanted to learn more about phosphorescent paint.

Met Sting and wife Trudie Styler.

Met William and Karen Lauder.

Designed windows at Bergdorf Goodman, New York, New York.

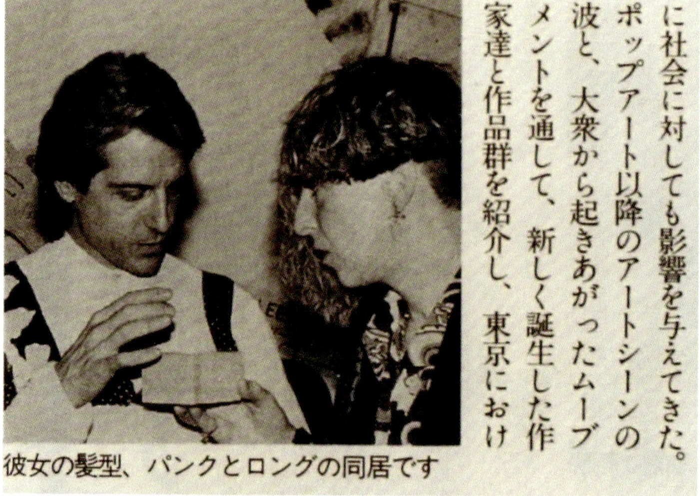

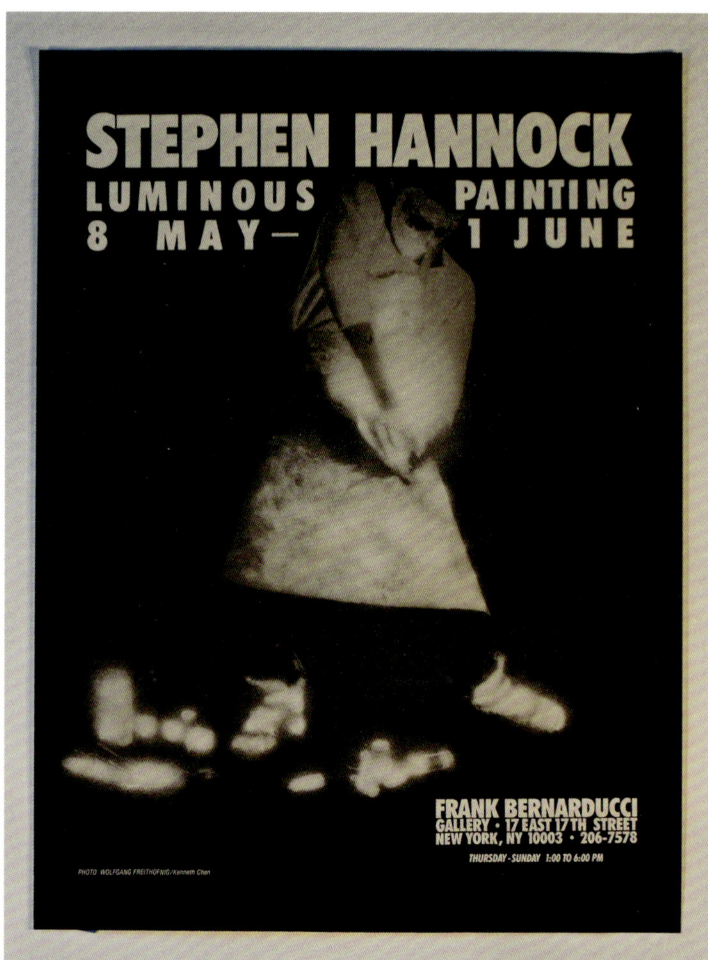

1988 *American Pop Culture Now* exhibition at Laforet Museum in Tokyo, Japan.

Featured in *Newsweek* magazine article on neo-Romantic landscape.

1990 MTV news feature, produced by Buddy Squires.

First show of polished oil work at Tibor De Nagy Gallery, New York, New York.

1992 125 High Street Tower, Boston; installation with Florentine Films documentary, produced by Roger Sherman.

The Metropolitan Museum of Art acquires the first painting from Hannock, *Vortex at Dawn Collapsed*.

1993 Five-painting permanent installation at the Knickerbocker Club, New York, New York.

1994 First collaboration with restaurateurs Tom Colicchio and Danny Meyer.

Agnes Mongan dies.

First Oxbow painting exhibited at Salander-O'Reilly Galleries, New York, New York.

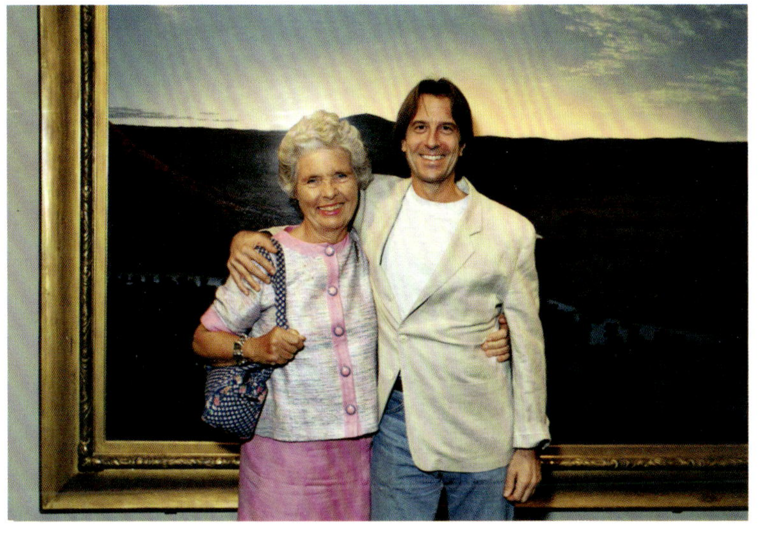

1995   First Oxbow painting acquired by Irene Hunter for the Smith College Museum of Art.

1996   Began work on film *What Dreams May Come*. Develops "Painted World" special effects with Joel Hynek and Nicholas Brooks from Mass Illusions.

1997   Jodie Faison dies. Oxbow drawing donated to Smith College Museum of Art in her memory.

Meets Bridget Watkins.

1998   Designs set for Stephen Petronio Dance Company production of *Not Garden*.

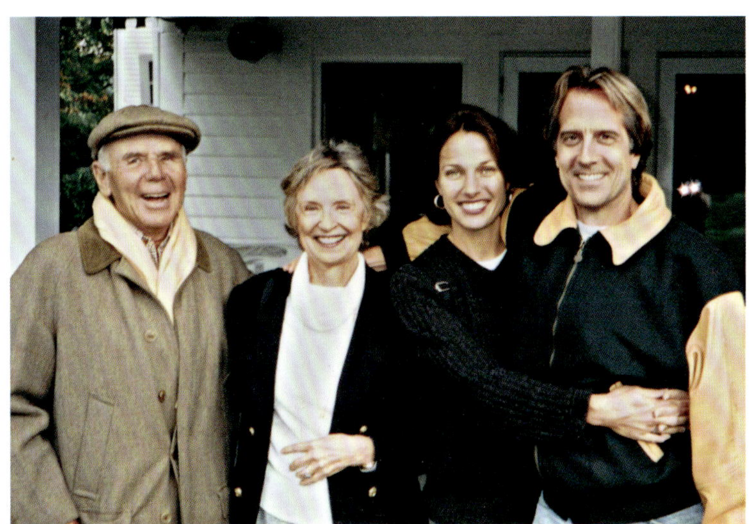

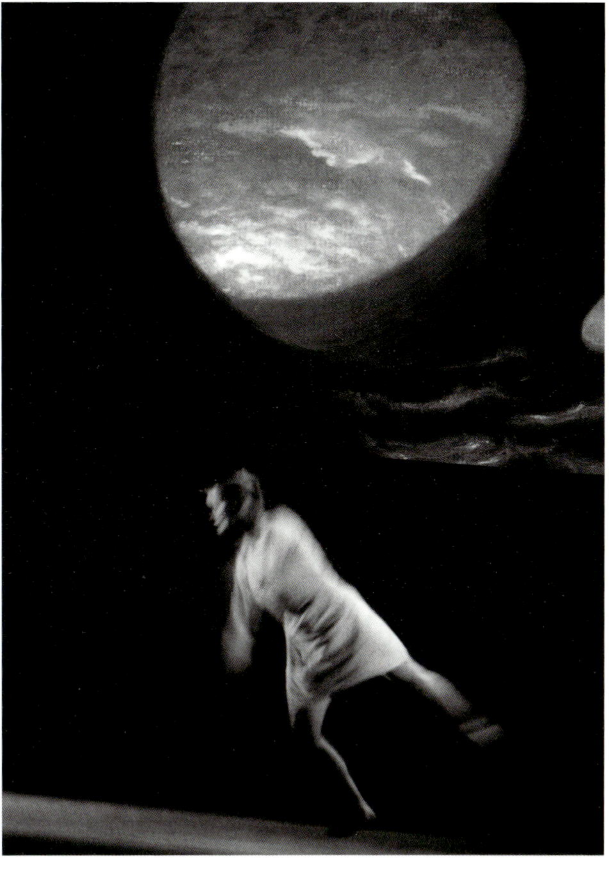

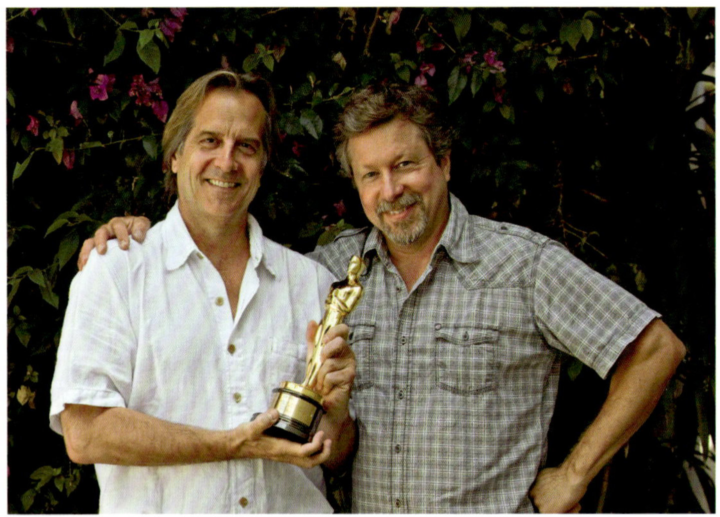

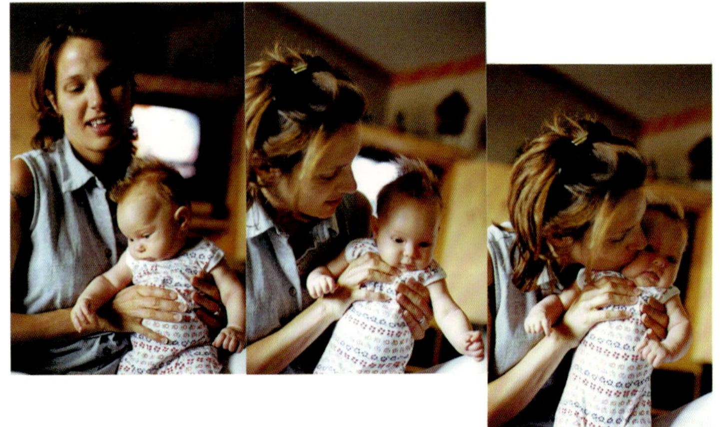

1999 Receives Academy Award for Special Visual Effects.

Wrote *Luminosity*, published by Chronicle Books.

Daniel Hodermarsky dies.

2000 Marries Bridget Watkins. Daughter Georgia is born.

Leonard Baskin dies.

Elizabeth Mongan dies.

The Metropolitan Museum of Art acquires *Oxbow with Green Light*.

2001 Morning of 9/11, alerted to Bridget's brain tumor during terrorist attacks on World Trade Center.

2002 Tribeca Film Festival has first event; began art prize program with Jane Rosenthal and Craig Hatkoff.

First year for Stephen Hannock Scholarship at Cornish College of Art, Seattle, Washington, in memory of his Aunt Evelyn Jordan.

Bought house in Williamstown, Massachusetts.

2003 Opens studio in North Adams near Mass MoCA.

Museum of Contemporary Art San Diego, California, acquires *I Miss My Friends* installation.

2004 Marshall Hannock dies.

Bridget Watkins Hannock dies.

Heroic Woman donated to Deerfield Academy.

2005 The dedication of Bridget's Garden in Madison Square Park, New York, New York.

Sting and Dominick Miller perform at the dedication.

National Gallery of Art in Washington, DC, acquires *A Recent History of Art in Western Massachusetts; Flooded River for Lane Faison (Mass MoCA #12)*.

2006 *Stephen Hannock: A Survey* at The Butler Institute of American Art, Youngstown, Ohio, curated by Dr. Lou Zona.

Lane Faison dies.

Sundance Canyon at Dawn, completed to benefit the 25th anniversary of Sundance Institute, Utah, supported by William and Karen Lauder.

The Metropolitan Museum of Art acquires *Kaaterskill Falls for Frank Moore and Dan Hodermarsky*.

2007 Bowdoin College Museum of Art, Brunswick, Maine, acquires *Oxbow for Bowdoin College; Flooded River for Leonard Baskin and David P. Becker (Mass MoCA #84)*.

Stephen Hannock: A Survey at Albany Institute of History & Art, Albany, New York.

Whitney Museum of American Art acquires *Maternal Nocturne*.

2008 The new Grand Rapids Art Museum opens with *Luminous Afternoon in Western Michigan for Bridget*, in memory of Bridget Watkins Hannock.

The First Green Art Museum, a documentary of Grand Rapids Art Museum (GRAM), produced and directed by David Lachman.

Unveiling of *Northern City Renaissance* at the Laing Art Gallery, Newcastle-upon-Tyne, United Kingdom.

2009 Documentary of *Northern City Renaissance* by Wolfram Hissen for estWest Films.

Major monograph *Stephen Hannock* published by Hudson Hills Press.

Received honorary Doctorate in Fine Arts degree from Bowdoin College, Brunswick, Maine.

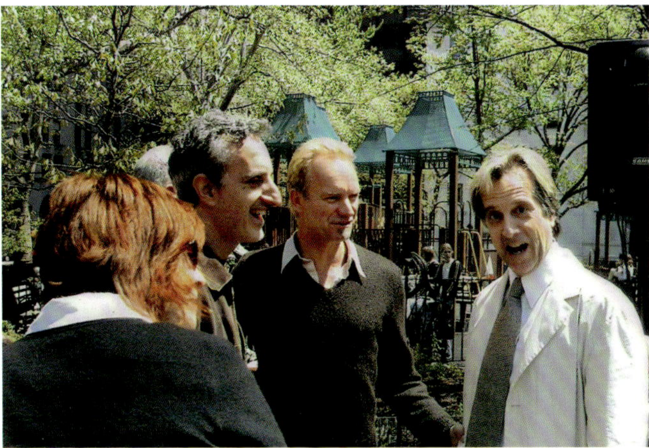

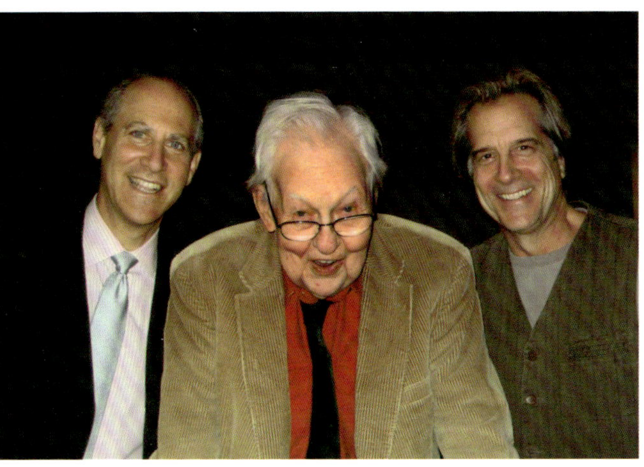

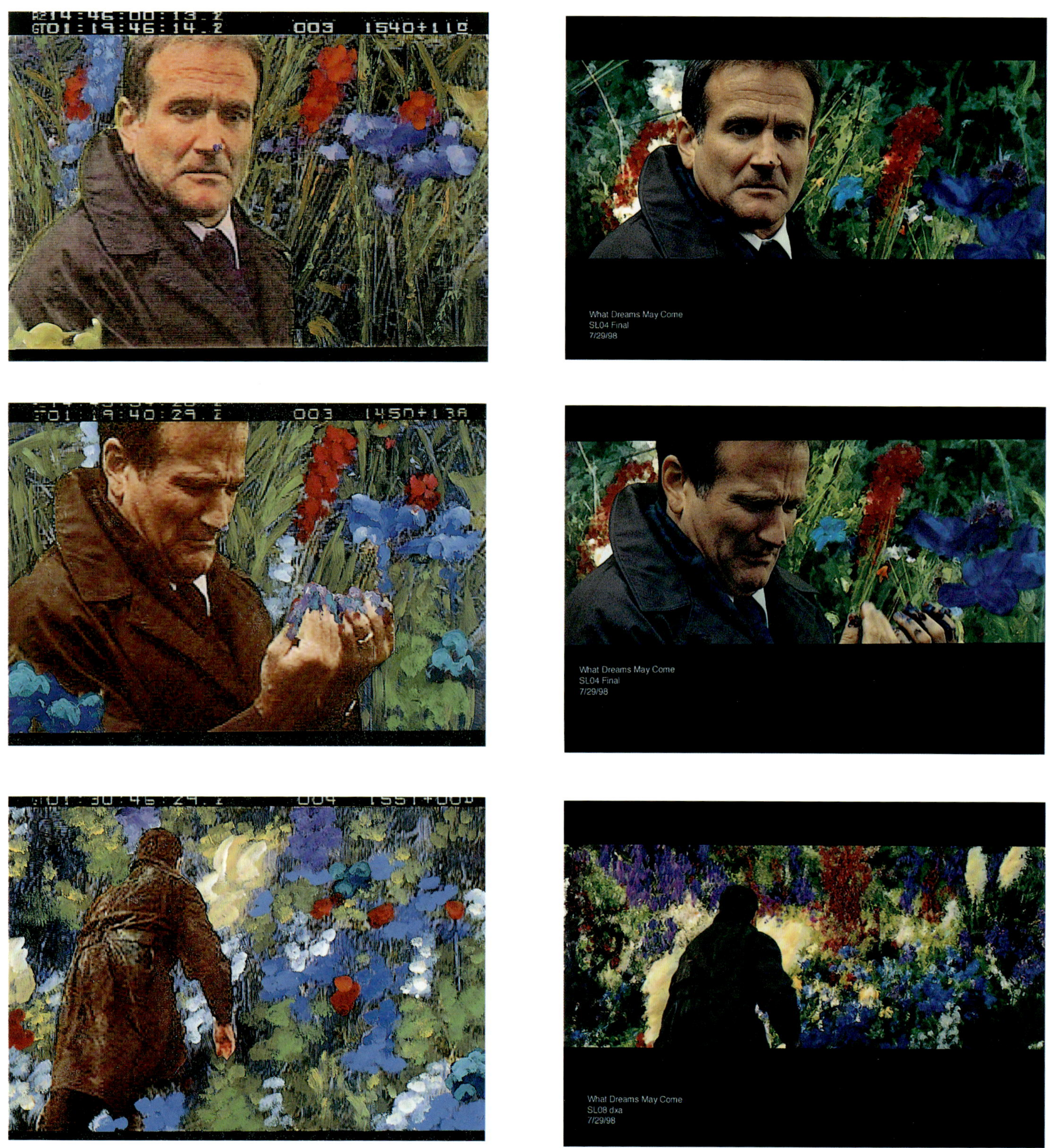

Film Stills from *What Dreams May Come* featuring Robin Williams, 1997
Courtesy of Universal Studios Licensing LLLP

Selected Exhibitions, Installations, Awards & Collections

Selected Solo Exhibitions

2007

The Albany Institute of History & Art, Albany, NY, "Luminosity: Paintings by Stephen Hannock"

The Berkshire Museum, Pittsfield, MA, "Northern City Renaissance at the Berkshire Museum"

2006

Butler Institute of American Art, Youngstown, OH, "Stephen Hannock: A Survey"

2005

McKenzie Fine Art, New York, NY

The Harrison Gallery, Williamstown, MA

2002

McKenzie Fine Art, New York, NY

Michael Kohn Gallery, Los Angeles, CA

Meredith Long and Company, Houston, TX

2001

Winston Wachter Fine Art, Seattle, WA

John Berggruen Gallery, San Francisco, CA

2000

James Graham & Sons, New York, NY

Quint Contemporary Art, La Jolla, CA

1999

Winston Wachter Fine Art, Seattle, WA, "Recent Nocturnes"

Kohn Turner Gallery, Los Angeles, CA, "Nocturnes and Flooded Rivers"

Robert Berman Gallery, Santa Monica, CA

Meredith Long and Company, Houston, TX

1998

Charles P. Russell Gallery, Deerfield Academy, Deerfield, MA, "Space and Time" traveled to: Dayton Art Institute, Dayton, OH

James Graham & Sons, New York, NY

1997

Meredith Long and Company, Houston, TX

The Ralls Collection, Washington, DC

John Berggruen Gallery, San Francisco, CA, "Nocturnes: From Tuscany to Napa"

1996

James Graham & Sons, New York, NY

1995

Timken Museum of Art, San Diego, CA, "After Church, After Cole, Stephen Hannock's Oxbow"

1994

Salander O'Reilly Galleries, New York, NY

1993

John Berggruen Gallery, San Francisco, CA

Gallery One, Toronto, Canada

1992

Meredith Long and Company, Houston, TX, "Recent Paintings:
Stephen Hannock"

1990

Tibor de Nagy Gallery, New York, NY

Joseph V. Reed Center for the Arts, Deerfield, MA, "Selected
Works, 1970–1990" traveled to: Robert Berman Gallery, Santa
Monica, CA

1989

Frank Bernarducci Gallery, New York, NY

1988

Wallace Wentworth Gallery, Washington, DC

1987

Frank Bernarducci Gallery, New York, NY

1986

B-1 Gallery, Santa Monica, CA

1983

Deerfield Academy, Deerfield, MA

Frank Bernarducci Gallery, New York, NY

1982

Carpenter Center for the Visual Arts, Harvard University,
Cambridge, MA

Albany Institute of History & Art, Albany, NY

Williams College Museum of Art, Williamstown, MA

1981

Greenspace Gallery, New York, NY

1980

St. George's School, Newport, RI

Warberg Center, Middlesex School, Concord, MA

Deerfield Academy, Deerfield, MA

Northfield-Mount Herman, Northfield, MA

Williston Academy, Easthampton, MA

Paul Mellon Center, Wallingford, PA

1979

Hood Museum of Art, Dartmouth College, Hanover, NH

1978

Massachusetts Institute of Technology, Cambridge, MA

Boston Center for the Arts, Boston, MA

1976

Smith College Museum of Art, Northampton, MA

University of Massachusetts, Amherst, MA

Selected Group Exhibitions

2007

The Harrison Gallery, Williamstown, MA, "Friends from Northampton"

James Graham & Sons, New York, NY, "One Hundred Fifty Years in the Art Business"

McKenzie Fine Art, New York, NY, "The Story Goes"

Ferrin Gallery, Pittsfield, MA, "We are Here"

Barn Gallery at Stonover Farm, Lenox, MA, "The Art of Night: Sunrise to Sunset"

2006

The Harrison Gallery, Williamstown, MA, "Nightscapes"

2004

The Harrison Gallery, Williamstown, MA, "Friends from New York"

2003

The Harrison Gallery, Williamstown, MA, "Waterscapes"

James Graham & Sons, New York, NY, "Grisaille"

Winston Wachter Mayer Fine Art, New York, NY, "Rotations"

2002

Brattleboro Museum, Brattleboro, VT, "The American River" traveled to: Wood Art Gallery, Vermont College, Montpelier, VT; Montshire Museum, Norwich, VT; Philadelphia Art Alliance, Philadelphia, PA; Florence Griswold Museum, Lyme, CT

Mount Holyoke College Art Museum, South Hadley, MA, "Changing Prospects: The View from Mount Holyoke"

2000

University of Wyoming Art Museum, Laramie, WY, "Landscape 2000: Late 20th-Century American Landscape Painting"

University Art Gallery, San Diego State University, San Diego, CA, "Transcending Earth and Sky"

James Graham & Sons, New York, NY, "Fluid Flow"

1999

Gibbes Museum of Art, Charleston, SC, "Water: A Contemporary American View," traveled to: Mobile Museum of Art, Mobile, AL; Leigh Yawkey Woodson Art Museum, Wausau, WI

Philbrook Museum of Art, Tulsa, OK, "Green Woods & Crystal Waters: The American Landscape Tradition Since 1950" traveled to: Davenport Museum of Art, Davenport, IA; Ringling Museum of Art, Sarasota, FL

Mandeville Gallery, Union College, Schenectady, NY, "Enduring Vision: Contemporary Painters in the Tradition of the Hudson River School"

1998

Hampshire College Art Gallery, Amherst, MA, "Master & Apprentice, Selected Works from Leonard Baskin & Stephen Hannock

South Bend Regional Museum of Art, South Bend, IN, "Remembering Beauty: American Landscapes"

Winston Wachter Fine Art, New York, NY, "Movements of Grace: Spirit in the American Landscape"

1997

James Graham & Sons, New York, NY, "Landscape as Abstraction"

The Kitchen, New York, NY, "Derriere Garde Festival"

The Cumberland Gallery, Nashville, TN, "Choice Cuts"

1996

James Graham & Sons, New York, NY, "Water"

1995

James Graham & Sons, New York, NY, "Contemporary Landscape: Topography and Imagination"

1993

Salander O'Reilly Galleries, Beverly Hills, CA, "Hollywood Collects"

1992

The X - Art Foundation, New York, NY, "Blast Art Benefit"

Salander O'Reilly Galleries, Beverly Hills, CA, "Gallery Selections"

Salander O'Reilly Galleries, New York, NY, "Stephen Hannock/Ralph Blakelock"

1991

Salander O'Reilly Galleries, Beverly Hills, CA, "Figurative Paintings"

Lintas Worldwide, New York, NY, "Lights in Darkness"

Tibor de Nagy Gallery, New York, NY, "Biennial"

1990

Tibor de Nagy Gallery, New York, NY, "Season's Best"

Virginia Museum of Fine Arts, Richmond, VA, "Harmony and Discord: American Landscape Painting Today"

Graham Modern Gallery, New York, NY, "Landscape on Paper"

1989

Williams Center for the Arts, Lafayette College, Easton, PA, "Neo-Romantic Landscape and Still Life"

1988

Hampden Gallery, University of Massachusetts, Amherst, MA, "Luminous Painting and Sculpture"

1987

Le Fouret Museum, Tokyo, Japan, "American Pop Culture Today"

University Center Gallery, Adelphi University, Garden City, NY, "Urban Visions"

Park Avenue Atrium, New York, NY, "Light"

1986

55 Bleeker Gallery, New York, NY, "Mainly on the Plane"

High-Tech Exhibition Space, San Francisco, CA, "Luminous Painting"

Frank Bernarducci Gallery, New York, NY, "American Cityscape"

Schreiber Cutler Gallery, New York, NY

1985

Frank Bernarducci Gallery, New York, NY, "Major Works"

1983

Brooklyn Museum of Art, Brooklyn, NY

SELECTED INSTALLATIONS

2007

Pace Wildenstein, New York, NY, installation for the Sundance Institute

The Olana Partnership, Hudson, NY

2002

Ethical Culture, New York, NY, Set design for the opera *Mary Shelley*

1998

Joyce Theater, New York, NY, Set design for Stephen Petronio Dance Company

1993

The Knickerbocker Club, New York, NY

1988

Georgetown University Convention Center, Washington, DC

1987

Tunnel, New York, NY, "Art against AIDS"

Bergdorf Goodman, New York, NY, Fifth Avenue windows

1986

Vertigo, Los Angeles, CA

AREA, New York, NY

Limelight, New York, NY

1977

Charles River Esplanade, Boston Common, Boston, MA

Awards

1998

Academy Award for special effects for film *What Dreams May Come*

Public Collections

Albany Institute of History & Art, Albany, NY

Bowdoin College Museum of Art, Brunswick, ME

Butler Institute of American Art, Youngstown, OH

Dayton Art Institute, Dayton, OH

Grand Rapids Art Museum, Grand Rapids, MI

The Metropolitan Museum of Art, New York, NY

Museum of Contemporary Art, San Diego, CA

Museum of Fine Arts, Boston, MA

Museum of Fine Arts, Houston, TX

National Gallery of Art, Washington, DC

Princeton University Art Museum, Princeton, NJ

Reader's Digest Collection, Pleasantville, NY

Smith College Museum of Art, Northampton, MA

Smithsonian American Art Museum, Washington, DC

Williams College Museum of Art, Williamstown, MA

Worcester Art Museum, Worcester, MA

Selected Bibliography

Exhibition Catalogues

American Pop Culture Today, Volume Two. Tokyo, Japan: U. S. S.O. Co., Ltd., 1988.

Arthur, John. *Green Woods & Crystal Waters, The American Landscape Tradition*. Tulsa, OK: Philbrook Museum of Art, 1999.

Atkins, Robert. *After Church, after Cole: Stephen Hannock's Oxbow*. San Diego, CA: Timken Museum of Art, 1995.

Atkins, Robert, and Hugh Davies. *Stephen Hannock*. New York, NY: James Graham & Sons, 1996.

Baskin, Hosea. *Master & Apprentice, Selected Works from Leonard Baskin & Stephen Hannock*. Amherst, MA: Hampshire College Art Gallery, 1998.

Fahlman, Betsy. *James Graham & Sons: A Century and a Half in the Art Business, 1857–2007*. New York, NY: James Graham & Sons, 2007.

Fischer, Hal. *Stephen Hannock: Space & Time*. Deerfield, MA: Deerfield Academy, 1998.

Garver, Thomas. *Water: A Contemporary American View*. Charleston, SC: Gibbes Museum of Art, 1999.

Rosenfeld, Jason. *Stephen Hannock*. New York, NY: McKenzie Fine Art, Inc., 2002.

Williams, Mara. *The American River*. Brattleboro, VT: Brattleboro Museum, 2002.

Books and Articles

Berman, Ann. "In Plein Sight." *The Shuttle Sheet* (April 2007): 8–9.

__________. "The New Old School." *Traditional Home* (September 2007): 126–33.

Cahill, Timothy. "July Portfolio: Stephen Hannock." *Chronogram* (July 2007): 44–45.

Christy, Duncan. *Luminosity: The Paintings of Stephen Hannock*. San Francisco, CA: Chronicle Books, 2000.

Driscoll, John, and Arnold Skolnick. *The Artist and the American Landscape*. Cobb, CA: First Glance Books, 1998.

Faison, Jr., S. Lane, and Stephen Hannock. "A Conversation on Landscape." In *The Harrison Gallery*. Williamstown, MA: The Harrison Gallery, 2004.

Giuliano, Charles. "The Palimpsests of Stephen Hannock." *Maverick Arts* 361 (September 30, 2007).

Genocchio, Benjamin. "The River: An Object of Beauty, and a Mode of Transport." *New York Times*, October 26, 2003, CT10.

Glueck, Grace. "Hymning a Mountain in Many Views." *New York Times,* September 13, 2002, E32.

Hoppin, Martha. "Depicting Mount Holyoke: A Dialogue with the Past." In *Changing Prospects: The View from Mount Holyoke*. Ithaca, NY: Cornell University Press, 2002.

Little, Carl, and Arnold Skolnick. *Paintings of New England*. Camden, ME: Down East Books, 1996.

"Luminosity: Paintings by Stephen Hannock." *Panorama* (Spring/Summer 2007), 7.

McGuigan, Cathleen. "Transforming the Landscape." *Newsweek* (December 26, 1988): 60–62.

Miliard, Mike. "An Artist in Demand." *Bowdoin Magazine* (November 2006): 10–17

Rewald, Sabine. "Stephen Hannock." *The Metropolitan Museum of Art Bulletin* 59 (Fall 2001): 70.

Rosenblum, Robert. "Art: Contemporary Romantic Landscapes." *Architectural Digest* (May 1993): 193–230.

Serwer, Andy. "Portrait of an A-List Artist." *Fortune Magazine* 152 (October 17, 2005): 124–36.

<h1 style="text-align:center">INDEX</h1>

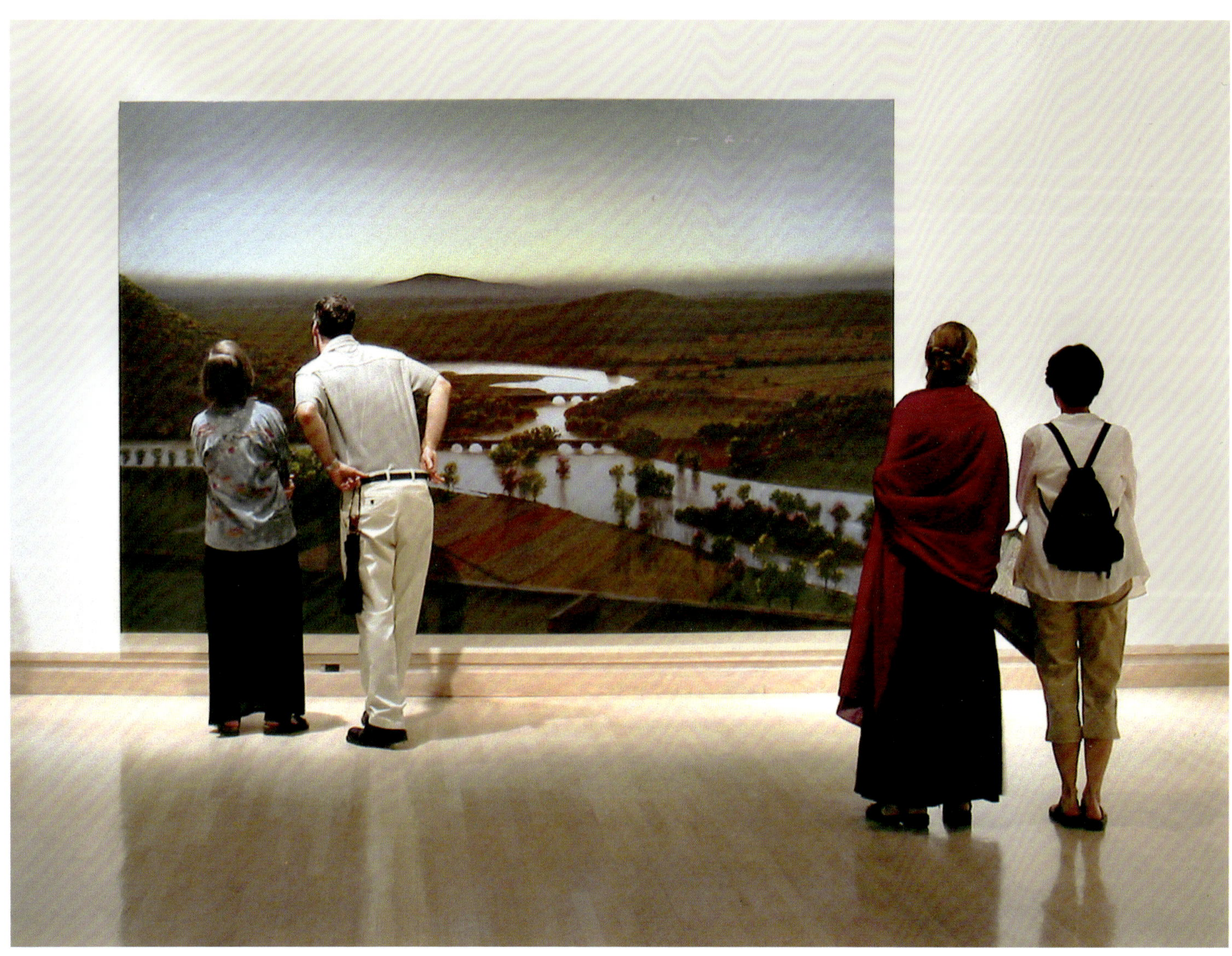

Oxbow Painting at The Metropolitan Museum of Art, New York, 2001